POLITICAL CHOICE IN

Political Choice in Britain

Harold D. Clarke
David Sanders
Marianne C. Stewart
Paul F. Whiteley

OXFORD
UNIVERSITY PRESS

OXFORD

UNIVERSITY PRESS

Great Clarendon Street, Oxford OX2 6DP

Oxford university press is a department of the University of Oxford.

It furthers the University's objective of excellence in research, scholarship,
and education by publishing worldwide in

Oxford New York

Auckland Bangkok Buenos Aires Cape Town Chennai
Dar es Salaam Delhi Hong Kong Istanbul Karachi Kolkata
Kuala Lumpur Madrid Melbourne Mexico City Mumbai Nairobi
São Paulo Shanghai Taipei Tokyo Toronto

Oxford is a registered trade mark of Oxford University Press
in the UK and in certain other countries

Published in the United States
by Oxford University Press Inc., New York

British Library Cataloguing in Publication Data
Data available

Library of Congress Cataloguing in Publication Data
Data available

ISBN 0-19-924488-X
ISBN 0-19-926654-9 (pbk.)

1 3 5 7 9 10 8 6 4 2

Typeset by Newgen Imaging Systems (P) Ltd., Chennai, India
Printed in Great Britain
on acid-free paper by
Biddles Ltd., King's Lynn, Norfolk

To the BES Respondents

Preface

This is a book about the political choices that British voters make. More precisely, it is about the decisions that they make in successive general elections. In each election, voters have two choices—first, whether to cast a ballot, and second, which party to choose. Since the first British Election Study (BES) some four decades ago, the emphasis has been very much on the second of these decisions, party choice. The prior, turnout decision has received very little attention. In the 1950s and 1960s, neglecting turnout seemed reasonable, or at least acceptable, since the vast majority of people regularly voted in general elections. That has changed. In 2001, less than three in five members of the eligible electorate went to the polls, thereby clearly signalling that the turnout decision has become an important aspect of electoral choice in contemporary Britain. Turnout and party choice both merit attention.

Viewed generally, the literature on electoral choice is dominated by two theoretical perspectives—what we call the *sociological* and *individual rationality* frameworks. These two frameworks subsume a wide variety of explanatory models. Historically, most studies of voting behaviour in Britain and elsewhere have adopted, and then strongly advocated, a single model within one of these two frameworks. Ensuing empirical analyses typically, and predictably, demonstrate the power of the preferred model. We contend that this research strategy imposes undesirable theoretical costs because the explanatory contributions and potential superiority of rival models are ignored. These costs may not be recoverable because national election studies are a very scarce commodity. Almost always there is only one study per research community per election cycle. When used to guide the construction of the survey instruments, the 'single model' approach means that the data needed to investigate the utility of a range of alternative models are often unavailable.

In *Political Choice in Britain*, we specify and test several rival explanatory models of electoral choice. As principal investigators of the 2001 BES, we explicitly designed the survey instruments with this goal in mind. Since electoral participation had been largely ignored in previous studies, we constructed substantial batteries of new questions to generate the data needed to test alternative models of turnout. In the same spirit, extensive additions were made to the set of questions designed to operationalize various models of party choice. New questions designed to locate elections within, and gauge their impact on, the broader political culture were also included. These surveys are described in Appendix A. The data and questionnaires are available from the UK Data Archive at the University of Essex and the 2001 BES website: www.essex.ac.uk/bes.

The analyses in the pages that follow do not rely exclusively on data gathered in the 2001 BES. Indeed, some of the most important findings are only possible because of the availability of the now lengthy set of BES surveys initiated in the early 1960s. These data are especially useful because they include multi-wave panels that facilitate analyses of the individual-level dynamics of partisanship and other important political orientations. Additional leverage for these analyses is provided by the 1992–2001 BEPS (British Election Panel Studies). Important also are data that we gathered in a series of monthly surveys conducted by the British Gallup organization between January 1992 and December 2002. The data enable us to investigate the aggregate-level dynamics of party support over a decade that witnessed the sharp reversal of the fortunes of the erstwhile hegemonic Conservatives, as well as the emergence and rise to power of New Labour.

Analyses using varying combinations of these data sets challenge sociological models of party choice. In Britain, the long-dominant sociological model is motivated by one key observation and one key hypothesis; the former being that class is the dominant politically relevant social cleavage, and the latter being that class location drives party choice. Since the inception of British electoral research in the 1950s, many analysts have adopted this model, and Butler and Stokes made it the centrepiece of their classic study, *Political Change in Britain* (1969). Ironically, the title of their book suggests the fundamental weakness of class-based models, namely their inability to account for more than very slowly paced change. Since the class locations of the vast majority of voters do not change, other explanatory factors must be employed to account for the variations—sometimes sharp—in party support across successive elections. Although this logic is eminently transparent, and empirical evidence documenting the weakening of the class x party choice nexus has been available since the 1970s, proponents of the class voting model have continued to insist that it constitutes the canonical account of political choice in Britain. Our analyses indicate that this is incorrect.

Sociological accounts of voting behaviour are dominated by models located in the individual rationality tradition. Particularly important are valence models, early examples of which were developed by Donald Stokes (1963, 1992). These models do not place unreasonable requirements on the cognitive capacities of voters or impose exorbitant deliberation costs on them. Rather than being omniscient utility maximizers, voters are only required to recognize that they possess limited information about alternative political futures. They react to these limitations by focussing on competing parties' managerial teams, paying particular attention to the competence of rival party leaders. They look for a 'safe pair of hands'. In making judgements about which party and which leader can do the best job, voters do not ignore performance. Rather, they store and update information about party and party leader performance and, in so doing, they develop—and sometimes change—their partisan attachments. Nor is the case that the dominant model of party choice in Britain has moved from 'class' to 'choice' over time. Although the relationship between class and party support has weakened significantly since the 1960s, we contend that it was never as strong as many have presumed. Valence models provide a superior account of past as well as present party choice.

What about turnout? Analyses of rival models in the sociological and individual rationality frameworks reveal that choice-based models perform relatively well. But, this is only possible if one circumvents a fundamental empirical problem with classic rational-choice models of electoral participation. As is well known, these models suffer from the 'paradox of participation'—millions of people do vote even though their vanishingly small probability of decisively affecting the election outcome means that it is irrational to do so. However, by collectivizing the concept of political influence, it is possible to specify a simple cost-benefit model that explains a substantial portion of the variance in individual-level electoral participation in 2001, as well as aggregate-level variations in turnout over time.

There is more to this story—various individual and collective incentives also have significant effects on turnout. Especially important are system incentives that revolve around the notion of civic duty. There is a strong correlation between sense of civic duty and age in the 2001 BES data, with younger voters having substantially lower levels of civic duty than older ones. Analyses suggest that this relationship has a significant generational component. If so, then it cannot be easily assumed that people in what we call the 'Thatcher' and 'Blair' generations will eventually become as participatory as the generations that preceded them.

Reflecting on these various findings, a colleague in political philosophy might politely inquire, 'what, then, is your psephological anthropology?' Translating this pointed, if arcanely worded, question as a request for a 'bottom line' description of the typical British voter, our answer is a combination of famous aphorisms by V. O. Key (1968) and Amartya Sen (1977). British voters are neither 'fools', nor are they 'rational fools'. The dominance of the valence model of party choice testifies that Key was correct to argue that voters are sensible people whose behaviour in a political world of uncertainty and limited information is guided by a rough and ready rationality. At the same time, voters respond to what we call 'general incentives', that is, they are motivated by collective considerations as well as egocentric concerns. As a result, the British electorate does not exhibit a pernicious individual rationality that prompts the collective irrationality of undermining a democratic polity by draining it of citizen participation.

In reaching this conclusion, we recognize that generational replacement is a motor of political change. Thus, the fact that many young people do not view voting as a serious civic duty becomes cause for concern. That said, there is no indication of a wholesale retreat from citizenship or deep-seated disaffection with the political system. Indeed, data gathered in the 2001 BES show that levels of psychological involvement in political life, views of the self as a political actor and satisfaction with the performance of British democracy are quite similar, and in some cases, superior to those measured by national surveys conducted over the past four decades. It is essential to calibrate—not celebrate—this finding. Contemporary Britain is hardly a political Arcadia, overflowing in a bounty of social capital, citizen participation, and enthusiasm for the political system. But, insofar as we can tell, it never has been—Britain's 'civic culture' is now and has always been considerably more minimalist and rougher than that.

Thus, our story of political choice in Britain is one that has elements of both change and continuity. Readily acknowledging that the economic and social contexts in which political choice occurs have changed greatly since national election studies began in the 1960s, we nevertheless contend that the present is like the past in important respects, but both are different than often supposed. In the pages that follow, we present the evidence that prompts this conclusion.

However, before doing so, there is another order of business. A large number of individuals and organizations contributed to making this book a reality. We are very pleased to acknowledge their assistance. First, we wish to thank the Economic and Social Research Council (ESRC) for its generous funding of the 2001 BES. We also wish to thank the ESRC for funding the Dynamics of Democracy project as part of the Participation and Democracy programme. This enabled us to gather the 2000–2 monthly survey data on the inter-election dynamics of party support in Britain. ESRC officers Gary Williams and Jennifer Edwards deserve special notes of thanks for their interest in and support of these projects. We also benefited from research awards from the National Science Foundation (SES-9309018, SES-9600018, SES-9710148) that helped us to fund the 1992–9 monthly Gallup surveys that tracked the evolution of party support during a crucial period. NSF Political Science officer Frank Scioli's efforts are much appreciated. Our universities also offered significant assistance. Program support at the University of Texas at Dallas has been especially important—bolstering the available funds for surveys and enabling two of the authors, Clarke and Stewart, to travel to Britain to work on the project.

Members of the 2001 BES Advisory Board deserve special recognition. Board members included John Bartle, Alice Brown, Ivor Crewe, Russell Dalton, David Denver, Cees van der Eijk, Mark Franklin, Peter Kellner, Anthony King, Richard Johnston, Ron Johnston, Lawrence LeDuc, William Miller, Anthony Mughan, Pippa Norris, Charles Pattie, Elinor Scarbrough, Patrick Seyd, and David Walker. In the design stage of the project, several members of the board met at the University of Sheffield and at the University of Essex to provide suggestions about the content and structure of the survey instruments, and the aims of the project as a whole. Their willingness to spend valuable time sharing their insights and wisdom with us is much appreciated.

We also wish to thank the individuals and research organizations that did the field work for the several surveys that are the centrepiece of the 2001 BES. The pre- and post-election cross-sectional and panel surveys were conducted by Nick Moon and his staff at NOP. Simon Sarkar and Colleen Sullivan directed the Gallup staff that conducted the rolling cross-section telephone campaign survey and follow-up post-election survey. FDS did the post-election telephone survey in Northern Ireland. Thanks are also due to Joe Twyman who generously offered to help us with a mode experiment by placing a web version of the post-election survey on the Yougov site.

As the surveys prepared to go into the field, we were very fortunate to secure the services of Jonathan Burton. Jonathan's careful checking of the CAPI programs proved invaluable. During the data collection phase of the project, we had the assistance of three extremely able research officers—Antony Billinghurst, Jane Carr, and Rob Johns. Antony worked on the 'data cam' project, putting the daily updated results of the rolling cross-sectional campaign survey on the BES website. Jane and Rob performed a variety of crucial data collection tasks with skill and enthusiasm, including visiting the Lord Chancellor's Office in London and, in Rob's case, local sheriff's offices throughout Scotland, to gather vote validation data. We also thank Ben Sanders and Carole Welge. Ben assisted Rob in maximizing return rates on the mailback questionnaire, and Carole maintained project records.

In addition to the BES board members mentioned above, other individuals have helped to develop our thinking about electoral choice and how to study it. In this regard, we especially wish to acknowledge Jim Alt, Chris Anderson, André Blais, Ian Budge, John Curtice, Ray Duch, Euel Elliott, Geoff Evans, Frank Feigert, Jim Granato, Anthony Heath, Jane Jenson, Allan Kornberg, Allan McCutcheon, William Mishler, Jon Pammett, Colin Rallings, Norman Schofield, Paul Sniderman, Michael Thrasher, and Guy Whitten. One organization deserves special thanks too—the EPOP (Elections, Public Opinion, and Parties) section of the Political Studies Association. Participation in the EPOP annual conference has provided us with many valuable learning opportunities, and the conference is invariably an enjoyable experience. The hard work of David Denver, Justin Fisher, Jon Tonge, and other EPOP organizing officers is much appreciated. Another person deserving special thanks is Bob Wybrow who was director of British Gallup for many years. At an early EPOP meeting at Worcester College, Oxford, Bob listened to our idea of using Gallup surveys to do a mini-election study every month. His enthusiasm and support did much to make the ensuing eleven-year project on the dynamics of party support in contemporary Britain a reality.

Special thanks are also due to our editors at Oxford University Press, Dominic Byatt, and Claire Croft. Their initial enthusiasm for, and continuing interest, in this book spurred our efforts. In addition, we thank Stuart Fowkes, Oxford University

Preface

Press, and Vanessa Villaverde, University of Texas at Dallas. Stuart guided the book through the production process, and Vanessa prepared the indexes.

Last, but certainly not least, we wish to thank Gillian Sanders and Sue Whiteley. Their patience and support over the several years that it has taken to complete the project are deeply appreciated.

Political Choice in Britain has been a genuine collaborative effort among the four authors. The project's base at the University of Essex has provided Clarke and Stewart with many opportunities to visit Wivenhoe Park. Indeed, Wivenhoe House has become their 'home away from home' and a rendezvous point for all of us. Our evening debriefing sessions there, as well as at the Rose and Crown in Wivenhoe, The Marlborough in Dedham, and other nearby establishments, have been sources of intellectual and social capital and much good fun. All are important for a project like this.

Harold Clarke
David Sanders
Marianne Stewart
Paul Whiteley
Wivenhoe House, July 18, 2003

Contents

List of Figures

List of Figures

List of Figures

List of Tables

List of Tables

List of Tables

ONE

Political Choice in Britain

Jim Hill voted Labour in the 1955 general election. Jim worked as a welder for a Midlands company that was founded in 1912 and made castings for the motor industry. He belonged to the Transport and General Workers' Union. He rented a house, which he shared with his wife and three daughters, from the local council. Jim's wife, who had stopped working when they had their first baby, shopped at 'the stores'—the local Co-op that was 5 minutes' walk from their house. Jim did not think much about politics—although he paid his union dues and occasionally talked politics with his mates in the local pub. Like most people he knew, Jim had always thought of himself as 'Labour'. He thought that a Labour government was more likely to look after the interests of working class people like himself. Even so, he did not expect much to change if a Labour government was elected. Life in Britain would carry on pretty much as it had since the end of the war, regardless of which party was in power. There was bound to be the occasional spot of trouble in the empire, and you could never be sure what the Russians might do in Eastern Europe. But he could not be bothered with all that. The foundry where he worked would keep him employed, with reasonable pay, until he retired with his company pension. His family would get better (and free) medical treatment than anything he had experienced as a child in the 1920s and early 1930s. And his daughters would certainly be better educated than he was. He expected that they would marry local boys from the same sort of working class background that he had come from. He also expected that they would live quite close to him and his wife when they brought up their own families.

Jim's granddaughter, Melanie, still lives today in the Midlands town where her grandfather spent his life, although the foundry where he worked closed in the early 1980s. She lives in her own terraced house, which she is buying with her partner, in an area where 40 per cent of the population is Asian. After graduating from university in the early 1990s, she became a teacher. She left in 1996, disillusioned with work in the public sector, to become a customer services manager at a nearby airport. She expects to change her job again within the next five years.

Melanie occasionally uses the local corner shop, but she buys most of her food and household goods from a superstore complex on the outskirts of town. As soon as she can afford it, she intends to buy a second house, which she will rent out and keep as an investment for her retirement. In the 1997 general election, Melanie voted Labour. In 2001, she thought about not voting at all, but finally opted for the Liberal Democrats.

It is clear that, in the early twenty-first century, Melanie's world lacks the social and economic certainty and cohesion that characterized her grandfather's life in the 1950s. Her employment position is far less secure. She has to plan for her retirement and her own healthcare in ways that her grandfather never thought necessary. She does not have one social milieu, but several: her extended family; her friends, who are scattered across Europe; her Asian neighbours; and her diverse set of colleagues at the airport, who travel to work daily from all over the region. She lives in an economic and social world that both enables and requires her constantly to make choices: which supermarket, which consumer goods, which television channel, which healthcare package, and so on. She has grown up in a world in which rights, and especially consumer rights, have become increasingly important; where class boundaries have become increasingly fluid; where alternative lifestyles have abounded; and where information sources have multiplied enormously.

When Butler and Stokes began their classic study of British voting behaviour in 1963, what appeared to be the relatively stable social and economic world of Jim Hill provided the backdrop to the 'tribal' pattern of British party politics that they depicted. Party preferences were certainly not *just* about class. Nonetheless, class was believed to be a very important determinant of the way that most people thought about the political world and, compared with other socio-demographic characteristics, it appeared to be strongly correlated with the way they voted. Butler and Stokes found that a substantial majority of the working class typically supported Labour and a similar proportion of the (numerically smaller) middle class supported the Conservatives. Objective class positions, class identities, party identifications and voting preferences were all intimately related in ways that lent considerable credence to the 'sociological' approach to British electoral politics. According to Butler and Stokes, most people had relatively stable views both of themselves and of the main parties as political actors. Since these views were rooted in the social structure, it followed that important political changes in Britain were likely to be rooted in long-term—and almost inevitably very slow—changes in the social fabric.

It would be surprising if the economic and social changes that Britain has experienced over the last fifty years have left the political realm untouched. Indeed, in the 1970s, observers were already charting the decline of class voting and of party identification (or 'partisanship') in Britain. At the same time, other analysts were beginning to talk about the voter as consumer. Voters were appearing to become less tribal, and they were increasingly prepared to make choices between political parties based on the attractiveness of the alternative policy packages being offered.

2

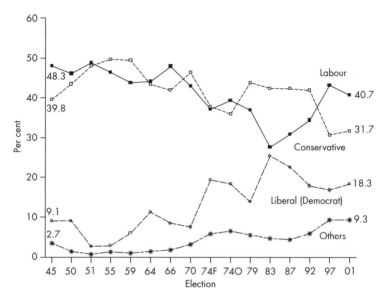

Figure 1.1 Vote shares, United Kingdom, 1945–2001 general elections
Source: Butler and Kavanagh (2002: Appendix 1).

The patterns of party support that analysts have sought to explain are shown in Figure 1.1. In the fifteen general elections between 1945 and 1997, voting for the two major parties has been very similar—averaging slightly over 41 per cent for Labour and slightly over 42 per cent for the Conservatives. This is not to say that party support levels have not varied. Labour voting has ranged from a low of 28 per cent in 1983 to a high of nearly 49 per cent in 1951. The comparable figures for the Conservatives are 31 per cent in 1997 and almost 50 per cent in 1955; and, for the Liberals (Democrats), approximately 3 per cent in 1951 and 25 per cent in 1983. In 2001, the Labour, Conservative, and Liberal Democrat vote shares were 41 per cent, 32 per cent, and 18 per cent, respectively. The remarkable change in the fortunes of the main political parties—not just Labour's victory in 2001—clearly requires more attention.

The attendant levels of turnout in general elections are displayed in Figure 1.2. Between 1945 and 1997, turnout averaged just over 76 per cent, ranging from a low of slightly over 71 per cent in 1997 to a high of 84 per cent in 1950. Although there was a gentle downward trend, movements over time were irregular—if turnout fell in one election, then it tended to rebound in the next one. However, this did not happen in 2001 when the turnout rate dropped to 59.4 per cent (Electoral Commission 2001: 11–12). This was the lowest since the 'Khaki' election of 1918 and certainly since the end of Second World War. The dramatic decline in

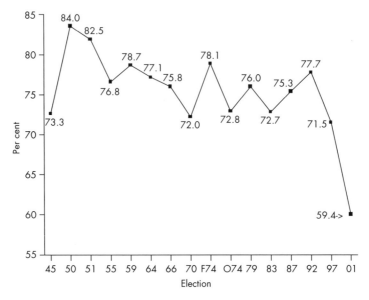

Figure 1.2   Voting turnout, United Kingdom, 1945–2001 general elections
Source: Butler and Kavanagh (2002: Appendix 1).

voter turnout in the two most recent general elections has provoked interest in the questions of why some people vote and others do not.

In this book, we analyze the changing political choices that voters in Britain have made over the last four decades. In particular, we explain why voters made the party choices that they did in the 2001 general election, and why many people chose not to vote at all in that contest. We recognize that the social and economic context in which contemporary voters think and act is very different from that of their grand-parents. The electoral context has also changed, in part because of the choices that were made by earlier cohorts of voters and to which political parties have responded. Notwithstanding this changing context and the changing way in which scholars have sought to understand why voters behave as they do, we argue that the core calculus of voting in Britain has not changed substantially since at least the early 1960s. Indeed, it is questionable whether, even in the 1950s, people like Jim Hill were on the sort of sociological autopilot that often has been assumed in analyses of British voting behaviour. On the contrary, we argue that the most important influences on voting have always been based on a reasoned calculation made by the voter. In mak-ing these claims, we do not espouse a narrowly cast rational choice approach. Rather, following broadly in the tradition established by Donald Stokes, we see voters as making summary judgements based primarily on what he called 'valence'—on their perceptions of the likely competence of competing parties' managerial teams.

4

This chapter discusses the main theoretical frameworks that inform our analysis. It then describes the principal data sets that are used to conduct the analyses and to ascertain which framework tells the better story of electoral choice. The chapter concludes with an overview of the specific arguments and findings that are presented in the following chapters of the book.

SOCIOLOGISTS, ECONOMISTS AND VOTING

The Sociological Framework

Since the 1950s, two theoretical frameworks have informed most electoral research conducted in advanced democracies—in Brian Barry's terms, the frameworks of 'sociologists' and 'economists' (Barry 1971). The sociological framework has represented the orthodoxy in British electoral research since the early 1960s (Butler and Stokes 1969). This framework contains three core ideas. The first is that relatively fixed social characteristics, such as social class or region, work through long-term socialization processes to predispose individuals to support one party rather than another. Second, the results of these socialization processes can be either reinforced or undermined by the individual's social context—for example, by the kind of work the individual does, the sort of neighbourhood he or she lives in, and the informal groups to which he or she belongs. The third idea is that there is a distinctive social psychology of voting. Over time, and again largely as a result of socialization, most individuals tend to develop stable and enduring affective attachments to particular political parties. These party identifications serve both to colour the ways in which individuals interpret political information and to predispose them to vote for the same party in successive elections.

Proponents of the sociological approach argue that it offers a plausible and parsimonious account of the relative electoral stability that, in their view, has characterized British party politics for much of the post-war period. The proportions of votes secured by the major parties, although they have varied enough to produce periodic changes in government, never fluctuated dramatically. Indeed, the parties' vote shares at successive elections were marked more by their stability than their volatility. This was entirely consistent with the claim of the sociological approach that people's political preferences are rooted in their positions in the social structure. The approach never claimed that all variation in voting preferences would be determined by social structure. Other contingent factors, such as the condition of the economy, specific issues, perceptions of party leaders, or events, would cause some people to switch their votes between elections. However, most people would continue to vote according to their structural positions and their party identifications and this, in turn, would be associated with relative electoral stability. Electoral change would be glacial because social structure, and the patterns of partisanship that depend on it, evolve slowly.

The sociological account of British electoral behaviour began to be challenged soon after it was proposed. First, Crewe, Sarlvik, and Alt (1977) observed a marked decline in the strength of party identification, although there was little evidence of the extensive social structural change that might have been expected to produce it. Second, the correlation between vote and the key social structural variable in the sociological framework—social class—began to weaken (e.g. Franklin 1985; Rose and McAllister 1986). In subsequent decades, the strength of party identification has continued to decline, and the correspondence between class and voting has continued to weaken. As a result, many electoral analysts in Britain—like their counterparts in many other advanced democracies—have moved away from models of the vote that place primary importance on sociological factors such as social location and long-term partisan attachments. Instead, they specify voting models where the principal explanatory variables are leader and party images, issue perceptions, and assessments of economic performance.

The sociologists' response to the above findings has taken several forms. The response to declining levels of party identification has been to focus more attention on the role of ideology and values (Rose and McAllister 1990; Heath et al. 1991, 1994; see also Scarbrough 1985). One response to the weakening correlation between class and vote has been to investigate the electoral impact of 'class-related' cleavages such private versus public sector statuses (Dunleavy and Husbands 1985). Another response has been to 'save the relationship', by developing a more elaborate conceptualization of social class, and new measures of the correlation between class and vote. With regard to the latter approach, the argument is that, once class is properly conceptualized and the correlation between class and vote is properly calculated, the class–vote relationship remains strong, subject only to periodic obfuscation by policy convergence among the competing parties (Heath, Jowell, and Curtice 1985, 2001). However, there are difficulties. The dilution of the simple equation of 'middle class equals Conservative, working class equals Labour' substantially weakens the theoretical parsimony and explanatory power of the concept of class. Moreover, as shown in Chapter Three, alternative measures of the correlation between class and vote do not negate the key fact that non-manual workers have become less inclined to support their 'natural' party, the Conservatives, while manual workers have become less likely to support their 'natural' party, Labour. However measured, the correlation between class and vote has weakened substantially since the 1960s.

The Individual Rationality Framework

Although social–structural factors play a role in voting, in our view, they are not as important as the ideas associated with a second framework, that is, the individual rationality framework. Some of these ideas derive from the 'economic' or rational choice approach, as articulated in Downs' classic study, *An Economic Theory of Democracy* (1957). First, the act of voting depends on a calculation of the personal costs and benefits of voting—a calculation that takes account of the perceived probability that the individual's vote will have a decisive effect on the election outcome. The fact that this probability is usually miniscule creates a 'paradox of voting' in which it is irrational to vote even when there are substantial differences in the benefits that would be received were alternative parties to hold office (see Aldrich 1993). The implication of this paradox is that the decision to vote must involve something more than a narrowly rational, personalized calculation. Second, people support the party that they perceive to be closest to their own positions in the dominant issue space, a space that is typically best represented by a unidimensional, left–right continuum. Third, rational vote-seeking parties, *ceteris paribus*, position themselves in the dominant issue space such that they can maximize the number of votes they receive.

Downs' ideas about individual rationality have informed many studies of voting behaviour. His analysis of costs and benefits has been featured in several subsequent studies of voting turnout—although analysts have also followed Riker and Ordeshook's (1968, 1973) strategy of adding 'efficacy' and 'citizen duty' terms to the core cost–benefit calculation. The cost–benefit approach also has been used to explore the role of economic performance as a determinant of voting preferences. This has generated a debate over whether voters are mainly egocentric or sociotropic, and prospective or retrospective, when forming their political judgements (e.g. see Lewis-Beck 1988). In addition, the suggestion that voters prefer the party closest to them in the dominant issue space has spawned a long-running series of issue-proximity voting studies, where rival groups of scholars have sought to establish whether 'closeness' to a party matters more or less for voters than being broadly on the same side of the ideological divide. Downs' claim that successful vote-seeking parties shift their own general ideological or more specific issue positions in response to changes in voters' policy preferences has been used, in the British context, to analyze a number of major electoral changes. These have included the Conservatives' acceptance of Keynesian demand management and the welfare state after 1945; the Conservatives' success, under Margaret Thatcher, in recognizing that the centre of gravity of British public opinion had shifted to the right, and that the electorate was now ready to embrace monetarist economics and trade union reform; and Labour's move to the centre under Blair in the 1990s, which helped to produce Labour's general election successes in 1997 and 2001 (Heath, Jowell, and Curtice 2001). Finally, some scholars have developed a rational choice interpretation of party identification. The idea is that people can develop a habit of voting for one party as a way of reducing the costs of continuously collecting and evaluating political information (e.g. see Key 1968). Relatively early in their political lives, they make judgements about which party is closest to their own ideological and issue positions, and they tend subsequently to continue to support that party unless a major political trauma causes them to reassess their early judgements. These ideas have been developed further by Fiorina (1981), who argues that party identification is best seen as a running tally, or an accumulation, of voters' retrospective evaluations of the performance of major parties and their leaders. In this sense, partisanship is a rational, rather than an affective, sociologically driven, phenomenon.

The rational choice approach to electoral behaviour has been criticized from several perspectives (for a review, see Green and Shapiro 1994). Two major weaknesses stand out. First, the approach seriously understates the extent to which people, as political actors, perceive and evaluate the world in non-rational terms. Critics argue that the political arena is not directly analogous to the economic realm where fairly narrow self-interested calculation can be assumed to underpin both consumer and producer/supplier behaviour. Moreover, to the extent that rational choice models include non-rational elements, they lose their theoretically distinctive and rigorous character. The second weakness follows from the first. Since rational choice models ignore substantively important, non-rational factors that motivate behaviour, attempts to operationalize and test rational choice voting models rarely, if ever, provide satisfactory explanations of the phenomena under investigation. Simply put, critics argue that rational choice accounts of voting tend to fail empirically.

The limitations of the rational choice approach have led a number of scholars to propose alternative models of turnout and party support. In doing so, they have maintained their distance from sociological determinism while recognizing that voters' cost–benefit calculations are more indecisive, impressionistic, and sometimes emotionally laden than rational choice theory would allow. Ironically, Donald Stokes, one of the most influential advocates of the social–psychological approach, articulated an early version of a broader model of voter rationality. Stokes (1963, 1992) distinguished between what he termed 'position' and 'valence' issues. Position issues typically require the voter to make a spatial assessment, such as the extent to which government should redistribute income from rich to poor. On such issues, the parties can be expected to take differing positions, and in Downsian fashion, voters determine which party is closest to their own preferred positions when making their electoral choices. In contrast, valence issues arise when there is broad agreement about the desired policy outcome—such as the achievement (or maintenance) of low unemployment, low inflation, high educational standards, or good healthcare. Voters support the party that appears to offer the best chance of delivering competent performance in these policy areas.

Recent proponents of more general models of voter rationality have placed particular emphasis on the heuristics or cognitive shortcuts that individuals employ in order to make electoral choices under conditions of uncertainty (e.g. Sniderman, Brody, and Tetlock 1991). Voters often have neither the resources nor the inclination to inform themselves fully about the political choices that are available to them in any given election. As a result, they contrive to use judgemental shortcuts that enable them to avoid or reduce the transaction costs of constantly updating their stock of political information.

Here, we propose an approach that combines a focus on valence issues with the idea that voters use such shortcuts when making their electoral decisions. In our view, the most important factor underlying electoral choice is valence—people's judgements of the overall competence of the rival political parties. These judgements, in turn, are arrived at through two principal and related shortcuts: leadership evaluations and party identification. The importance of voters' perceptions of party leaders as heuristic devices derives in part from the fact that parties themselves can be highly amorphous institutions. Parties typically have local, regional, and national organizations that do not always convey a single, unified political message. The platform that a party presents at election time is frequently the result of public, intra-party debate among competing personalities who have previously articulated different policy positions and even represented different intellectual traditions. In these circumstances, it is not always clear to voters what 'the party' actually stands for. How better, then, to crystallize one's view of a party than by making a judgement about the character and competence of its leader? The leader is not an amorphous, vaguely perceived entity. Rather, he or she is a clearly identified, single individual who, if elected, will take ultimate responsibility for any hard choices that the government needs to make. For many voters, then, assessing the leader is a very convenient way of assessing the likely competence of the party in office.

However, leader images are not the only heuristic that voters use in order to estimate parties' likely performance. As noted above, voters' competence assessments are also informed by their party identifications. Following Fiorina (1981) and others who have conceptualized partisanship in terms of an individual rationality approach, we view party identification as a store of accumulated information about political parties. Partisan attachments are frequently updated on the basis of a voter's assessment of the parties' political and economic performance, and these updated attachments inform electoral choice.

Our approach to political choice also contributes to the understanding of people's decisions to vote. In addition to the narrow calculation of the personal costs and benefits associated with the act of voting, it is possible that people consider the group and system-wide benefits that might accrue from their participation. Some people believe, for example, that the legitimacy and successful functioning of the political system require widespread citizen participation. Such individuals might be expected to vote—even if the personal benefits of voting were substantially outweighed by the time and effort involved in doing so. By taking a broader view of political calculation, we believe that it is possible to offer a more plausible characterization of the psychology of political participation.

In sum, our investigation is guided by three sets of theoretical ideas. Following the sociological tradition, we assess the extent to which electoral choices are determined by voters' social locations, in particular by their class location. Following the individual rationality approach pioneered by Downs, we investigate the extent to which people's issue positions—and their closeness to the different parties on key issues—affect their vote choices. We also use this approach to explore costs and benefits associated with the decision to go to the polls. Finally, and consistent with the work of Stokes, Fiorina and others, we examine the relevance of broader notions of individual rationality. Voting models informed by these ideas are what we call *valence politics* models. They focus on how judgements about parties' likely performance in office affect electoral choice, how such judgements are conditioned by cognitive shortcuts, such as leadership images and party identification, and how perceptions of group and system benefits affect citizens' decisions to vote.

QUESTIONS, DATA, AND METHODOLOGY

Two key questions addressed in this book are why British citizens vote and why they make the particular party choices that they do. We also address a third set of questions. To what extent do British citizens engage with the political process beyond participation in elections? And, what does the pattern of engagement over the last four decades tell us about the health of contemporary British democracy? To answer these questions, we draw on the two theoretical frameworks discussed above, and we use as much representative data as we can to test their competing claims. Data gathered in the 2001 British Election Study (BES) are particularly useful since the study was explicitly designed to test rival explanations of voter turnout and party choice. The core data set in the 2001 BES is a two-wave panel in which respondents were interviewed face-to-face both before (in March–May) and after (June–September) the 2001 election. The post-election wave, with an additional top-up sample to compensate for panel attrition, is also used as a free-standing, post-election cross-section. In addition, we employ a second data set—completely separate from the first—based on a rolling cross-section survey conducted during the 2001 campaign. In this survey an average of 160 respondents was interviewed by telephone each day during the official 4-week campaign. Many of these respondents (78 per cent) were re-interviewed immediately after the election.

We extend our analyses of voting behaviour to earlier elections for two reasons. One is that some of the voting patterns observed in 2001 originate in earlier changes in the attitudes and preferences of the British electorate—and these changes must be analyzed to provide a compelling account of what happened in that election. Another reason is that we make claims about the sources of party support that run counter to many previous BES-based analyses. In particular, and as discussed above, emphasis is placed on the importance of valence judgements.

10

Accordingly, we analyze earlier data to ascertain whether the factors affecting electoral choice in 2001 differed from those operating in earlier elections, or whether valence and alternative choice calculations have always been at the core of voting decisions in Britain.

To provide a longer-term perspective on the 2001 findings, several additional data sets are used extensively. We rely heavily on data gathered in the previous BES post-election cross-sectional surveys conducted since 1964. These data are vital for mapping changes in the distribution of theoretically important variables, as well as over-time changes in the relationships between such variables and voting behaviour. We also employ BES and British Election Panel Study (BEPS) data sets gathered over the 1963–70, 1974–9, 1992–7, and 1997–2001 periods. These multi-wave panels are crucial for investigating the dynamics and determinants of party identification in Britain over the past four decades. A third important data set is based on monthly Gallup surveys, which we conducted between January 1992 and December 2002. These data are employed in both aggregate- and individual-level forms. The aggregate-level Gallup data enable us to document changes in electoral preferences in the wake of the 1992 Exchange Rate Mechanism (ERM) crisis. These aggregate data also shed light on whether the factors that produced Labour's victory in 2001 were a continuation of those at work before the 1997 general election. Individual-level analyses of the Gallup data are valuable for assessing whether the effects of theoretically interesting explanatory variables observed in analyses of various BES data sets are consistently evident during the 1992–2001 period that witnessed the rise of New Labour.

Other types of data are also employed. Information gathered in annual British Social Attitudes (BSA) surveys helps us to gauge levels of participation in various kinds of political activities, and augments our investigation of the nature of partisanship in Britain. Data from the British Household Panel Surveys (BHPS) and special surveys commissioned by Sanders et al. (2002) are used for the latter purpose as well. In addition, we marshal aggregate-level data from numerous surveys conducted by various organizations over the 1947–2001 period. These data permit us to develop a long-term perspective on electoral politics and democratic life in Britain. Some of these data were collected by commercial polling agencies, such as Gallup, MORI, NOP, and ICM, and some were gathered in Eurobarometer surveys conducted by the European Commission. Data on parties' ideological positions gathered in the Manifestos Project (Budge et al. 2001) play a significant role in our analyses of the dynamics and determinants of voting turnout between 1945 and 2001.

POLITICAL CHOICE IN BRITAIN CONSIDERED

Chapters Two to Four of this book begin the empirical analyses of political choice in Britain by addressing the main question in electoral research: why do voters make the party choices that they do? Chapter Two discusses the theoretical frameworks outlined above. The sociological framework identifies various aspects of an individual's social location as potential sources of differential voting patterns. These aspects include social class as well as region, gender, ethnicity, age, and home ownership. The sociological approach also claims party identification to be a key explanatory variable. However, since the individual rationality framework makes a similar claim, we treat partisanship as a 'signature variable' of both approaches. This framework contains both the Downsian and the valence approaches. Our characterization of the Downsian approach focuses on issue positions and proximities; that is, the closer that an individual voter locates him or herself to a particular party on a key issue dimension, such as the left–right continuum, the more likely he or she is to vote for that party in an election. The valence approach specifies that heuristics and other types of calculation inform voters' party preferences. In addition to partisanship, these include leadership images, evaluations of economic performance, and assessments of issue competence.

Chapter Three assesses the extent to which the sociological, Downsian, and valence perspectives explain patterns of party support in the United Kingdom between 1964 and 2001. The chapter is divided into three parts. The first part develops a set of 'consistency measures' that explore the degree of bivariate association between vote choice and the key signature variables associated with each perspective. The empirical results show that all three approaches are relevant for understanding vote choice in Britain. Between 1964 and 2001, leader images and partisanship consistently have the largest effects on voting while issue proximities and social location are significant but less important. However, the relationship between vote and social class progressively weakens over time. This decline in the role of class is not matched by a compensating rise in the explanatory power of other social location variables. This implies that the overall importance of the sociological approach has declined since 1964. The second part of Chapter Three presents multivariate models that build on the bivariate analyses conducted in the first part. The results support the notion that, with the exception of the declining role of social class, the relative importance of the various signature variables associated with the sociological and individual rationality frameworks has remained more or less constant from the mid-1960s onwards.

This conclusion is reinforced in the final part of Chapter Three, which examines the calculus of party support using individual-level monthly data for the period between 1992 and 2001. The results show that leader images, partisanship, and evaluations of economic competence consistently exert large and significant effects on party preferences, with a secondary role being played by social location. Important changes in party preference occurred in the wake of the September 1992 ERM crisis. This crisis, in combination with New Labour's move to the right under Tony Blair after 1994, helped to produce shifts in voters' leadership perceptions, their party identifications, and their economic competence perceptions that endured through to 2001.

Chapter Four provides a detailed analysis of the sources of party support in 2001. We concentrate on the main UK-wide choices that were available to most voters—Labour, the Conservatives, and the Liberal Democrats. Although the Scottish National Party (SNP) and Plaid Cymru are significant forces in their respective national assemblies, they are relatively minor players in Westminster politics. Accordingly, perceptions of these parties played a small part in the calculations of an overwhelming majority of British voters. Our analysis of vote choice in 2001 specifies a series of multivariate models that capture the effects of the key variables from each of the models in the sociological and individual rationality frameworks. As in Chapter Three, the evidence provides some support for both. Party identification, leader images, issue positions and proximities, and economic evaluations all exerted sizeable effects on vote choice. Tactical voting was also in evidence, benefiting the Liberal Democrats at the expense of Labour and the Conservatives. Our summary conclusion about the outcome of the 2001 election is that Labour won because it held all of the important cards—it enjoyed substantial leads over its competitors on all of the key determinants of vote choice. In contrast to many earlier studies of British electoral politics, we make strong claims about the effects of evaluations of party leaders on electoral choice. Since voters' reactions to the leaders might be rationalizations of pre-existing voting preferences, we conduct a variety of statistical tests to determine whether our inferences regarding the effects of leader evaluations are warranted.

Chapter Five provides an analysis of the impact of the 2001 election campaign. The analysis focuses on two questions. Did the campaign mobilize political interest and participation? And, did it sway voters' political choices? Data from the BES pre-post-election panel survey and the BES rolling cross-section campaign survey are used to investigate these questions. Contrary to what is commonly assumed about the function of election campaigns, the 2001 campaign did little to mobilize political interest or partisanship. Indeed, there is evidence of demobilization during the early part of the campaign, with interest in the election recovering only in the week prior to polling day. However, the local campaigns, conducted by party activists, contributed significantly to turnout and party choice. The analyses also indicate that tactical voting did not occur spontaneously but, rather, was driven by Liberal Democrat grassroots campaigning. More generally, campaigning by all of the major parties affected the vote shares that they received.

Chapter Six addresses important theoretical questions that arise from analyses in Chapters Three and Four, which document that party identification is a powerful predictor of electoral preference. This was true in the 1960s and it remains true today. The theoretical issue arises because models in the sociological and the individual rationality frameworks both claim party identification as a major explanatory variable. However, they conceptualize it differently. According to sociological models, party identification is a long-term, stable, affective orientation, whereas for models in the individual rationality framework, party identification is a summary, potentially mutable, tally of current and past party performance evaluations. Thus, an important observable difference concerns whether party identification manifests impressive levels of individual stability, as claimed by the sociological model, or whether it displays the substantial dynamics claimed by models in the individual rationality framework.

Analyses presented in Chapter Six show that, since the early 1960s, there has been considerable individual-level instability in party identification in Britain. Moreover, and contrary to the claims of some earlier studies (e.g. Green, Palmquist, and Schickler 2002), this instability is not simply a consequence of random measurement error. Analyses also show that partisanship can be effectively modelled as a response to judgements about party leader performance and economic evaluations. Taken together, these findings suggest that partisanship in Britain corresponds closely to the characterization provided by the valence politics model. Since the two other main predictors of vote choice—leader perceptions and economic evaluations—are also derived from the valence model, we conclude that electoral choice in Britain has been, and remains, primarily about valence.

Chapters Seven and Eight investigate determinants of voter turnout. Traditionally, turnout has not been regarded as a problem in Britain, and analysts have paid relatively little attention to it. As Figure 1.2 illustrates, turnout generally remained quite high throughout much of the post-Second World War period, although there was a gradual, if irregular, downward trend. However, in 1997 and especially in 2001, the decline accelerated sharply. These recent declines, combined with falling turnout in local elections and persistently low turnout in elections to the European Parliament, have led a number of academic analysts and media commentators to conclude that nonvoting has become a serious problem. Chapter Seven begins by relating voting to other forms of political participation. The analyses show that voting in various elections constitutes a distinctive type of political participation. We then discuss several models that purport to explain why people participate in democratic politics and why they decide to vote (or not to vote). The relative deprivation or equity-fairness model stresses the gap between what an individual expects and what he or she gets out of life. The civic voluntarism model focuses on the resources that individuals bring to bear on the decision to vote or not and the mobilization efforts that are made by other actors. The social capital model emphasizes social trust and the individual's involvement with social organizations. The cognitive mobilization model highlights the role of political interest, political knowledge, and media usage. Finally, the general incentives model supplements a broadly defined Downsian-style cost–benefit analysis with variables that take account of a variety of other incentives, such as 'doing one's democratic duty'.

Chapter Eight provides operational specifications for each of these models of the decision to vote. It then tests each model using data drawn from the 2001 BES pre- and post-election surveys. Because each model receives some support from the data, we conduct statistical tests to determine whether any model is superior to the others. The tests indicate that each model makes a significant contribution to the explanation of turnout. Accordingly, we estimate a composite model of turnout that combines elements of the several specific models. Analyses of the composite model reveal that the crucial individual-level influences on electoral turnout are calculations of efficacy-discounted benefits and costs of participation, sense of civic duty, and age. The final section of Chapter Eight analyzes the aggregate-level dynamics of turnout, using proxy variables for the efficacy and benefit terms in the individual-level models, as well as linear and quadratic trend terms to control for various long-term forces. These analyzes indicate a substantial portion (not all) of the decline in turnout in 1997 and 2001 was caused by the one-sided nature of the contests, coupled with the perception that the two major parties did not offer a menu of distinctive policy choices.

Chapter Nine extends our investigation to consider voters' orientations towards themselves as political actors, as well as their orientations towards elections, parties, various political institutions, and the wider democratic process. Using survey data gathered over the past four decades, we consider whether contemporary British voters are less interested in politics than their forebearers, less politically efficacious, less inclined to participate in various political activities, and less satisfied with the democratic process. Notwithstanding the declines in turnout in 1997 and 2001, we find that, in almost all of these respects, *contemporary Britons are almost indistinguishable from earlier generations.* Average levels of political interest and political efficacy, and willingness to engage in non-electoral actions, have changed little over the last forty years. Contemporary British voters are not particularly interested in politics and they do not feel particularly efficacious. But their predecessors felt almost exactly the same way. And, in terms of judgements about the overall performance of democracy in Britain, people were more satisfied in 2001 than at any time since 1973 when measures of democracy satisfaction were first recorded. We find that democratic satisfaction is largely driven by valence politics considerations. The main sources of satisfaction are positive evaluations of state institutions, economic and social policies, and political leadership in general.

Commentators have inferred from falling turnout in the two most recent general elections that British voters are increasingly disillusioned with the democratic process. The evidence presented in Chapter Nine indicates that this inference is incorrect. However, analyses in Chapter Eight do suggest that there is a dynamic in attitudes towards electoral participation and, by extension, to a citizen's role in the democratic process. That dynamic concerns sense of civic duty. Younger people are less likely to believe that voting is a civic duty, and less likely to believe that nonvoting is a serious violation of that duty. Moreover, there is evidence that these age differences reflect generational differences, rather than being wholly the result of life-cycle processes. If so, processes of generational replacement will eventually produce an electorate where average levels of civic duty are lower than is presently the case. Since a sense of civic duty is a primary determinant of turnout, *ceteris paribus*, such an electorate will be less likely to manifest high levels of electoral participation.

Finally, Chapter Ten concludes with a summary of major theoretical and empirical claims. Our analyses indicate that British electoral politics over the past forty years can be best understood using an individual rationality framework. The three major predictors of *electoral choice*—leadership images, partisanship, and evaluations of economic performance—are key elements of the valence model. Analyses of *turnout* demonstrate the explanatory power of cost–benefit calculations that are augmented by assessments of overall benefits to the political system in general—which are elements of the general incentives model. Beyond electoral participation, *satisfaction with the democratic process* itself depends primarily on assessments of institutional and policy performance—that is, on valence judgements. Thus, the individual rationality framework and, in particular, its valence politics model, provide powerful analytic leverage for explaining political choice in Britain. Contemporary voters, like Melanie, who reluctantly went to the polls in 2001, clearly live in a world of valence politics. Our analyses demonstrate that her grandfather, Jim, lived in a much more valenced world than many observers have assumed.

TWO

Theories and Models of Party Support

Over the past half-century, studies of why people vote as they do have accorded pride of place to explanatory models containing a variety of social, psychological, and economic variables (Dalton and Wattenberg 1993; Scarbrough 2000). Two major theoretical frameworks or approaches have informed the selection and specification of these models of electoral choice. In this chapter, we first discuss models located in what we call the sociological framework. These models emphasize the importance of social characteristics, social contexts, and social psychology for understanding voting behaviour and election outcomes. First introduced in studies conducted in the United States in the 1940s and 1950s, sociological models have heavily informed electoral research in that country and elsewhere. In Britain, sociological models have been very influential, and strong claims have been advanced for the influence of social class on voters' political attitudes and behaviour. Next, we consider what we call the individual rationality theoretical framework, and spatial and valence models within this framework. Since gaining popularity in the 1970s, models in this framework have attracted researchers with the promise of providing a logically coherent and empirically convincing account of the dynamics of party support in successive elections and in the periods between them. In this chapter, we discuss rival models of electoral choice grounded in the sociological and individual rationality frameworks in terms of core concepts and signature variables. Subsequent chapters assess the power of the various models to explain voting behaviour in the 2001 and earlier British general elections.

EXPLAINING PARTY SUPPORT

The Sociological Framework

The older, sociological tradition of electoral research emphasizes the *role of society*, notably the effects of social characteristics, social contexts, or social psychology on political choice. Given that much of the early research was conducted largely, although not exclusively, by sociologists whose interests focussed on group influences on the individual, the emphasis on social groups and community contexts does not surprise. For example, groups and contexts figured prominently in the studies of the 1940 and 1948 presidential elections in Erie County, Ohio (Lazarsfeld, Berelson, and Gaudet 1948) and Elmira, New York (Berelson, Lazarsfeld, and McPhee 1954), and the 1950–1 and 1955 general elections in the constituency of Bristol North-East (Milne and Mackenzie 1954, 1958; Milne 1959/1977). However, methodological and theoretical changes accompanied the shift of the locus of electoral research projects from the Office of Radio Research at Columbia to the Survey Research Center at Michigan. National sample surveys became the primary tool of data collection, and social–psychological or 'motivational' explanations of vote choice replaced the earlier emphasis on demographic characteristics and community contexts (Rossi 1959). Major early examples of research employing social–psychological approaches were the nationwide studies of the 1952, 1956, and 1960 American presidential elections by Angus Campbell and his colleagues (Campbell, Gurin, and Miller 1954; Campbell et al. 1960). The Michigan style of electoral research was soon exported to other countries including Britain. In the early 1960s, David Butler and Donald Stokes brought Michigan's election-study tool kit from Ann Arbor to Nuffield to conduct their pioneering studies of the 1964, 1966, and 1970 general elections (Butler and Stokes 1969; see also Butler and Stokes 1971, 1976).

In the sociological framework, *social characteristics*, such as class, ethnicity, gender, or race, anchor political preferences and, since the former change slowly, if at all, the dynamics of the latter must be constrained as well. But, analytical approaches involving social characteristics and *social contexts* overlap since both rely on social interaction and social identification to explain the communication and mobilization successes or failures of parties and other political organizations. The fundamental story of the social characteristics-contexts model is that communities provide a setting for group influences on political preference. That is, communities constitute spaces for interpersonal interaction, and these interactions are the medium by which social environments and social groups condition individual activity and group behaviour. This conditioning occurs in at least two ways. In one way, dominant social divisions contain varying parcels of historical experiences, socializing influences, and material interests. These experiences, environments, and interests among members of the same social group become matched to the policies and programmes expressed by a particular political party. As long as the party continues to advocate for the group, most of its members will continue to support it. For example, the standard Marxian view is that the social division of labour determines individuals' material interests, and the collectivization of work creates a shared awareness that fellow class members are deprived of both material goods and the symbolic value of these goods in society. This collective awareness makes class members receptive to mobilization for political activity by organizations, such as political parties and trade unions, that are capable of constructing bases of electoral support (e.g. Przeworski and Sprague 1986).

The second way in which conditioning occurs expands on the first. In this case, discussions within groups, group mobilization by parties, and group exposure to media have three related effects (Rossi 1959). These forms of communication transmit the prevailing political preference of the group to its members. They mediate the influence of socioeconomic status on political preference. And, they work to reinforce 'like-minded' views in the group while converting views that deviate from prevailing opinion about issues, candidates, and leaders. Contextual analysts also place considerable weight on 'conversations in contexts'. These conversations occur in workplaces and other settings such as those provided by families, churches, and neighbourhoods (Huckfeldt and Sprague 1995; Mutz 1998). Such discussions express affective orientations and social norms, and they provide guidelines for decision making. This is especially the case when a decision must be made with information that is unavailable or imperfect and in an environment of risk and uncertainty. In turn, the frequent use of these guidelines and their demonstrated reliability in decision making tend to strengthen ties among individuals, to engender policy agreement, and to mobilize political participation.

An explanation that supplements the social characteristics-contexts approach grounds voting behaviour 'more in social psychology than in sociology'. This *social psychology* explanation is 'guided by the philosophy that the immediate determinants of an individual's behaviour lie more clearly in his attitudes and his perceptual organization of his environment than in either his social position or other "objective" situational factors' (Rossi 1959: 37). Its proponents claim that this approach is superior to the social characteristics-contexts model because it can account for the impact of changing political events on people's attitudes about politics.

As indicated above, the evolution of voting behaviour research in the United States, Britain, and elsewhere has been associated closely with the development of social–psychological models of political support. One of the earliest of these models, developed at the University of Michigan, relied heavily on reference- and small-group theory (Belknap and Campbell 1952; see also Campbell, Gurin and Miller 1954; Campbell et al. 1960; Butler and Stokes 1969; Miller and Shanks 1996). Its central concept is *party identification* or, in the British case, what Butler and Stokes (1969: 37) called 'partisan self-image'. In its original formulation, party identification was defined as 'an individual's affective orientation to an important group-object in his environment . . . the political party serves as the group towards which the individual may develop an identification, positive or negative, of some degree of intensity' (Campbell et al. 1960: 121–2). This party identification is typically acquired as the result of childhood and adolescent socialization experiences that occur within families or other primary group settings (Campbell et al. 1960; see also Butler and Stokes 1969; Jennings and Niemi 1974). Once acquired, party

19

identifications are normally very stable in direction; that is, people who identify with a particular party continue to do so throughout their lives. However, party identifications tend to strengthen over the lifecycle as a result of adult experiences that include repeated exposure to, and participation in, the electoral process (Converse 1969, 1976).

As a core, stable element in public political psychology, Michigan-style party identification constitutes a powerful long-term force on voting behaviour. In addition to influencing electoral choice directly, party identification acts as a 'perceptual screen' that affects the acquisition and interpretation of political information. Party identification thereby exerts indirect effects on voting by shaping attitudes towards parties, their issue stands, and their candidates for public office. In Butler and Stokes' account, the perceptual screening functions of party identification help it to overcome the public's lack of political sophistication, particularly its 'remoteness . . . from the affairs of government', 'the limits of its political information', and 'the problem of causal reasoning' as reflected in the difficulties of attributing responsibility to parties for past action or of calculating probable future actions (Butler and Stokes 1969: ch. 2). Moreover, its status as an 'unmoved mover' means that party identification has significant system-level consequences in a democratic polity. When party identification is widespread in an electorate, it constitutes a powerful force working to restore long-term patterns of party competition (Stokes and Iversen 1966). Thus, it provides an important anchor for the existing party system in the minds of citizens and, hence, helps to promote the stability of the larger political order (Campbell et al. 1966).

After the publication of *The American Voter*, the social–psychological conception of party identification enjoyed widespread acceptance and was accorded the status of a key variable in models of electoral choice. However, starting in the 1970s, the popularity of the concept gradually waned as interest grew in individual rationality accounts of voting and other forms of political behaviour. Recently, two lines of theorizing have attempted to refurbish a Michigan-style concept of party identification. One involves schema theory in cognitive psychology. Schemas are cognitive structures that receive, process, and retrieve information for decision-making purposes. Partisan schemas are structures that contain perceptions of partisan differences related to interest in, experience with, and knowledge of political parties (Lodge and Hamill 1986). Voters employ partisan schemas to help them make sense of the political world. These schemas can also serve as heuristic devices—cost-effective shortcuts—that facilitate voters' reasoning about the electoral choices and other political decisions they are asked to make (e.g. Sniderman, Brody, and Tetlock 1991). As such, partisan schemas accord well with the multidimensional construct of partisan orientations towards candidates, groups, and issues developed in *The American Voter*.

Another recent theoretical account of partisanship has been proposed by Green, Palmquist, and Schickler (2002). Green and his colleagues attempt to rescue the social–psychological conception of party identification from the wholesale revisions proposed by members of the individual rationality school. Green et al.'s intellectual point of departure is clearly Ann Arbor: 'The most detailed explanation of the concept of identification, and the one we find most instructive for our own conceptualization, appears on page 121 of *The American Voter*' (Green, Palmquist, and Schickler 2002: 235, note 1; see also Miller and Shanks 1996). They observe that, although the conceptualization, operationalization, and analysis of partisanship have received much attention, there is relatively little work on party identification as a form of self-identification. Moreover, its relationship with other aspects of personal identity has not been thoroughly explored. Green, Palmquist, and Schickler's principal claim is that most people 'know' who they are, where they are located socially, which groups they like and which ones they dislike, and what political parties these groups support. Party identification flows from this mix of cognition and affect—it is a socially informed self-identification with cognitive and affective components.

Green, Palmquist, and Schickler also maintain that, since people typically lack a rich store of politically relevant information and are biased information processors, partisan attachments are relatively immune to changes in the political environment. Indeed, party identifications tend to persist even when people are dissatisfied with their party. Also, as in the Michigan account, party identification affects voting behaviour indirectly. It does so by influencing reactions to candidates and their policy proposals, and by affecting evaluations of important domestic and international events and prevailing economic and social conditions. The stability and filtering function of party identification make it a powerful force anchoring individual voting behaviour and limiting the extent of variation in election outcomes.

THE INDIVIDUAL RATIONALITY FRAMEWORK

The Individual Rationality Framework

The individual rationality framework encompasses a set of decision-making models. In addition to the standard, baseline model of expected utility maximization, the set consists of a variety of spatial and valence models that have been advanced to explain political choice. The standard model of rational decision-making incorporates an expected utility-maximizing strategy (e.g. von Neumann and Morgenstern 1947). In this strategy, a key role is played by preference which is 'a comparative evaluation of a set of objects stored in memory and drawn on when people make decisions' (Druckman and Lupia 2000: 2).[1] A rational person acts on his or her preference in such a way that he or she '(1) can always make a decision when confronted with a range of alternatives . . . . (2) ranks all the alternatives . . . in such a way that each is either preferred to, indifferent to, or inferior to each other . . . . (3) preference ranking is transitive . . . . (4) always chooses from among the possible

21

alternatives that which ranks highest . . . . (5) always makes the same decision each time . . . confronted with the same alternatives' (Downs 1957: 6).

One of the earliest applications of the standard model to the study of voting and elections was the *spatial model* developed by Anthony Downs (1957). This model has its origins in economic theories designed to explain the location decisions made by firms, particularly why businesses and stores tend to select locations in close proximity, such as across the street or next door, to their competitors (Hotelling 1929). Just as business competitors try to attract customers on High Street or Main Street, in Downs' model—sometimes referred to as the Downsian proximity model—political parties lure voters on an ideological ('left-right') continuum (Downs 1957; see also Key 1968; Shepsle and Boncheck 1997). Although the particulars of party strategy reflect contextual considerations, such as the distribution of voter preferences and the number of parties, the general idea motivating the model is simple. Positions on the ideological continuum are determined by preferences for different amounts of government-provided goods and services. Parties compete by moving their policy positions across the continuum to the point that attracts the maximum number of voters. In the classic situation of two-party competition, the expectation is that parties converge on the policy position of the 'median voter' (Black 1958); that is, the person whose policy preference is at the mid-point of the distribution of policy preferences in the electorate. By converging on the position of the median voter, a party maximizes the number of votes it receives.

According to the Downsian spatial model, a rational voter chooses the party that provides the most benefits or 'streams of utility derived from government activity' (Downs 1957: 36). More specifically, the voter chooses by calculating which candidate's or party's issue position is closest to his or her ideal point or preference for utility income on the ideological continuum. This calculation of distances or 'spaces' involves an assessment of 'current party differentials'; that is, comparisons of utility received under an incumbent with what would be obtained under other parties. Although the calculation is simple in principle, Downs and other spatial theorists recognize that, in practice, it can be difficult to compare the expected or future performance of alternative parties should they form a government. A voter may avoid this difficulty by using parties' over-time 'performance ratings'. In doing so, he or she extrapolates by estimating what the incumbent party would do in the future based on what it has done in the past. Another possibility is that the voter employs an 'objective' standard for increasing utility income. Or, he or she may try to determine the difference between utility income received in the present and what would have been received if the opposition had been in power. The result of the latter comparison is straightforward: 'If their present utility incomes are very low in their own eyes, they may believe that almost any change likely to be made will raise their incomes. In this case, it is rational for them to vote against the incumbents . . . On the other hand, men who are benefiting from the incumbents' policies may feel that change is likely to harm rather than help them . . . Hence, they rationally vote for the incumbents' (Downs 1957: 42).These various types of calculations are more easily made in two-party, 'winner-take-all' systems that clarify the locus of policy responsibility than in multi-party, coalitional ones which blur it (Powell and Whitten 1993; Anderson 1995).

Since first introduced, the spatial model has attracted both friends and foes. In one of the early critiques of the model, Stokes emphasized that much inter-party competition involves what he called 'valence issues'. He complained that '[i]t will not do simply to exclude valence-issues from the discussion of party competition' before concluding that such issues 'plainly do not fit the spatial scheme' (Stokes 1963: 373–4). For Stokes, the spatial model relied on four questionable assumptions of unidimensionality, fixed structure, ordered dimensions, and common reference. Contrary to these assumptions, politics often has multiple dimensions, variable issue content, positive or negative values, and spaces of competition that are per-ceived differently by politicians and voters (Stokes 1963, 1992). Stokes' *valence model* especially relies on the idea of positive and negative values. These values are attached to conditions or goals that nearly everyone shares. For example, nearly universal emphasis on the instrumental value of prosperity and individual economic well-being forges a broad consensus on the desirability of high rates of economic growth coupled with low rates of inflation and unemployment. Similarly, the high value placed on collective and individual security stimulates widespread agreement on the desirability of policy outcomes such as 'adequate' national defence, low crime rates, effective healthcare, disease prevention, and transport safety. Public opinion on all of these goals is very heavily skewed.

Stokes argues that the shared emphasis on the desirability of such goals, and their linkages with parties in people's minds, powerfully affect political issue agendas and the nature of inter-party competition. Parties and voters often do not disagree about goals. Rather, they debate which party, which party leader, and which policies are most likely to achieve the outcomes that virtually everyone wants.Voters are encouraged to differentiate leaders and parties on the basis of such qualities as ability or trustworthiness, and symbols of success and failure. The differentiation occurs 'from experiences with parties and leaders, and *the results that they achieve, over time* (emphasis added)' (Stokes 1992: 150). If these results occur in the past or present, then the electorate 'rewards a governing party for its success in bringing prosperity or holds a governing party responsible for its failure to avoid hard times' (Stokes 1992: 147). 'But if the condition is a future or potential one, the argument turns on which party, given possession of the government, is the more likely to bring it about' (Stokes 1963: 373). In sum, valence issues involve compar-ative judgements about party performance in areas on which public opinion is skewed heavily towards 'good' outcomes, notably peace, probity, and prosperity. 'The issue acquires its power from the fact that the parties may be very unequally linked in the public's mind with the universally approved condition of good times and the universally disapproved condition of bad times, and the difference between electoral success and disaster may turn on the parties' ability to strength or weaken these bonds or *valences* in the public's mind' (Stokes 1992: 144).

Although Downsian spatial and Stokesian valence models are often said to be very different, it is possible that they share a number of properties (for a discussion, see Schofield 2003). Both types of models specify the use of future 'utility' or anticipated performance assessments, and they also allow for past- or retrospectively focussed judgements. Moreover, both Downsian and Stokesian models recognize that voters pay attention to *incumbent* performance, and they attribute responsibility for this performance. If voters think that the incumbent party, regardless of partisanship or other political characteristics, *has performed well*, then they reward it for 'good times' and opposition parties lose support. Thus, the incumbent wins votes when inflation or unemployment declines and 'utility' as measured by prosperity improves. However, if voters think that the incumbent party *has performed poorly*, then they punish it for 'bad times' and an opposition party gains support. Accordingly, the incumbent loses votes when inflation and/or unemployment have increased and, hence, 'utility' has decreased. In these scenarios, responsibility attributions are the crucial link between issue evaluations and political choice. The idea of voters attributing credit or blame to an incumbent government for the state of the economy or other valence issues is the core concept that motivates Key's (1968) *reward–punishment model.*

There also is a similarity between Downs' notion of party differential and Stokes' concept of 'position-issues' on which 'parties or leaders are differentiated by their advocacy of alternative positions on an ordered dimension' (Stokes 1992: 143). Thus, the *issue–position model* posits that parties and leaders differ, and are perceived to differ, in their advocacy of alternative policies. More specifically, the issue–position model states that an issue must meet three criteria to affect voting and the outcome of an election. A voter must have a position on an issue, competing parties must have clearly different policies on the issue, and the voter must be able to link his or her position to the policy of one of the parties (Butler and Stokes 1969).

The *issue–priority model* also allows voters to disagree about policy priorities, policy implementation, and party competence (Budge and Farlie 1983; Clarke et al. 1992). The basic idea motivating the issue–priority model is that political parties develop policy agendas that they use to structure public debate, and they establish track records of dealing with a specific set of issues when in office. Parties thereby claim issue ownership and build policy reputations that become widely recognized by voters. A party mobilizes its supporters by emphasizing *its* issues, but not those of other parties and, hence, it benefits when its issues become salient on the political agenda. In contrast to a reward–punishment model, the issue–priority model can have counter-intuitive implications. This is because negative outcomes do not necessarily prompt punishment at the polls. Voters' decisions reflect both current conditions and the perceived issue-priorities of the competing parties. For example, when health services deteriorate or unemployment increases, the issue–priority model predicts that these conditions will become salient election issues, but that voters will not necessarily punish a governing left-of-centre party. The reason is that such parties have records and reputations for caring about these problems and, thus, are perceived as more willing and able to address them. Similarly, when crime worsens or inflation increases, the issue–priority model predicts that people who are concerned about these problems will not abandon an incumbent right-of-centre party because they view it as more willing and able to act on these issues than a left-of-centre party. These predictions of the issue–priority model are consistent with the empirical observation that social welfare and public service issues, such as health, education and welfare provision, traditionally benefit left-of-centre parties, whereas issues involving crime prevention and national defence work to the advantage of right-of-centre parties (e.g. Hibbs 1977, 1987).

To summarize, the basic Downsian spatial model portrays electoral politics as taking place on a unidimensional, left-right continuum.[2] Voters choose the party whose position is closest to them on this continuum. In contrast, the valence model argues that the issues that matter most are ones where public opinion is heavily skewed. For these issues, there is an overwhelming consensus concerning what constitutes a 'good' outcome, and parties are judged in terms of their ability to produce them. The valence model predicts that voters tend to reward an incumbent for good performance and certainly punish it for a bad one. The issue–priority model is a hybrid that incorporates shared goals and parties' reputations for policy competence. More specifically, the model distinguishes parties by the extent to which they care about particular issues and are seen as competent to address them. The issue–priority model suggests that voters are not necessarily wrathful—an incumbent party can survive bad times because 'there is no alternative' for dealing with an issue that is highly valued by a large segment of the electorate. Most fundamentally, all of the models concur that public perceptions of party performance matter when people make their voting decisions.

Economic Evaluations, Party Identification, and Party Leaders

Performance-based models have focussed heavily on the economy, partisanship, and party leader images. As noted, the earliest efforts to develop valence models of voting incorporated national 'economic outlook' (e.g. Campbell et al. 1960: ch.14) and 'the economy as an issue' (Butler and Stokes 1969: 390–4; Goodhart and Bhansali 1970). In the wake of these early efforts, *economic evaluation models* have received a great deal of attention. A key element of these models is voters' evaluations of economic conditions. A great deal of research has focussed on whether voters think primarily in terms of *egocentric* considerations (personal self-interest) or *sociotropic* ones (national economic conditions) (e.g. Kinder and Kiewiet 1979, 1981; Lewis-Beck 1988; Norpoth, Lewis-Beck, and Lafay 1991; Clarke et al. 1992).

An emphasis on egocentric evaluations fits well with the individual rationality framework in microeconomic theory that posits a world of self-interested, utility-maximizing, economic agents. However, an emphasis on sociotropic judgement does not have this close articulation with economic theory because voters are said to be people concerned about the provision of economic goods that flow to society as a whole. It has been hypothesized that part of the explanation of whether voters think socially or selfishly lies in their responsibility attributions for national economic conditions and personal economic circumstances (e.g. Lewis–Beck 1988; see also Sniderman and Brody 1977).

The relative importance of *past-* versus *future*-oriented economic evaluations is another important question in research on the political economy of party support. Downs argues that, if the retrospective–prospective distinction is interpreted to mean past performance versus future promises, then rational individuals will rely on the former when judging the economy. The reason is that the voter 'must either compare (*a*) two hypothetical future utility incomes or (*b*) one actual present utility income and one hypothetical present one. Without question, the latter comparison allows him to make more direct use of concrete facts than the former. Not only is one of its terms a real entity, but the other can be calculated in full view of the situation from which it springs' (Downs 1957: 40). If voters think that the only reliable information is that concerning actual party performance and they want to reduce information-processing costs, then they will rely on information about economic conditions while the present incumbent has been in office. Moreover, if voters suspect that parties will 'say anything', such as making insincere promises to win votes, then they use the credible information they have—which is about parties' past performance.

In contrast, some analysts stress that elections require voters to forecast what parties or leaders will do based on current information (Clarke et al. 1992). Rational voters have no interest in rewarding or punishing anybody. Rather, they wish to maximize their utilities and, to do so, they must make forecasts about what the future holds if an alternative party or leader is elected. These forecasts can be made in various ways. People can use an extrapolative expectations model whereby the future is forecast as a linear trend based on present and past information. Alternatively, they may implement an adaptive expectations model that updates expectations using information about economic performance with current performance being weighted more heavily than past performance. Or, they may use (or at least behave as if they used) a more demanding rational expectations model of how they think the economy works and use this model to make unbiased forecasts. Regardless of which model is employed, the assumption is that economic expectations matter for party support (e.g. MacKuen et al. 1992*b*, 1996; Clarke and Stewart 1994; Erikson, MacKuen, and Stimson 2000, 2002).

Efforts to explain how voters acquire and use economic information when making political support decisions have led to increasing interest in cognitive psychology. If the information required to make a decision is poor, and getting it is expensive, then a cognitively thrifty public can selectively consult trusted media for guidelines about what to think. People also may rely on leaders, party identification, or groups as heuristic devices, or they may employ their emotions for strategic decision-making purposes. With respect to the latter, several scholars have argued that economic (and other) evaluations have affective or emotional content (e.g. Conover and Feldman 1986; Frank 1988; Marcus, Neuman, and MacKuen 2000). That is, voters' thoughts about the economy and their personal economic situations generate emotional reactions that have important effects on how they process politically relevant information. In this regard, people can be confident, happy, hopeful, angry, anxious, or disgusted about economic circumstances even when these do not affect them personally (e.g. Marcus, Neuman, and MacKuen 2000: 169–70). These emotional reactions, in turn, may activate dispositional, surveillance, or other psychological systems by which individuals use either habit or reaction to threat to scan their environments for information that helps to make a decision (Marcus, Neuman, and MacKuen 2000).

The impact of evaluations of economic conditions and the performance of political parties and party leaders extends beyond the voting decision. These evaluations also have important roles in a *valence model of the dynamics of party identification*. As discussed above, Downs argues that the rational citizen compares utility received under an incumbent with what would have been obtained under another party. Current 'party differentials' are then calculated as the basis for choosing a party among competing alternatives (Downs 1957). Key (1968) thought somewhat similarly and anticipated a later, cognitive psychological view of partisanship. According to Key, the connection between policy preference and party identification develops in two ways. Either an identification develops first and the policy preference of the party is adopted next, or an initial preference leads to a subsequent identification. With respect to the latter, he hypothesized that: '[l]ike or dislike of a political personality or a party policy and many other factors bring shifts in party identification' (Key 1968: 298–9).

The ideas advanced in the early work of Downs, Key, and Stokes are echoed in later individual rationality models of partisanship. Among these models, the best known was developed by Fiorina (1981). In the addendum titled 'Valence Issues and Retrospective Voting' to *Retrospective Voting in American National Elections*, Fiorina presented several ideas that were regarded by Stokes as compatible with those expressed in the 'Spatial Competition' article and *Political Change in Britain* (Stokes 1992). For Fiorina, party identification is a storehouse of information about the (largely economic) performance of political parties and their leaders. Over time, voters update their partisanship as they acquire new information on economic conditions and parties' actual or expected performance. Voters make summary 'running tallies' of current and past party performance evaluations, giving more weight to recent, as opposed to earlier, information. Other analysts have proposed similar models (Franklin and Jackson 1983; Franklin 1984, 1992; Achen 1992, 2002; Stewart and Clarke 1998; see also MacKuen, Erikson, and Stimson 1989; Erikson, MacKuen, and Stimson 2000, 2002). Although differing in detail, these models agree that partisanship at any point in time is the product of voters using a utility-maximizing or satisficing strategy to process information. The core idea is that partisanship is not exclusively a product of early-life socialization but, rather, of information updating that produces changes in both the intensity and direction of partisan attachments. Stokes recognized that the possibility of partisan dynamics posed a major challenge to the Michigan model of party identification. Writing in the early 1990s, he concluded that '[t]he trend towards valence politics is plainly correlated with the weakening of the old-time party loyalties, which were rooted in strong position issues' (Stokes 1992: 158). As we show in Chapter Six, the consequences are not trivial; variations in economic conditions and attendant shifts in party performance evaluations are sufficient to produce consequential individual- and aggregate-level changes in partisanship.

A third area in which performance or valence judgements matter concerns how *party leader images* affect parties' standings with the electorate. It has traditionally been argued that leader images have small to null effects on voting behaviour and election outcomes in Britain (for a review, see King 2002*b*). The argument has two variations. One is that leader images are short-term, ephemeral factors that are easily overcome by the complex of powerful long-term forces summarized by voters' class locations. The other argument is that 'the pull of the leaders remains but one among the factors that determine transient shifts of party strength; it is easily out-weighed by other issues and events of concern to the public, including the movements of the economy which do so much to set the climate of the party battle' (Butler and Stokes 1969: 387–8). In recent years, this latter argument has contin-ued to resonate among observers of British politics—'issues of performance and issues of policy loom much larger in most voters' minds than do issues of person-ality' (King 2002: 220). The claim is that issue concerns, particularly those focussing on economic problems, and public perceptions of parties' abilities to handle these problems, deserve pride of place in models of electoral choice.

We propose that leader images matter as well. It has been claimed that leaders' personalities infrequently affect electoral choice and election outcomes directly, and that they can operate indirectly through leaders' influence on governments and parties (King 2002*b*). However, we contend that leader *images*—people's feelings of like or dislike of leaders and the standards of judgement that they bring to bear on leader performance—exert significant direct effects on party support. They do so for three reasons. The first pertains to the evolving roles of prime ministers in parliamentary systems. Over the past two decades, a variety of system-level and other factors, including constitutional developments, leadership style, party strategy, and public outreach activities, have contributed to the 'presidentialization' of the prime minister's role (e.g. Mughan 1993; Foley 2000). The media have also been an important factor by constantly shining the publicity spotlight on the prime minister. Consistent with recent empirical evidence, the presidentialization hypothesis states that prime ministers have significant effects on party support, but it does not require these effects to be equally strong regardless of who occupies Number 10 (Clarke, Ho, and Stewart 2000).

A second reason focuses on the conduct of election campaigns in parliamentary and presidential systems alike. In this regard, much has been made about the candidate-centered, versus party-oriented, election campaigns that have evolved in response to the primary election system and televised campaigning in the United States. In parliamentary systems, candidate- or leader-centered campaigning presumably would develop more slowly since leader behaviour is restrained by parliament (Wattenberg 1991; Dalton and Wattenberg 2000). However, campaign-related factors are influential in parliamentary systems (see Chapter Five). In the contemporary era, parties begin their 'long campaigns' months or even years before the writs are issued, and once the election is called, media coverage of the parties and their leaders intensifies greatly. The media encourage the 'personalization' of electoral politics by focussing heavily on the leaders' policy pronouncements, by conducting in-depth, sometimes provocative, interviews with them, and by monitoring their 'comings and goings' on the campaign trail. For their part, parties promote this tendency by fighting leader-centered national campaigns (Foley 2000; King 2002).

The third reason involves voter psychology. The contention that leader images have significant effects on electoral choice does not require the assumption that voters are responding irrationally to vacuous aspects of leader images dreamed up by advertising agencies and party spin doctors. It also is important to appreciate that 'issues' and 'parties' are essentially abstractions, not amenable to direct sensory perception. In contrast, party leaders are seen and heard frequently and, on occasion, spoken to and touched—they are highly visible embodiments of their parties (Miller, Wattenberg, and Malachuk 1986). Moreover, if an issue is particularly complicated, then voters may resort to heuristic devices, including leader images, to deal with too little or too much information, the uncertainty of the decision-making environment, and their aversion to risk (e.g. Sniderman, Brody, and Tetlock 1991). In this regard, party leader images provide helpful cues because they compress information into forms that can be conveniently and effectively used to make electoral choices.

We hypothesize that democratic norms, formal government processes that emphasize accountability, and intense media scrutiny of performance encourage voters to use standards of judgement that invoke two dimensions of leader images. These images are leaders' general effectiveness or *competence*, and their caring about or *responsiveness* to public concerns. Since governing leaders tend to have greater public salience and more established records than do opposition leaders, the two dimensions of the former's image may be more clearly defined and less strongly correlated than those of the latter. This was certainly the case for Margaret Thatcher whose 'conviction politics', notably her unrelenting advocacy of neoconservative policies, contributed to a sharp distinction in people's minds between her competence to manage the government, and her responsiveness to public needs and concerns (Stewart and Clarke 1992).

To illustrate the structure of party leader images in the British electorate, we conduct a confirmatory factor analysis[3] of the 2001 BES data. In the post-election wave of the survey, respondents were asked about six aspects of the leaders' images. We first test a baseline model that assumes all six aspects comprise a unidimensional leader image. This single-factor model has a poor fit for all three leaders. For example, for Tony Blair, the model's goodness-of-fit statistics are: $\chi^2 = 159.11$, $df = 14$, $p = 0.000$, and the RMSEA test decisively rejects the hypothesis of a close fit (Joreskog and Sorbom 1996). We next consider a model that specifies two separate, but interrelated, competence and responsiveness factors. This model hypothesizes that the 'keeps promises', 'decisive', and 'principled' items load on the competence factor whereas the 'caring', 'listens to reason', and 'not arrogant' items load on the responsiveness factor. This two-factor model is initially tested using data for Tony Blair.[4] As Table 2.1 shows, the model's fit is very good ($\chi^2 = 46.75$, $df = 11$, $p = 0.00$; see Table 2.1), and the RMSEA test indicates a close fit. Applying the two-factor model to the data for Hague and Kennedy also produces satisfactory results. In addition, the two-factor models for the three leaders explain substantial amounts of item variance, and all factor loadings are statistically significant. In all three cases, the strongest loadings on the competence factor are 'keeps promises' and 'principled', whereas 'caring' has the largest loading on the responsiveness factor. The inter-factor correlations are strong for all three leaders, but especially for Kennedy, thereby suggesting that the competence and responsiveness components of his image were less clearly separated in voters' minds than was the case for Blair and Hague. Overall, the results are consistent with the hypothesis that British voters' leader images are structured in terms of two, interrelated, competence and responsiveness dimensions. These results echo those produced by analyses of leader images during the Thatcher era (Stewart and Clarke 1992), thereby indicating that separate competence and responsiveness components are enduring features of party leader images in Britain.

SOCIAL DETERMINISM, VALENCE POLITICS, AND POLITICAL CHOICE IN BRITAIN

In the sociological tradition of electoral inquiry, social characteristics, social contexts, and social psychology drive political preference. As this tradition developed in Britain, class became the pre-eminent politically relevant social cleavage. Class provides beliefs, cues, interests, and values to members, and class identities

Table 2.1 Confirmatory factor analyses of party leader images

Image	Factor	
	Responsiveness	*Competence*
A. *Tony Blair*[a]		
Capable of strong leadership	0.00	0.76
Keeps promises	0.00	0.93
Caring	0.86	0.00
Decisive	0.00	0.68
Sticks to principles	0.00	0.89
Listens to reason	0.76	0.00
Not arrogant	0.67	0.00
B. *William Hague*[b]		
Capable of strong leadership	0.00	0.66
Keeps promises	0.00	0.82
Caring	0.85	0.00
Decisive	0.00	0.59
Sticks to principles	0.00	0.87
Listens to reason	0.72	0.00
Not arrogant	0.62	0.00
C. *Charles Kennedy*[c]		
Capable of strong leadership	0.00	0.60
Keeps promises	0.00	0.76
Caring	0.87	0.00
Decisive	0.00	0.66
Sticks to principles	0.00	0.85
Listens to reason	0.81	0.00
Not arrogant	0.66	0.00

Note: Weighted least squares estimates.
[a] Inter-factor correlation $(\phi) = 0.89$, $\chi^2 = 46.75$, $df = 11$, $p = 0.00$; RMSEA $= 0.03$, p (test for close fit) $= 1.0$; $N = 3010$.
[b] Inter-factor correlation $(\phi) = 0.79$, $\chi^2 = 46.89$, $df = 10$, $p = 0.00$; RMSEA $= 0.04$, p (test for close fit) $= 0.99$; $N = 3006$.
[c] Inter-factor correlation $(\phi) = 0.94$, $\chi^2 = 35.07$, $df = 11$, p $= 0.00$; RMSEA $= 0.03$, p (test for close fit) $= 1.0$; $N = 3013$.
Source: 2001 BES post-election survey.

and interests are the foundations of partisan attachments and reflected in images projected by political parties. Labour's commitment to redistributive policies and the welfare state, together with its trade-union associations, have distinguished it as the party of the working class. In contrast, the Conservative Party's commitment to property rights and business enterprise has helped to forge the link between itself and the middle class.

Theories and Models of Party Support

By making social class a principal explanatory factor in their models of electoral choice and political change, Butler and Stokes were very much in the mainstream of British political inquiry. But, there was a rather obvious irony in their doing so. If the class locations of most voters do not vary significantly and the choices presented by parties do not shift in major ways between consecutive general elections, then social class has very limited power to explain differences in successive election outcomes. However, Butler and Stokes seemingly stood on stronger ground when employing social class to explain party choice in a given election. To this end, they relied heavily on the social-psychological conceptualization of party identification. In Butler and Stokes' account, party identification converts voters' social class locations into long-term party support. In the political world that they described, tribal loyalties ruled—just as a vast majority of voters developed life-long identifications as middle or working class, they labelled themselves as Conservatives or Labour.

Although Butler and Stokes presented statistical evidence regarding the strength of the relationships among social class, party identification, and voting behaviour, the task of explaining variations in election outcomes and, hence, political change remained incomplete. In this regard, they claimed that demographic processes, such as those involving differential fertility and mortality rates in the working and middle classes, could shift the balance of party support (Butler and Stokes 1969: 265–74). However, such processes happen gradually and, hence, their impact on political change is felt only in the long run. If party identification is an influential, but very stable, element in voters' political psychology, then electoral change is bound to occur slowly. Barring major realigning events—such as a great depression or major war—which rapidly corrode longstanding party loyalties and forge new ones, the balance of party support will be a product of generational changes. What matters is the proportions of successive, differentially sized generations of working class Labour and middle class Conservative party identifiers entering and exiting the electorate. Thus, inserting party identification as a mediating variable in the social-class electoral choice causal chain is of little help in explaining short- and medium-term change. Butler and Stokes implicitly recognized the limitations of a class-based model of electoral change by devoting several later chapters of their book to analyses of the effects of potentially highly mutable variables such as voters' economic evaluations, party preferences on important issues, and party leader images.

Although it would appear that explanations of short- and medium-term change in party support have to look beyond the effects of social class, some analysts have remained staunch defenders of the sociological framework and, in particular, the class–vote model. Its defence has been made two ways. First, it has been suggested that '[i]t may be time to rehabilitate the idea of social determinism' (Weakliem and Heath 1994: 263). This suggestion hinges largely on the assumption that the relationship between class and voting is generally strong and, *ceteris paribus*, does not

32

vary systematically over time. The 'trendless fluctuation' observed in the relationship reflects the extent of convergence in various elections in competing parties'
policy programmes. The class–vote relationship strengthens when party programmes diverge and weakens when they converge (Heath, Jowell, and Curtice
2001; see also Evans, 1999). This approach is flawed because, as we show in Chapter
Three, the relationship between class and vote has weakened appreciably over time.
Moreover, over the entire period for which BES data are available, the relationship
has never been as strong as many observers have assumed. This also fails to explain
party choice in elections when there is a convergence in party programmes.

A second defence is mounted by analysts who are less concerned about the
strength of the class–vote relationship but unwilling to abandon the central role of
society in political choice. Some maintain that social interactions occurring in
neighbourhoods and other places are very important (e.g. Curtice and Park 1999).
Others claim that the class–vote relationship has actually strengthened at sub-national
aggregate levels, although this relationship may have weakened across the country as
a whole (e.g. Miller 1977). Still others have proposed alternative measures as ways of
capturing what they perceive to be the evolving social realities of British political
life. These include different measures of social class and other politically relevant
socioeconomic cleavages, such as voters' consumption and production relationships
to the public and private sectors (e.g. Dunleavy and Husbands 1985). Finally, there
are efforts to develop socio-cultural explanations of imperfections in class–vote
relationships following the tradition of the classic studies of working-class Tories and
silk-stocking socialists (Nordlinger 1967; McKenzie and Silver 1968). The newer
generation of such studies focusses on the confluence of family learning, socioeconomic interests, ideology and values (Rose and McAllister 1986, 1990).

Neither group of studies has overcome scepticism regarding the explanatory
power of social class in particular, or of sociological models of party support more
generally. This scepticism is now longstanding. In the short, five-year span after
Political Change in Britain first appeared, data from the two 1974 British Election
Studies showed that the social class–party support nexus had weakened significantly
(Crewe, Sarlvik, and Alt 1977; see also Sarlvik and Crewe 1983). Subsequent
election studies have shown further erosion of the relationship, thereby indicating
that class dealignment had become a prominent feature of British electoral politics
long before New Labour's victory in 1997 (e.g. Crewe 1974, 1986; Clarke and
Stewart 1984; Franklin 1985; Franklin, Mackie, and Valen 1992). National monthly
surveys conducted over the past decade demonstrate the continuing weakness
of ties between party and society. As discussed in Chapter Six, these time series data
reveal that the traditional BES measure of party identification manifests considerable short-term dynamism, and that aggregate-level partisanship reacts to changes
in economic evaluations and salient events such as the 1992 ERM crisis (see also
Clarke, Stewart, and Whiteley 1997, 1998). In sum, evidence gathered over the past
three decades indicates that attenuated relationships among class, partisanship, and

vote are not a short-lived period phenomenon or a methodological artefact of when and how the data were collected.

The questioning of sociological models has been accompanied by a growing interest in the power of the individual rationality framework to explain electoral choice and political change. For example, a recent spatial analysis suggests that New Labour successfully exploited the ideological space by moving to the centre where most voters resided, and thereby forced the Conservatives to rely on their core right-wing supporters in the 1997 general election (Sanders 1998). An alternative analytical approach recognizes that the links between valence politics and political choice have strong historical antecedents. Britain has long been characterized as having a political–cultural tradition in which liberal beliefs and principles have coexisted with significant elements of conservatism and socialism (Beer 1965, 1982). This political–cultural mix has required a balance between ideas about government's role in economy and society and those about individuals' responsibility for their own welfare.

Whatever may be the equilibrium between these positions at any particular point in time, the Keynesian macroeconomic revolution, and the expansion of government economic management, have been accompanied by rising public expectations about what government could, and should, do to improve economic performance and personal well-being. In the aftermath of the Second World War, political parties, regardless of ideological principles, were convinced that economic-management techniques were the navigational instruments for steering around the pernicious effects of an economic downturn and directing course towards prosperity. Perhaps not surprisingly, many people in Britain came to believe that government can, and should, be deeply involved in economy and society. As a result, they came to demand more prosperity and more programmes requiring more growth. In the 1970s, when growth yielded to stagnation, there was a rising tide of public discontent and an increasing debate about government overload and the fiscal crisis of the welfare state (O'Connor 1973; Habermas 1975; King 1975; Brittan 1983). At the same time, interest grew in the ideas of neoconservative politicians who rejected the post-Second World War accord on the role of government. But, through the ebbs and flows of political debate and economic misfortune, the British public has held fast to its expectations that government can, and should, be involved in a wide variety of important policy areas (Clarke, Stewart, and Zuk 1988; Borre and Scarbrough 1995; Kaase and Newton 1995).

This public emphasis on performance is particularly evident in findings from analyses of the effects of economic evaluations on party support decisions. Research demonstrates that geographic variations in perceived economic performance and efficacy are the principal determinants of cross-constituency differences in voting behaviour (e.g. Johnston, Pattie, and Allsopp 1988). Aggregate-level time series analyses of the dynamics of party support also indicate the importance of economic evaluations. For example, the 'Essex Model' hypothesizes that macroeconomic conditions, particularly interest rates and taxation rates, strongly influence voters' expectations about their personal financial circumstances, and these expectations, in turn, propel the dynamics of governing party support (e.g. Sanders et al. 1987; Sanders 1991, 1993, 1995). Although differing in detail, other time series models have also shown that economic evaluations have significant effects on support for parties and their leaders (e.g. Clarke and Stewart 1995; Clarke, Stewart, and Whiteley, 1997, 1998; Norpoth 1997).

There is additional evidence that emotional reactions to economic conditions matter. In this regard, the British media typically conflate the concepts of evaluation and emotion by applying the label 'feel-good factor' to voters' personal economic expectations. However, the feel-good factor does not explicitly tap emotional responses to economic performance. There are surveys that employ direct measures of emotional reactions to national and personal economic conditions (Clarke, Stewart, and Whiteley 1997, 1998). This research finds that British voters' emotional reactions to the national economy are more often negative than positive, and these reactions, in turn, typically are more negative than personal ones. Both personal and national emotional reactions became markedly more negative at the time of the September 1992 currency crisis and increasingly positive in the months before the 1997 election. These findings agree with the argument that emotional reactions are not simply static reflections of deep-seated personality traits. Rather, these reactions have dynamic properties and are triggered by dramatic events as well as ongoing movements in the economy. Moreover, controlling for economic evaluations and several other variables, emotional reactions to economic circumstances significantly influence aggregate movements in partisanship and evaluations of party leader performance.

The argument that variations in party support are strongly affected by valence politics is strengthened by research on the impact of leader images. As noted, it has long been conventional wisdom among British political scientists that evaluations of leaders do not matter much as determinants of voting behaviour. Certainly, the model of long-term factors associated with social class had little room for short-term forces involving leader effects on political choice. When short-term forces received consideration, issue concerns, particularly those focussing on economic problems, and public perceptions of parties' abilities to handle these problems, were thought to dominate effects associated with the images of the party leaders (Butler and Stokes 1969: 387–8). However, mounting evidence points to quite different conclusions. Studies conducted over the past two decades show that perceptions of governing and opposition party leaders strongly influence electoral choice and levels of party support in inter-election periods (Miller et al. 1990; Stewart and Clarke 1992; Clarke, Stewart, and Whiteley 1997, 1998). These British findings that 'leaders matter' accord well with the results of research in other Anglo-American democracies such as the United States, Canada, and Australia (e.g. Clarke et al. 1979; Miller, Wattenberg, and Malanchuk 1986; Marcus 1988; Bean and Mughan 1989; Clarke, Kornberg, and Wearing 2000). In all of these countries, voters' perceptions of leader competence are important elements in the set of 'valence politics' forces that do much to shape voting behaviour and election outcomes.

In sum, we argue that sociological models can tell only a limited part of the story of political choice in Britain. This is true now and it was true some four decades ago, when the first national election studies were conducted. The fundamental limitations of sociological models are their inability to deal with information that lacks an obvious social group referent, and their inability to keep pace with the short- and medium-term changes in the variables they purport to explain (Dalton and Wattenberg 1993). As noted, Butler and Stokes were well aware that polity and economy move faster than society. Hence, the later chapters of their book effectively abandoned their sociological model and turned attention to potentially mutable factors such as party–issue linkages, party leader images, economic conditions, and election campaigns. As Stokes (1992: 141–2) observed, these components of the valence framework acquired even more prominence in subsequent editions of *Political Change in Britain*. We believe that it was right to do so. But, beliefs about facts, and facts themselves, can be two quite different things. Accordingly, in the following chapters, we investigate the ability of various sociological and individual rationality models to explain political choice in the 2001 and earlier British elections.

NOTES

1. Preferences require comparison among alternatives; dominance by a superior strategy; invariance in relation to how alternatives are presented; strictness in ordering so that if P_1 is preferred strictly to P_2, then P_2 cannot be preferred strictly to P_1; and transitivity so that if P_1 is preferred to P_2 and P_2 is preferred to P_3, then P_1 must be preferred to P_3 (Plous 1993: 82–3; Druckman and Lupia 2000: 12–13; Saari 2001: 34–6).

2. Subsequent spatial models posit that inter-party competition and electoral choice occur on more complex, multidimensional, political landscapes (Merrill and Grofman 1999; see also Miller, Page, and Kollman 1998). Political parties roam over these landscapes, with some models permitting parties to 'leapfrog' each other to get closer to the ideal points of particular groups of voters. But, long jumps and extreme positions may be counterproductive. For example, the Macdonald and Rabinowitz (1993) directional model warns that a voter will not support a party that takes a position 'too far' from his or her preferred outcome.

3. CFA tests hypothesized measurement models. In these models, the observed variables are assumed to be caused by latent constructs or 'factors' (e.g. Joreskog and Sorbom 1996: ch. 3). CFA goodness-of-fit tests inform the researcher regarding the degree to which a hypothesized measurement model accurately reproduces the covariance structure of the observed data. Since CFA inter-factor correlations are population parameter estimates rather than arbitrary values, they provide important information about relationships between hypothesized latent factors. Here, CFA is implemented using LISREL 8.53's

weighted least squares (WLS) procedure that does not require the assumptions of interval-level measurement and multivariate normal distributions. It is particularly appropriate for analyses of ordinal or dichotomous survey data that have skewed response distributions.

4. The two-factor model for Blair is first tested using data drawn from one random half-sample of the survey respondents. Data from the remaining half-sample then are used to repeat the test and check the results. In comparison with the one-factor baseline model, the two-factor model for Blair does much better for the first half-sample ($\chi^2 = 28.44$, $df = 11, p = 0.01$) as well as the second ($\chi^2 = 28.92, df = 11, p = 0.001$). In both cases, the RMSEA test indicates a close fit. We therefore proceed to assess the fit of the model for Blair using data from the entire sample.

THREE

Party Support in Britain, 1964–2001

In Chapter Two, we discussed two major theoretical frameworks or approaches that have informed the study of electoral choice. These are the sociological framework and the individual rationality framework. This chapter explores the relevance of models of electoral choice located in these frameworks for understanding party support in Britain since 1964. The exploration is motivated by two considerations. First, since an important substantive aim of this book is to explain the outcome of the 2001 British general election, we need to understand why New Labour enjoyed an almost continuous opinion poll lead over the Conservatives throughout the 1997 parliament. We suggest that the origins of this sustained period of government popularity and New Labour's victory in 2001 lay in earlier changes in the electorate's economic evaluations and political preferences. Second, a principal theoretical goal of this study is to examine the relative importance of alternative theoretical accounts of electoral choice. We begin this examination here by considering the main changes that have occurred over the last four decades in relationships between party choice and the explanatory 'signature' variables that characterize sociological, issue–proximity, and valence models. Our analysis draws primarily on data gathered in successive British Election Study (BES) surveys conducted at each general election since 1964. These data are supplemented by evidence from a new data set based on over 127,000 interviews carried out by the Gallup Organization in monthly surveys between 1992 and 2002.

The chapter first considers the changing character and importance of models located in the sociological framework. We show that, although certain sociodemographic characteristics, notably region, became increasingly important predictors of voting after the 1960s, the explanatory power of social class—the core signature variable of the dominant sociological model—weakened appreciably. The strength of party identification, another major component of the model, has also fallen continuously since the mid-1960s. These declines in class-based voting and partisanship suggest, in turn, that the sociological approach is less relevant now than it was in the 1960s. The second part of the chapter examines the issue–proximity model. Data from the 1983–2001 BES surveys reveal that Labour's shift to the right in the 1990s brought the party much closer to the issue preferences of much of the electorate. This change was an important precondition for Labour's success in both 1997 and 2001. The third part of the chapter considers the valence model. We argue that the impact of issue priorities on voting for the two major parties has changed very little since the 1960s. More importantly, using evaluations of party leaders as a proxy for more general judgements about party *competence*, we show that competence perceptions have played a key role in determining electoral choice since at least the 1960s. In addition, Gallup data document the crucial reversal in public perceptions of the Conservatives and of Labour as managers of the economy that occurred in the early 1990s—a reversal that underpinned Labour's successes and the Conservatives' failures in 1997 and 2001. We then analyze a series of multivariate models to investigate changes in the importance of various factors that have affected party support between 1992 and 2001. These analyses indicate that the sociological, issue–proximity, and valence approaches all have some explanatory leverage. However, the valence model performs best—providing a plausible and consistently powerful explanation of voting behaviour over the past four decades.

THE SOCIOLOGICAL APPROACH

As discussed in Chapter Two, the sociological approach dominated research on voting behaviour in Britain in the 1960s (Pulzer 1968; Butler and Stokes 1969). Its account of the effects of social structure hypothesizes strong linkages among class identities, partisan identities, and electoral choice. Class was the departure point. British electoral politics were said to be strongly 'tribal', with large majorities of voters identifying themselves as members of either the working class or the middle class. Evidence from the early BES surveys was interpreted as supporting this claim. Thus, Butler and Stokes (1969: 66–7) emphasized that only one person in twelve refused to volunteer or, at least, accept a working or middle class label when requested to do so. The party system mirrored the dichotomous pattern of class identification. Labour's historic commitment to the redistribution of wealth through the instruments of progressive taxation and the welfare state, together with its close association with the trade union movement, clearly marked it as the champion of the working class. Similarly, the Conservative Party's commitment to property rights, business, and free enterprise firmly established it as the defender of the middle class. The result was that the vast majority of voters easily translated their class identifications into political preferences by developing strong and stable identifications with one of these parties. Guided by partisan attachments reflecting their class identities, voters supported the same party in one election after the next.

This portrait of the forces driving electoral choice in Britain is parsimonious, but inaccurate. The 1964–2001 BES surveys reveal that both party identification

Party Support in Britain, 1964–2001

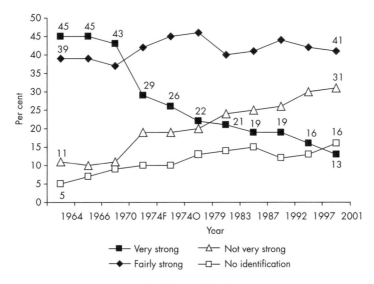

Figure 3.1 Strength of party identification, 1964–2001

Source: 1964–2001 BES post-election surveys.

and class-based voting have declined significantly over the past four decades. As Figure 3.1 shows, the percentage of the electorate who identified 'very strongly' with a party fell from 45 per cent in 1964 to 22 per cent in 1979. The decline continued thereafter—albeit more slowly—so that by 2001, only 13 per cent regarded themselves as very strong party identifiers. A similar pattern emerges when 'fairly strong' identifiers are considered in conjunction with 'very strong' ones. In 1964, very strong and fairly strong identifiers together constituted over 80 per cent of the electorate. By 2001, this figure had fallen to 54 per cent.[1]

This decrease in the strength of partisanship has been accompanied by a long-term decline in class-based voting, that is, in the tendency for the working class to support Labour, and for the middle class to support the Conservatives. Table 3.1 contrasts the class–vote relationship in 1964 with that in 2001.[2] In 1964, approximately two-thirds of the working class (people with manual occupations) supported Labour, and slightly over three-fifths of the middle class (those with non-manual occupations) supported the Conservatives. In 2001, although Labour still retained a disproportionate share of working class support, the Conservatives' lead among the middle class had disappeared.

Using cross-tabulations such as the one in Table 3.1, it is possible to construct various measures of the strength of class-based voting that can be tracked over time. One such measure is the *Alford index* of 'absolute class voting'. As used in the British context, the Alford index is designed to gauge the extent to which

41

Party Support in Britain, 1964–2001

Table 3.1   Class voting, 1964 and 2001 (Column percentages)

	1964		2001	
	Social class		Social class	
Vote	Non-Manual	Manual	Non-Manual	Manual
Conservative	62(a)	28(c)	34	20
Labour	22(b)	64(d)	38	61
Other	16	8	28	19

Note: Non-manual occupations are categories A, B, and C1 of the social class variable; manual categories are categories C2, D, and E. The Alford Index of absolute class voting is calculated as d−b (see Alford 1964: 79–80). The consistency index of absolute class voting is calculated as (a−c) + (d−b). A relative class-voting index (the odds ratio) can be calculated as (a/b)/(c/d). See Heath, Jowell, and Curtice (1985: 31).

Source: 1964 and 2001 BES post-election surveys.

working class people are differentially predisposed to support the Labour Party. The index, which varies from 0 to 100, is computed by subtracting the percentage of middle class people (i.e. those with non-manual occupations) who voted for the Labour Party from the percentage of working class people (i.e. those with manual occupations) who voted Labour. In addition, we compute a generalized version of the Alford index, which we call the *consistency index*. This index, which varies from 0 to 200, equals the Alford index plus a number computed by subtracting the percentage of working class respondents who voted for the Conservative Party from the percentage of middle class respondents who voted Conservative.[3] The rationale for this index derives from the fact that voters can choose a party other than Labour or the Conservatives. Hence, the consistency index provides a more comprehensive measure of class voting conceived as the extent to which both middle and working class people support the 'natural' party of their class. Finally, since part of the long-lived controversy concerning the decline in class voting in Britain has focussed on how the relationship is measured, we also compute the index of *relative class voting* suggested by one of the major participants in the debate (e.g. see, Heath, Jowell, and Curtice 1985).[4] This relative index is the odds of a middle class person voting Conservative rather than Labour divided by the odds of a working class person doing so.

Figure 3.2(a) traces the values of the three indices using data gathered in the eleven BES post-election surveys conducted between 1964 and 2001. There are three important points to note. First, all three indices indicate that the strength of class-voting has declined substantially. The value of the Alford index has fallen from 42 to 23, the consistency index has fallen from 76 to 37, and the relative index has fallen from 6.4 to 2.7. Second, the three indices are very strongly correlated—indeed, their

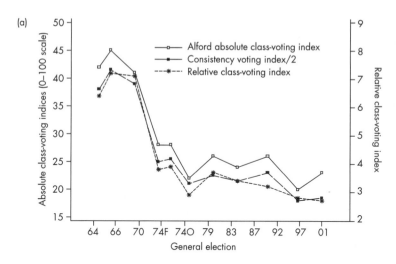

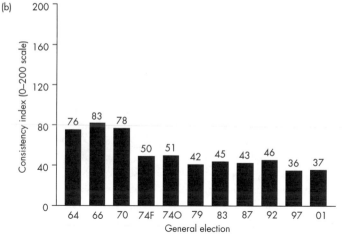

Figure 3.2 The decline of class voting, 1964–2001 general elections (a) Three measures of class voting, 1964–2001 general election (b) Consistency index of class voting, 1964–2001 (0–200) scale

Source: 1964–2001 BES post-election surveys.

average inter-correlation (r) is fully +0.99. The virtually identical patterns produced by the three indices suggest that using an absolute or a relative class voting index makes no substantive difference for portraying the dynamics of class voting. All three indices show that class has become less important as a source of party preferences since the mid-1960s. Over time, British voters have become less 'tribal'—less class-driven—in their electoral choices.

Third, when calibrating the decline in the strength of class voting, it is important to note the starting point relative to the scale on which the relationship is being measured. As Figure 3.2(b) illustrates, the Alford index and the consistency index never approached their maximum values. The Alford index fell from 42 in 1964 to 23 in 2001, but this is on a scale ranging from 0 to 100. Similarly, the consistency index fell from 76 to 37 on a scale ranging from 0 to 200. Another way of making the point is to observe that well over one-third of those casting a ballot in 1964 did not support their 'natural' class party. Twenty-six per cent were 'cross-voters'; that is, members of the working class who voted Conservative or members of the middle class who voted Labour. An additional 11 per cent voted for the Liberals or another party. The comparable figures for 2001 are 31 per cent and 24 per cent, respectively. The absolute class–voting indices clearly testify that there is less class-based political 'tribalism' now than there used to be, but equally clearly, they tell us that class voting was not pervasive when the BES began some four decades ago.

It is possible to go further. The tribal metaphor implies that people identify *themselves* as well as the Conservative and Labour parties in class terms. As noted above, Butler and Stokes were impressed that large percentages of BES respondents have been willing to accept middle or working class labels if prompted to do so by interviewers. But, the key words here are 'willing' and 'prompted'. When not cued to adopt a class label in an initial question or being requested to do so in a follow-up one, BES respondents indicate that the extent of class self-identification is much more limited. For example, random half-samples of the 1964 and 1966 BES respondents were asked: 'Do you ever think of yourself as belonging to a particular social class?' Fully 50 per cent, and 54 per cent, respectively, said 'no'.[5] More recent data indicate little has changed. For the six BES conducted between February 1974 and 1992, on average 53 per cent responded to an initial open-ended class identification question by saying that they never thought of themselves in class terms. The comparable figures for the two most recent studies are 48 per cent for 1997 and 50 per cent for 2001. Thus, for at least the past four decades, there always have been large numbers of BES respondents whose class identifications are artefacts—products of a question sequence that forces them to choose either the middle or working class.[6] This observation, in turn, prompts the inference that the 'class tribes' always have been considerably smaller than commonly supposed. If upwards of one-half of the British electorate lack class self-identifications, a model of their voting behaviour in which (absent) class identities drive party support cannot be correct.

The BES data also tell us that the decline of class voting has not affected the Conservative and Labour parties in equal measure. Figure 3.3 displays how Conservative middle class voting and Labour working class voting varied between 1964 and 2001. Until 1987, levels of Conservative support in the middle class and Labour support in working class support tended to move together. Although Labour's working class vote increased progressively thereafter, the Conservatives' support among the middle class fell dramatically in 1997 and remained low in 2001.

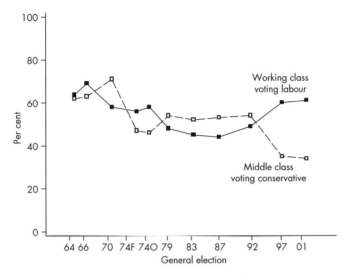

Figure 3.3   Middle class support for Conservatives and working class support
for Labour, 1964–2001 general elections

Source: 1964–2001 BES post-election surveys.

Figure 3.3 thereby suggests that, although both major parties have been adversely affected by the long-term decline in class voting, since 1992 the Conservatives have suffered a serious loss of 'natural' class support. The evidence in Figure 3.4 supports this conclusion. The figure indicates that Conservative election victories (in 1970 and 1979–92) were associated with increased working class support for the Tories and reduced middle class support for Labour, whereas Labour victories were associated with the reverse pattern. The trendless 'mirror-imaging' of Labour and Conservative support in Figure 3.4 indicates that, since 1964, there have been no systematic long-term changes in either working class Conservative or middle class Labour support. The crucial changes, as displayed in Figure 3.3, have been the decline in the Conservatives' share of the middle class vote, and the rebound in Labour's share of the working class vote.

But, if both partisanship and class-based voting were already in decline by the 1970s, what was happening to the other aspects of social–structural position? Were they, too, becoming less important? Or, did the decline of class voting and partisanship mean that other social–structural factors were becoming increasingly significant? Class has undoubtedly never been the only source of social–structural cleavage in British electoral politics, and some analysts have argued that other sources have become more important over time (e.g. Dunleavy and Husbands 1985; Johnston and Pattie 1995). Moreover, a full specification of the sociological framework requires more than just a consideration of the role of class.[7] In the

45

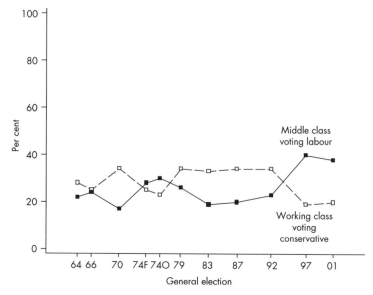

Figure 3.4 Working class support for Conservatives and middle class support
for Labour, 1964–2001 general elections

Source: 1964–2001 BES post-election surveys.

1960s, both the Conservatives and Labour had distinctive socio-demographic
support profiles that extended beyond their class bases of support. The
Conservatives drew support disproportionately from homeowners (who, until the
1970s, were themselves overwhelmingly middle class), from England (especially
outside the major urban centres), from women, and from older voters. Labour was
supported disproportionately by people living in rented accommodation, by voters
living in Northern England, Scotland or Wales, by men, and by younger voters.
The Liberal Democrats, for their part, were notable for not having a strong socio-
demographic constituency, although they enjoyed disproportionate support among
the middle class and in the Southwest of England and Scotland. How, if at all, did
the social characteristics of support change between the 1960s and 2001?

Figure 3.5 displays consistency indices for homeownership, region, gender,
and age for each election between 1964 and 2001.[8] The homeownership line on
the figure denotes the proclivity for homeowners disproportionately to vote
Conservative and for those living in rented accommodation to vote Labour. The
line for region represents the extent to which Labour voting was concentrated in
the North of England, Scotland, and Wales, and Conservative voting was
concentrated in England. The gender line indicates the tendency for women to
disproportionately support the Conservatives and for men to support Labour. And,

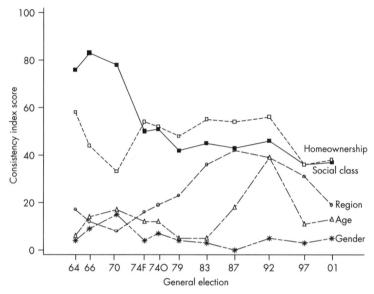

Figure 3.5 Effects of socio-demographic characteristics on Conservative versus Labour voting, 1964–2001 general elections

Source: 1964–2001 BES post-election surveys.

the line for age represents the extent to which Labour support was concentrated among people under the age of 35 and Conservative support among those over 35.

Several features of these data are noteworthy. First, recalling that the strength of the relationship between class and vote declined over time, Figure 3.5 shows that the relationships between other socio-demographic characteristics and voting have tended either to increase and then decline or to fluctuate more or less randomly. This pattern reinforces the distinctiveness of the decline in the class–vote relationship. Second, the effect of region strengthened progressively through the 1970s and 1980s and then weakened slightly during the 1990s (see also Johnston and Pattie 1995). Third, the homeownership effect remained broadly constant throughout the period with the result that, by 1983, it was actually larger than the class effect. Note, however, that the level of homeownership increased significantly between 1970, when homeowners represented 50 per cent of the electorate, and the mid-1980s, when the figure was almost 70 per cent. This extension of homeownership, the direct consequence of the Thatcher government's policy of selling council houses to former tenants, diluted the previous association between class and home-ownership.[9] This, in turn, means that the homeownership effect cannot be regarded as a surrogate for the (declining) class effect since homeownership was distributed much more evenly across the classes by the mid-1980s. Finally, the effects of age

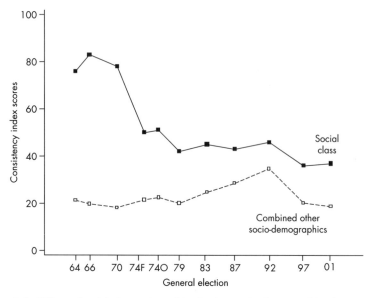

Figure 3.6   Effects of social class and combined other socio-demographic characteristics
on Conservative versus Labour voting, 1964–2001 general elections

Source: 1964–2001 BES post-election surveys.

and gender on vote are generally quite limited and, with the exception of age in 1992, do not change significantly over time.

Figure 3.6 provides a more concise view of the evidence reported in Figure 3.5. It compares the consistency index measure of class voting with a single index that represents the *average* of the other socio-demographic effects (ownership, region, gender, age). These data reveal that, as the class effect falls, the combined other socio-demographic effects rise very gradually. However, after 1992, the 'other effects' line also declines, so that by 2001, its value is almost identical to that recorded in 1964. This pattern leads to an important overall conclusion. The decline in class-based voting after 1970 was *not* accompanied by a compensating and sustained rise in the importance of other socio-demographic sources of voting. On the contrary, while class-based voting fell, other socio-demographic factors, considered in the aggregate, remained relatively minor influences on the vote. The clear implication is that, between 1964 and 2001, social–structural factors collectively exerted a declining influence on the vote. The sociological approach—always less important than often assumed—became less relevant to the explanation of British electoral behaviour.

This conclusion is reinforced by the more detailed analysis of the relationship between class and party support provided in Figures 3.7, 3.8, and 3.9. These figures, based on Gallup survey data, report monthly voting intentions for the Conservative,

Party Support in Britain, 1964–2001

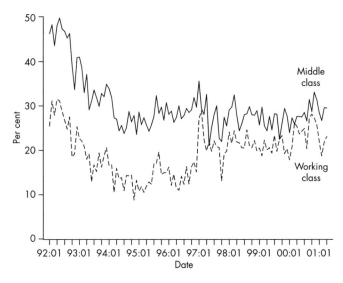

Figure 3.7   Conservative support in middle and working classes,
January 1992–April 2001

Source: January 1992–April 2001 monthly PSCB and P&D surveys.

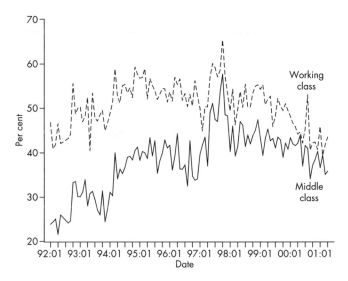

Figure 3.8   Labour support in middle and working classes, January
1992–April 2001

Source: January 1992–April 2001 monthly PSCB and P&D surveys.

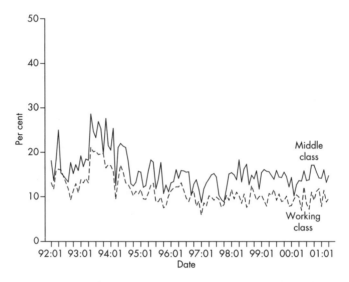

Figure 3.9   Liberal Democrat support in middle and working classes,
January 1992–April 2001

Source: January 1992–April 2001 monthly PSCB and P&D surveys.

Labour, and Liberal Democrat parties among middle class and working class voters from January 1992 to April 2001. The patterns in Figures 3.7 and 3.8 indicate how the long-term decline in class voting observed earlier continued during the 1990s. In both figures the gap between middle class and working class support narrows over time, particularly after 1997. This suggests that class has continued to decline in importance as an influence on both Labour and Conservative support. With these more recent data, we can also include the Liberal Democrats in the analysis (Figure 3.9). The gap between their vote intention share among middle class versus working class people is more or less constant throughout the 1992–2001 period. The effect of class on Liberal Democrat support does not appear to have declined— but it was not very strong in the first place. However, the important point about Figures 3.7, 3.8, and 3.9 is that this more detailed evidence leads to the same con-clusion as that suggested by the BES surveys. At the end of the twentieth century, class had come to play a very limited role in determining the voting preferences of the British electorate.[10]

THE ISSUE–PROXIMITY MODEL

The classic spatial or issue–proximity model is based on three simple propositions. First, a single, left–right ideological or issue space underlies party competition.

Second, voters tend to support the party they perceive as being closest to their own position in this left–right space. Third, vote-seeking parties attempt to position themselves in the left–right space such that they maximize their (relative) attractiveness to as many voters as possible. The BES began to collect systematic data on people's perceptions of their own and the main parties' positions on key issues in 1983, but due to differences in the scales used to measure issue positions, comparative analyses can only be performed for the 1987–2001 period.[11] Before presenting the evidence on how and why these perceptions changed between 1987 and 2001, we engage in a modest amount of story telling. More specifically, we describe how the parties have sought to present themselves to the electorate over the long term—and, in particular, how Labour has shifted its ideological centre of gravity in recent years.

During the 1950s, British party politics were often characterized by the term 'Butskellism'. The term, an amalgam of the names of the Labour leader (Hugh Gaitskell) and a leading Conservative (R. A. Butler), conveyed the idea that both the Conservatives and Labour were moderate, centrist parties whose policies in government were unlikely to differ radically from one another. Although the two parties never leapfrogged each other on the ideological continuum, they continued to share a broad consensus on most major economic and social policies throughout the 1950s and 1960s. This was partially due to the Conservatives' acceptance of social welfare and state-run enterprise (Budge et al. 2001: 26). For its part, the 1964 Labour government under Harold Wilson, with its commitment to economic planning and its desire to harness 'the white heat of technology', promised radical reform that would rejuvenate British industry and significantly increase the country's rate of economic growth.

However, Labour's periods in office between 1964 and 1970 and then between 1974 and 1979 proved especially disappointing. In the face of foreign competition, British industry continued to lose market share both at home and abroad. Growth rates stubbornly failed to improve. To make matters worse, during the 1970s Labour seemed hopelessly unable to deal with the new phenomenon of 'stagflation', a condition in which levels of both inflation and unemployment remained high for protracted periods. Given the economic difficulties that Labour encountered between 1974 and 1979, it was not surprising that the Callaghan government lost the general election in May 1979.

The Conservatives' response to their victory in 1979 was to push ahead with the strong, neo-conservative policy agenda of the 'Thatcher revolution' (Budge, Robertson, and Hearl 1987; Crewe and Searing 1988; Budge et al. 2001). Mrs Thatcher's uncompromising advocacy of market principles, and her government's attempts to implement free enterprise solutions to Britain's economic and social problems, included the sale of council housing and confrontation with the trade unions. As a consequence, the 1980s witnessed the erosion of the broad party consensus that had existed in the 1950s and 1960s. Both Mrs Thatcher and her Labour opponents were determined to practice the politics of ideological conviction.

For its part, Labour responded to its defeat in 1979 by moving its policy stances and overall image to the left (Budge, Robertson, and Hearl 1987; Budge et al. 2001; see also Figure 8.7). A critical mass of Labour activists—including MPs—was convinced that Labour lost in 1979 because the Wilson and Callaghan governments had been insufficiently radical. In particular, they believed that there was an urgent need for higher and more progressive taxation that could be used to fund higher state spending on education, health, and social welfare. Labour's left-wing had long sought to establish its dominance within the parliamentary party and to ensure that Labour stood for election on a genuinely radical, socialist policy platform that would be fully implemented if the party was elected. Their hopes were strengthened when a group of leading members of the party's right wing defected from the party to form the Social Democratic Party (Crewe and King 1996). Labour's 1983 party manifesto fulfilled the left's dreams. The manifesto promised an enhanced role for the state in the economy, including the re-nationalization of industries that the Conservatives planned to privatize; the restoration of trade union power; the abandonment of tenants' right to buy council housing; and increases in taxation to pay for improved social policy provision. Uncertain as to how any or all of this was going to be either paid for or managed, voters deserted Labour on an unprecedented scale. In June 1983, Labour obtained its lowest share of the popular vote (28 per cent) in post-war history. It was one of the great ironies of British twentieth-century politics that the Labour left, having finally established its dominance within the party, should have found that very dominance rendered Labour completely unelectable.

Following Labour's defeat in 1983, the Conservatives pressed ahead with their privatization programme and their strategy for reducing trade union power while Labour began the process of restoring its electoral appeal. The process was both slow and difficult. It was not until the 1989 Policy Review—after yet another general election defeat in 1987—that Labour began seriously to shift its policy positions towards the centre ground of UK politics. In preparation for the 1992 general election, the party discarded its commitment to unilateral disarmament. It softened its position on restoring all of the trade union rights that had been curtailed by Conservative legislation in 1981 and 1984. And, the party abandoned its intention to re-nationalize the major utilities that the Conservatives had privatized. However, Labour refused to compromise with its past over the question of taxation and public expenditure. The party leader, Neil Kinnock, made it clear that a massive improvement in Britain's public service provision—in education, health, and social welfare—would be Labour's top priority and that a Labour government was prepared to increase taxation in order to achieve it. This continued commitment to 'tax and spend' proved to be Labour's Achilles heel. Its opponents in the Conservative Party and in the press presented Labour's policy on taxation as evidence that the party had not really changed its 'ideological spots'. It was argued that the Policy Review might have transformed Labour's rhetoric and tamed some of its wilder policy aspirations. But fundamentally, the party was still committed to the sort of fiscal profligacy that had led to economic crisis and Britain's relative economic decline in the 1960s and 1970s. Labour was still too dangerously left-wing for voters to entrust it with the reigns of government. This message was not lost on the electorate, particularly at a time when the economy was just emerging from the 1990–1 recession. In the 1992 general election, the Conservatives were re-elected with a substantially reduced Commons majority, but Labour trailed by 7 per cent in the popular vote.

Four successive defeats had a searing effect on Labour. It was widely recognized that the party had to work harder to convince voters that it had genuinely moved towards the political centre. The party's immediate response was to elect its 'safest pair of hands'—John Smith—as leader. Smith had the advantage of looking and sounding like a respectable Scottish bank manager. He made an important gesture towards moderation during his brief period of leadership by introducing the principle of OMOV—one member one vote—for elections for the party leadership in 1993. By empowering the rank-and-file membership, OMOV was a convenient device for curtailing the frequently disruptive influence of the grass roots activists, who were typically more left-wing than Labour's voters. Smith died prematurely in the spring of 1994. He was replaced by another moderate—Tony Blair.

Blair took the constitutional changes within the Labour Party even further. Between his election in July and his first conference as party leader in October, 1994, he campaigned vigorously for the abolition of Clause IV of the party's constitution. To those unfamiliar with the intricacies of twentieth-century Labour politics, the debate appeared both arcane and obscure. Yet, it was very important. Clause IV embodied Marxist economic doctrine by formally committing the Labour Party in power to the public ownership of the means of production, distribution, and exchange. It was reproduced on every Labour Party membership card. Even if no actual Labour government had come close to implementing it (although Attlee's administration after 1945 made a start), Clause IV represented a crucial symbol, especially for Labour activists, of where they would like to go in an ideal world. Blair won the debate on the abolition of Clause IV overwhelmingly. This victory proclaimed to the British electorate—via a broadly sympathetic and understanding phalanx of print and electronic journalists—that *this* Labour leader was not afraid to jettison the ideological baggage of Labour's past.

Moreover, Blair had the political skill to build on this early victory. He was convinced that Labour had to appeal successfully to 'middle Britain'. Changes in Britain's economy and society over the previous three decades had led to a considerable expansion in the size of the middle class and a corresponding decline in the size of the working class. Labour would never win another election if it simply appealed to the working class, to the dispossessed and marginalized, and to that small fraction of the middle class that, for reasons of either altruism or identity, sided with the 'underdog'. Victory for any party depended increasingly on appealing to self-interested middle class as well as working class voters. Accordingly, the party was swiftly re-positioned across a wide range of policy areas. New Labour embraced the principles of private enterprise and recognized the importance of sustaining a business environment in which wealth creation could flourish. It emphasized that, in areas where the state was or had been involved in public service provision, what mattered was the quality of service delivery, not whether the service provider was privately or publicly owned—accordingly, privatization could be freely accepted. The trade unions were told publicly that they could expect no special favours from a New Labour government and that they should certainly not expect to see a repeal of the 1981 and 1984 Trades Union Acts that had exercised the Labour left so strongly during the early Thatcher years. Finally, New Labour warmly embraced the need for a strong approach to criminals. The New Labour government would be 'tough on crime' as well as being—in a gesture designed to placate Old Labour supporters—'tough on the causes of crime'.

A considerable amount of evidence shows that the electorate began to see a real change in Labour's ideological position after 1992. As noted above, since 1987 the BES has used 11-point scales to track movements in voters' ideological positions and their perceptions of the positions adopted by the major parties. Although the issues considered have not always been the same, data exist for some issues over at least three elections. Here, we consider two issues. The first is privatization/nationalization, that is, the extent to which the state should own significant parts of the economy. Respondents were asked to place themselves and the parties on an 11-point scale, on which the left-wing position indicated a preference for more nationalization of major industries and utilities, and the right-wing position indicated a preference for more privatization. Table 3.2 shows how the perceived positions of the parties changed between 1987 and 1997. The top part of the table

Table 3.2 Average scores on nationalization–privatization scales, 1987–97

	1987	*1992*	*1997*
Average perception of position of			
Labour	2.9	3.6	4.5
Liberal/Alliance/Liberal Democrats	5.6	5.4	5.1
Conservatives	9.2	8.4	7.7
Average self-placement	6.4	5.7	5.1
Labour to the left of the average			
respondent by	3.5	2.1	0.6
Conservative to the right of the average			
respondent by	2.8	2.7	2.7

Note: Eleven-point (1–11) scales; a low score indicates a preference for nationalization, and a high score indicates a preference for privatization.

Source: 1987–97 BES post-election surveys.

displays the average positions of the parties and of the average respondent. The bottom part compares the extent to which Labour was perceived as being to the left of the average respondent with the extent to which the Conservatives were perceived as being to the right. In 1987, Labour was perceived as being well to the left. Its average score on the 11-point scale was 2.9, substantially to the left of the average respondent's position of 6.4. By 1992, following the Policy Review, Labour was seen as having moved towards the centre—but not by much. Its average score on the 11-point scale was 3.6, compared with a mean respondent position of 5.7. However, by 1997, Labour's mean score was 4.5—only 0.6 away from the average respondent's self-placement score of 5.1. These data thereby suggest a gradual convergence between the perceptions of Labour and the average respondent on this particular ideological measure after 1987. The pattern for the Conservatives is quite different, with the gap between the average self-placement score and the average placement of the Conservatives being virtually identical in all three years (2.8 in 1987, 2.7 in 1992, and 2.7 in 1997).

A second position issue concerns the extent of state involvement in redistributive service provision. Respondents in the 1987–2001 BES were asked their preferences for increasing taxes to pay for improved services ('health and social services') versus cutting taxes and reducing services. Similar to the privatization/ nationalization measure, respondents were asked to indicate their own position on this issue, as well as their perceptions of the positions adopted by various political parties. Table 3.3 shows that the average person has consistently been closer to Labour on this issue than she or he has been to the Conservatives. In 1987, for example, the gap between Labour and the average self-placement score was 1.5, compared with a gap of 2.7 for the Conservatives. The interesting point

Table 3.3 Average scores on increase taxes and services versus reduce taxes and services scales, 1987–2001

	1987	*1992*	*1997*	*2001*
Average perception of:				
Labour's position	3.0	2.8	3.5	5.0
Alliance/Liberal Democrat position	4.4	4.0	3.7	4.4
Conservative position	7.2	7.7	6.7	6.4
Average self-placement	4.5	4.1	3.6	4.5
Number of points Labour to the				
left of average respondent	1.5	1.3	0.2	−0.5
Number of points Conservatives to the				
right of average respondent	2.7	3.6	3.0	2.9

Note: Eleven-point (1–11) scales; a low score indicates a preference for higher taxation to improve services, and a high score indicates a preference for lower taxation and no improvement in services.

Source: 1987–2001 BES post-election surveys.

here is that—despite its proximity to the average voter—Labour was unable to shake off the detrimental effects of its image as the party of 'tax and spend'. It was only by 1997, when the gap had narrowed to 0.2, that the party could neutralize accusations that a Labour government would inevitably lack fiscal discipline. By 2001, under Blair's transformation of Labour's image, the average respondent actually placed Labour 0.5 points to her or his *right* on the taxation/spending scale.

In sum, the issue-proximity model helps us to describe how the electorate's view of the parties changed between 1987 and 2001. But, how well does the model explain electoral choice? Do people vote for the party that is closest to them on a salient issue-position dimension? As discussed above, the issue of taxes versus services has been important in British politics since at least the early 1980s. Table 3.4 presents evidence from the 1987 BES on the relationship between vote and issue proximity, that is, respondents' perceptions as to which party is closest to them on the tax versus services issue. To illustrate, the number in the top left cell of the table indicates that 81 per cent of the respondents who placed themselves closest to the Conservatives on this issue voted Conservative. Similarly, 65 per cent of those who placed themselves closest to Labour voted Labour. However, only 44 per cent of those who placed themselves closest to the (then) Alliance voted Alliance. The overall relationship in this table is quite similar to that reported earlier for the consistency index of class voting and the equivalent indices for other social characteristics. Although three categories now are involved in the construction of the independent variable, it is possible to calculate a simple 'consistency index' comparable with our earlier measures.[12] As shown in Figure 3.10, issue proximity consistently affected party support in every election for which suitable data are available, and at levels comparable with the effects exerted by social class.[13] However, it also appears that the effect weakened during the 1990s—the score for 1997 is noticeably lower than those for four elections between 1979 and 1992.

The above findings lead to a somewhat mixed verdict on the explanatory potential of the issue–proximity model. In accordance with the third proposition stated at the beginning of this discussion, the model is very useful for characterizing the way

Table 3.4   Voting behaviour and proximity of parties to voter on reduce taxation versus increase services scale, 1987 (Column percentages)

	Party respondent is closest to on taxation versus services scale		
Vote	*Conservative*	*Labour*	*Alliance*
Conservative	81	14	34
Labour	8	65	22
Alliance	12	21	44

Note: Eleven-point reduce taxation versus increase services scale.

Source: 1987 BES post-election survey.

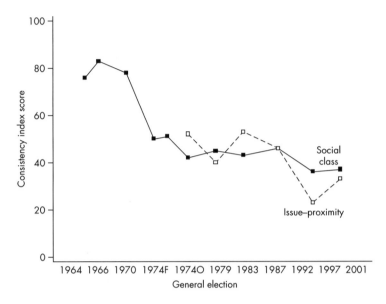

Figure 3.10   Effects of social class and issue proximity on Conservative versus Labour voting, 1964–2001 general elections

Source: 1964–2001 BES post-election surveys.

that the major parties, and especially Labour, responded to the electoral realities of the 1980s and early 1990s. In true Downsian fashion, after 1983 Labour shifted its position towards the ideological centre ground, and thereby more closely approached the position of the 'median voter'. As shown in Tables 3.2 and 3.3, the acceleration of the process after 1992 under Smith and Blair finally convinced voters that Labour had genuinely moved towards the centre. However, the second proposition of the issue–proximity model appears less convincing. A majority of electors do vote for the party that is closest to them on the tax-spend scale, but a substantial and growing minority, as shown by the falling consistency scores displayed in Figure 3.10, do not. This suggests that factors other than issue proximity led British voters to support Labour strongly in 1997 and 2001. In the next section we argue that these factors are connected to the general question of managerial competence.

THE VALENCE MODEL

Valence issues refer to areas of policy where there is widespread agreement about the desirability of general goals. As discussed earlier, the valence model has two main features. One feature involves perceptions of the actual or anticipated performance in office of the competing political parties. The key proposition here is that voters tend to support the party whose leadership they regard as *most competent* to deal with the important issues of the day. A second feature is that the valence model nests (contains) several submodels, one of which is the particularly interesting case of issue priority. The basic claim of the issue–priority model is that political parties benefit differentially from the salience of particular valence issues. Because of consistency in the images that they project over time, parties come to have an edge on some issues, and to be disadvantaged on others. It has traditionally been assumed that an emphasis on social issues such as health, education, and welfare benefits left-of-centre parties, whereas an emphasis on national defence, crime, and economic issues, especially taxation and inflation, benefits right-of-centre ones (Hibbs 1977, 1987; Budge and Farlie 1983; Clarke et al. 1992).

To assess the long-term significance of the valence model to British electoral politics, we need to consider the extent to which voting correlates over time with people's assessments of the performance capabilities of the rival front-bench teams and with their issue priorities. Although this exercise cannot be conducted with many competence measures or with many policy areas, we can still offer a cross-time analysis of the utility of the valence model. To assess the importance of competence judgements, we focus on perceptions of party leaders (using BES data) and views of parties' economic management skills (using Gallup data). Leadership perceptions constitute the simplest, most consistently available, summary measure of voters' competence judgements over the 1964–2001 period. Although the specific BES questions about party leaders vary over time, we can determine whether the respondent has a positive, neutral, or negative view of each major party leader.[14] The expectation is that, *ceteris paribus*, someone who has a positive view of the leader of a particular party will be more likely to vote for that party, whereas someone who takes a neutral or negative view will be less likely to vote for it.

We investigate the issue–priority claims of the valence model by contrasting voters who prioritize health, education, or welfare (HEW) issues with those who do not.[15] This investigation requires us to assume that voters who prioritize HEW issues also perceive Labour as the party most competent to deal with these issues. The assumption is necessary because the 1964–97 BES did not ask questions that link issue priorities to perceptions of which party is most able to handle those issues. However, the 2001 BES includes specific questions about these connections. Given the focus of this chapter, we hypothesize that people who prioritize HEW issues tend to support Labour; whereas those who emphasize other issues support the Conservatives or another party.

Figure 3.11 reports the results of calculating consistency scores for leadership evaluations (a surrogate competence measure) and HEW issue prioritization for each general election between 1964 and 2001. As a point of reference, the figure also displays the consistency index scores for social class. Two aspects of the figure

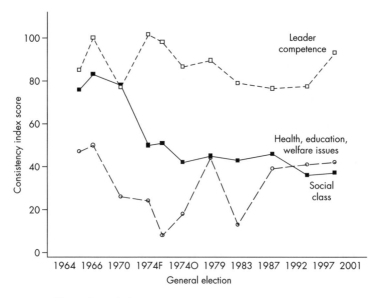

Figure 3.11 Effects of social class, leader competence and health, education, and welfare
issues on Conservative versus Labour voting, 1964–2001 general elections
Source: 1964–2001 BES post-election surveys.

are noteworthy. First, with the sole exception of 1970 when the effects are equal,
leadership effects (an average of the effects for Conservative and Labour leaders
only) are always greater than those associated with class. And, from the mid-1970s
onward, the difference in the magnitude of class and leadership effects is always
substantial. Moreover, unlike those for class, leadership effects do not decline over
time. These consistently strong leadership effects suggest that, at least since the
mid-1960s, voters' perceptions of leader competence have played an important role
in the determination of electoral choice. Second, the HEW issue–priority effect
starts out smaller than that for class. It fluctuates more or less trendlessly over time,
and is actually larger than the class effect in 1997 and 2001. Thus, it appears that the
priorities accorded to particular valence issues influence electoral choice, although
their impact is considerably smaller than that for leader competence. Overall, the
results lend considerable credence to the valence model.

The competence aspects of the valence model are especially important for
understanding developments in British party politics during the 1990s. In addition
to Labour's widely recognized ideological shift, public perceptions of the parties'
perceived economic management capabilities turned. Before presenting the relevant
data, a brief narrative is again in order.

Party Support in Britain, 1964–2001

Since the end of Second World War, the Conservatives had enjoyed a reputation for sound economic management, and Mrs Thatcher's neo-conservative rhetoric stressed this aspect of the party's image. However, her two terms of government between 1979 and 1987 witnessed sharp variations in both objective economic conditions and public economic perceptions. As a result of spikes in inflation and then unemployment, the economy often controlled the agenda and negative economic evaluations frequently prevailed. Yet, the prime minister and her party were not pushed from the commanding heights. Conflict within the opposition parties, coupled with a decisive victory in the 1982 Falklands War, did much to boost public confidence in the Conservatives generally, and Mrs Thatcher, in particular (Norpoth 1987, 1997; Clarke, Mishler, and Whiteley 1990). However, this was not the case when the Conservative government led by Mrs Thatcher's successor, John Major, confronted the Exchange Rate Mechanism (ERM) crisis in September, 1992.

Britain had joined the ERM of the European Monetary System in October 1990, when Major was Chancellor of the Exchequer, on the grounds that the country's long-term economic stability was best served by the alignment of the UK's currency with those of its EU partners. Unfortunately, the exchange rate when Britain acceded to the ERM was too high. British exporters found it increasingly difficult to compete in European markets. Export orders were lost and an economic downturn intensified into recession. By September of 1992, the foreign exchange markets had lost confidence in the government's ability to sustain the external value of sterling at the rate required by membership of the ERM. A run on sterling provoked the government into formally withdrawing from the ERM and allowing sterling to float.

Taken separately, these events might have had little impact on public opinion. After all, sterling had in effect been a floating currency for much of the 1968–90 period. But, the impact on elite discourse and public opinion was significant for at least three reasons. It was the first time since 1945 that a Conservative government was associated with a serious currency crisis. The three previous crises—the devaluations of 1947 and 1967 and the IMF loan negotiations to bail out a bankrupt Exchequer in 1976—took place under Labour governments. On each of these occasions, a Labour government gave the impression that it was in office but not in power. Now, a Conservative government exhibited a similar failure to control events, and an important psychological barrier had been breached.

A second factor was that the government was obliged to reverse its dominant macroeconomic story overnight. Prior to the ERM crisis, the Conservatives insisted in the strongest terms that Britain's membership of the ERM was essential to the country's economic stability and growth. Currency stability, supported by all of the EU countries' central banks, would replace the uncertainties and high transaction costs, previously faced by exporters and importers, of a varying exchange rate supported only by the Bank of England. In the aftermath of the crisis, the government had to change its story radically. Growth and stability would now be best achieved outside the ERM through currency flexibility. In the difficult and uncertain world of economics, it is possible that the government was right: British interests were best served by ERM membership before September 1992 and by non-membership thereafter. However, the voters were not forgiving. For three years, they had been told one thing and, now, they were being told the opposite. Yet, no one in the government had apparently made a mistake, no one apologized, and the Chancellor of the Exchequer, Norman Lamont, did not resign. On the contrary, for several months after the crisis, Prime Minister Major consistently and publicly expressed his confidence in his chancellor's abilities—although the continuing pressure on Lamont eventually led to his resignation in early 1993. These developments conspired to weaken the electorate's confidence in the government's economic and political judgement—a lack of confidence that affected the overall image of the Conservative Party and its leader in voters' minds.

A third factor that underpinned the effect of the ERM crisis on public opinion was connected with the recession that transpired in 1990–1. Although this was the second recession since the Conservatives took office in 1979, the party went largely unpunished because many people were not convinced by Labour's claims that it was capable of providing a responsible government. Accordingly, they gave the Conservatives 'the benefit of the doubt'. They voted Conservative in 1992 for lack of a plausible alternative rather than because of any deep conviction that the party deserved their support as a reward for its previous performance in office. In this sense, there was a predisposition among many voters to turn on the Conservatives if they failed to display the policy-making assurance that Labour had apparently lacked. The government's mishandling of the ERM crisis was precisely the sort of event that could prompt people to downgrade their image of the competence of the Conservative Party and its leader.

However, it should be stressed that the Conservatives' lost reputation was not a sufficient condition for the rejuvenation of Labour, although it may have been a necessary one. John Smith and, subsequently, Tony Blair sought to bring Labour's policies in line with the changed economic and political climate that had resulted first from Thatcherism and more recently, on a wider canvass, from both globalization and the growing powers of the European Union. In particular, Blair was aware from the outset that the key to Labour's medium-term electoral success lay in convincing people that his party had broken decisively with its 'tax-and-spend' past—that it was now as much concerned with wealth creation as it was with income redistribution. The image of presbyterian fiscal rectitude that John Smith had projected was developed further. Well in advance of the 1997 election campaign, Blair's shadow chancellor, Gordon Brown, firmly committed a Labour government to keeping within the public expenditure levels then being planned by the Conservatives for a period of at least two years. Once in office, this commitment was rigorously upheld. Indeed, fiscal prudence—with the Chancellor agreeing only to a level of public expenditure that could be funded from either current

Party Support in Britain, 1964–2001

Table 3.5   Party best able to manage the economy, 1964–91 (Horizontal percentages)

Date	Party			Conservative minus Labour (%)
	Conservative	Labour	Neither	
January 1964	44	32	5	+12
October 1964	45	34	5	+11
November 1964	49	30	10	+19
September 1989	57	23	9	+34
November 1989	47	37	10	+10
March 1990	35	46	10	−11
October 1990	42	38	13	+6
January 1991	50	34	7	+16

Note: 'Do not know' responses included in calculation of percentages, but not shown in table.
Source: King and Wybrow (2001: 116).

or publicly announced tax levels—became the watchword of New Labour's first term.[16]

Under Blair and Brown, first in opposition and then in government, Labour successfully projected an image of managerial competence. The fact that its overall macroeconomic performance between 1997 and 2001, was not much different from that of John Major's government between 1992 and 1997, went largely unnoticed by the electorate (Sanders et al. 2001). Labour's prudent approach to public spending and macroeconomic management enabled it to sustain its lead over the Conservatives in the economic competence stakes that the ERM crisis had engendered.

The consequences of these considerations can be seen in Table 3.5 and Figure 3.12 which report responses to a Gallup question that was asked occasionally before 1991 and monthly since then (King and Wybrow 2001: 116–17). The question reads: 'With Britain in economic difficulties, which party do you think could handle the problem best—the Conservative Party or the Labour Party?' As Table 3.5 indicates, with the exception of March, 1990—the month in which Margaret Thatcher introduced the widely resented and soon-to-be-abandoned poll tax—and December 1992, the Conservatives were always preferred to Labour in terms of their economic management skills. Even in 1964, when voters elected the first Labour government in thirteen years, they still considered the Conservatives better at handling economic difficulties than Labour. This reputation was a tremendous resource for the Conservatives, even if it failed always to guarantee them victory in the 1960s and 1970s.

The data displayed in Figure 3.12 are the balance of responses, that is, the percentage of respondents who think the Conservatives would be best on the economy minus the percentage that consider Labour would be best. When the balance

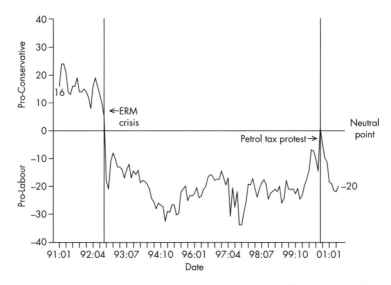

Figure 3.12   Conservatives versus Labour as party best able to manage the
economy, January 1991–May 2001

Source: January 1991–May 2001 monthly Gallup, PSCB, and P&D surveys.

of opinion is above the zero line, the Conservatives are regarded as best; when the balance is below it, Labour is seen as best. The overwhelming message of Figure 3.12 is that from September 1992 onwards, Labour supplanted the Conservatives as the party of economic competence in the minds of the electorate. The ERM crisis was the pivot for a fundamental change in the images of Britain's two major parties, and it clearly undermined the Conservatives' economic reputation. In the aftermath of the crisis, it was not a coincidence that the 'poll of polls'—the average of the monthly vote intention percentages reported by major polling agencies—revealed that the Tory vote intention share had dropped sharply (Figure 3.13). Labour's share rose dramatically, and its commanding lead over both the Conservatives and Liberal Democrats continued virtually uninterrupted throughout the 1992–2001 period. Labour's image of economic competence and its substantial edge in the polls became the backdrop against which the party decisively won the 1997 and 2001 elections.

The above discussion suggests two simple conclusions about the valence model. First, as our analysis of the impact of leader evaluations and issue priorities on voting between 1964 and 2001 shows, the model always has been as, or more, compelling statistically as either models in the sociological framework or the issue–proximity model. Second, as the discussion of Labour's efforts to capitalize on the Conservatives' post-ERM difficulties indicates, the valence model provides

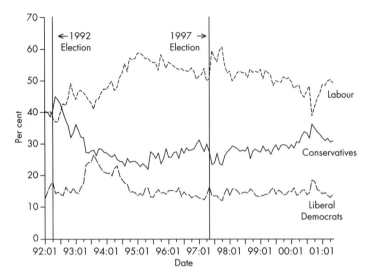

Figure 3.13 Voting intentions: Conservative, Labour, and Liberal Democrat support
in public opinion polls, January 1992–May 2001

Source: Average monthly vote intention percentages in Gallup, Harris ICM, MORI, NOP,
ORB, and Rasmussen Research polls.

powerful leverage for understanding the dynamics of party choice during the
1990s. The change in public perceptions of economic management competence
was crucial to the subsequent electoral fortunes of both major parties.

MULTIVARIATE MODELS OF PARTY SUPPORT

Figure 3.14 summarizes our efforts thus far to evaluate sociological, issue–proximity,
and valence models. It describes the over-time variations in the relationship between
vote and the signature variables in each of the three models. Apart from the declining
impact of class, the overwhelming impression conveyed by the figure is the relative
stability of most of the effects. There are short-term perturbations, but little evidence
of long-term trends. The other noteworthy feature of the figure is that the leader
effect is noticeably stronger than other effects, which by 1997 all tend to cluster
together.

However, the evidence presented thus far has involved bivariate relationships. To
explore the determinants of party support in greater detail, we develop two sets of
multivariate models. The first uses data from the 1966, 1992, and 1997 BES surveys
to investigate how the performance of key variables changed between the mid-1960s
and the late-1990s. Although we do not report equivalent findings for analyses of

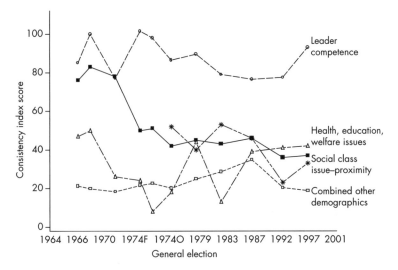

Figure 3.14   Effects of social class and other factors on Conservative versus Labour voting, 1964–2001 general elections

Source: 1964–2001 BES post-election surveys.

other BES data, the results are very similar to those presented here. Since the BES surveys provide only occasional snapshots of the state of public opinion, the second set of models employs the Gallup data introduced earlier. Since the Gallup data were gathered monthly over the entire 1992–2001 period, they allow us to explore the changing relevance of the different models in the decade before the 2001 election.

Modelling Electoral Support in 1966, 1992, and 1997

The specifications of models of voting in the 1966, 1992, and 1997 elections include the several variables shown in Figure 3.14 and reported in Table 3.6. For each year, separate analyses are conducted for Conservative, Labour, and Liberal (Democrat) voting. There are four noteworthy aspects of these models. First, all of the models include a party identification variable. There is an ambiguity associated with this variable. As observed earlier, party identification is an important element of the sociological approach, which regards party identification as an enduring, affective attachment that develops as a result of early life socialization (e.g. Campbell et al. 1960). Party identification is also claimed as a significant component of the valence model, which conceptualizes it as a running tally of retrospective assessments of party performance (e.g. Fiorina 1981). Party identification thus can be interpreted

65

Table 3.6 Models of Conservative, Labour, and Liberal (Democrat) voting, 1966, 1992, 1997

	1966			1992			1997		
	Conservative	Labour	Liberal	Conservative	Labour	Liberal	Conservative	Labour	Liberal
Conservative party Id	4.91**			3.67**			4.30**		
Labour party Id		4.50**			3.84**			3.08**	
Liberal (Dem) party Id			3.45**			4.12**			3.25**
Middle class (ABC1)	1.12**	−1.22**	0.62*	0.34	−0.57**	0.06	0.34*	−0.09	0.12
Owner-occupier	0.29	−0.27	0.33	0.73**	−0.46*	0.03	0.44*	0.32**	0.39*
North, Scotland, Wales	−0.29	0.15	0.35	−0.65**	0.24	−0.17	−0.50**	0.27**	−0.49**
Age	0.01	−0.01	−0.02	0.01	0.00	−0.02*	0.01**	0.00	0.00
Gender (man)	0.37	−0.29	0.19	−0.28	−0.23	0.14	−0.27	−0.15	−0.02
Positive view of:									
Conservative leader	1.26**	−1.22**	−0.67*	1.24**	−0.58**	0.20	1.04**	−0.56**	−0.13
Labour leader	−1.29**	1.15**	0.30	−0.65**	1.05**	0.02	−0.78**	1.84**	0.71*
Top issue priority, Health, education, welfare	−1.42**	0.77**	−0.00	−0.72**	0.35*	0.81**	—	—	—

Constant	−2.90**	1.57*	−1.78*	−4.25**	−2.74**	−2.68**	−4.52**	−5.73**	−4.27**
Per cent correct	94	92	93	89	91	92	91	83	90
McFadden R^2	0.70	0.66	0.36	0.54	0.55	0.40	0.58	0.37	0.30
Variables added to 1992 and 1997 models									
Party nearest on tax-spend:									
Conservatives				1.03**			0.64**		
Labour					1.50**			0.47**	
Liberals						0.72**			0.62**
Ethnic minority				−0.52	1.18	0.26	−0.43	0.36	−0.70
McFadden R^2 with added predictors				0.57	0.61	0.41	0.61	0.40	0.31

** $p \leq 0.01$; * $p \leq 0.05$; one-tailed test.

Source: 1966, 1992, 1997 BES post-election surveys.

as a signature variable for both the sociological and valence models. Second, all three specifications include socio-demographic characteristics (class, homeownership, region, gender, age) designed to capture a variety of sociological effects. Third, since the necessary data were not collected until the 1980s, the 1966 voting models do not contain an issue–proximity variable, whereas the 1992 and 1997 models do have variables that measure proximity to the parties on the taxation-spending scale. Fourth, the valence indicators include evaluations of the Conservative and Labour leaders, and an issue–priority variable for 1966 and 1992. For example, the 1966 Conservative voting model is specified as follows:

$$\text{VOTE} = f(\beta_0 + \beta_1\text{PID} + \beta_2\text{CLASS} + \beta_3\text{HOME} + \beta_4\text{REGION} + \beta_5\text{GENDER} + \beta_6\text{AGE} + \beta_7\text{CONLEADER} + \beta_8\text{LABLEADER} + \beta_9\text{HEWPRIORITY})$$

where,

VOTE = scored 1 if respondent voted Conservative, and 0 if respondent voted for another party;

PID = party identification, those identifying with the Conservative Party are scored 1, others are scored 0;

CLASS = middle class (A, B, C1—scored 1), working class (C2, D, E—scored 0);

HOME = own home outright or mortgage (scored 1), rent or other accommodation (scored 0);

REGION = a dummy variable scored 1 for Scotland, Wales, and the North of England, and 0 otherwise;

GENDER = gender (men scored 1, women scored 0);

AGE = age (in years);

CONLEADER = evaluation of the Conservative leader (positive scored 1; neutral or negative, scored 0);

LABLEADER = evaluation of the Labour leader (positive scored 1; neutral or negative, scored 0);

HEWPRIORITY = accords priority to health, education, and welfare issues (scored 1), or not (scored 0).

Since the dependent variable is a dichotomy, binomial logit analysis is used to estimate model parameters (Long 1997: ch. 3).

Table 3.6 presents the results of the Conservative, Labour, and Liberal (Democrat) analyses. These results lend some credence to all three models. The party identification variables are significant and properly signed. This provides *prima facie* support for both the sociological and valence models. Also, as anticipated in our earlier discussion, the effects of class decline over time. Although the class coefficients in the Conservative and Labour models are correctly signed in 1992 and 1997, they are much smaller than in 1966—and in the 1990s' models, most of the class coefficients do not achieve statistical significance. However, the effects of homeownership and region, which are not significant in the 1966 Conservative and Labour models, are significant in one or both of these models in 1992 and

1997. This suggests that, although the importance of the class component of the sociological approach declined between the 1960s and the early 1990s, the decline was compensated for to a limited extent by the increasing importance of other social characteristics. Third, the leadership coefficients are significant and correctly signed for the Conservative and Labour models in all three elections. This suggests the continuing importance of the performance component of the valence model. Fourth, the health, education, and welfare variable has significant negative effects on Conservative voting, but significant positive effects on Labour voting in 1966 and 1992. Thus, consonant with the issue–priority hypothesis, people who prioritized HEW issues were less likely to support the Conservatives and more likely to support Labour. This finding lends additional credence to the issue–priority component of the valence model. Finally, additional analyses of the 1992 and 1997 models indicate that the issue–proximity variable also achieves statistical significance in the Conservative, Labour, and Liberal Democrat models. Thus, the issue–proximity model is supported by the data. In sum, the multivariate analyses reveal that all three theoretical accounts are relevant for understanding electoral choice in Britain.

Modelling Electoral Support Between 1992 and 2001

The specification of the 1992–2001 voting intentions models is similar to that for the BES voting models described above. However, there are some minor differences that reflect the properties of the Gallup data. The Gallup measures of partisanship, class, homeownership, region, and gender are identical to those employed in the BES analyses. As discussed above, party identification may measure either sociological or valence effects. Class, homeownership, region, and gender, together with age cohort, are also included to capture sociological effects. However, since the Gallup data do not contain issue–proximity measures, we cannot evaluate the explanatory power of the issue–proximity model. Although the Gallup data also do not include an issue–priority variable, the valence model can be accessed with measures of partisanship, leadership competence, and perceived economic management competence. For the Liberal Democrats, the latter variable is proxied by the view that *neither* Labour *nor* the Conservatives are competent economic managers. An example model (of Labour voting intentions) is as follows:

$$\text{VOTEINT} = f(\beta_0 + \beta_1 \text{PID} + \beta_2 \text{CLASS} + \beta_3 \text{HOME} + \beta_4 \text{REGION} + \beta_5 \text{GENDER} + \beta_6 \text{AGE} + \beta_7 \text{BESTPM} + \beta_8 \text{PTYEC})$$

where, VOTEINT = whether a respondent intended to vote Labour (scored 1), or not (scored 0);

PID = party identification, whether a voter identified with the Labour Party (scored 1) or not (scored 0);

CLASS = middle class (A, B, C1—scored 1), working class (C2, D, E— scored 0);

HOME = own home outright or mortgage (scored 1), rent or other accommodation (scored 0);

REGION = a dummy variable scored 1 for Scotland, Wales, and the North of England, and 0 otherwise;

GENDER = gender (men scored 1, women scored 0);

AGE = age (in years);

BESTPM = Labour leader would make the best prime minister scored 1, other responses scored 0;

PTYEC = Labour seen as best on the economy scored 1, other responses scored 0.

Table 3.7 reports the parameter estimates using data for the entire 1992–2001 period (the 'All' row in each sub-table) and separate estimates using data for each year.[17] These estimates enable us to detect the extent to which the model parameters fluctuate over time, and thereby assess the extent to which various influences on party support changed during the 1990s. Most of the effects shown in Table 3.7 are relatively stable over time, although there are one or two notable exceptions. This stability suggests that, on the whole, the factors affecting party support did not change noticeably during the 1990s. The stability is most evident in relation to the party identification terms in the Conservative, Labour, and Liberal Democrat models. The significance of the effects of partisanship on voting intentions throughout the period is consistent with both the sociological and valence models.

The socio-demographic variables, signature variables in sociological models, produce mixed results. In the analyses for all three parties, the effects of gender and age are either insignificant or unstable over time. However, the effects of region change systematically. Until 1996, controlling for other relevant variables, Labour derived proportionately more support in the North, Scotland, and Wales—areas where the Conservatives and Liberal Democrats received proportionately less support. After 1996, this pattern was reversed, with Labour attracting disproportionate support in Southern England. It seems likely that this change reflects the success of Tony Blair's attempts to attract 'middle England' voters to New Labour. Class and homeownership effects are fairly similar over time in all three models, with middle class people and homeowners being more likely to support either the Conservatives or Liberal Democrats, and less likely to support Labour. Although the effects of class on Conservative voting appeared to decline during the mid-1990s, the effect was restored in 2001. Overall, these socio-demographic results for 1992–2001 are similar to those reported for 1992 in Table 3.6. In turn, this suggests that, although the sociological model was less powerful in the early 1990s than it had been in the 1960s, its explanatory power did not weaken much during the remainder of the decade.

Party Support in Britain, 1964–2001

Table 3.7 Annual and pooled models of party support, 1992–2001

	Party Identifier[a]	Class ABC1	Owns Home	North or Celtic	Age	Gender (Man)	Best PM[a]	Best on Economy[a]
A. Conservative models								
1992	2.63**	0.24*	0.14	−0.34**	−0.13**	−0.13	2.03**	2.37**
1993	2.82**	0.28**	0.43**	0.05	−0.05*	−0.25*	1.89**	2.08**
1994	2.51**	0.32**	0.34**	−0.39**	−0.01	−0.36**	1.73**	2.29**
1995	2.76**	0.35**	0.42**	−0.21**	−0.03	−0.30**	1.86**	2.25**
1996	2.63**	0.34**	0.39**	−0.29**	−0.04	−0.21**	1.78**	2.37**
1997	2.54**	0.10	0.41**	0.58**	−0.00	−0.23**	1.89**	2.36**
1998	2.61**	0.18**	0.40**	0.13	−0.08**	−0.25**	2.07**	2.33**
1999	2.60**	0.01	0.65**	0.15*	−0.05**	−0.15*	1.77**	2.25**
2000	2.61**	0.17*	0.48**	0.23**	0.01	−0.12	1.86**	2.18**
2001	2.98**	0.31**	0.55**	0.22	0.16**	−0.09	1.96**	1.92**
All	2.67**	0.21**	0.46**	0.03	−0.02**	−0.22**	1.81**	2.27**
B. Labour models								
1992	3.14**	−0.36**	−0.33	0.11	−0.04	−0.18	1.52**	2.27**
1993	3.79**	−0.37**	−0.25**	0.27**	−0.08**	−0.08	1.58**	1.68**
1994	3.52**	−0.26**	−0.05	0.30**	−0.10**	−0.03	1.58**	1.90**
1995	3.33**	−0.32**	−0.21**	0.28**	−0.06**	0.04	1.58**	1.81**
1996	3.28**	−0.40**	−0.22**	0.21	−0.03*	0.09	1.64**	1.77**
1997	2.69**	−0.09	−0.18**	−0.43**	0.08**	0.00	1.87**	1.45**
1998	2.59**	−0.21**	−0.14**	−0.23**	0.04*	0.05	2.06**	1.51**
1999	2.59**	−0.14**	−0.24**	−0.10	0.09**	−0.04	1.88**	1.41**
2000	2.26**	−0.25**	−0.24**	−0.18**	0.04*	0.03	2.02**	1.47**
2001	2.37**	−0.19	−0.19	−0.32**	−0.13**	−0.22**	2.08**	1.25**
All	2.85**	−0.26**	−0.24**	0.07**	−0.03**	0.01	1.71**	1.60**
C. Liberal Democrat models								
1992	3.37**	−0.06	0.36**	−0.45**	0.03	−0.11	2.00**	1.03**
1993	3.29**	0.25**	0.22**	−0.61**	0.02	−0.13	1.94**	1.04**
1994	3.48**	0.29**	0.25**	−0.36**	0.02	−0.16*	1.87**	0.96**
1995	3.40**	0.36**	0.25**	−0.57**	−0.02	−0.11	1.87**	0.79**
1996	3.32**	0.27**	0.22**	−0.37**	0.03	−0.23**	1.93**	0.78**
1997	2.87**	0.24**	0.06	0.34**	0.03	−0.10	2.02**	0.42**
1998	3.00**	0.47**	0.02	0.31**	0.03	0.01	2.14**	0.45**
1999	3.10**	0.42**	0.16*	0.34**	0.01	0.04	2.12**	0.33**
2000	3.04**	0.44*	0.22**	0.27**	−0.04	−0.07	2.03**	0.49**
2001	3.10**	0.37**	0.32*	0.46**	−0.01	0.11	2.29**	−0.06
All	3.17**	0.34**	0.20**	−0.07**	0.00	−0.08**	2.01**	0.73**

** $p \leq 0.01$; * $p \leq 0.05$; one-tailed test.

[a] Conservative, Labour or Liberal Democrat depending upon which party's vote is being analyzed.

Source: Gallup monthly surveys during 1992–2001.

With regard to the valence model, the leadership effects in Table 3.7 are generally constant over time. The 'best prime minister' coefficients are fairly stable in both the Conservative and Liberal Democrat analyses. In the Labour analysis, the 'best prime minister' effect increases modestly during the period—a reflection of Tony Blair's increasing impact on support for Labour. Finally, the influence of the 'best on economy' variable is generally consistent in both the Conservative and Labour models. The only exceptions to this pattern are the coefficients for 1992. Since the 1992 data cover the period of the ERM crisis, it is likely that these temporary perturbations are the result of voters' short-term reactions to the crisis. For the Liberal Democrats, the declining importance of the 'neither best on economy' term presumably reflects an increasing sense that, once in office, Labour demonstrated its ability to manage the economy competently.

In sum, analyses of the Gallup data indicate that the fundamental calculus of party support was largely unaltered between 1992 and 2001. The importance of specific aspects of the sociological and valence models varied little, and key variables in both approaches continued to demonstrate their ability to shape electoral preferences. Unlike the BES analyses, the Gallup analyses indicate that social class continued to exert some influence. In addition, party indentification was consistently in evidence in the Gallup analyses. The valence model, which shares party identification as a signature variable with the sociological approach, also receives support. In addition to partisanship, leadership evaluations and economic competence judgements were consistently influential.

CONCLUSIONS: PARTY SUPPORT THEN AND NOW

This chapter has two main objectives. The first is to tell a substantive story that identifies the key medium-term changes in party strategy and in voters' perceptions that underpinned Labour's general election victories in 1997 and 2001. Electoral outcomes are results of a complex interplay between voters and political parties. By their behaviour over time, and various other ways, voters convey messages about their policy preferences to parties. In turn, parties seek to respond to voters' messages and to persuade them to embrace their ideas and principles. The result of this interplay is that the context of electoral competition is, to a greater or lesser degree, in a continuous state of flux. Moreover, in the British context, declines in the strength of party identification and the linkage between social class and party support mean that more voters than ever before are subject to the effects of short-term forces operating in the electoral arena at particular points in time.

Despite this potential volatility, the nature of major party competition was fairly stable in Britain during the 1980s and early 1990s. The Conservatives consistently advocated rolling back the state—particularly the privatization of state-owned industries—and strengthening Britain's private enterprise economy. Labour generally opposed the privatization programme and stressed the need for wealth redistribution rather than wealth creation. The response of the electorate to these sharply contrasting alternatives was also relatively consistent. From 1979 to 1992, 42–44 per cent of voters opted for the Conservatives—sufficient for them to achieve a series of comfortable victories given Britain's first-past-the-post electoral system. For its part, Labour secured between 28 and 37 per cent of the vote over the same period— enough to keep the Liberal Democrats in third place but not enough to disrupt what appeared to be an emergent Conservative electoral hegemony.

It was precisely this series of disheartening electoral defeats that led the Labour Party to decide that, if it were ever to regain power, it had to radically transform itself. It had to recognize the realities of voters' policy preferences and offer them a plausible alternative when it came to choosing a government. Accordingly, Labour sought to change the choice it presented to the electorate. It moved to the centre ground, embracing some of the principles of privatization and free enterprise that had proved so successful for the Conservatives. Labour also recognized that it had to establish in the public mind that it was competent to manage the economy. Under the leadership of John Smith and Tony Blair, it did so. Assisted by the Conservatives' serious mishandling of the September 1992 ERM crisis, Labour succeeded in presenting itself as 'New Labour'—a moderate, fiscally responsible alternative that would not rock the national economic boat.

To turn this image of a competent, responsible government into a reality, Labour had to broaden the socio-demographic basis of its electoral appeal. It had to reach beyond its traditional heartlands in the urban working class. This is precisely what it did. After 1992, voters generally—and especially middle class people in southern England—began to recognize that Labour had moved to the ideological centre of British politics. They also came to the view that Labour was competent to handle the economy. And, they developed a high regard for Tony Blair. In this changed context, it came as no surprise that people were prepared to reconsider their electoral choices. In 1997, Labour used its newfound reputation for ideological moderation, managerial acumen and competent leadership to create a broad-based coalition that ensured an overwhelming victory. In 2001, the party replayed this script with nearly identical results.

But, although the substantive story is important, the second objective in this chapter has more general significance. We have investigated which rival approach to the study of electoral choice is most relevant for understanding British voting behaviour over the past four decades. We have shown that the dominant variable in the sociological approach—social class—has lost a good deal of its explanatory power since 1964. Moreover, we have shown that social class was never as important as many analysts have contended. The declining effects of class have not been compensated for by any systematic increase in the importance of other social cleavages. Other socio-demographic variables are correlated with the vote, but they are generally no more important now than they were forty years ago. Party identification is another variable claimed by the sociological approach. In this chapter we have shown that although party identification has declined in strength, it continues to be strongly associated with electoral choice. But, is party identification properly categorized as a signature variable of the sociological approach? Chapter Six addresses this important question.

Efforts to evaluate the Downsian issue–proximity model are constrained by the lack of suitable data prior to 1979. However, our operationalization of the model— which identifies the party that each respondent is closest to on the taxation/ spending scale—suggests that issue proximity has consistently affected electoral choice since at least the 1970s. Finally, an analysis of the valence model indicates that it, too, has considerable explanatory power. In particular, perceptions of leader competence— which proxy more general perceptions of party competence—and issue priorities, are two variables which have consistently significant effects on party support.

The sociological framework dominated the analysis of British voting behaviour for much of the period after the first national election study was conducted in 1964. Analyses presented in this chapter have shown that although sociological models should not be dismissed as irrelevant, their ability to explain electoral choice is limited. These limitations are not novel; rather they are longstanding. Accordingly, a comprehensive analysis of electoral choice needs to consider the contributions of the issue–proximity and valence models that are crucial parts of the individual rationality framework. We undertake this analysis in the chapters that follow.

NOTES

1. See Appendix B for the wording of the 1964–2001 BES party identification question sequences.

2. Class is operationalized in terms of the distinction between manual and non-manual occupations. Although there are several ways of measuring social class (e.g. see, Heath et al. 1991), we chose the simple manual or non-manual distinction for two reasons. First, it is the only operational definition for which comparable data are available throughout the 1964–2001 period. Second, as we show in Chapter Four with data from the 2001 general election, using a more elaborate class measure (the five-category Heath-Goldthorpe scale) makes virtually no difference to the strength of the relationship between class and vote.

3. The consistency index is necessarily the Alford index × 2 when an analysis is confined to voting for two parties. This is not true when voting for three or more parties is considered.

4. The controversy between Crewe (1986) and Heath et al. (1985, 1987, 1991) hinges on how the class–vote relationship should be interpreted. Crewe favours an absolute index on the grounds of simplicity and clarity. It shows unambiguously that class location, defined in the same way over time, has become much less important as a determinant of vote since the 1960s. In turn, this reflects the fact that the decision calculus of the typical voter has changed. Heath et al. argue that changes in the political landscape, such as the increasing role played by the Liberal Democrats and nationalist parties, as well as the disastrous performance of Labour in 1983 and 1987, have obfuscated rather than eroded the class–vote relationship.

They suggest that the use of a relative index, *inter alia*, takes account of these changing circumstances. Heath et al. conclude that the social psychology of voting, as reflected in the class–vote relationship, remained broadly constant from the 1960s to the 1990s. Crewe's response (1992) is that their analysis confuses cause and effect. He contends that the emergence of the Liberals and nationalists in the 1970s and Labour's failure in the 1980s were, in part, the results of class dealignment, not factors that need to be controlled for when a suitable measure of class voting is being devised.

5. In the 1964 BES, respondents in a second random sample were asked a class identity question which clearly cued them that saying that they belonged to the middle or working class was an appropriate answer. 'There's quite a bit of talk these days about different social classes. Most people say they belong to either the middle class or to the working class. Do you ever think of yourself as being in one of these classes?' Even with this cue, 40 per cent denied that they thought of themselves as a member of a social class.

6. For example, the class identification question sequence in the 1987 BES is: '(a) Do you ever think of yourself as belonging to any particular class? [IF "YES"] Which class is that? (b) "[IF OTHER, OR NO, OR DON'T KNOW]" Most people say they belong to either the middle class or the working class. If you *had* [emphasis in original] to make a choice, would you call yourself middle class, or working class?' See Health et al. (1991: 280).

7. This analysis focusses on homeownership, region, gender, and age. Ethnicity is an important socio-demographic variable (Saggar 1997), but it is not included in the analysis because of the small proportions of ethnic minority respondents in BES surveys before 1992. The public/private sector employment distinction (Dunleavy and Husbands 1985) is omitted because, although data are available since 1979, its effects have tended to be statistically insignificant in most general elections since then. The exceptions were 1983 (when public sector employees were significantly less likely to vote Conservative) and 1992 (when public sector employees were significantly more likely to vote Labour).

8. For example, the region data for Figure 3.5 are calculated by constructing a series of tables, one for each election, in which vote (Labour/Conservative/other) is cross-tabulated with region (the north of England plus Scotland plus Wales versus the rest of England). The consistency index score for region-based voting is then calculated as discussed in the note to Table 3.1. Thus, the score is the sum of (*a*) the percentage of North/Scots/Welsh who vote Labour minus the percentage of that group who vote Conservative and (*b*) the percentage of Southern England voters who vote Conservative minus the percentage of that group who vote Labour.

9. These changes were partly the result of an explicit electoral calculation by the Conservative Party. In the 1980s, Margaret Thatcher's reforming Conservative governments sought to curtail the power of the trade unions and to reinvigorate Britain's economic competitiveness by reducing the level of state involvement in the economy. In electoral terms, Thatcherism aimed to broaden the appeal of the Conservatives among working class voters in particular. Around one-third of the working class had traditionally supported the Tories. That proportion could be significantly—and perhaps permanently—increased by an appeal to those working class voters who were disillusioned with the economic failures of the 1974–9 Labour government and who wished to take advantage of the more market-driven and mobile economic climate that the Conservatives were intent on creating. The key symbol of this new economic mobility was homeownership. Britain had always had a relatively high proportion of owner-occupiers (50% in 1970) compared with other European countries.

Moreover, homeowners had tended to be both middle class and disproportionately Conservative supporters. Largely as a result of the Conservatives' introduction of the right of tenants to buy their council houses, homeownership increased from 55% of the electorate in 1979 to 70% in 1987. And, as the new property owners disproportionately switched their partisan loyalties to the Conservatives along with their new homeowner status, the Conservatives reaped their electoral reward with four successive general election victories.

10. Equivalent analyses to those shown in Figures 3.7–3.9 for each social characteristic examined earlier (homeownership, region, gender, age) are not shown to conserve space. However, we can confirm that the results support the inferences drawn from Figures 3.5 and 3.9. The homeownership graphs are very similar to the patterns for social class in Figures 3.7–3.9. As the 1990s progressed, the Conservatives and Labour drew support from both homeowners and renters in increasingly similar proportions—which the Liberal Democrats did throughout the 1992–2001 period. The region graphs show that, in 1992, the Conservatives and Liberal Democrats enjoyed distinctly higher levels of support in southern England than they did in the North, Scotland, and Wales. Labour's position was the exact opposite: its support was higher in the North, Scotland, and Wales than in the South. However, in the aftermath of the 1997 election, the positions of the two major parties were completely reversed. Labour began to draw proportionately more of its support from the South, while the Conservatives and Liberal Democrats depended increasingly (the latter only marginally) on the North, Scotland, and Wales. The gender graphs indicate that all three parties attracted support equally from men and women throughout the period. The age graphs reveal that the Liberal Democrats were supported equally among all age groups, whereas the Conservatives continued to receive slightly more support from the over-35s than from the under-35s, and Labour drew slightly more support from the under-35s than from the over-35s.

11. The 1983 BES used 21-point (-10 to $+10$) issue–proximity scales (Heath, Jowell, and Curtice 1985: 223–9). More recent BES have used 11-point scales, with the 1987, 1992, and 1997 surveys using 1–11 scales and the 2001 survey using a 0–10 scale. We add 1 to the 2001 scores and then reflex them to match the scales used in 1987, 1992, and 1997.

12. When three parties are involved in the construction of issue–proximity consistency measures, we need to take account of the fact that the distributions of three columns of numbers (one for each party) are being summed to produce the consistency score. (With the two-party consistency scores, the distributions of only two columns of numbers are summed.) To render the three-party scores comparable with the two-party scores, we multiply the former by two-thirds (0.67).

13. As noted above, the data for 1983 are based on a 21-point, issue-position scale whereas the data for 1987–2001 are based on 11-point issue-position scales. Nonetheless, the table for 1983 is identical in structure to Table 3.4. As a result, the consistency scores, are directly comparable with one another. The 1979 data are based on a question that directly asks respondents which party is preferred on the taxation versus social services issue.

14. The leader effects are restricted to Conservative and Labour leaders only. Since the questions asked about leaders on the BES surveys have changed over time, we selected measures that allowed a determination of whether the respondent took either a positive or a neutral/negative view of the leader concerned. For 1964–70, we use the 10-point leader

76

thermometer scores constructed by Butler and Stokes. Scores of 1–5 indicate negative or neutral, and scores of 6–10 indicate positive views. For 1974 and 1979, we use the 'marks out of 10' that respondents were invited to give for each leader. Again, 1–5 connotes a negative or neutral view; 6–10, a positive view. For 1983, we use respondents' views of the putative 'effectiveness . . . [of the leader] . . . as prime minister'. 'Effective' is taken to connote a positive view; not 'effective' or 'no opinion' is taken to imply a negative or neutral view. For 1987, we use whether or not the leader is perceived to be 'good at getting things done'; being 'good . . . ' is positive, and not being 'good' is negative or neutral. For 1992 and 1997, we use whether or not the respondent views the leader as being 'capable of strong leadership': if he is, then this connotes a positive view; if not, then a negative view. For 2001, we use the 0–10 point feeling thermometer scores. A score of 0–5 points connotes a negative or neutral view of the leader; a score of 6–10 means a positive view.

15. We recognize that the issue–priority model may refer to a larger set of issues but, in the British case, health, education, and welfare have been particularly salient and, to some extent, contentious issues. As with the leadership variables, question-wording differences across BES surveys necessitated flexible measurement of HEW priorities. For each survey, we identify those respondents who placed greatest priority on health, education, or other social welfare issues such as social service, housing, and pensions. For 1964–70, we used the panel responses because, in 1966, panel respondents were asked to specify what they thought were the most important campaign issues. We used this 1966 measure (variable V0200a) as an indicator of respondents' HEW views over the 1964–70 period (respondents who were coded as categories 27–29 were regarded as prioritizing HEW issues; those in other categories were not). For the two 1974 elections, respondents who cited pensions, housing, or social services as 'the most important thing' in the election were identified as people who accorded priority to HEW issues. For 1979, respondents who cited 'social services' as being 'extremely important' in determining their vote were regarded as prioritizing HEW issues. For 1983, we used 'the most important issue' in deciding your vote: respondents who cited 'health' or 'social services' were regarded as prioritizing HEW issues. In 1987, respondents who cited 'education', 'health', or 'social service' as 'the most important issue' were defined as prioritizing HEW issues. In 1992, those who mentioned 'education', 'health' or 'social service' as 'extremely important' were defined as prioritizing HEW issues. Since the 1997 survey did not include a measure, the graphs that display HEW priorities interpolate the 1997 figure as the mid-point between the 1992 and 2001 figures. For 2001, we used responses to the 'most important issue' question. People who mentioned education, pensions, health, or social services were regarded as giving priority to HEW issues.

16. Brown's first major act within a week of becoming Chancellor in May 1997 gave full autonomy to the Bank of England to set UK interest rates. This was a huge policy innovation. In the past, governments of all parties had been suspected of using interest rate policy to serve their narrow party political ends rather than the country's long-term economic needs. The suspicion was not completely unfounded. For at least the previous twenty years, governments had sought to reduce interest rates in advance of general elections to generate a political–business cycle effect—a sort of feel-good economic atmosphere that would lead voters to support the incumbent government (Clarke et al. 1992: ch. 8; see, more generally, Alesina, Roubin, and Cohen 1997). However, Blair's New Labour

government voluntarily deprived itself of a key policy instrument that had been (ab)used for short-term electoral goals and longer-term economic ones. The financial markets were clearly impressed by the simple message that Bank of England autonomy was intended to convey.

17. The number of cases for each annual model is approximately 10,000; for the 1992–2001 period, 98,000. For presentational purposes, goodness-of-fit measures and other model diagnostics are not reported.

FOUR

Electoral Choice in 2001

Numerous competing models of electoral choice jostle for attention in the literature on voting and elections. In this chapter, we assess the adequacy of several of these models for explaining voting in the 2001 British general election. We begin by marshalling data gathered in the 2001 BES pre- and post-election surveys to describe the forces at work as voters prepared to go to the polls. These data clearly show that Labour was in a very advantageous position in the run-up to the election. Next, we analyze the competing models of electoral choice delineated in Chapter Two. The first is the social class model. This model constituted the conceptual core of Butler and Stokes' pioneering study, and it has heavily influenced subsequent research on voting and elections in Britain. Analyses reveal that, as in other recent elections, the impact of social class on voting was quite feeble in 2001. Although some of the other models considered have substantial explanatory power, statistical tests indicate that none of them can tell the whole story of electoral choice. To better appreciate the perform-ance of the competing models, we compute changes in the probabilities of voting for various parties when the values of signature variables in the models are varied. These calculations indicate that partisanship and feelings about party leaders have particularly strong effects. Since data to be presented in Chapter Six demonstrate that partisanship has dynamic qualities that contradict the sociological account of the nature of party identification, we conclude that valence models provide a superior explanation of electoral choice in contemporary Britain.

LABOUR'S COMMANDING LEAD

Data collected in the BES surveys and selected monthly public opinion polls enable us to sketch a portrait of key elements in public political psychology as voters prepared to cast their ballots in 2001. These data clearly show that Labour was well-positioned for victory. With few exceptions, the party held substantial leads over its rivals with regard to all of the variables that matter for electoral choice. We begin with partisanship.

Partisanship

In the four decades since Butler and Stokes brought the concept of party identification from Ann Arbor to Nuffield, the cross-sectional relationship between partisan attachments and voting behaviour has always been impressive. Although the extent of individual-level stability of partisan orientations remains an important and controversial topic, at any point in time a party with a large cohort of party identifiers is likely to be very competitive. In this regard, party identification data gathered in successive monthly Gallup polls document that a sizeable shift in the balance of partisan forces occurred in the early 1990s.[1] Just before the September, 1992 ERM crisis, the two major parties' shares of identifiers were nearly equal but, since then, Labour has consistently enjoyed an advantage. Although the extent of that advantage has varied, it has typically been substantial, and this was certainly the case in the spring of 2001. Figure 4.1 shows that, in the 2001 BES pre-election survey, 42 per cent reported that they identified with Labour, whereas 25 per cent said they were Conservatives, 9 per cent claimed to be Liberal Democrats, and 3 per cent identified with one of

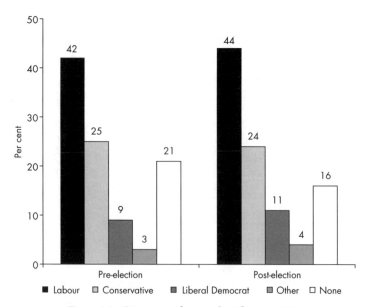

Figure 4.1 Direction of party identification, 2001

Source: 2001 BES pre- and post-election surveys.

several smaller parties.[2] One person in five did not identify with a party. As Figure 4.1 also shows, Labour maintained its partisan edge during the ensuing election campaign, with the percentages identifying with various parties remaining substantially unchanged. Labour's partisan lead was consequential. In Chapter Six, we demonstrate that partisan orientations have always been considerably more mutable than the traditional Michigan model allows. However, we also contend that the Michigan model is correct to stress the relevance of current partisan orientations for explaining voting behaviour in a given election. And, as is demonstrated later in this chapter, partisan orientations had substantial effects on electoral choice in 2001.

Spatial Models and Tactical Voting

Downs' (1957) pathbreaking study spurred interest in spatial models of party competition and electoral choice. In what quickly became the canonical statement of the spatial modelling approach, Downs proposed that voters attempt to maximize their utilities by taking into account their proximity to various parties on one or more issues of interest. After assessing the positions of competing parties on these issues, voters choose the party that is closest to their preferred position(s). Thus, the calculus of voting involves choosing a party that is minimally distant from one's ideal point in a uni- or multi-dimensional issue space. To operationalize key features of this spatial model, the 2001 BES employed two 11-point scales to summarize the perceived issue positions of voters and of parties. As discussed in Chapter Three, one scale concerns preferences for greater government spending versus tax reduction.[3] It is designed to capture respondents' perceptions of self and party positions on a complex of issues related to the scope and efficacy of government action. The second scale is a general 'left–right' dimension that has long had considerable currency in political discourse in Britain and most other established democracies.[4] Respondents were asked to place themselves and each of the parties on the two scales. Computing the absolute distance between voters and parties on the left–right dimension shows that, on average, voters were closest (1.3 points) to the Liberal Democrats, with Labour (1.6 points) and the Conservatives (2.4 points) in second and third places, respectively (Figure 4.2). The pattern for the tax-versus-spend dimension is the same—on average, voters saw themselves as slightly closer to the Liberal Democrats than Labour and, again, the Conservatives were seen as more distant (see also Table 3.5).

To the extent that voters adhere to a Downsian utility-maximizing logic when making their decisions, these figures suggest that the Conservatives were at a disadvantage, not only relative to Labour, but also to the Liberal Democrats. As discussed in Chapter Three, in 2001 the latter party was seen as somewhat further to the left than Labour and more strongly in favour of additional government spending rather than tax reductions. With the Liberal Democrats outflanking

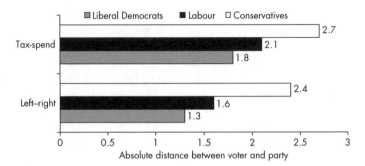

Figure 4.2   Average distances between voters and parties on the left–right and
tax-spend dimensions

Source: 2001 BES post-election survey, supplemented with data from 2001 BES pre-election survey.

Labour, the Conservatives were the only major party seen as being to the right of the government on these scales. Although some voters also placed themselves on the right of the scales, many more occupied centre-left or left positions that put them closer to the Liberal Democrats and to Labour.

A variant of the general utility-maximizing approach to electoral choice involves the hypothesis that some voters cast their ballots *tactically*. The basic idea that underpins this hypothesis is that voters take into account the competitive status of the parties in their constituencies when deciding what to do. Voting *sincerely*, that is, voting for a preferred party, does not maximize utility if that party is unlikely to win. In such a situation, a sincere vote is a 'wasted vote'. People maximize their expected utilities by choosing from the subset of parties that are competitive in their constituencies.

In the British case, analyses of constituency-level electoral data have prompted some commentators to argue that sizeable numbers of voters behaved tactically in the 1997 and 2001 general elections (e.g. Curtice and Steed 1997, 2002). More specifically, it appears that part of the Liberal Democrats' success in increasing their seat share in 1997 may be attributed to the party's ability to convince groups of voters in selected marginal constituencies to cast their ballots tactically. In situations where the Liberal Democrats were one of two competitive parties, they advocated a tactical vote for their party by people whose sincere preference was for another party—the Conservatives or Labour—that was seen as having little or no chance of winning. By so doing, voters could keep the party they least preferred from winning in that constituency. It also appears that Labour benefited from tactical voting in 1997. In constituencies where the battle was between Labour and the Conservatives, Liberal Democrats motivated by tactical considerations tended to opt for Labour to defeat the local Tory candidate and thereby help to oust a very unpopular government (Curtice and Steed 1997).

Electoral Choice in 2001

Data gathered in the 2001 BES post-election survey suggest that a minority of voters behaved tactically. Based on answers to a question designed to detect if tactical considerations motivated electoral choices,[5] we classify 86 per cent as sincere voters and 14 per cent as tactical voters. Figure 4.3 shows that fully two-fifths of the latter group but slightly less than one-fifth of the former one reported casting their ballot for a Liberal Democrat candidate. In contrast, vote shares for both the Conservatives and Labour were substantially larger among sincere than among tactical voters. These sizeable percentage differences in the behaviour of self-reported tactical and sincere voters argue that a variable identifying the two groups should be included in the multivariate models of voting behaviour analyzed later in this chapter.

Economic Evaluations

In Chapter Two, we observed that there is broad agreement that the economy matters—both for voting behaviour and for shifts in party support in the interims between elections. However, considerable controversy remains concerning the specifics of economic voting models, with the mechanisms by which economic conditions are translated into political support being a subject of sharp debate. In the British case, Butler and Stokes (1969) conducted one of the early analyses of how macroeconomic conditions affect the dynamics of party popularity. Tacitly acknowledging the inadequacy of a class-based political psychology for explaining how party fortunes waxed and waned from one election to the next, they identified changes in

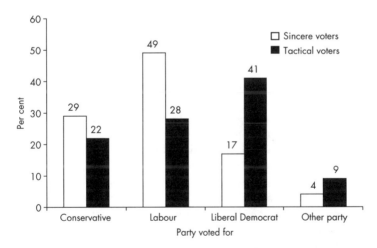

Figure 4.3 Electoral choice—sincere and tactical voting in the 2001 general election
Source: 2001 BES post-election survey.

the macroeconomy as a factor with considerable potential to affect inter-election variations in party support. As the prosperous 1960s gave way to the stagflated 1970s, their decision to investigate linkages between economics and elections seemed eminently plausible.

If the general proposition that economic conditions typically affect party support is accepted, then it follows that Labour was in an enviable position in the spring of 2001. The unemployment rate, which had fallen significantly well before Labour's massive victory in May, 1997, remained low during the Blair government's first term in office. Joblessness stood at only 3.3 per cent when the pre-election BES benchmark survey was conducted in March, 2001. Unlike the late 1970s, rival parties had no grounds for claiming that 'Labour's not working'. Other aspects of the economy's performance were favourable as well. Inflation—another serious problem for Labour governments in the 1970s—was a modest 3.2 per cent when the 2001 campaign began. The story for interest rates was the same. The cost of borrowing had fallen far below what it had been in the early 1990s, and the base rate was only 5.5 per cent when the writs for the 2001 election were issued.

Thus, economic news in the run-up to the election was generally very good. It could be interpreted as providing convincing evidence that New Labour was a 'safe pair of hands', capable of continuing to deliver on Tony Blair's often-articulated promise of economic prosperity without the 'boom and bust' cycles that had bedevilled earlier governments, Conservative and Labour alike. The only possible cloud on the economic horizon was taxation. Discontent with high taxes on petrol had fuelled a more general impression that Chancellor of the Exchequer, Gordon Brown, had introduced a number of 'stealth taxes' that were inhibiting the ability of ordinary people to enjoy the good times that had been the hallmark of New Labour's first term in office.

Data from the 2001 BES suggest that these misgivings had not translated into a more general pessimism. Figure 4.4 shows that just before the election campaign began less than one respondent in three believed that the economy had deteriorated over the past year, and only about one in four believed this about their personal economic circumstances.[6] As for the future, only about one in three thought the economy would weaken in the year ahead, and less than one in five judged that their personal financial situation would worsen.[7] Reflecting the buoyant economy, most of those interviewed thought that national and personal economic conditions had stayed the same or improved during the past year and would continue to do so.[8] Widespread optimism remained the norm in the BES post-election survey. As Figure 4.4 illustrates, the distribution of positive and negative economic judgements was nearly the same as it had been before the election. This is true both with respect to the object of evaluation (the country or the individual) and the time horizon (past or future).

There is additional evidence that Labour was poised to benefit from the wide-spread economic optimism. In Chapter Three, we observed that the balance of

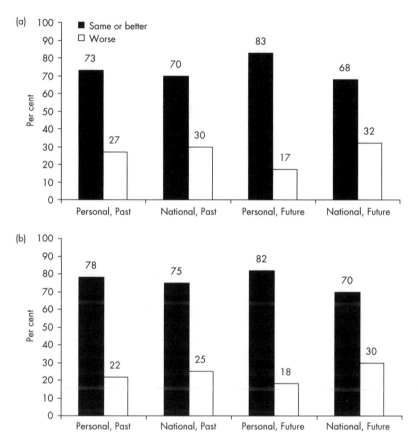

Figure 4.4 Economic evaluations, 2001 (a) Pre-election survey (b) Post-election survey
Source: 2001 BES pre- and post-election surveys.

opinion regarding which party would do the best job in handling the economy had shifted sharply from the Conservatives to Labour around the time of the September, 1992 ERM crisis. As with party identification, the Labour lead in the public mind as the party best able to manage the economy had been sustained thereafter, and Blair and Brown did not squander it after taking power in May 1997. In the pre-election survey, nearly one-half of the respondents judged Labour to be the best party on the economy, less than one-third picked the Conservatives, and one-quarter said they were 'undecided' or 'didn't know'.[9] Again, Labour did not lose this edge during the ensuing campaign; indeed, they widened it. In the post-election survey, a clear majority said Labour was best on the economy and only one respondent in four selected the Conservatives.

The positive economic evaluations and frequent endorsements of Labour's stewardship of the economy were accompanied by positive emotional reactions.[10] Many voters 'felt good' about personal and national economic conditions. When asked in the post-election survey to describe their emotional reactions to their own economic circumstances, over three-quarters of the respondents said they were 'hopeful', over one-half said they were 'happy' or 'confident', and over one-third said they were 'proud'. Negative reactions were much less common—less than one-third reported they were 'uneasy', and less than one-fifth mentioned that they were 'afraid', 'angry', or 'disgusted'. Overall, over 60 per cent of those interviewed offered two or more positive answers and less than 20 per cent failed to give at least one positive answer. The distribution of the number of negative responses is exactly reversed—over 60 per cent said they experienced no negative emotional reactions, and less than 20 per cent cited two or more negative reactions. The distribution of reactions to the national economy is very similar, with positive reactions being much more common than negative ones.

Taken together, the survey data make a compelling case that Labour occupied a commanding position on the economy as the 2001 campaign began. Most voters judged that things would stay the same or get even better, and many also felt good about both the national economy and their personal situation. However, as argued below, the 'good times' were not necessarily a pure 'political plus' for Labour. The continuing supply of economic well-being was accompanied by, and arguably magnified, the demand for more and better public services.

Government Performance Evaluations

Despite Margaret Thatcher's persistent efforts to convince the British electorate of the dangers of relying on the 'nanny state', even at the high tide of her influence in the 1980s many voters continued to believe that government had a leading role to play in the provision of healthcare, education, pensions, transportation, and other public services (Clarke, Stewart, and Zuk 1988; Crewe and Searing 1988). Moreover, recent research makes a strong case that demand for such services has a 'luxury good' quality, that is, demand rises in circumstances of perceived economic well-being (Stevenson 2001, 2002). These findings suggest that the widespread economic optimism that characterized the public mood in the run-up to the 2001 general election would be accompanied by strong demand for public services. If so, judgements about Labour's record in various non-economic areas could have been of considerable importance when voters went to the polls.

However, the impact of robust demand for, and the accompanying salience of, public services is difficult to forecast. As election issues, such services are heavily valenced since virtually everyone sees them as desirable. Overwhelming majorities favour the provision of public services and, hence, debate focuses on how best to provide them, who is most competent to do so, and who is most likely to deliver on their promises. As discussed in Chapters Two and Three, in the context of debates about public services, Labour has almost always had significant advantages. The party has traditionally emphasized the role of government in providing a broad array of social welfare programmes and other public services. These programmes and services have been high priorities for Labour leaders and activists, and have occupied prominent positions in Labour election manifestos (Bara and Budge 2001; Budge et al. 2001). In turn, the electorate has responded by recognizing that the provision of these programmes and services has been a core concern for the party. In a sense, Labour has 'owned' public service provision issues for much of the past century and, therefore, the party could be expected to benefit whenever they have become salient in the public mind. Other things being equal, placing these issues high on the election agenda was likely to be good politics for Labour.

However, other things were not always equal. Historically, voters may have appreciated that Labour really cared about public services, but they were less sure about the party's competence to deliver them. As noted above, the economic difficulties besetting Labour governments in the 1960s and 1970s had helped to create the impression that a Labour government, however well intentioned, would not be able to deliver on its promises. Failure to manage the economy effectively would doom public service policy initiatives and threaten existing services as well. A Labour government could be trusted to try to do what is right, but it could not be trusted to do it.

Starting in the early 1990s, this caring–competence imbalance in Labour's image began to shift. On the competence side, the ERM crisis did much to change public opinion about Labour's managerial acumen relative to the Conservatives. Then, following their electoral victory in 1997, Prime Minister Blair and his colleagues were able to claim credit for delivering a strong and stable economy. At the same time, some voters were becoming concerned that New Labour lacked the passionate commitment to public services that had characterized Old Labour. As prosperity continued, such voters—many of whom were long-term Labour loyalists—wondered why the new tax revenues were not being used to achieve the party's historic policy goals. New Labour's combination of capitalist economics and tightly controlled public spending did not sit well with such people. According to their logic, since the Blair government could afford to invest in public services, its failure to do so must mean that it no longer cared. New Labour and Labour were not the same thing.

The prime minister and his advisors were aware of these emergent changes in the party's image. Continuing the campaign strategy in 2001 that had proved so effective in the 1997 election, Blair stressed two themes. First, every time Conservative Leader, William Hague, tried to castigate the government for problems in areas such as the NHS, education or transport, the prime minister reminded everyone that the Conservatives had been in power for nearly two decades prior to 1997, and they, not Labour, had overseen a massive disinvestment in, and consequent erosion of, the quality and quantity of public services (Butler and Kavanagh 2002).

The Conservatives and, more particularly, Lady Thatcher's ideological heir, party leader William Hague, were the ones who *really did not care*. New Labour did care. The needed investment would be made, but the situation was so bad when the party came to power, that it would take time—another term in office—to set things right. When making this argument, Blair did not miss the opportunity to claim credit for the healthy economy that would provide the funds needed to rebuild and extend public service programmes. The prime minister encouraged voters to conclude that New Labour was both competent and responsive.

In the early spring of 2001, it was not obvious how the electorate would react to the arguments advanced by the rival parties. First, there was the matter of how the government's record would be judged. As Figure 4.5 shows, the BES pre-election survey confirms that Labour received very high grades for its performance on the economy. Substantial majorities thought that the government had done a good job in handling inflation and unemployment, and only small minorities thought other-wise.[11] The balance of opinion on taxation was much narrower, with one-third approving of Labour's record, one-third being unsure, and one-third disapproving. Judgements about most public services were much more negative. On the NHS, 31 per cent of the respondents thought that Labour had done very well, but nearly

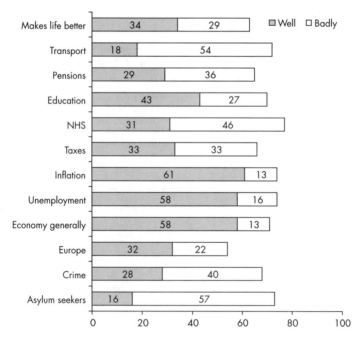

Figure 4.5 Government performance evaluations, 2001 BES pre-election survey

Source: 2001 BES pre-election survey.

46 per cent thought that the party had done badly. The distributions of judgements for transportation, pensions, crime, and asylum seekers were also negative, the latter massively so. Only on education was the picture brighter, with a sizeable plurality stating the government had done either very or fairly well, and slightly over one-quarter saying it had done fairly or very poorly. Finally, on an issue that the opposition Conservatives believed that they had considerable potential appeal—relations with the European Union (EU)—Labour held an edge, but many voters were unsure. Evaluations of government performance did not change markedly between the pre- and post-election surveys. Labour continued to receive high grades for its handling of the economy, but less enthusiastic endorsements for its work on education, taxes, and Europe. Many voters persisted in giving the government low marks for its performance on a variety of public services, including crime, heath care, pensions, and transport. Widespread dissatisfaction was also voiced over asylum seekers and the foot and mouth crisis.

Issue Priorities

The fact that New Labour's report card for its first term in office was mixed does not mean that voters thought another party would do a better job. As observed, traditionally Labour has 'owned' crucial issues such as healthcare and education and, as noted, Tony Blair had worked assiduously to remind voters that the Conservatives, not Labour, were responsible for allowing public services to run down in the 1980s and 1990s. Moreover, even if the Conservatives concluded that they were vulnerable on public services, their ability to shape an agenda around issues traditionally favourable to them—such as crime and taxes—remained to be tested. In the BES pre-election survey, the magnitude of the task confronting the Conservatives in the run-up to the election became apparent. The NHS, education, and other public services were chosen by 38 per cent of the respondents as the most important issues in the forthcoming election, but Labour held enormous leads on these issues over the Conservatives, the Liberal Democrats, and other parties[12] (see Table 4.1, Panel A). Labour was also overwhelmingly favoured by people concerned about the economy, and it held smaller leads among those worried about crime and transport. The Conservatives did lead Labour among the groups designating Europe or asylum seekers as most important, but these groups were quite small, collectively constituting less than one in ten of those answering the most important election issue question. Overall, 34 per cent favoured Labour on the most important issue, with only 15 per cent, 4 per cent, and 3 per cent choosing the Conservatives, Liberal Democrats, or other parties, respectively. However, the pre-election survey also reveals that many voters had not made linkages between issues and parties. Fully 30 per cent stated that they either did not know which party would do the best job on the issue they believed was most important

Table 4.1 Most important election issue in 2001 general election and party best able to handle it

	Party best able to handle issue					
	Labour	Conservative	Liberal Democrat	Other	D.K. None	Total
A. Pre-election survey						
Most important issue						
National health service	45[a]	10	4	2	39	21[b]
Education	47	10	10	2	31	10
Other social services	48	14	5	2	31	7
Crime	29	17	2	2	49	6
Transport	30	14	7	2	46	2
Economy	52	14	3	2	29	14
Taxes	29	30	3	1	36	7
EURO, Europe	24	42	6	2	24	7
Asylum seekers	9	56	0	7	27	2
Other issues	26	18	5	12	39	10
No important issue	—	—	—	—	—	15

	Labour	Conservative	Liberal Democrat	Other	D.K. None	No Important Issue
Overall party preference, Most important issue	34[a]	15	4	3	30	15

	Party best able to handle issue					
	Labour	Conservative	Liberal Democrat	Other	D.K. None	Total
B. Post-election survey						
Most important issue						
National health service	55[a]	10	8	1	26	29[b]
Education	59	7	13	1	20	12
Other social services	61	7	7	3	23	6
Crime	38	21	1	3	37	3
Transport	6	16	7	2	69	2
Economy	66	10	4	1	19	6
Taxes	26	33	12	3	26	4
EURO, Europe	26	40	6	3	26	13
Asylum seekers	18	33	10	16	23	2
Other issues	35	14	10	11	30	7
No important issue	—	—	—	—	—	17

	Labour	Conservative	Liberal Democrat	Other	D.K. None	No Important Issue
Overall party preference, Most important issue	39[a]	14	7	3	21	17

[a] Horizontal percentages.
[b] Vertical percentages; weighted N's pre = 3223, post = 3025.

Source: 2001 BES pre- and post-election surveys.

or that no party would do a good job. An additional 15 per cent said there were no important issues. Clearly, there was considerable 'play' in public opinion on the issues before the election campaign began.

Much of this looseness in issue–party linkages had not evaporated by the time voters went to the polls. In the post-election survey, 21 per cent of those interviewed said they either 'didn't know' which party was best able to handle the issue deemed most important, or 'no party' could handle the issue (Table 4.1, Panel B). Another 17 per cent stated that there was no important issue. Moreover, among those selecting a party, Labour continued to hold a large lead over other parties—39 per cent thought that Labour was best on the issue they selected as most important. The comparable percentages for the Conservatives, Liberal Democrats, and other parties were close to what they had been before the campaign began. Labour's overwhelming lead on the issues reflected the inability of other parties, particularly the Conservatives, to shape the election debate. Although the Tories continued to be favoured by people concerned about issues such as Europe, asylum seekers, and taxes, relatively few voiced these concerns. Despite the Conservatives' efforts to make Britain's possible adoption of the Euro a major campaign issue, only about one person in eight said this or some other aspect of the country's relationship with the EU was an important issue. Even smaller numbers mentioned asylum seekers and taxes. To the extent that issue priorities drove electoral choice, the Conservatives and other opposition parties were in very weak positions.

Party Leader Images

As discussed in Chapters Two and Three, there is now considerable evidence that orientations toward party leaders influence party support in Britain. In this regard, surveys conducted prior to the 2001 election indicated that Tony Blair was an important asset for Labour. Since becoming prime minister in May 1997 and, indeed, since he had won the party leadership in July 1994, Blair consistently scored well when voters were asked to judge his leadership abilities relative to those of his counterparts. For example, in monthly Gallup polls carried out since he became party leader, on average nearly one-half of those interviewed thought that Blair would make the 'best prime minister'.[13] In contrast, less than one respondent in six opted for either the Conservative or the Liberal Democrat leader. Blair continued to be well received in the run-up to the 2001 general election. In our April 2001 Gallup survey, 51 per cent thought Blair would be the best prime minister, whereas only 21 per cent chose William Hague, and 15 per cent favoured Charles Kennedy. Also, although Blair was not especially warmly received, feelings about him were more positive than those about the other leaders (see Figure 4.6). Kennedy's average score was just slightly below the mid-point (5) on the 'like–dislike' scale, and Hague's was decidedly in the negative range.[14]

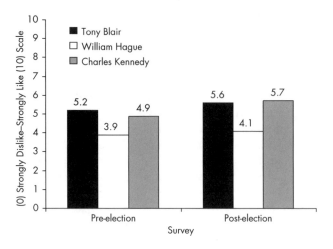

Figure 4.6 Feelings about party leaders in 2001

Source: 2001 BES pre- and post-election surveys.

Analyses of data gathered in the 2001 BES post-election survey show that party leader images are structured in terms of two strongly interrelated competence and responsiveness dimensions[15] (see Chapter Two). Over the course of the campaign, Blair maintained a very sizeable edge over Hague on both components of leader image. On the competence dimension, 77 per cent of those participating in the post-election survey believed that the prime minister was a 'strong leader', but only 29 per cent perceived Hague this way (Figure 4.7). Blair also outscored his Conservative rival, albeit not as conclusively, on the other competence indicators—'keeps promises', 'decisive', and 'sticks to principles'. On the responsiveness dimension, Blair led Hague on both the 'caring' and 'listens to reason' items, and the two were tied on the 'not arrogant' one. Moreover, as Figure 4.6 indicates, Blair continued to receive higher scores on the like–dislike scale than did Hague, their average scores being 5.6 and 4.1, respectively.

Charles Kennedy's ratings were closer to those of his Labour rival. In addition to having a slightly higher affect score than Blair, he outperformed Blair on the responsiveness dimension, with more voters thinking that he was caring, listened to reason, and was not arrogant (Figure 4.7). Kennedy's performance on the competence dimension was less consistent. Although more voters thought he would keep promises and stick to principles, he trailed the Labour leader on decisiveness and strong leadership, with the gap in the latter area being quite substantial. Competitive with Blair, Kennedy conclusively outperformed Hague. In the post-election survey, Kennedy had a considerably higher average affect score than Hague, and he led the Conservative leader on all indicators of competence and responsiveness. In several instances, the differences were sizeable.

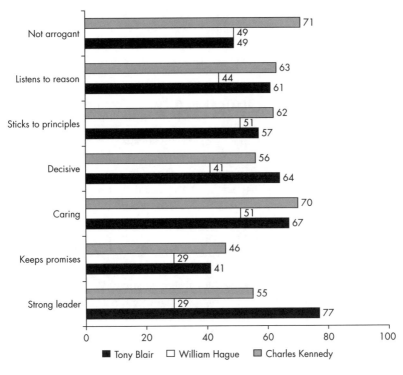

Figure 4.7 Party leader images in 2001

Source: 2001 BES post-election survey.

Viewed generally, the party leader image data show that although large numbers of voters judged that both Blair and Kennedy had at least some of the qualities needed to be a successful party leader and prime minister, many expressed serious reservations about Hague. On only two indicators (caring and sticks to principles) did even bare majorities give the Conservative leader a 'thumbs up', and his decidedly low affect scores both before and after the election suggest that many voters disliked him. Hague's failure to make a positive impression with much of the electorate meant that the Conservatives were faced with the unenviable task of trying to win in 2001 with a leader that many voters found unappealing.

In sum, it is evident that Labour was in a strong position coming into the 2001 election. The party had substantially more party identifiers than its rivals. Although issue proximities were very slightly more favourable to the Liberal Democrats, Labour was considerably closer than the Conservatives to the average voter's ideal point. National and personal economic evaluations mirrored a healthy economy. In addition, although voters gave the Blair government mixed grades for its perform-ance in office, Labour had a large lead over the Conservatives and the Liberal

93

Democrats as the party best able to handle the election issues that voters considered most important. And, the prime minister's image was much more positive than that of his chief rival, William Hague. In the next section, we determine the extent to which each of these several advantages mattered when voters cast their ballots.

COMPETING MODELS OF ELECTORAL CHOICE

The analysis of the explanatory power of various sociological, issue-proximity, and valence models of electoral choice begins with models in which social class and other socio-demographic characteristics are the only right-hand side variables. Then, we consider models that feature party identification, issue proximities, evaluations of and emotional reactions to economic conditions, party performance on important election issues, and party leader images. Each of the several models is analyzed individually, and in each case two dependent variables are used. First, since a fundamental decision concerns whether to vote for the governing party or an opposition party, we investigate models in which the dependent variable is dichotomous, with the voting choices being: (*a*) Labour, (*b*) any of the opposition parties. For this first set of analyses, binomial logit is used to estimate model parameters.[16] Second, recognizing that the British party system offers choices among several opposition parties, we analyze models whose dependent variable has four vote categories: (*a*) Labour, (*b*) Conservative, (*c*) Liberal Democrat, (*d*) other parties. In this second set of analyses, Labour voting is treated as a 'reference category' to determine how various predictor variables affect voting for different opposition parties. Multinomial logit is employed to estimate model parameters.[17]

Before presenting the results of these analyses, we summarize the models of interest in equation form.[18] For each equation, the left-hand side (dependent) variable VOTE is the voter's electoral choice in 2001. This is either the two-category choice (Labour, opposition parties) or the four-category choice (Labour, Conservative, Liberal Democrat, various other parties). The models are:

Social Class:
$$\text{VOTE} = f(\beta_0 + \beta_1 \text{CLASS})$$
where
CLASS = social class.

Social Class and Other Socio-Demographics:
$$\text{VOTE} = f(\beta_0 + \beta_1 \text{AGE} + \beta_2 \text{CLASS} + \beta_3 \text{ETHNICITY} + \beta_4 \text{GENDER} + \beta_5 \text{HOME} + \beta_6 \text{SECTOR} + \Sigma \beta_{7-12} \text{REGION})$$
where
$$\begin{aligned} \text{AGE} &= \text{age;} \\ \text{CLASS} &= \text{social class;} \\ \text{ETHNICITY} &= \text{ethnicity;} \\ \text{GENDER} &= \text{gender;} \\ \text{HOME} &= \text{own (outright or mortgage) or rent home;} \end{aligned}$$

SECTOR = employment sector (private/public);

REGION = a set of regional dummy variables for South East, South West, Midlands, North, Wales, Scotland (Greater London is the reference category).

Party Identification:

$$VOTE = f(\beta_0 + \beta_1 LABPID + \beta_2 CONPID + \beta_3 LIBPID + \beta_4 OPID)$$

where

LABPID = Labour party identification;

CONPID = Conservative party identification;

LIBPID = Liberal Democrat party identification;

OPID = identification with another party (SNP, Plaid Cymru, Greens, UK Independence Party, etc.).

Issue Proximities:

$$VOTE = f(\beta_0 + \beta_1 LABPROX + \beta_2 CONPROX + \beta_3 LIBPROX)$$

where

LABPROX = summed absolute distance between respondent and Labour Party on left–right and tax-spend scales;

CONPROX = summed absolute distance between respondent and Conservative Party on left–right and tax-spend scales;

LIBPROX = summed absolute distance between respondent and Liberal Democrat Party on left–right and tax-spend scales.

Economic Evaluations and Emotional Reactions to Economic Conditions:

$$VOTE = f(\beta_0 + \beta_1 PPROS + \beta_2 NPROS + \beta_3 PRET + \beta_4 NRET + \beta_5 PEMOT + \beta_6 NEMOT + \beta_7 LABEC)$$

where

PPROS = personal prospective economic evaluations;

NPROS = national prospective economic evaluations;

PRET = personal retrospective economic evaluations;

NRET = national retrospective economic evaluations;

PEMOT = emotional reactions to personal economic conditions;

NEMOT = emotional reactions to national economic conditions;

LABEC = Labour judged best able to handle the economy.

Party Performance on Most Important Election Issues:

$$VOTE = f(\beta_0 + \beta_1 LABIS + \beta_2 CONIS + \beta_3 LDEMIS + \beta_4 OTHERIS)$$

where

LABIS = Labour best able to handle most important election issue;

CONIS = Conservatives best able to handle most important election issue;

LIDIS = Liberal Democrats best able to handle most important election issue;

OTHERIS = other party (SNP, Plaid Cymru, Greens, UK Independence Party, etc.) best able to handle most important election issue.

Party Leader Images:

$$VOTE = f(B_0 + \beta_1 BLAIR + \beta_2 HAGUE + \beta_3 KENNEDY)$$

where

BLAIR = like/dislike Tony Blair;

HAGUE = like/dislike William Hague;

KENNEDY = like/dislike Charles Kennedy.

We first analyze a baseline sociological model that specifies voting for Labour as opposed to voting for any of the opposition parties as the dependent variable, and social class as the only independent variable.[19] Given that one aspect of the controversy regarding the impact of social class on electoral choice has focussed on measurement issues, we use two alternative measures of social class. The first is the standard six-category Market Research Society variable, with categories 'A', 'B', 'C1', 'C2', 'D' and 'E' (e.g. Butler and Stokes 1969: 70–1). The second is the five-category measure developed by Heath and Goldthorpe, with categories 'salariat', 'routine non-manual', 'petty bourgeois', 'foremen and technicians', and 'working class' (e.g. Heath, Jowell and Curtice 2001: 29–30). Table 4.2, Panel A shows the results of the analyses that employ the Market Research Society measure.[20] Model A in this panel contrasts

Table 4.2   Logit models of the effects of social class on voting in the 2001 general election

	Model A		Model B					
	Labour		Conservative		Liberal Democrat		Other	
	β	SE	β	SE	β	SE	β	SE
A. Market research society measure of social class								
Social class	−0.34***	0.04	0.41***	0.05	0.35***	0.05	0.10	0.09
Constant	−1.35***	0.15	0.85***	0.18	0.42*	0.19	−1.82***	0.34
McFadden R^2	0.04				0.03			
% Correctly classified	61.3				47.1			
Lambda	0.16				0.02			
AIC	1968.31				3458.57			
B. Heath-goldthorpe five-category measure of social class[a]								
Salariat	−1.01***	0.14	1.06***	0.18	1.16***	0.19	0.32	0.30
Routine non-manual	−0.87***	0.17	0.96***	0.21	0.97***	0.22	0.15	0.38
Petty bourgeois	−1.25***	0.24	1.67***	0.27	0.44	0.38	0.98*	0.46
Foremen and technicians	−0.60**	0.21	0.52*	0.27	0.81***	0.27	0.20	0.46
Constant	−0.51***	0.11	−1.27***	0.14	−1.48***	0.16	−2.36***	0.23
McFadden R^2	0.03				0.03			
% Correctly classified	61.2				47.1			
Lambda	0.14				0.02			
AIC	1906.83				3374.59			

Note: Two analyses are presented in each panel: (*a*) Model A—a binomial logit analysis of voting for Labour (the governing party) versus voting for any of the opposition parties; (*b*) Model B—a multinomial logit analysis of Conservative, Liberal Democrat, and other party voting, with Labour voting as the reference category.
* $p \leq 0.05$; ** $p \leq 0.01$; *** $p \leq 0.001$; pre-post panel $N = 1479$; validated voters only.
[a] Working class is the reference category.

Source: 2001 BES pre–post panel survey.

Labour voting with voting for any other party. In this model the coefficient for social class is statistically significant and negative. This means that, in 2001, working class people were more likely to vote for Labour than the other parties (considered as a group). However, the fit of the model is very poor—the estimated (McFadden) R^2 is merely 0.04, and the percentage of voters whose behaviour is correctly classified is only 61 per cent.[21] The latter is only 16 per cent better than could be done using a 'naïve' model that placed all of the survey respondents in the model category of the dependent variable (that is, guessing that all respondents were Labour voters). Model B in Panel A analyzes how the Market Research Society social class variable affects support for various opposition parties (with voting for Labour as the reference category). As expected, the effects of social class on Conservative and Liberal Democrat voting are positive and statistically significant, indicating that middle- and upper-class people were more likely than those in the working class to vote for one of these parties than for Labour (the reference category). However, the fit of the model again leaves much to be desired. The estimated R^2 is 0.03, and merely 47 per cent of the voters are correctly classified—only 2 per cent better than could be done using a simple mode-guessing model.

The analyses in Panel B of Table 4.2 demonstrate that it would be incorrect to conclude that the weakness of the social class–vote relationship in 2001 is simply an artefact of how class is measured. Model A in Panel B shows that, compared to those in the working class, people in any of the other Heath–Golthorpe class categories were significantly less likely to vote Labour. But, once more, the relationship is very weak, with the estimated R^2 being only 0.03, and only 62 per cent being correctly classified. The situation does not improve in the analysis of voting for various opposition parties. Although there are several statistically significant coefficients, the goodness-of-fit statistics are disappointing. The conclusion that social class cannot explain electoral choice in 2001 is inescapable.

The weakness of the relationship between social class and electoral choice should not prompt the inference that other socio–demographic variables, such as age, ethnicity, gender, home ownership, occupational sector, or region now occupy positions of centrality in a well-specified model of the vote. As discussed in Chapter Three, evidence from earlier BES surveys shows that socio–demographic variables do not tell the whole story of electoral choice. The analyses of the 2001 BES data reported in Table 4.3, Panel A reinforce the point. Focussing first on voting for the governing Labour Party versus all of the opposition parties, it can be seen that, in addition to the social class relationship, Labour voting is significantly associated with ethnicity, employment sector, home ownership, and region. Non-white British, council tenants, public sector workers and Londoners (Greater London is the reference region category) were more likely to vote Labour than white British, home owners, private sector workers and those living in the South East, the South West, or the Midlands. Although statistically significant, these relationships do not impress. The estimated R^2 is only 0.07, and the percentage correctly classified is only marginally greater than

Table 4.3 Logit models of the effects of socio-demographic characteristics on voting in the 2001 general election

| | Panel A | | | | Panel B | | | |
| | Labour | | Conservative | | Liberal Democrat | | Other | |
	β	SE	β	SE	β	SE	β	SE
Predictor variables								
Age	0.00	0.00	0.01★★★	0.00	−0.02★★★	0.00	−0.01★	0.00
Ethnicity	−0.72★★★	0.23	1.12★★★	0.35	0.50★	0.28	0.51	0.54
Gender	0.17	0.11	−0.23★	0.13	−0.19	0.14	0.24	0.26
Region[a]								
South East	−0.51★★	0.21	0.79★★★	0.26	0.31	0.25	0.08	0.49
South West	−0.63★★	0.27	0.67★	0.33	0.80★★	0.32	−0.49	0.80
Midlands	−0.41★	0.22	0.67★★	0.28	0.29	0.27	−0.51	0.59
North	0.11	0.21	0.14	0.26	−0.19	0.26	−1.03★	0.57
Wales	−0.23	0.29	−0.05	0.41	0.14	0.37	1.06★	0.55
Scotland	−0.28	0.25	−0.06	0.34	−0.43	0.35	1.73★★★	0.47
Social class	−0.29★★★	0.04	0.36★★★	0.06	0.27★★★	0.06	0.09	0.11
Home ownership	−0.50★★★	0.14	0.92★★★	0.20	0.31★	0.18	−0.03	0.30
Employment sector	0.23★	0.12	−0.42★★	0.15	−0.04	0.15	0.02	0.27
Constant	−0.13	0.33	−1.88★★★	0.47	0.48★★★	0.18	−2.03★★	0.74
McFadden R^2	0.07				0.09			
% correctly classified	62.7				49.5			
Lambda	0.31				0.27			
AIC	1932.64				3299.14			

Note: Two analyses are presented: (*a*) Panel A—a binomial logit analysis of voting for Labour (the governing party) versus voting for any of the opposition parties; (*b*) Panel B—a multinomial logit analysis of Conservative, Liberal Democrat and other party voting, with Labour voting as the reference category. [a] Greater London is the reference category.

★ $p \leq 0.05$; ★★ $p \leq 0.01$; ★★★ $p \leq 0.001$; pre-post panel $N = 1479$; validated voters only.

Source: 2001 BES pre–post panel survey.

when social class is the only explanatory variable. Table 4.3, Panel B reports the results of the analysis that differentiates among voters for the Conservatives, the Liberal Democrats, and other parties as opposed to Labour. This model's fit also is poor. The estimated R^2 is only 0.09, and slightly less than half of the respondents are correctly classified. Socio-demographic characteristics cannot explain voting behaviour in 2001.

The next task is to estimate each of remaining models individually in analyses of voting for Labour versus any of the opposition parties. The results are presented in Table 4.4. Most of the variables in the various models perform as expected, with coefficients being statistically significant and properly signed. Thus, Labour identification has a statistically significant, positive impact on Labour voting, whereas

Table 4.4 Rival models of Labour versus other party voting in the 2001 general election

	β	SE
A. Party identification model		
Labour identification	1.74★★★	0.18
Conservative identification	−2.29★★★	0.24
Liberal Democrat identification	−1.41★★★	0.30
Other party identification	−2.47★★★	0.90
Constant	−0.58★★★	0.10
McFadden R^2 = 0.38		
% correctly classified = 82.3, λ = 0.67		
B. Issue–proximity model		
Proximity to Labour	0.27★★★	0.03
Proximity to Conservatives	−0.19★★★	0.02
Proximity to Liberal Democrats	−0.04★	0.02
Constant	−0.33★★	0.12
McFadden R^2 = 0.10		
% correctly classified = 66.2, λ = 0.37		
C. Economic voting model		
Retrospective Evaluations—national economy	0.17★★	0.07
Retrospective Evaluations—personal conditions	0.17★★	0.07
Prospective Evaluations—national economy	0.41★★★	0.07
Prospective Evaluations—personal economic conditions	−0.06	0.09
Labour Party best on economy	1.81★★★	0.15
Emotional Reactions—national economy	0.20★★★	0.04
Emotional Reactions—personal economic conditions	−0.06	0.09
Constant	−1.54★★★	0.13
McFadden R^2 = 0.27		
% correctly classified = 75.9, λ = 0.55		
D. Issue performance model		
Party Best on Most Important Issue		
Labour	1.74★★★	0.13
Conservatives	−1.97★★★	0.27
Liberal Democrats	−1.41★★★	0.30
Other party	−2.47★★	0.90
Constant	−0.58★★★	0.10
McFadden R^2 = 0.25		
% correctly classified = 76.3, λ = 0.56		
E. Party leader model		
Feelings about Tony Blair	0.79★★★	0.04
William Hague	−0.15★★★	0.03
Charles Kennedy	−0.30★★★	0.04
Constant	−2.57★★★	0.34
McFadden R^2 = 0.41		
% correctly classified = 82.1, λ = 0.67		

★ $p \leq 0.05$; ★★ $p \leq 0.01$; ★★★ $p \leq 0.001$; one-tailed test.

Source: 2001 BES pre–post election panel survey.

the effects of Conservative, Liberal Democrat, and other party identifications are significant and negatively signed. Issue proximities (measured as absolute distances) also act as anticipated. The closer respondents were to Labour, the more likely they were to cast a Labour ballot, whereas the closer they were to other parties, the less likely they were to vote Labour.[22] Exactly the same pattern characterizes the 'party best on the most important election issue' variables. Favouring Labour on the most important issue prompts a Labour vote, whereas judging that another party is most capable prompts a vote for it. Leader images also work as expected. Increasingly positive feelings about Tony Blair enhance the probability of a Labour vote, and increasingly positive feelings about William Hague or Charles Kennedy decrease that probability.

Finally, most of the variables in the economic voting model work as expected. Positive retrospective and positive prospective economic evaluations of the national economy encourage a Labour vote, as do positive retrospective evaluations of personal economic conditions. Also as hypothesized, perceptions that Labour is the party best able to handle the economy are positively associated with voting for the party. Emotional reactions to national, but not to personal, economic conditions matter as well. Positive reactions to the national economy increase the likelihood of voting Labour, and negative reactions increase the likelihood of voting for another party. Net of other types of economic judgements, personal prospections do not achieve statistical significance.

A large majority of the variables that work in the Labour voting models are also influential in the models of voting for the Conservatives, Liberal Democrats, and miscellaneous other parties (Tables 4.5 and 4.6). In virtually every case, the direction of the effects is as anticipated. Positive feelings about Blair and Kennedy decrease, and positive feelings about Hague increase, the probability of voting Conservative. Similarly, positive feelings about Blair and Hague reduce the chances of voting Liberal Democrat, whereas positive feelings about Kennedy increase them. For the most part, party identification also acts predictably, with identification with the Conservatives or Liberal Democrats increasing the likelihood of voting for those parties, and identification with Labour decreasing that likelihood. An exception occurs in the Liberal Democrat model: Conservative identifiers are more, not less, likely to vote Liberal Democrat than are nonidentifiers (the reference category).

Issues matter as well. Both issue proximities and judgements regarding which party is best able to handle the most important election issue have the expected influences. Being close to the Conservatives or Liberal Democrats, respectively, on the left–right and tax-spend scales increases the chances of a Tory or Liberal Democrat vote; being close to another party reduces those chances. Similarly, people who believed that the Conservatives or Liberal Democrats were best able to handle what they considered to be the most important election issue were more likely to vote for those parties; people who judged another party to be more capable were more likely to vote for that party.

Once more, most of the variables measuring evaluative or emotional reactions to economic conditions have predictable effects. These effects are the mirror image

Table 4.5 Rival logit models[a] of Conservative voting in the 2001 general election

	β	SE
A. Party identification model		
Labour identification	−3.48★★★	0.37
Conservative identification	3.00★★★	0.27
Liberal Democrat identification	0.13	0.40
Other party identification	−1.05	0.70
Constant	−0.54★★★	0.18
McFadden $R^2 = 0.39$		
% correctly classified = 75.1, $\lambda = 0.54$		
B. Issue–proximity model		
Proximity to Labour	−0.31★★★	0.04
Proximity to Conservatives	0.48★★★	0.03
Proximity to Liberal Democrats	−0.13★★★	0.03
Constant	0.05	0.16
McFadden $R^2 = 0.14$		
% correctly classified = 56.7, $\lambda = 0.20$		
C. Economic voting model		
Retrospective evaluations—national economy	−0.27★★	0.09
Retrospective evaluations—personal conditions	−0.22★	0.10
Prospective evaluations—national economy	−0.50★★★	0.10
Prospective evaluations—personal economic conditions	−0.17	0.11
Labour party best on economy	−3.19★★★	0.20
Emotional reactions—national economy	−0.21★★★	0.05
Emotional reactions—personal economic conditions	0.12★★	0.05
Constant	1.04★★★	0.14
McFadden $R^2 = 0.23$		
% correctly classified = 64.4, $\lambda = 0.34$		
D. Issue performance model		
Party best on most important issue		
Labour	−2.79★★★	0.22
Conservatives	2.43★★★	0.28
Liberal Democrats	−1.01★	0.53
Other party	2.02★	0.93
Constant	−0.00	0.11
McFadden $R^2 = 0.25$		
% correctly classified = 64.3, $\lambda = 0.34$		
E. Party leader model		
Feelings about Tony Blair	−0.84★★★	0.04
William Hague	0.59★★★	0.03
Charles Kennedy	−0.10★	0.06

Table 4.5   Continued

	β	SE
Constant	1.96★★★	0.43

McFadden R^2 = 0.39
% correctly classified = 73.0, λ = 0.50

★ $p \leq 0.05$; ★★ $p \leq 0.01$; ★★★ $p \leq 0.001$; one-tailed test.
[a] Multinomial logit model; Labour voting is the reference category.

Source: 2001 BES pre–post election panel survey.

Table 4.6   Rival logit models[a] of Liberal Democrat voting in 2001 general election

	β	SE
A. Party identification model		
Labour identification	−1.38★★★	0.21
Conservative identification	0.90★★★	0.30
Liberal democrat identification	2.32★★★	0.30
Other party identification	−1.74★	0.88
Constant	−0.43★★	0.17

McFadden R^2 = 0.39
% correctly classified = 75.1, λ = 0.54

B. Issue–proximity model		
Proximity to Labour	−0.23★★★	0.03
Proximity to Conservatives	0.04★	0.02
Proximity to Liberal Democrats	0.20★★★	0.03
Constant	−0.72	0.15

McFadden R^2 = 0.14
% correctly classified = 56.7, λ = 0.20

C. Economic voting model		
Retrospective evaluations—national economy	−0.16★	0.08
Retrospective evaluations—personal conditions	−0.08	0.08
Prospective evaluations—national economy	−0.39★★★	0.08
Prospective evaluations—personal economic conditions	0.17★	0.10
Labour party best on economy	−0.90★★★	0.18
Emotional reactions—national economy	−0.19★★★	0.05
Emotional reactions—personal economic conditions	0.04	0.04
Constant	0.21	0.15

McFadden R^2 = 0.23
% correctly classified = 64.4, λ = 0.34

D. Issue performance model		
Party Best on Most Important Issue		
Labour	−1.11★★★	0.17
Conservatives	0.27	0.38
Liberal Democrats	2.37★★★	0.31

Table 4.6 Continued

	β	SE
Other party	1.27	1.05
Constant	−0.45★★★	0.12
McFadden R^2 = 0.25		
% correctly classified = 64.3, λ = 0.34		
E. Party leader model		
Feelings about Tony Blair	−0.72★★★	0.05
William Hague	−0.09★	0.04
Charles Kennedy	0.61★★★	0.05
Constant	0.22	0.42
McFadden R^2 = 0.39		
% correctly classified = 73.0, λ = 0.50		

★ $p \leq 0.05$; ★★ $p \leq 0.01$; ★★★ $p \leq 0.001$; one-tailed test.
[a] Multinomial logit model; Labour voting is the reference category.

Source: 2001 BES pre–post election panel survey.

of those in the Labour voting analysis described above. Believing that Labour is the party best suited to handle the economy negatively influences Conservative and Liberal Democrat voting. As in the analysis of Labour voting, reactions to the national economy have the strongest and most consistent effects. Specifically, prospective and retrospective judgements about national economic conditions are negatively associated with voting Conservative or Liberal Democrat. And, as also expected, positive emotional reactions to national economic conditions are associated with a lower probability of voting for these parties. The influence of reactions to personal economic circumstances is weaker, with some coefficients being insignificant or signed incorrectly. In sum, the overall message conveyed by the economic voting models is that how voters reacted to the national economy, rather than personal economic circumstances, mattered most in 2001.

A Tournament of Models

The preceding analyses indicate that all of the voting models (party identification, issue proximities, issue priorities/performance, leader images, economic evaluations) work reasonably well, in the sense that many of the coefficients are statistically significant and properly signed. However, as summarized in Table 4.7, the explanatory power of the models varies considerably. The party identification and party leader models fare best. In the binomial logit analysis (Labour versus opposition party voting), these models have estimated R^2s of 0.38 and 0.41, respectively, and over 80 per cent of the cases are correctly classified. In the multinomial logit analyses (voting for Conservatives, Liberal Democrats, or other parties), the estimated R^2s

Table 4.7 Goodness-of-fit statistics for rival models of electoral choice

			Fit statistics		
	AIC	BIC	McFadden R^2	% Correctly Classified	λ
A. Voting for Labour versus voting for other parties					
Model					
Social class[a]	1968.31	1978.91	0.04	61.3	0.28
All Socio-Demographics	1932.64	2001.53	0.07	62.7	0.31
Party Identification	1271.39	1297.85	0.38	82.3	0.67
Party Leaders	1205.69	1226.89	0.41	82.1	0.67
Issue Proximity	1837.14	1858.34	0.10	66.2	0.37
Issue Performance	1532.38	1558.88	0.25	76.3	0.56
Economic Conditions	1511.68	1554.05	0.27	75.9	0.55
Composite	937.82	1117.69	0.57	87.7	0.77
Composite + tactical voting	927.12	1112.28	0.58	87.6	0.77
B. Voting for Conservatives, Liberal Democrats or other parties[b]					
Model					
Social class[a]	3458.57	3479.77	0.03	47.1	0.02
All socio-demographics	3299.14	3225.14	0.09	49.5	0.06
Party identification	2168.59	2237.35	0.39	75.1	0.53
Party leaders	2187.41	2240.40	0.39	73.0	0.50
Issue proximity	3048.21	3101.21	0.14	56.7	0.20
Issue performance	2663.66	2732.55	0.26	64.3	0.34
Economic conditions	2761.51	2878.03	0.23	64.4	0.34
Composite	1607.94	2136.97	0.60	82.1	0.67
Composite + tactical voting	1567.54	2112.44	0.61	82.3	0.67

Note: For the Akaike Information Criterion (AIC) and Schwartz Bayesian Criterion (BIC), smaller values are preferable; for the McFadden R^2, larger values indicate a better fit.
[a] Market research society measure.
[b] Voting for Labour is the reference category.
Source: 2001 BES pre–post election panel survey.

equal 0.39, and the percentages correctly classified are in the mid-seventies. R^2s for the economic voting and election issue models are lower, varying from 0.23 to 0.27, and the percentages correctly classified range from 64 to 76. The figures for the issue-proximity model are even lower. In the case of Labour voting, the R^2 is only 0.10, and 66 per cent of the cases are correctly classified. Comparable numbers for the issue-proximity model of Conservative, Liberal Democrat, and other party voting are 0.14 and 57 per cent. These latter statistics are similar to those for the social class and 'all demographic characteristics' models presented above.

The Akaike Information Criterion (AIC) and Bayesian Information Criterion (BIC) provide additional leverage for discriminating among competing models

(Burnham and Anderson 1998). When the AIC (or BIC) is computed for two or more competing models, the model with the smallest AIC (or BIC) value is considered best.[23] As Table 4.7 shows, AIC and BIC values for the competing models of Labour versus other party voting favour the party leaders model, with the party identification model a relatively close second. Although the economic conditions and issue performance models are less attractive (they have larger AIC and BIC values), they are considerably more attractive than those for the issue-proximity model. Consistent with their small estimated R^2s and poor performance in correctly classifying voting behaviour, the pure social class and general demographic models trail badly in the competition.

Almost exactly the same story is told by the AIC and BIC for the models of Conservative, Liberal Democrat, and other party voting. Both criteria indicate that the party identification and party leader models are best, with the AIC providing marginally greater support for the party identification model, whereas the BIC favours the party leaders model by a very narrow margin. Again, the economic voting, issue-performance, and issue-proximity models occupy intermediate positions, and the social and general demographic models bring up the rear.

Overall, there is a high degree of agreement among the various evaluation criteria regarding which models perform best. The clear winners are the party leader and party identification models, and the clear losers are the social class and general demographic models. Three other models occupy intermediate positions. Two of them explicitly concern issues, and the third (economic voting) involves economic conditions that frequently become election issues. These models have nontrivial explanatory power—more than social class or other demographics, but appreciably less than leader images and partisanship.

The finding that the competing models differ considerably in their explanatory power does not mean that the weaker ones make no independent contribution to understanding electoral choice in 2001. Thus far, each of the models is used in its pure form. It remains to be seen whether any particular model contributes to the explanation of the vote over and above the contribution made by one or more of its rivals. We first perform a series of pairwise comparisons. In each of these comparisons, we investigate whether adding the explanatory variables from a particular model (A) to another model (B) results in a significant reduction in the deviance calculated when the second model is estimated using only its explanatory variables.[24] If such a reduction occurs, then we conclude that Model A 'encompasses' Model B in the sense that it accounts for variance in the dependent variable (electoral choice) that cannot be explained by Model B (Charemza and Deadman 1997: 250).[25] We also run the test the other way—adding the variables from Model B to Model A to determine whether the former encompasses the latter.

The results of these tests reveal that, in every comparison, the models encompass one another (Tables 4.8 and 4.9). For example, consider the comparison of the general demographics model and the party identification model as competing explanations of Labour versus other party voting (Table 4.8). If we add the party identification variables to the demographics model, the resulting reduction in deviance (which constitutes the test statistic, distributed as chi-square) is 691.93. With four degrees of freedom (the number of party identification variables), this reduction is statistically significant ($p < 0.001$). Doing the test the other way— adding the demographic variables to the party identification model—produces a chi-square of 56.68 with 12 degrees of freedom (the 12 variables in the demographic model). Again, this is significant ($p < 0.001$). What these tests say is that a joint model including the party identification and demographic variables has greater explanatory power than either model considered by itself.

Table 4.8   Encompassing tests, rival models of voting for Labour versus other parties

Model encompassed?	Encompassing model?					
	Socio-demos	Party Id	Party leaders	Issue proximity	Issue performance	Economic conditions
Socio-demographics						
$\Delta \chi^2$	X	691.93	771.70	209.96	472.22	520.46
df:		4	3	3	4	7
Party identification						
$\Delta \chi^2$	56.68	X	286.69	36.97	125.48	139.01
df:	12		3	3	4	7
Party leaders						
$\Delta \chi^2$	62.75	222.99	X	31.71	103.96	73.11
df:	12	4		3	4	7
Issue proximity						
$\Delta \chi^2$	132.45	604.71	663.15	X	367.51	391.91
df:	12	4	3		4	7
Issue performance						
$\Delta \chi^2$	87.96	386.47	428.65	60.75	X	215.31
df:	12	4	3	3		7
Economic conditions						
$\Delta \chi^2$	109.50	373.30	371.10	58.45	188.62	X
df:	12	4	3	3	4	

Note: Test statistic is distributed as χ^2 (difference in deviance (-2*log likelihood) between restricted and joint nesting model); all tests are statistically significant, $p \leq 0.001$.

Source: 2001 BES pre–post election panel survey.

Table 4.9 Encompassing tests, rival models of voting for the Conservatives, Liberal Democrats, or other parties[a]

Model encompassed?	Encompassing model?					
	Socio-demos	Party Id	Party leaders	Issue proximity	Issue performance	Economic conditions
Socio-demographics						
$\Delta \chi^2$	X	1196.27	1256.27	470.35	805.80	754.08
df:		4	3	3	4	7
Party identification						
$\Delta \chi^2$	113.72	X	472.26	95.39	259.61	227.49
df:	12		3	3	4	7
Party leaders						
$\Delta \chi^2$	198.54	497.09	X	97.20	204.83	150.52
df:	12	4		3	4	7
Issue proximity						
$\Delta \chi^2$	273.42	981.02	958.00	X	584.95	517.03
df:	12	4	3		4	7
Issue performance						
$\Delta \chi^2$	218.32	754.69	675.08	194.40	X	350.98
df:	12	4	3	3		7
Economic conditions						
$\Delta \chi^2$	300.44	802.41	700.61	206.33	430.82	X
df:	12	4	3	3	4	

Note: Test statistic is distributed as χ^2 (difference in deviance ($-2\star$log likelihood) between restricted and joint nesting model); all tests are statistically significant, $p \leq 0.001$.
[a] Voting for Labour is the reference category.

Source: 2001 BES pre–post election panel survey.

As a second example, consider the comparison of the party identification and party leader models in the analysis of Conservative, Liberal Democrat, and other party voting. As noted above, both of these models have considerably greater explanatory power than any of their rivals. But, how do the party identification and leader models fare when pitted against one another? Specifically, do we gain explanatory leverage by adding the party identification variables to the leader model? What about adding leader variables to the party identification model? The test statistics (Table 4.9) indicate that the answers to the latter two questions are affirmative. Adding the party leader variables to the party identification model yields a statistically significant chi-square of 472.26 (df = 3, $p < 0.001$). Similarly, adding the party iden-tification variables to the party leader model produces a significant test statistic (479.09, df = 4, $p < 0.001$). These results indicate that neither model is redundant. Information about both party identification and feelings about party leaders increases our ability to explain voting for the Conservatives, Liberal Democrats, and other parties over and above the explanations provided by each set of variables separately.

A Composite Model

Each model makes a contribution to the explanation of electoral choice. However, since the preceding analyses involve pairwise comparisons of various models, a more general test specifies a composite model that incorporates all of the variables from the several specialised models. As Table 4.7 shows, this composite model for Labour versus opposition party voting is superior to any of the models considered thus far. The estimated R^2 is 0.57, and nearly 90 per cent of the cases are correctly classified. Moreover, although the composite model is much larger than any of the specialised models, and thereby incurs a much heavier parameterisation penalty, its AIC and BIC values are smaller than that for any other model. The story is the same for the composite model of Conservative, Liberal Democrat, and other party voting. The estimated R^2 and percentages of cases correctly classified are substan-tially larger than those for the specialised models, and the AIC and BIC values are smaller. The composite model testifies that all of the specialised models have stories to tell about electoral choice in 2001.

These specifics of these stories may be appreciated with the help of the para-meter estimates for the composite models (Table 4.10). Turning first to the analysis of Labour versus other party voting, we see that two of the party leader variables have significant effects. As expected, more positive feelings about Tony Blair enhance the probability of a Labour vote, whereas more positive feelings about Charles Kennedy diminish it. Three of the party identification variables are signifi-cant, and they behave as expected. Labour identifiers were more likely to vote for 'their' party, and Conservative and Liberal Democrat identifiers were less likely to do so. Issue proximities matter as well. As the distance between a voter and the perceived position of the Conservatives or Liberal Democrats decreases, the likeli-hood of a Labour vote decreases. Issue-priority or performance variables also behave as hypothesized. The perception that the Conservatives or Liberal Democrats are best able to handle the voter's most important election issue reduces the likelihood of a Labour vote. Among the economic voting variables, positive reactions to national economic conditions have positive effects on Labour voting, as do perceptions that Labour is most competent to handle the economy. Most social characteristics, including social class, do not exert significant effects. Two exceptions are ethnicity and home ownership; people who describe themselves as 'white British' and

Table 4.10 Binomial[a] and multinomial logit models[b] of voting in the 2001 general election, composite specification

| | Panel A | | Panel B | | | | | |
| | Labour | | Conservative | | Liberal Democrat | | Other | |
	β	SE	β	SE	β	SE	β	SE
Predictor Variables								
Age	0.01	0.01	0.01	0.01	−0.01	0.01	−0.01	0.01
Ethnicity	−0.75*	0.34	2.03***	0.61	0.43	0.40	0.55	0.74
Gender	0.01	0.18	−0.07	0.28	−0.02	0.21	0.12	0.36
Home ownership	−0.58**	0.24	0.64	0.40	0.46*	0.28	0.26	0.45
Occupational sector	−0.13	0.19	0.39	0.31	0.07	0.22	0.34	0.38
Region[b]								
South East	0.08	0.33	−0.18	0.54	−0.14	0.86	1.01	0.81
South West	−0.33	0.43	−0.28	0.69	0.56	0.47	0.77	1.06
Midlands	0.65*	0.37	−0.82	0.58	−0.62	0.42	−0.11	0.90
North	0.68*	0.34	−1.62**	0.57	−0.37	0.38	−0.12	0.88
Wales	0.06	0.46	−0.92	0.77	0.10	0.51	1.84*	0.90
Scotland	0.44	0.42	−0.92	0.70	−0.88*	0.51	1.75*	0.86
Social class	−0.04	0.08	0.09	0.12	0.04	0.09	−0.12	0.15
Party identification								
Conservative	−1.50***	0.33	1.46***	0.39	0.77*	0.40	−0.05	0.63
Labour	1.14***	0.24	−2.54***	0.48	−0.91***	0.28	−0.57	0.50
Liberal Democrat	−0.99**	0.35	−0.69	0.54	1.48***	0.37	−0.77	0.81
Other Party	−1.11*	0.49	−0.79	0.88	−1.74	1.08	2.78***	0.63

Table 4.10 Continued

	Panel A				Panel B			
	Labour		Conservative		Liberal Democrat		Other	
	β	SE	β	SE	β	SE	β	SE
Party leader affect								
Blair	0.46***	0.05	−0.52***	0.07	−0.41***	0.06	−0.67***	0.09
Hague	0.01	0.04	0.32***	0.07	−0.12*	0.05	0.03	0.09
Kennedy	−0.28***	0.06	−0.09	0.09	0.43***	0.07	0.18*	0.10
Party best on most Important issue								
Conservative	−0.97**	0.35	0.73	0.45	−0.02	0.51	1.24*	0.62
Labour	0.38*	0.20	−0.92**	0.38	−0.28	0.25	−0.26	0.44
Liberal Democrat	−0.78*	0.36	−1.40*	0.72	1.36***	0.41	−0.51	0.89
Other Party	−1.06	0.75	1.81	1.38	1.42	1.35	3.25**	0.63
Party-issue proximity								
Conservative	−1.02**	0.38	0.17**	0.06	0.04	0.04	0.04	0.07
Labour	0.33	0.22	−0.13*	0.07	−0.06	0.05	−0.01	0.08
Liberal Democrat	−1.12**	0.40	0.11	0.07	0.09*	0.05	−0.05	0.08

Economic evaluations								
National retrospective	0.17*	0.10	−0.04	0.14	−0.20*	0.07	0.01	0.19
Personal retrospective	0.15	0.10	−0.25	0.16	−0.04	0.11	−0.56	0.19
National prospective	0.19*	0.10	−0.38**	0.16	−0.14	0.11	−0.23	0.20
Personal prospective	−0.15	0.13	0.01	0.19	0.19	0.14	0.33	0.22
Emotional reactions to Economic conditions								
National	0.01	0.06	0.09	0.10	−0.07	0.07	0.09	0.12
Personal	−0.08	0.06	0.12	0.09	0.12*	0.07	0.03	0.11
Labour best on economy	0.54*	0.24	−1.29***	0.32	−0.09	0.28	0.03	0.44
Tactical voting	−0.85***	0.24	−0.77*	0.38	1.12***	0.25	1.03**	0.42
McFadden pseudo R^2	0.58				0.61			
% Correctly classified	87.6				82.3			
Lambda	0.74				0.67			

* $p \leq 0.05$; ** $p \leq 0.01$; *** $p \leq 0.001$; pre–post panel, validated voters, $N = 1466$.

[a] The results of two analyses are presented: (a) binomial logit analysis of voting for Labour (the governing party) versus voting for any of the opposition parties; (b) multinomial logit analysis of Conservative, Liberal Democrat, and other party voting, with Labour voting as the reference category.

[b] Greater London is the reference category.

Source: 2001 BES pre–post election panel survey.

homeowners were less likely to vote Labour than those in other ethnic groups and renters. Net of all these relationships, there is evidence of tactical voting, with those classified as tactical voters being less likely than others to cast a Labour ballot.

The composite model of Conservative, Liberal Democrat, and other party voting yields similar results. Once again, several variables from the party leader and party identification models have significant effects. With regard to leaders, positive feelings about Blair decrease the probability of voting for any of the opposition parties, whereas positive feelings about Hague increase the probability of voting Conservative and lessen the probability of voting Liberal Democrat. Positive feelings about Kennedy do not diminish the likelihood of voting for the Conservatives or one of the minor parties, but they do enhance the probability of voting Liberal Democrat. The party identification effects are such that identification with the Conservatives, Liberal Democrats, or one of the minor parties boosts the likelihood of voting for those parties. Identification with Labour lessens those likelihoods. Other variables also have significant effects. People who judged that Labour or the Liberal Democrats were best on the most important election issues were less likely to cast a Conservative ballot; those who thought that the Liberal Democrats were most competent were more likely to vote Liberal Democrat. Issue proximities are influential, with people closest to the Conservatives being more likely to vote Conservative, and people closest to Labour being less likely to do so. Those who were closest to the Liberal Democrats were more likely to support that party.

Most economic variables do not achieve significance, but it is noteworthy that those that do involve judgements about the national economy rather than personal economic circumstances. Judging that Labour is best on the economy also decreases the likelihood of a Conservative vote. Tactical voting is evident. As expected, the Conservatives suffered because of it, whereas the Liberal Democrats and the minor parties benefited. Demographic variables perform poorly; of 36 coefficients estimated, only five are significant. Social class is not significant in any of the models. Finally, as in the case of the Labour versus opposition party voting, the composite model for Conservative, Liberal Democrat, and other party voting outperforms any of the specialised models. The estimated R^2 and the percentage of cases correctly classified are higher than for any of those models, and the AIC and BIC values are lower.[26]

Voting Probabilities

The preceding analyses tell us that numerous variables influenced electoral choice in 2001. But, how strong are these relationships? The answer is not immediately apparent because, unlike the coefficients generated by OLS regression, the coefficients from logit analyses do not have a straightforward interpretation. This is because the impact of any one variable depends not only on its values, but also on the values assumed by other variables (Long 1997). To discern the impact of a variable, we fix the values of other variables at their means or other plausible values,[27] and calculate the probability of voting for a party when the variable of interest is set at its minimum value.[28] We then recalculate the probability when the latter variable is set at its maximum value. The results of these calculations for the significant predictors in the model of Labour versus other party voting are shown in Figure 4.8.

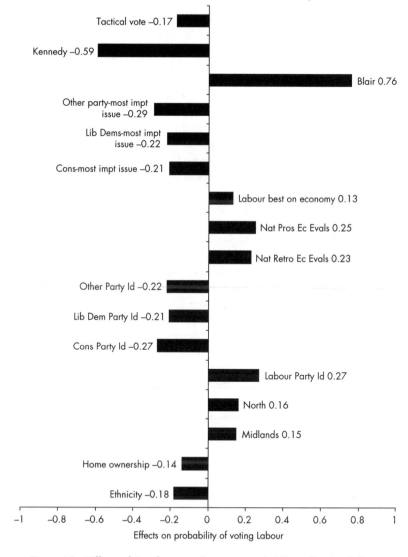

Figure 4.8 Effects of significant predictors on probability of voting Labour, composite voting model

Most immediately evident from this figure are the very strong effects of feelings about Tony Blair and Charles Kennedy. *Ceteris paribus*, increasing feelings about Blair from their minimum value to their maximum value boosts the probability of voting Labour by fully 76 points. A similar increase in feelings about Kennedy reduces that probability by 59 points. Several other predictor variables are capable of shifting the probability of voting Labour by lesser, albeit decidedly non-trivial, amounts. Changes in prospective and retrospective evaluations of national economic conditions alter the probability of voting Labour by 23 and 25 points, respectively. Judging that an opposition party is best able to handle the issue deemed most important in the election lowers the likelihood of voting Labour by similar amounts. Party identifications are important as well. Being a Labour identifier raises the likelihood of voting Labour by 27 points, and identifying with one of the opposition parties lowers that probability by over 20 points. The effects of other variables are smaller. Being a homeowner decreases the probability of a Labour vote by 14 points, and white British ethnicity does so by a slightly larger amount. Residents of the Midlands and the North are more likely to vote Labour than Londoners by 15 and 16 points, respectively. Finally, net of all other effects, deciding to vote tactically lowers the probability of voting Labour by 17 points.

Feelings about party leaders also have sizeable effects on Conservative voting (see Figure 4.9). None of the effects is as strong as those in the Labour voting model, but feelings about Hague have the largest impact and are capable of shifting the probability of a Tory vote by 37 points. Feelings about Blair can shift that probability by about half as much. Another relatively important variable is issue proximity to Labour. Voters who perceived that Labour was exactly where it should be (at the voter's ideal point) on the issues summarized by the left–right and tax–spend scales were 31 points less likely to vote Conservative. The impact of the distance between the voter and his or her perception of the Conservative Party on these scales is about half as large, and the effect of party selected on the most important election issue is smaller still. Selecting either Labour or the Liberal Democrats as best able to handle the most important election issue, rather than selecting no party or thinking there is no important issue, lowers the likelihood of a Tory vote by 9 points. Economic evaluations display slightly stronger effects. Increasingly positive national prospective economic evaluations lower the chances of a Tory vote by 16 points; perceiving that Labour is best on the economy lowers them by a slightly smaller amount. Party identification matters as well, with Conservative identifiers being 21 points more likely than nonidentifiers to vote Conservative, and Labour identifiers 14 points less likely to do so. The effects of other variables are quite small, with residence in the North reducing the likelihood of Conservative voting by 12 points, and white British ethnic identification raising it by 6 points. Tactical voters were 6 points less likely to cast a Conservative ballot than sincere ones.

The relatively strong influence of feelings about party leaders is also apparent in the Liberal Democrat analysis (see Figure 4.10). People who give Charles Kennedy

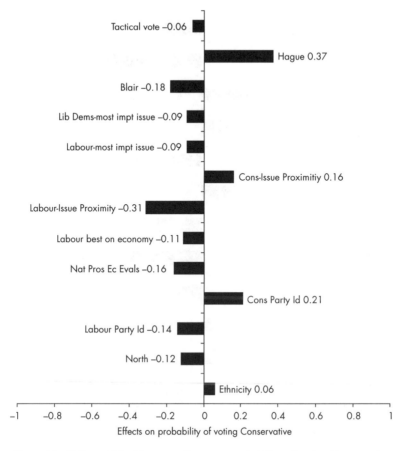

Figure 4.9 Effects of significant predictors on probability of voting Conservative, composite voting model

the lowest rating on the party-leader-affect scale are 64 points less likely to vote for the Liberal Democrats than those who gave him the maximum score. Feelings about the other leaders matter as well and are capable of changing the probability of supporting the Liberal Democrats by 27 points. Two other variables have sizeable effects. Identifying with the Liberal Democrats raises the probability of voting for the party by 38 points, and selecting it as best able to handle the most important election issue raises that probability by nearly the same amount. The effects of proximity to the Liberal Democrats on the left–right and tax-spend scales and national retrospective economic evaluations are also significant. The former changes the probability of voting Liberal Democrat by 24 points, and the latter by 22 points. Residence in Scotland and homeownership are considerably less important, but the

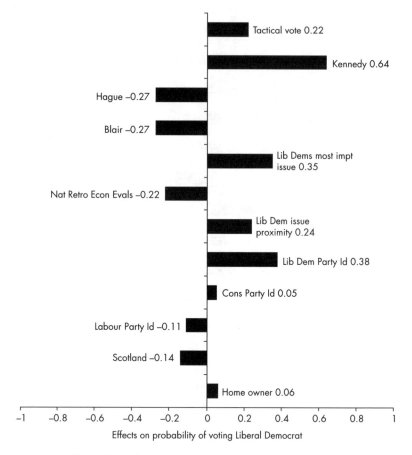

Figure 4.10 Effects of significant predictors on probability of voting Liberal Democrat, composite voting model

impact of tactical voting is sizeable. Persons motivated by tactical considerations are 22 points more likely than others to opt for the Liberal Democrats.

PARTY LEADERS: EFFECTS, CAUSES, CONSEQUENCES

Effects

The preceding analyses indicate that feelings about party leaders had strong effects. Since the impact of party leaders on electoral choice has been a topic of considerable controversy, we conduct supplementary diagnostic tests to check the validity of our findings. The first test involves adding a variable measuring pre-election vote intentions to our composite model. This variable helps to control for the possibility that feelings about party leaders reflect, rather than cause, vote decisions. That this is conceivable for at least some of the respondents in the 2001 BES is suggested by the fact that a majority (53 per cent) of those in the pre-election benchmark survey stated that they already had decided how to vote. However, as Table 4.11 (Panel A) shows, every leader variable that is significant in our earlier analyses (see Table 4.10) remains so when pre-election vote intentions are controlled.[29]

In a second diagnostic test, we reestimate our composite model using an alternative measure of party identification. Some researchers have claimed that the traditional BES measure of party identification is flawed. If they are correct, then this measure would not provide an accurate estimate of the effects of partisan attachments in a multivariate model of voting behaviour. As a consequence, the estimated effects of party leader images on the vote could be exaggerated because the effects of partisanship had not been adequately controlled. As discussed in Chapter Six, we included a new measure of party identification in the 2001 BES to see whether it performs differently from the traditional one.[30] Here, we use the new measure to

Table 4.11   Tests of party leader effects on voting

| | Vote | | | | | | | |
| | Labour | | Conservative | | Liberal Democrat | | Other party | |
Party Leader	β	SE	β	SE	β	SE	β	SE
A. Leader effects in vote models with controls for pre-election vote intentions								
Blair	0.44***	0.06	−0.50***	0.08	−0.38***	0.06	−0.61***	0.10
Hague	0.02	0.05	0.32***	0.08	−0.13*	0.05	0.01	0.09
Kennedy	−0.27***	0.06	−0.14	0.10	0.43***	0.07	0.19*	0.11
B. Leader effects in vote models with alternative measure of party identification								
Blair	0.40***	0.06	−0.44***	0.08	−0.37***	0.06	−0.59***	0.10
Hague	−0.01	0.05	0.36***	0.08	−0.12*	0.05	0.07	0.09
Kennedy	−0.19***	0.06	−0.08	0.09	0.33***	0.07	0.05	0.11
C. Exogeneity tests for party leader variables in vote models								
Blair	0.01	0.22	−0.96	0.89	−0.61	0.68	−0.39	1.12
Hague	0.15	0.52	−1.85	1.15	−0.06	0.75	0.91	1.35
Kennedy	0.04	0.50	0.68	1.23	0.19	0.71	1.17	1.33

Note: Logit estimates, Labour versus all other parties; multinomial logit estimates, Conservative, Liberal Democrat and other party voting with Labour voting as the reference category.
* $p \leq 0.05$; ** $p \leq 0.01$; *** $p \leq 0.001$; pre-post panel, $N = 1469$.

Source: 2001 BES pre–post election panel survey.

determine whether its presence in the composite model influences the magnitude of the estimated effects of feelings about party leaders. Table 4.11 (Panel B) shows that the answer is 'no'. Using the alternative measure of party identification reduces the size of the party leader coefficients only slightly (by an average of 0.08 points) and, with one exception (the impact of feelings about Charles Kennedy on 'other party' voting), all of the leader coefficients that are significant in the earlier analyses remain so.

As a third diagnostic test, we check whether our analyses suffer from 'simultaneity bias' that would undermine the credibility of the estimated effects of the several variables in the composite model (Greene 2003). The simultaneity bias conjecture is that feelings about leaders may affect voting behaviour, but voting also affects feelings about leaders. Testing for simultaneity bias requires that we develop models for feelings about party leaders. The substantive results of analysing these leader models are presented below. We use the residuals from these models to test for simultaneity bias. As should be the case if there is no simultaneity bias, Table 4.11, Panel C shows that these residuals are statistically insignificant when they are added to the composite models of the vote. These results are consistent with the idea that feelings about party leaders are weakly exogenous to electoral choice,[31] and that the impressive relationships between feelings about party leaders and voting behaviour documented above are not a statistical artefact.

Causes

Models of the factors that affect feelings about party leaders are interesting beyond their utility for conducting simultaneity bias tests. Our specification of these models is informed by the fact that leaders speak on behalf of their parties, and their pronouncements receive heavy and continuous media coverage both during election campaigns and in the interim between these events. As the leader of the governing party, the prime minister is constantly called on to explain government policies and to defend its performance on the economy, public services, foreign affairs, and other topics, great and small. Opposition party leaders work assiduously to capture media attention, to criticize the government on all these matters, and to shape the issue agenda to their party's advantage.

The salience of the leaders and the strong linkages that the media forge among leaders, issues, and policy performance suggest that variables such as party–issue proximities and perceptions of party best able to handle the issue designated as most important influence how voters feel about the leaders. In the contemporary British context (see Chapter Three), another potentially relevant variable concerns attitudes towards the desirability of joining the European Monetary Union (EMU).[32] It can also be anticipated that reactions to economic conditions influence voters' orientations towards the leaders. Given the political importance of the state of the economy, and its often-demonstrated influence on the dynamics of party support, it is not surprising that numerous studies have found that feelings about the leaders are affected by voters' economic evaluations. As discussed in Chapter Two, emotional reactions to economic conditions have received much less attention in this regard, but it may be hypothesized that they have similar effects. And, because the leaders inevitably are branded by their party's label, voters' party identifications will serve as a heuristic device that influence how they react to the leaders. Measures of age, ethnicity, gender, and social class are also included in the leader models to determine if feelings about the leaders vary across important socio-demographic groups in the electorate.

As shown in Table 4.12, a wide variety of factors affects feelings about Blair, Hague, and Kennedy. As hypothesized, voters who preferred Labour on the most important election issue preferred Blair more than those who preferred another party or thought

Table 4.12   Factors affecting feelings about party leaders

			Party Leader			
	Blair		Hague		Kennedy	
	β	SE	β	SE	β	SE
Predictor variables						
Age	0.01***	0.00	0.01***	0.00	0.01***	0.00
Ethnicity	−0.43***	0.14	−0.70***	0.16	−0.15	0.13
Gender	0.02	0.08	−0.09	0.09	−0.06	0.07
Social class	−0.19***	0.03	0.03	0.03	0.14***	0.03
Party identification						
Conservative	−0.24*	0.13	0.96***	0.15	−0.06	0.12
Labour	1.15***	0.12	−0.26*	0.13	−0.05	0.10
Liberal Democrat	−0.25	0.16	−0.30	0.18	0.82***	0.15
Other party	0.06	0.22	−0.25	0.25	−0.41*	0.20
Party best on most important issue						
Conservative	−0.31*	0.13	0.86***	0.16	−0.13	0.13
Labour	0.63***	0.11	−0.21*	0.11	0.19*	0.09
Liberal Democrat	−0.31*	0.17	−0.13	0.19	1.60***	0.16
Other party	−0.74**	0.26	−0.28	0.29	0.28	0.23
Party-issue proximity						
Conservative	−0.01	0.01	0.16***	0.02	−0.06***	0.01
Labour	0.14**	0.02	−0.04**	0.02	−0.04**	0.01
Liberal Democrat	−0.01	0.01	−0.07***	0.02	0.15***	0.02
Economic evaluations						
National retrospective	0.03	0.04	0.01	0.05	0.05	0.04
Personal retrospective	0.04	0.05	−0.01	0.05	−0.01	0.04

Table 4.12   Continued

| | Party Leader | | | | | |
| | Blair | | Hague | | Kennedy | |
	β	SE	β	SE	β	SE
National prospective	0.30★★★	0.04	−0.21★★★	0.05	−0.09★★	0.04
Personal prospective	−0.04	0.05	−0.01	0.06	0.09★	0.05
Emotional reactions to economic conditions						
National	0.28★★★	0.03	0.01	0.03	0.02	0.02
Personal	0.01	0.02	0.08★★★	0.02	0.02	0.02
Labour best on economy	1.02★★★	0.10	−0.68★★★	0.12	0.03	0.09
Attitude towards EMU[a]						
Definitely join	0.13	0.23	0.32	0.26	0.39★	0.21
Join if conditions right	−0.14	0.18	0.41★	0.20	−0.00	0.16
Out next 4–5 Years	0.06	0.18	0.56★★	0.20	−0.04	0.16
Out on principle	−0.38★	0.18	0.55★★	0.20	−0.37★	0.16
Constant	4.03★★★	0.27	4.45★★★	0.34	5.54★★★	0.25
R^2	0.54		0.32		0.21	
Adjusted R^2	0.54		0.31		0.20	

Note: OLS estimates.

★ $p \leq 0.05$; ★★ $p \leq 0.01$; ★★★ $p \leq 0.001$; pre-post panel, $N = 2314$.

[a] 'Don't know' is the reference category.

Source: 2001 BES pre–post election panel survey.

that there was no important issue or no party capable of handling it. Comparable effects are present in the models of feelings about Hague and Kennedy. Issue-proximity effects operate as well. People who placed themselves closer to a particular party's leader on the tax-spend and left–right scales tended to feel more warmly towards that party than those who put themselves further away from the party on these scales. Expectations about the national economy have a highly significant positive impact on feelings about Blair, as do emotional reactions to national economic conditions. Similarly, people who judged that the Labour Party was best able to handle the economy felt more warmly toward Blair and more coolly towards Hague. Party identification also works as hypothesized; identifiers with a particular party tended to like the leader of that party more than nonidentifiers and people who identified with another party.

In addition, attitudes towards the EMU make a difference, especially in the case of William Hague. As might be expected given his strident opposition to the Euro, people who expressed reservations about joining the EMU tended to feel more positive about the Conservative leader than those who were unsure or thought that Britain should join immediately. Also, as might be anticipated given Kennedy's strong pro-Europe stand, individuals who favoured joining the EMU were more positively disposed towards him, and those who definitely wished to stay out were more negatively disposed towards him. The latter group also tended to have more negative feelings about Tony Blair.

Some of the socio-demographic variables have significant effects. Although gender is not influential, older voters had more positive feelings towards all three leaders than younger ones. People who identified themselves as white British were more negative towards both Hague and Blair than those with other ethnic identifications. Finally, social class effects are evident; working class people were more favourably disposed towards Blair than middle class individuals. In contrast, feelings about Kennedy tended to be more positive among the latter group than the former one. Feelings about Hague were not significantly affected by social class. More generally, as in the voting analyses, the explanatory power of social class and other demographic variables is quite weak. Using class as the only predictor variable shows that it can account for only 2 per cent of the variance in feelings about Blair and Kennedy, and less than 0.5 per cent the variance in feelings about Hague. When all the demographics are employed as predictors, the explained variance in feelings about the leaders remains small, reaching a maximum of 5 per cent in Kennedy's case. In 2001, feelings about the party leaders were substantially decoupled from socio-demographic characteristics.

Consequences

The preceding analyses clearly indicate that several variables in the composite model exert both direct and indirect effects on voting, with the latter being mediated by feelings about the party leaders. In this regard, the direct and indirect effects of voters' reactions to the economy among different groups of party identifiers are particularly interesting. We gauge the size of these effects by setting the values of all of the predictor variables in the leader models to their mean values, except for party identification. Then, for each group of party identifiers, we increase the values of three of the economic variables—expectations about the national economy, emotional reactions to national economic conditions, and perceptions that Labour is best able to handle the economy—from their minimum to their maximum values. In every case, feelings about Blair become substantially more positive. For example, among Labour identifiers, feelings about Blair climb by five points (from 3.6 to 8.6) on the 11-point scale. Blair's gains among other groups of identifiers are of similar magnitudes.

We may better appreciate the electoral import of such changes by constructing scenarios in which we calculate the probability of voting Labour as the values of the economic variables are manipulated. We consider two alternative scenarios— one bleak and one rosy. The first envisages a situation where the Conservatives' 1997 campaign advertising, which predicted that 'it all would end in tears' if Labour was put in charge of the economy, was, in fact, correct. A voter, when confronted with dismal economic news, evaluated the prospects for the national economy very negatively, became angry and uneasy, and concluded that Labour was incapable of handling the country's economic affairs.[33] We contrast this with a situation similar to the one that actually occurred in 2001. Here, the voter reacted to a healthy economy by evaluating its prospects very positively, being confident and hopeful, and endorsing Labour as the party best able to handle the economy.[34]

When calculating how these alternative scenarios affect the probability of voting Labour, we begin by considering an otherwise average voter who is a member of the crucial swing group of people who lacks any generalized commitment to a political party (as indicated by the lack of a party identification). Without considering the impact of these economic variables on feelings about Prime Minister Blair, the probability that such a voter would cast a Labour ballot increases by 37 points (from 0.21 to 0.58) as reactions to the economy change from negative to positive (Figure 4.11, Panel A). However, taking into account the indirect effects of economic reactions, via their effects on feelings about Blair, the increase in the

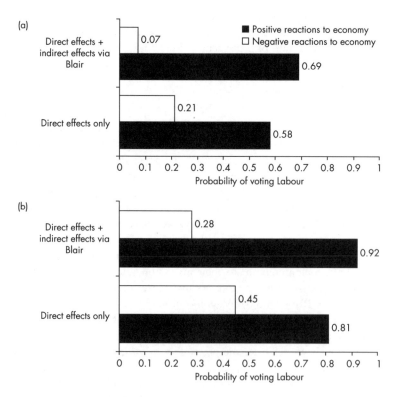

Figure 4.11 Direct and Blair-mediated effects of reactions to the economy on probability of voting Labour among nonidentifiers and Labour party identifiers (a) nonidentifiers, (b) Labour identifiers

probability of voting Labour is nearly twice as large—64 points (from 0.07 to 0.69). Figure 4.11, Panel B shows a second scenario that replicates the one just described, but which assumes that the voter is a member of the large group of Labour identifiers in the electorate. If we ignore the fact that feelings about the prime minister provide an indirect path for reactions to the economy to influence the vote, when such reactions change from negative to positive, the probability of voting Labour increases by 36 points (from 0.45 to 0.81). However, allowing the impact of reactions to the economy to be mediated via affect for Blair increases the probability by a much greater amount—64 points (from 0.28 to 0.92).

Both scenarios reinforce the general point that reactions to the economy had substantial effects on electoral choice in 2001. Since such reactions also influenced feelings about party leaders, the effects were both direct and indirect. In 2001, a buoyant economy provided major benefits for the governing Labour Party and its leader. However, the scenarios illustrate that there was considerable downside potential as well. If the Conservatives had been correct in their 1997 prediction that the election of a Labour government would be a prelude to economic misery similar to what beset the country in the 1970s, then Labour would have paid a substantial price at the polls. The probability of voting Labour would have dropped precipitously, not only among people lacking a party identification, but also among the large group of Labour partisans that constitute the core of the party's support in any given election.

CONCLUSION: WHAT MATTERED IN 2001

This chapter investigates the determinants of voting in the 2001 general election. Consonant with evidence presented in Chapter Three and earlier studies that have documented the weakening of the class–vote nexus, a social class model provides a very poor explanation of how voters behaved in 2001. Nor is it the case that the role of social class is usurped by other socio-demographic variables. Both alone and in combination, demographic characteristics leave much of the variance in voting unexplained. Those wishing to understand electoral choice in present-day Britain must look elsewhere.

Whichever model of electoral choice is investigated, Labour had a substantial edge over its rivals in 2001. As the election approached, Labour held a commanding lead in party identifiers. And, although sizeable groups had reservations about Labour's performance in delivering public services in areas such as health, transport, and crime, large majorities did not think that any of the other parties could do better. The result was that Labour maintained a large lead over its rivals as the party best able to handle a wide variety of issues that people judged important. Labour held an additional, related advantage in terms of its proximity to many voters on general left–right and tax-spend dimensions. Although the Liberal Democrats also were close to a large segment of the electorate on these dimensions, Labour's principal rivals, the Conservatives, were more distant. The robust economy was yet another trump in Labour's hand. Economic evaluations were positive, emotional reactions to national and personal economic conditions were sanguine, and Labour held a massive edge in judgements of which party was most competent to manage the economy. Labour's leader was another asset. Tony Blair held a marked advantage over William Hague on virtually every component of the competence and responsiveness dimensions of leader image. Although Blair was not especially warmly received by the voters, he generated considerably more positive affect than did Hague. Liberal Democrat leader, Charles Kennedy, was a stronger competitor—particularly as the campaign progressed—but, ultimately, his image was as good as, not better than, Blair's.

What then mattered for electoral choice in 2001? Our analyses strongly suggest two major conclusions. First, several things mattered—all of the voting models have something to say. Second, and equally clearly, some models have much more to say than others. The party leader and party identification models provide the strongest explanations. The economic voting and issue priority/performance models exhibit intermediate strength, and the issue-proximity model trails all of its competitors, except for the social class and general socio-demographics models. In keeping with the idea that all of the competing models make some contribution, a composite model that incorporates variables from the several models has the strongest explanatory power. Finally, net of everything else, there is evidence that the Liberal Democrats and minor parties benefitted at the expense of Labour and the Conservatives because of tactical voting.

We use parameter estimates from the composite model to calculate how much the probability of voting for a party changes when the values of significant predictor variables are changed. This exercise reinforces the conclusion that party identifications and feelings about the party leaders were particularly significant factors in 2001. In addition, positive reactions to the economy, which significantly raised the probability of a Labour vote, operated in part through their impact on feelings about Tony Blair. Indeed, both the prime minister and his party benefited handsomely from the mood of economic optimism that was a product of the 'good times' that voters enjoyed as they went to the polls in 2001. The healthy economy forcefully refuted the charges made by the Conservatives in 1997 that a New Labour government would revisit the economic difficulties that had afflicted the country when Labour had held the reins of power in the 1970s. In 2001, the continuing good economic news after four years in office made it possible for the prime minister to overcome widespread unhappiness that he and his party had failed to deliver the highly valued public services expected of a Labour government. In the end, the strong economy enabled the prime minister to convince large numbers of voters that another New Labour ballot was not a ticket to an impoverished past but, rather, a passport to a prosperous future—a future in which Labour would honour its commitment to improve public services.

Viewed generally, the analyses provide little comfort for proponents of socio-logical approaches to electoral choice. Party identification is a relatively strong pre-dictor of voting behaviour, but as shown in Chapter Six, partisan attachments are more mutable than sociological models allow. Within the individual rationality framework, valence models perform better than spatial ones. In particular, the explanatory power of party identification and feelings about party leaders testifies that voters' judgements about actual and anticipated party performance are what matter most for electoral choice. The credibility of this testimony is reinforced by the fact that feelings about party leaders are strongly influenced by economic evalu-ations and emotional reactions to economic conditions. Analyses presented in Chapter Six strengthen this interpretation by demonstrating that economic evalu-ations and party performance assessments do much to account for the dynamics of party identification. First, however, Chapter Five considers the determinants of voting in greater depth by investigating the impact of the 2001 election campaign.

NOTES

1. The Gallup party identification sequence is the same as that used in the 2001 BES. See note 2 for wording.

2. The 2001 BES party identification sequence is: (*a*) 'Generally speaking, do you think of yourself as Labour, Conservative, Liberal Democrat, Scottish Nationalist [in Scotland only], Plaid Cymru [in Wales only], or what? (*b*) [If 'None,' 'Don't Know', or 'Refused'] Do you generally think of yourself as a little closer to one of the parties than the others?' (*c*) [If 'Yes'] Which party is that? (iv) 'Would you call yourself very strong [PARTY GIVEN in (*a*) or (*b*)], fairly strong or not very strong?'

3. The question wording is: 'On a scale from 0 to 10, where 0 means government should cut taxes a lot and spend much less on health and social services, and 10 means government should raise taxes a lot and spend much more, where would you put the views of: (a) yourself, (b) the Labour Party, (c) the Conservative Party, (d) the Liberal Democrats, (e) the SNP [in Scotland only], (f) Plaid Cymru [in Wales only]'. Order of presentation of (a)–(f) is randomized.

4. The question wording is: 'In politics, people sometimes talk of left and right. Using the scale from 0 to 10, where would you place: (a) the Labour Party, (b) the Conservative Party, (c) the Liberal Democrats, (d) the SNP [in Scotland only], (e) Plaid Cymru [in Wales only], (f) yourself'. Order of presentation of (a)–(f) is randomized.

5. The question wording is: 'People give different reasons for why they vote for one party rather than another. Which of the following best describes your reasons? (a) the party has the best policies; (b) the party has the best leader; (c) I really preferred another party but it stood no chance of winning in my constituency'. All those citing (c) were classified as tactical voters. Some respondents did not choose (a), (b), or (c), but offered other reasons. If these answers indicated a tactical vote, the respondents were placed in the tactical voter category.

6. The questions are: 'How does the financial situation of your household now com-pare with what it was 12 months ago?' 'How do you think the general economic situation

in this country has changed over the last 12 months?' Response categories for both questions are 'got a lot worse', 'got a little worse', 'stayed the same', 'got a little better', 'got a lot better'.

7. The questions are: 'How do you think the financial situation of your household will change over the next 12 months?' 'How do you think the general economic situation in this country will develop over the next 12 months?' Response categories for both questions are 'get a lot worse', 'get a little worse', 'stay the same', 'get a little better', 'get a lot better'.

8. Attention must be paid to the context in which the economic evaluation questions were asked. Given the robust performance of the economy, 'stay the same' responses are interpreted as positive evaluations.

9. The question wording is: 'If Britain were in economic difficulties, which party do you think would be able to handle the situation best—Labour or the Conservatives?'

10. The wording of the question regarding emotional reactions to national economic conditions is: 'Which, if any, of the following words describe your feelings about the country's general economic situation?' The list of words includes: 'angry', 'happy', 'disgusted', 'hopeful', 'uneasy', 'confident', 'afraid', 'proud'. For reactions to personal economic conditions, the wording is: 'This time, please tell me if any of them describe your feelings about the financial condition of your household. If they do, please tell me which ones'.

11. The question wording is: 'How well do you think the present government has handled each of the following issues?' Issues include: asylum seekers and refugees, crime, the economy in general, education, relations with the European Union, inflation, the National Health Service, pensions, taxes, transport, unemployment, making life better for people like me, foot and mouth disease. Response categories are: 'very well', 'fairly well', 'neither well nor badly', 'fairly badly', 'very badly'. The order of presentation of the issues was randomized.

12. The question wording is: 'In your opinion, what is/was the single most important issue in the general election?' Respondents mentioning an issue were then asked: 'Which party is best able to handle this issue?'

13. The question wording is: 'Who would make the best prime minister—Mr. Blair, Mr. Hague, Mr. Kennedy?'

14. The question wording is: 'Using a scale that runs from 0 to 10, where 0 means *strongly dislike* and 10 means *strongly like*, how do you feel about: (a) Tony Blair, (b) William Hague, (c) Charles Kennedy, (d) John Swinney [in Scotland only], (e) Wyn Jones [in Wales only]'. The order of (a)–(c) was randomized.

15. The question wording is: 'Now, some questions about the *party leaders*. On the whole, would you describe [LEADER] as . . . .' Leader traits included: (a) '(not) capable of being a strong leader', (b) 'keeps/breaks his promises', (c) '(not) caring', (d) '(not) decisive', (e) 'someone who (does not) stick(s) to his principles', (f) '(does not) listen to reason', (g) '(not) arrogant'. For each item, the order in which the leaders were mentioned was randomized.

16. The binomial logit model is:

$$\Pr(\text{Vote}_i = m \mid \mathbf{x}_i) = 1/(1 + \exp(-\mathbf{x}_i\beta))$$

which says that the probability of individual i voting for party m, as opposed to voting for any other party, is conditional upon a set of predictor variables $\mathbf{x}_i$. This conditional probability equals 1 divided by quantity $1 + $ exponential $-\mathbf{x}_i\beta$ where $\mathbf{x}_i$ is the set of predictor variables, and β is a vector of coefficients estimated from the data (Long 1997: 49).

17. The multinomial logit model is:

$$Pr(\text{Vote}_i = m \mid \mathbf{x}) = \exp(\mathbf{x}_i \beta_m)/(1 + \Sigma \exp(\mathbf{x}_i \beta_j))$$

The probability of individual i voting for party m (Conservative, Liberal Democrat, other party) conditional on predictor variables **x** equals the ratio of two quantities. One quantity (the numerator) is exponential $\mathbf{x}_i \beta_m$ where **x** is the set of predictor variables multiplied by β_M which is a vector of estimated coefficients for party m in the set of parties j (Conservative, Liberal Democrat, other). The other quantity (the denominator), $1 + \Sigma \exp(\mathbf{x}_i \beta_j)$, is a sum where the **x**'s are the predictor variables and the β_j's are the vectors of estimated coefficients for the j parties. In the present application of this model, Labour voting is the reference category, and statistical identification is achieved by normalizing Labour's β vector to 0 (Long 1997: 153–54).

18. Variables in various models are coded as follows:

(a) Social Class—the six-category classification ranging from A (scored 6) to E (scored 1);

(b) Age—in years;

(c) Ethnicity—a dichotomy with 'white British' scored 1, and other groups scored 0;

(d) Homeownership—homeowners and those with mortgages are scored 1, renters and others are scored 0;

(e) Sector—employment sector scored: public = 1, private/other = 0;

(f) Region—a set of 0–1 dummy variables for the South East, South West, Midlands, North, Wales, and Scotland. Greater London is the reference category;

(g) Party Identification—a set of 0–1 dummy variables for Labour, the Conservatives, the Liberal Democrats, and other parties (collectively). Nonidentifiers are the reference category. The pre-election party identification data are used to construct these variables;

(h) Issue Proximities—three issue–proximity variables are computed as −1 the average absolute distance on the left–right and tax-spend scales between the respondent and the Labour, Conservative, and Liberal Democrat parties. Data for these variables are taken from the post-election BES survey. For respondents with missing data, data gathered in the pre-election survey are used if these data are available. Data still missing are recoded to mean values;

(i) Economic variables: (*a*) Labour best on the economy is a 0–1 dummy variable; (*b*) national retrospective, national prospective, personal retrospective, and personal prospective economic evaluation variables are constructed by coding these variables as: 'lot better' = 2, 'little better' = 1, 'same' or 'don't know' = 0, 'little worse' = −1, 'lot worse' = −2. The recoded national economic evaluation variables were then multiplied by variables constructed on the basis of answers to the following question: 'To what extent do you think that the government's policies affect the overall performance of the British economy?' Response categories were coded: 'a great deal' = 2, 'a fair amount' = 1 'not very much', 'not at all', 'don't know' = 0. The personal economic evaluation variables were multiplied by variables constructed on the basis of answers to: 'To what extent do you think that the government's policies affect the financial situation of your household'. The response categories were identical to those for the preceding question about government's impact on the national economy. The result of these procedures was to create four economic evaluation indices ranging from +4 (conditions are/will be 'a lot better' and government has a great deal of responsibility) to −4 (conditions are/will be 'a lot worse' and government has a great deal of responsibility); (*c*) emotional reactions to national and personal economic conditions: two indices are created by summing the number of positive ('happy', 'hopeful', 'confident', 'proud') and negative ('angry', 'disgusted', 'uneasy', 'afraid') emotions mentioned. The latter sum is subtracted from the former one.

(j) Party Best Able to Handle Most Important Election Issue—a series of 0–1 dummy variables are created for mentions of Labour, the Conservatives, the Liberal Democrats, or (collectively) one of the other parties as best able to handle the election issue that the respondent deems most important. Data from the post-election survey are used to construct these variables.

(k) Feelings about Party Leaders—the 11-point (0–10) leader 'like–dislike' scales from the post-election survey are used. Missing data are recoded to mean values.

19. Model parameters are estimated using STATA 7 SE. The 2001 BES pre-post panel is used to minimize possible endogeneity problems that might arise when using party identification as predictor variable. By using the pre-election wave of the panel, party identification is measured prior to measuring the vote decision. The analyses are restricted to validated voters to have the best possible measure of actual voting behaviour.

20. See Appendix C for crosstabulations of voting behaviour by measures of social class and other socio-demographic variables.

21. Unlike the popular McKelvey R^2, the McFadden R^2 can be computed for both binomial and multinomial logit analyses. The McFadden R^2 is calculated as: $1 - \ln(L(\theta|\mathbf{x})_\beta / \ln(L(\theta|\mathbf{x})_\alpha$ where $\ln(L(\theta|\mathbf{x})_\beta$ is the loglikelihood for the model of interest and $\ln(L(\theta|\mathbf{x})_\alpha$ is the loglikelihood for a model that includes only a constant. See Long (1997: 104).

22. We also constructed alternative issue-proximity variables using the summed squared absolute distances between a respondent's position on the tax-spend and left–right scales and the positions assigned the parties. These quadratic variables performed similarly to their non-squared counterparts, although their effects were marginally weaker.

23. The AIC is computed as AIC $= -2*\ln(L(\theta|\mathbf{x})) + 2k$, where $\ln(L(\theta|\mathbf{x}))$ is the value of the loglikelihood for a particular model, and k is the number of estimated parameters in the model (see, for example, Burnham and Anderson 1998:47–8). The BIC $= -2*\ln(L(\theta|\mathbf{x})) + k*\ln N$ where $\ln N$ is the log of the sample size N and other quantities are as just described (Burnham and Anderson 1998: 68). The k term in the formulae for AIC and BIC means that, *ceteris paribus*, parsimonious models are favoured, with the parameterization penalty for BIC being heavier than that for AIC for all but extremely small ($N < 8$) samples.

24. The deviance is computed as $-2*\ln(L(\theta|\mathbf{x}))$. Differences in the deviance produced by adding the variables from a model (B) to those in a model (A) are distributed as chi-square, with degrees of freedom equal to the number of variables in model B.

25. The encompassing test used is the joint nesting model chi-square test. It provides a summary test for variance encompassing in the context of a multinomial logit model.

26. Some analysts prefer multinomial probit to multinomial logit methods because of concerns about possible violation of the IIA (independence of irrelevant alternatives) assumption (see, for example, Breslaw 2002). Accordingly, the composite voting model was also estimated using multinomial probit procedures. The results are substantially the same as those reported in Table 4.10. The vast majority of coefficients that are significant and properly signed using multinomial logit are also significant and properly signed using multinomial probit. Similarly, the vast majority of coefficients that are insignificant using the former technique remain insignificant using the latter one. Details are available upon request.

27. For these analyses, the effects of a particular party identification (e.g. being or not being a Labour identifier) on the probability of voting for a given party are assessed by setting other party identification variables at a value of 0, rather than a mean value. This procedure shows what difference it makes to have a given party identification, rather than being a nonidentifier. The same approach is used for assessing the effects of selecting a party as best able to handle what a respondent believes to be the most important election issue. In this case, the analysis shows what difference it makes to select a given party rather than to select no party, or to believe there is no important election issue. Other variables are set at their mean values.

28. Probabilities of voting for a party are computed using STATA 7 SE and CLARIFY (see Tomz Wittenberg and King 2001).

29. In analyses where a predictor variable is a lagged version of the dependent variable, the nature of the simultaneity bias is to exaggerate the magnitude of the coefficient associated with the lagged variable, and to depress the magnitude of other predictor variables. Thus, if including vote intentions as an additional predictor produces simultaneity bias, then the effect is to make the significance tests for the party leader variables more conservative than they otherwise would be (see Greene 2003).

30. The alternative measure of partisanship does not prompt respondents by offering them a list of parties. The wording is: 'Some people think of themselves as usually being a supporter of one political party rather than another. Do you usually think of yourself as being a supporter of one particular party or not?' Respondents answering affirmatively are then asked 'Which party is that?' Here, we use responses to these questions to construct a series of 0–1 dummy variables for Labour, Conservative, Liberal Democrat, and 'other' party identifiers. Nonidentifiers are the reference group.

31. A variable X is said to be weakly exogenous to a variable Y if X affects Y at time t, but Y does not affect X at time t. Demonstrating weak exogeneity is required to warrant single-equation inferences regarding the effects of X on Y. Note that Y may affect X at time $t + i$, but this is a problem only if one wants to use a model for forecasting purposes. If Y does not affect X with a lag, then X is said to be strongly exogenous to Y, or that Y does not Granger-cause X (see Charemza and Deadman 1997).

32. The serious divisions that the issue has caused in the Conservative Party over the past decade demonstrate its potential to prompt strong and politically consequential reactions. Thus, although British membership in the EMU was not a major issue in the 2001 election, it may be hypothesized that attitudes towards the Euro affect voters' feelings about the party leaders. Respondents were requested to think about the Euro, and asked which of four options came closest to their view. The options were: (a) 'definitely join as soon as possible'; (b) 'join if and when the economic conditions are right'; (c) 'stay out for at least the next four or five years'; (d) 'rule out on principle'. Here, we construct 0–1 dummy variables for these options, with 'don't know' responses treated as the reference category.

33. In the bleak economic scenario, the expectations about the national economy variable was scored -3, the emotional reactions to national economic conditions variable was scored -2, and the dummy variable for Labour as the best party on the economy was scored 0.

34. In the rosy economic scenario, the expectations about the national economy variable was scored $+3$, the emotional reactions to national economic conditions variable was scored $+2$, and the dummy variable for Labour as the best party on the economy was scored 1.

FIVE

Electoral Choice and the 2001 Campaign

This chapter focuses on two related questions. First, what is the role of political parties in mobilizing support during the run-up to an election? Second, and related, how much did campaigning influence electoral choice in 2001? When addressing these questions, it is important to remember that, although commentators often describe a UK general election campaign in the singular, general elections are actually fought in 659 separate constituencies. Although some features of campaigns are the same regardless of locality, there are enough differences in campaigning efforts and styles across the country to make it useful to describe an election campaign as a set of local contests. Variations in these local campaigns depend on a range of factors, including geographic location, level of inter-party competition, the state of local party organizations, and the calibre and commitment of the candidates.

There is a longstanding debate in Britain about the extent to which campaigns influence voting behaviour, with one school of thought arguing that campaigns are irrelevant, and another contending that they are important. In this chapter, we address this debate in the context of the 2001 general election. After discussing the controversy over campaign effects in Britain, we examine aggregate evidence on voting behaviour and consider what this tells us about variations in campaigning across the country. Next, we investigate the dynamics of the 2001 campaign, using BES data from the pre- and post-election surveys and data from the rolling cross-section campaign survey. This leads to an examination of patterns of candidate expenditures in 2001. Finally, we specify and test models of the relationship between campaigning and party choice.

THE DEBATE ABOUT CAMPAIGNS

The debate about the importance of election campaigns involves two rival arguments. One is that campaigning makes little or no difference to the election outcome. This argument takes into account several considerations (Dalton, McAllister, and

Electoral Choice and the 2001 Campaign

Wattenberg 2000). Most people are inattentive to politics in general and to campaigns in particular. They have other and better things to do with their time. Parties and politicians are irrelevant at best and untrustworthy at worst. And, in an era of class and partisan dealignment, few people see parties as offering real choices in elections.

In the British case and, indeed, in most parliamentary systems, it is also argued that, by the time the election is called and the official campaign starts, it is too late for national or local campaigning to make any significant difference to the outcome. The campaign is, at best, marginally significant and typically irrelevant since election outcomes are largely determined by events in the years prior to polling day. A case in point was the 1997 British general election, which was regarded as a 'done deal' when it was called (Butler and Kavanagh 1997; more generally, see Denver 1998). In this particular election, Labour's landslide victory owed much to the Conservative government's dismal performance after 1992. In September of that year, Britain's ejection from the European exchange rate mechanism was a crucial factor in under-mining public confidence in Conservative economic management abilities (see Chapter Three). In addition, the Conservative government broke promises, especially on taxes and the public services, and a climate of bitter intra-party conflict developed over the Euro and Britain's role in Europe. These factors, together with the well-pub-licized financial irregularities of some Conservative MPs, did much to discredit the government and its leader, John Major. Moreover, Tony Blair's election as Labour leader in July, 1994 and his subsequent creation of New Labour were important fac-tors that occurred long before the official campaign got underway. Thus, in writing about the 1997 election campaign, Anthony King concluded:

The politicians, as they always do on these occasions, puffed, panted, and rushed about the country. They stretched every sinew and strained every nerve. They gave speeches, they gave interviews, they gave their all. No camera angle was neglected, no photo opportunity was missed. At times the politicians resembled those manic characters in the jerky, speeded-up film comedies of the 1920s. But nothing happened. The audience, for whose benefit all these entertainments were laid on, remained almost completely inert. Scarcely a cough or a sneeze could be heard from the pit (King 1998: 179).

The Nuffield election studies also have maintained that campaigns are marginal or irrelevant in influencing election outcomes (e.g. Nicholas 1951; Butler 1952; Butler and Kavanagh 1992). In their statistical appendix to the 1997 Nuffield study, Curtice and Steed concluded that '[t]he 1997 election does not appear to support claims made that local campaigning can make a difference in respect of other parties' performances too. The Labour party targeted 90, mostly marginal Conservative constituen-cies . . . Yet . . . the performance in these constituencies was very similar to that in other Conservative/Labour contests' (Curtice and Steed 1997: 312). And, the next Nuffield report described the 2001 election campaign as boring and predictable:

Inevitably, the conduct of the 2001 campaign must be considered in the context of a poor turnout. Had it encouraged apathy or at least failed to foster enough interest to overcome indifference? The public was perhaps becoming bored with the ritual of modern campaigns. The morning press conferences, the set-piece media interviews with prominent politicians, the party leaders' bus trips to encounters with voters (largely staged for the benefit of the cameras), instant rebuttals and the speeches before invited and largely sympathetic audiences may now be past their sell-by date (Butler and Kavanagh 2002: 249).

In contrast, other observers have argued that campaigns matter. Political scientists have typically emphasized the mobilization functions of election campaigns, finding that they can heighten interest, strengthen partisanship, and encourage turnout (Rosenstone and Hansen 1993; see also Leighley 1995). Moreover, when competition is close, the efforts of rival parties and their candidates can be an important factor in deciding who wins. In Britain, there are at least two reasons for this. First, it may be argued that there is limited scope for local campaign effects when swings in party support from one election to the next are quite uniform across the country. However, the amount of variation in swing has tended to be larger since the 1970s than it was in the 1950s and 1960s (Denver 2003). For example, in the 1955 general election, the variation in the two-party (Conservative-Labour) swing, as measured by its standard deviation, was 1.4 per cent (Butler and Stokes 1969: 135). In 1997, the comparable figure was 4.3 per cent, and in 2001, it was 3.7 per cent (Curtice and Steed 1997: 297, 2002: 305). Clearly, there is a stronger *prima facie* case for local effects when changes in party support are quite variable across the country.

Several empirical studies have found that local campaigns are important. One line of inquiry uses campaign spending as a surrogate measure of party activity (Johnston, Pattie, and Johnston 1989; Whiteley, Seyd, and Richardson 1994; Johnston and Pattie 1995, 1997, 2002; Pattie, Fieldhouse, and Johnston 1995; Pattie and Johnston 2002). This is spending that the local constituency parties are legally allowed during an election, and it is fairly tightly regulated. Other research is based on surveys of party members and assesses local campaign effects by measuring their activity levels in various constituencies (Seyd and Whiteley 1992, 2002; Whiteley and Seyd, 1994, 2003). Yet another approach uses surveys of the parties' local constituency agents, the persons who run the local campaigns (Denver and Hands 1985, 1997; Denver et al. 2002). The general conclusion of these investigations is that 'the easy generalization made in many academic studies—that, in modern conditions, local campaigning is merely a ritual, a small and insignificant side show to the main event—is seriously misleading' (Denver and Hands 1997: 305).

A second reason why campaigns matter involves the growth of political communications and the decline of the strength of party identification in the British electorate (see Chapters Three and Six). In Britain and most other parliamentary systems, campaigns remain party-oriented events: 'parties organize and structure the activities that take place during parliamentary elections, from local meetings addressed by constituency candidates to nationally televised public events, such as debates between major party leaders' (Dalton, McAllister, and Wattenberg 2000: 52). To do so, parties must rely on cadres of grassroots party members as well as media, political, and public relations consultants who must strategically use their resources to 'sell' the leader and the party's policies to targeted voters (Dalton and Wattenberg 2000; Farrell and Webb 2000). It presumably is easier to undertake these activities and to influence voter decision making during periods of class and partisan dealignment. Accordingly, over time, the context in which British elections take place has become more favourable for campaigns to matter.

In this chapter, the argument is that the campaign influenced electoral choice in 2001. We investigate several types of campaign effects. First, as discussed in reference to local versus national campaigns, we are interested in *when* campaigns matter—the timing of their effects—and *where* they matter. As depicted in Table 5.1, in any general election, there are both temporal and spatial dimensions to the campaign. With regard to the temporal dimension, campaigning is now a permanent feature of political life—the day after a general election, the parties start the process of preparing for the next one. Thus, the long campaign involves constant news and opinion management over the lifetime of a parliament (Miller et al. 1990). There are also medium-term and short-term campaigns. It seems reasonable to define the beginning of the medium-term campaign as the budget month in the year preceding an election (e.g. March 2000 vis-à-vis the June 2001 election). This is the last budget that can influence policy outcomes if an election is called the following year. So, the parties step up their efforts with this in mind. Once this medium-term campaign commences, parties establish their overall organizational structures, select their main policy themes, designate personnel for key roles, select target constituencies for particular attention, and decide which voters will be contacted. During the short or official campaign, which starts as soon as an election is called, parties issue their manifestos, conduct press conferences, arrange leadership tours and key speeches, make party political broadcasts, increase their advertising and private polling, and intensify their efforts to contact the voters.

Viewed spatially, there are several types of geographically defined general election campaigns (Seyd 2001; Whiteley and Seyd 2003). As shown in Table 5.1, there is the national campaign that is organized from party headquarters and concentrated largely around the party leadership. There are centrally coordinated local campaigns in which party headquarters provide local parties with personnel, technical support, services and literature. In these campaigns, local efforts are controlled from party headquarters. There also are purely locally directed campaigns in which the activists organize their efforts according to their own priorities and resources. Most attention has been concentrated on the national campaigns, in part because of a longstanding view among both politicians and academic observers that, to the extent to which campaigns are influential, the parties' national-level activities are all that matter. More attention is now given to local campaigns because of growing evidence that they can significantly influence voting behaviour and, in a close contest, the election outcome (Seyd and Whiteley 1992; Whiteley, Seyd, and Richardson 1994; Pattie, Fieldhouse, and Johnston 1995; Denver and Hands 1997).

Table 5.1 Spatial and temporal dimensions of the 2001 general election campaign

Spatial dimension	Temporal dimension		
	Long campaign (May 1997–June 2001)	Medium campaign (March 2000–April 2001)	Short campaign (May 2001–June 2001)
Central	Government policies Government annual reports Government news management Sampling of public opinion Party management Fighting elections (European, Scotland, Wales, London, local government)	HQ organizational structures established Preparation of election manifesto Advertising agency employed Priority constituencies selected National telephone bank established Training of full-time organizers	Ministerial policy initiatives Publication of election manifesto News conferences Speeches and interviews Party election broadcasts Party advertising Party opinion polling
Centrally-co-ordinated Local	Reselection of constituency MPs/candidates	Agreement on priority targets Commencement of voter identification First direct mailing to targeted voters	Production and coordinated distribution of candidates' election addresses Registration of postal voters

Table 5.1 Continued

	Temporal dimension		
Spatial dimension	Long campaign (May 1997–June 2001)	Medium campaign (March 2000–April 2001)	Short campaign (May 2001–June 2001)
			Direct mailings and leaflet distributions
			Candidates' news releases, meetings and interviews
Local	Selection of candidates		Production and distribution of candidates' election addresses
			Registration of postal voters
			Leaflet distributions
			Candidates' news releases, meetings and interviews

Second, we are interested in conversion and activation effects. *Conversion* is designed to persuade supporters of other parties to switch their votes, whereas *activation* is aimed at mobilizing or reinforcing existing support (Alsop and Weisberg 1988; Farah and Klein 1989; Finkel 1993). On the face of it, a party should find it easier to reinforce voting decisions or to win the support of people who do not identify with a party than to convert supporters of a rival party. With this in mind, campaign activities aimed at opposition party supporters who were inefficiently targeted. On the other hand, given that canvassing is designed to identify supporters as much as to convert people, parties have only limited ability to choose between these alternatives. Parties that start with only relatively small numbers of supporters have no choice but to try to convert other people to their cause.

Third, we are interested in direct and indirect campaign effects. *Direct* effects result from activities such as canvassing, exposing people to party political broadcasts, and reminding them to get out to the polls. In each case, the party appeals directly to the electorate. *Indirect* effects are reflected in changes in important explanatory variables such as party identification, issue perceptions, and evaluations of the competence of the competing parties and their leaders. Here, we specify dynamic models of the effects of campaigning on party choice in 2001. Its impact on turnout is examined in Chapter Eight.

PARTY CAMPAIGNING IN 2001

In most of the general elections held since the end of the Second World War, the Conservative Party has been the principal campaign innovator. For example, the Conservatives first developed modern political advertising in the 1950s. The party's relative abundance of resources and its links with business, in particular the advertising industry, explain much of its post-war campaigning dominance. But this changed in the 1990s, and Labour was generally perceived to have performed better than the Conservatives in the 1992 general election (Butler and Kavanagh 1992). Labour's superiority was maintained in both 1997 and 2001. In addition, the Liberal Democrats, even with their limited resources, have concentrated effectively on local campaigning, and this won them seats in 1997 and 2001 (Whiteley and Seyd 2003). The two major parties have learned from the Liberal Democrats' methods.

In 2001, Labour's strategy was to try to hold on to the seats gained in the 1997 landslide, so the party essentially ran a defensive campaign (Seyd 2001). Recognizing that turnout was a potential problem, Labour organized 'Operation Turnout', targeting weak Labour supporters to encourage them to go to the polls. The party's strategy document made the point that if one in five of Labour's supporters who turned out in 1997 stayed home, and even if there was no switching to the Conservatives, then the party would lose 60 seats (Labour Party 2000). As part of the defensive effort, resources from the national party were concentrated in seats won in 1997, which were described as 'priority seats'. In fact, Labour had been fighting a defensive campaign ever since the 1997 election. The party had such a large majority in the House of Commons that it had encouraged its newly elected members to spend long periods in their constituencies, since they were not required in Westminster to maintain the government's majority. In this way Labour MPs directed the local campaigns that ran during the long campaign. As we see below, this strategy proved to be effective.

If Labour aimed to fight defensively, then clearly the Conservatives had to go on the offensive to win back seats lost in the 1997 landslide. In the event, their campaign was widely criticized as being too narrow and lacking in themes that resonated with the electorate. Kenneth Clarke, the former Conservative Chancellor of the Exchequer, criticized his party's campaign for being a continuation of 'four wasted years for the Tory party' (Collins and Seldon 2001: 66). Certainly the Conservatives' decision to concentrate on saving the pound, which became their principal theme as polling day approached, did not reflect the priorities of most people. As discussed in Chapter Four, voters were mainly concerned with issues such as the state of the National Health Service (NHS), the educational system, and other public services.

The Conservatives launched their campaign with an attack on Labour's 'stealth taxes' using an issue that had worked well for them in 1992 (Butler and Kavanagh 1992). William Hague promised tax cuts of £8 billion, which included a populist commitment to cut fuel taxes. But the campaign began to unravel as different individuals speaking on behalf of the party made conflicting claims about the size of the proposed tax cuts, and failed to answer questions about what services would have to be curtailed to pay for them. In particular, Oliver Letwin suggested to the *Financial Times* that his party might reduce taxes by £20 billion. Labour leaders were quick to point out that such cuts would decimate the public services, and the Conservatives were immediately put on the defensive on the tax issue. Overall, as the data presented below indicate, the Conservatives were unable to land any serious blows on Labour. Their attack strategy did not really work.

As Labour ran a defensive campaign and the Conservatives tried to go on the offensive, the Liberal Democrats took a different approach. Essentially, they had to run an insurgency campaign which focussed on maintaining the gains achieved in 1997 while at the same time targeting Conservative-held constituencies where the Liberal Democrats had a chance of winning. Since the Liberal Democrats were second to the Conservatives in 144 seats in 1997 and second to Labour in only eight, their strategy had to be predominantly anti-Conservative. They had abandoned the policy of equidistance between Labour and the Conservatives after the 1992 general election (Denver 2001). This had paid dividends in 1997, and so they continued with this approach in 2001. However, the Liberal Democrats risked being seen as too close to Labour. Their strategy was to criticize both parties at the national level, but to target the Conservatives at the local level. This approach both encouraged, and was encouraged by, the rise of tactical voting, which is estimated to have involved approximately 14 per cent of those who voted in 2001 (see Chapter Four).

CAMPAIGNING AND PARTY CHOICE

This section begins the analysis of campaign effects by reviewing constituency-level data on voting behaviour in 2001. This is a useful way of assessing the impact of campaigns, but it has three limitations. First, aggregate analyses of this type provide somewhat roundabout, rather than straightforward, evidence about the link between campaigning and voting behaviour. Second, constituency-level variations in voting speak primarily to the impact of local, as opposed to national, campaigns since the impact of the latter may be broadly uniform across the country. Third, if local party organizations are effectively directed from the centre, then the parties would concentrate their resources exclusively on marginal constituencies where seats can be won. If all the parties are equally efficient at this exercise and have the same resources, then there would be little or no impact on parties' vote shares because the campaigns would tend to cancel each other out. However, there would be a significant relationship between the marginality of a constituency and turnout, caused, in part, by the mobilizing effects of the relatively intense local campaigns. Denver and Hands (1985, 1997) first identified this relationship in their research on elections held in the 1970s.

Perhaps unsurprisingly, previous studies have shown that parties vary in their local campaigning efficiency. In 1997, the Conservatives tended to campaign more extensively in their own safe seats than they did in marginal seats (Denver and Hands 1997). The Liberal Democrats were more effective at concentrating their efforts on winnable seats than Labour; and Labour, in turn, was more effective than the Conservatives (Whiteley and Seyd 2003). The evidence presented below indicates that Labour became even more effective in 2001, with Labour MPs playing key roles in organizing and sustaining campaigns in their constituencies (Seyd 2001; Johnston et al. 2002). With this point in mind, if local campaigning is concentrated on the marginal seats and Labour is more effective at it than the Conservatives, then this should be apparent in the constituency results. Specifically, we would expect to find that Labour increased its vote share in its marginals more than the Conservatives did in theirs.

Table 5.2 examines the relationship between the size of the majority in 1997 and changes in turnout and vote shares in seats captured by Labour in 2001. It is evident that both turnout and party choice are significantly associated with marginality. Turnout tended to fall by a smaller amount in the Labour marginals, that is, seats with majorities less than 5 per cent of the total vote, than it did in safe seats. Similarly, Labour's vote share actually rose by nearly 4 per cent in these Labour marginals and fell by an equal amount in safe Labour seats. The same point cannot be made about the Conservatives (see Table 5.3). The Conservatives' vote share increased less in their marginals than it did in their safe seats, and the change in turnout was the same in the Conservatives' marginals as it was in their safe seats.

Table 5.2   Changes in turnout and Labour vote share between 1997 and 2001 by marginality of seats captured by Labour in 1997

Marginality of seat in 1997	Change in Labour vote share 1997–2001	Change in turnout 1997–2001
Majority under 5%	3.6	−10.4
Majority from 5% to 10%	2.0	−11.8
Majority from 10% to 15%	−1.1	−13.3
Majority from 15% to 20%	−1.5	−13.3
Majority over 20%	−3.9	−13.6
Mean change	−2.6	−13.2

Source: British Parliamentary Constituency Database, 1992–2001.

Table 5.3   Changes in turnout and Conservative vote share between 1997 and 2001 by marginality of seats captured by Conservatives in 1997

Marginality of seat in 1997	Change in Conservative vote share 1997–2001	Change in turnout 1997–2001
Majority under 5%	2.6	−11.3
Majority from 5% to 10%	2.8	−10.7
Majority from 10% to 15%	2.7	−11.8
Majority from 15% to 20%	2.9	−11.7
Majority over 20%	3.0	−11.4
Mean change	2.8	−11.4

Source: British Parliamentary Constituency Database, 1992–2001.

This suggests that Labour campaigned more effectively in its marginals than the Conservatives did in theirs. The Liberal Democrats resembled Labour, and achieved an increase in their vote share of 2.6 per cent in the seats they were defending but only 1.5 per cent elsewhere. Again, their success was likely spearheaded by the activities of incumbent MPs (Denver 2001).

These constituency-level patterns are interesting, but individual-level survey data are needed to examine campaigning effects on electoral choice in depth. A series of questions was asked in the 2001 BES post-election survey to find out whether people had been contacted directly by the parties during the campaign.[1] Evidence of the results of the parties' campaign efforts is shown in Figure 5.1. Just over three-fifths of those interviewed reported seeing a party political broadcast, just under one-quarter were canvassed in person, less than one in ten was canvassed by phone, and one in twenty was contacted on polling day. It is also apparent that the parties were more likely to try to mobilize voters in marginal seats than they

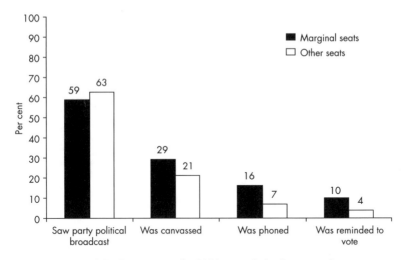

Figure 5.1 Exposure to the 2001 general election campaign

Note: A marginal seat is defined as one in which the gap in vote shares between the first and second party in the preceding (1997) general election is less than 10%.

Source: 2001 BES post-election survey.

were in safe seats.[2] As Figure 5.1 illustrates, rates of face-to-face canvassing, phone canvassing, and contacting on polling day were higher in the marginals than elsewhere. Only in the case of party political broadcasts were exposure rates slightly greater in safe seats than in marginal ones, and this was true for the obvious reason that such broadcasts cannot be targeted at the marginals.

Table 5.4 shows campaigning activities by the different parties, as reported by BES respondents. It is clear that Labour was more active than its rivals. Labour was ahead of the Conservatives in terms of the percentage of people who saw its party political broadcasts. It was slightly ahead of the Conservatives in doorstep canvassing and well ahead of them on telephone canvassing and contacting electors on polling day. The Conservatives came second with significant leads over the Liberal Democrats in canvassing both face-to-face and by telephone. Interestingly, the Conservative lead over the Liberal Democrats in contacting people on polling day was much slimmer than was true for canvassing. This is consistent with the idea that the Liberal Democrats make very strong efforts to get their vote out. The Nationalist parties succeeded in reaching a majority of the Scottish and Welsh electors via their party political broadcasts, and they did reasonably well in canvassing.[3]

Table 5.5 presents an analysis of the extent to which the parties tried to activate their own supporters as opposed to converting supporters of rival parties.[4]

141

Table 5.4   Exposure to the 2001 general election campaign (in %)

Of the 63% who saw a party political broadcast, the following saw:	
A Labour party political broadcast	84
A Conservative party political broadcast	78
A Liberal Democrat party political broadcast	66
A SNP party political broadcast (in Scotland)	57
A Plaid Cymru party political broadcast (in Wales)	51
Of the 23% canvassed face-to-face, the following were:	
Canvassed by Labour	50
Canvassed by the Conservatives	47
Canvassed by the Liberal Democrats	32
Canvassed by the SNP (in Scotland)	42
Canvassed by Plaid Cymru (in Wales)	37
Of the 8% canvassed by telephone, the following were:	
Telephoned by Labour	48
Telephoned by the Conservatives	34
Telephoned by the Liberal Democrats	11
Of the 5% reminded to vote, the following were:	
Reminded to vote by Labour	49
Reminded to vote by the Conservatives	27
Reminded to vote by the Liberal Democrats	21

Source: 2001 BES post-election survey.

The table shows that 42 per cent of the individuals canvassed face-to-face by Labour were already Labour supporters, and a further 34 per cent were supporters of no party. In contrast, 19 per cent and 5 per cent of those canvassed by Labour were Conservatives or Liberal Democrats, respectively. Thus, it can be argued that three-quarters of Labour's canvassing efforts were efficient since they were not aimed at converting the adherents of rival parties but, rather, at activating Labour supporters or attracting people who were not predisposed towards any party. In contrast to Labour, Table 5.5 shows that only about two-thirds of the Conservatives' face-to-face canvassing were efficient in the above sense, since about one-third of their canvassing efforts was directed at the supporters of their main rivals. Liberal Democrat campaign efforts were the least efficiently allocated, since only about four of ten people targeted were either Liberal Democrat supporters or favoured no party at all. However, since there are significantly fewer Liberal Democrats than Labour or Conservative supporters, it is not surprising that the Liberal Democrats had more difficulty identifying their electoral base. For the same reason, if the party wishes to be successful, then it needs to make converts rather than just relying on mobilizing the party faithful.

Table 5.5 Conversion and reinforcement in constituency campaigns

	Per cent of people canvassed by a party who were supporters of:			
	Labour	*Conservatives*	*Liberal Democrats*	*No Party*
Party doing the canvassing				
Labour	42	18	6	34
Conservatives	34	27	9	31
Liberal Democrats	38	25	7	30
Party doing phoning				
Labour	46	21	3	31
Conservatives	20	32	12	36
Party reminding voters to turn out				
Labour	51	7	0	42
Conservatives	18	50	0	32

Source: 2001 BES post-election survey.

Labour was similarly effective in its telephone canvassing, and the Conservatives did better in this particular mode by targeting a higher proportion of their own or non-party supporters. There are too few cases to evaluate Liberal Democrat efforts at telephone canvassing or encouraging people to turn out on polling day. But again, Labour was more effective than the Conservatives at reminding their own supporters to go to the polls. The fact that some 18 per cent of Conservative reminders were targeted at Labour supporters calls into question the effectiveness of Conservative efforts to identify their own supporters in the first place. Overall, the data in Table 5.5 suggest that Labour did more to activate its base than its main rivals did to activate theirs.

To analyze the impact of campaigning on turnout and party choice, we combine the information in Table 5.5 into summary mobilization indices.[5] These indices are displayed in Figure 5.2 and they represent the cumulative exposure of the 2001 BES post-election respondents to the parties' campaign activities. The data reveal that 28 per cent were exposed to none of the four forms of campaign activity. These people did not see a party political broadcast, they were not canvassed either face-to-face or by telephone, and they were not reminded to vote on polling day. At the other end of the scale, less than 1 per cent were exposed to all four forms of activity. As Figure 5.2 indicates, the modal category was exposure to one activity, usually a party political broadcast. Our hypothesis about the influence of parties' campaign efforts is simple—*ceteris paribus*, the more activities by a particular party to which a person was exposed, the more likely he or she was to vote for it.

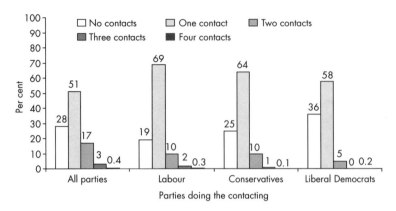

Figure 5.2 Number of contacts with party mobilizing activities during the 2001 general election campaign

Note: Entries are percentages of survey respondents with different number of contacts with various parties. For example, 19% had no contacts with Labour, 69% had one contact with that party, 10% had two contacts and 0.3% had four contacts.

Source: 2001 BES post-election survey.

DYNAMIC EVIDENCE OF CAMPAIGNING AND PARTY CHOICE

Cross-sectional data on exposure to parties' campaign activities are informative, but dynamic evidence is required to evaluate the impact of campaigning on electoral choice. Clearly, a necessary condition for campaign effects to exist is that there should be changes in the run-up to polling day in the percentage of people intending to cast a ballot, in patterns of party support, and in the distributions of key variables that determine voting behaviour. So, a good starting point for the analysis is to assess how much electors appeared willing to change their minds during the campaign. In the 2001 BES pre-election survey, where the vast majority of interviews were completed before the official campaign began, 53 per cent stated that they had decided how to vote, 40 per cent were undecided, and 7 per cent said they would not cast a ballot.[6] The conclusion that there was substantial potential for changes in party support in the run-up to the election is reinforced by answers to a question in the 2001 BES post-election survey that asked respondents when they made their decision to vote.[7] Fifty-four per cent said that they had decided a 'long time ago', and an additional 8 per cent said 'last year'. However, 14 per cent said that they had made up their minds 'this year', and 24 per cent said they had done so during the official (short) campaign. Given the assumption that the medium-term campaign

144

started roughly a year before polling day (see Table 5.1), it appears that between 38 and 46 per cent of those who cast a ballot in 2001 decided during this period.

We can probe the timing of vote decisions in greater detail by examining the intentions and subsequent behaviour of participants in the 2001 pre–post-election panel survey. Table 5.6 shows how pre-election intentions translated into votes or, in some cases, nonvotes. There was considerable movement in the 3 months preceding polling day. Seventy per cent of those who intended to vote Labour before the official campaign began actually did so, but 8 per cent switched to another party, and 22 per cent did not vote at all. Conservative vote intenders exhibited similarly high rates of volatility; 67 per cent stuck with the party, but 12 per cent moved to another party, and 21 per cent stayed home. Although the Liberal Democrat loyalty rate was higher than those for the other parties, 8 per cent switched and 16 per cent abstained. Considering all of the panelists, nearly one-third of those in the pre-election survey who reported that they had decided how to vote either supported another party or did not vote at all. The large undecided group—fully two-fifths of pre-election respondents—provided additional dynamics. In the event, 61 per cent of these people actually cast a ballot, with Labour having a slight edge over both the Conservatives and Liberal Democrats in gaining their support.

Data from the 2001 BES rolling cross-sectional survey provide a more finely grained portrait of the evolution of party support and political attitudes during the official campaign. This survey was designed such that every day during the campaign, national samples (average $N = 160$) were interviewed. Figure 5.3 tracks voting intentions over this period by plotting the percentages of respondents in the daily surveys who said they would vote for various parties.[8] 'Nearest neighbour'

Table 5.6   Pre-campaign vote intentions and voting behaviour in 2001
(Horizontal percentages)

Vote intentions (Pre-election survey)	Voting behaviour (Post-election survey)				
	Labour	Conservative	Liberal Democrat	Other Party	Did not vote
Labour	70	1	6	1	22
Conservative	4	67	6	2	21
Liberal Democrat	4	1	77	3	16
Other Party	3	0	3	64	31
Undecided	22	17	18	4	39
Will not vote	6	6	3	1	84

Note: Validated voters and non-voters, $N = 2112$ with missing data removed.

Source: 2001 BES pre–post election panel survey.

regression lines are superimposed on the scatter of daily data points to show underlying trends.[9] These lines reveal that there were significant movements in party support as the campaign progressed. Labour's vote intention share increased until about the middle of the campaign, but then receded so that the party finished about where it began. However, the Conservatives appear to have lost ground. Their voting intentions declined in the early part of the campaign, only to rally slightly at the end of May, before declining again immediately prior to polling day. In contrast, the Liberal Democrats made gains in voting intentions throughout much of the campaign.

Figure 5.4 examines changes in orientations towards the party leaders, one of the key determinants of voting discussed in Chapter Four. Figure 5.4 plots the

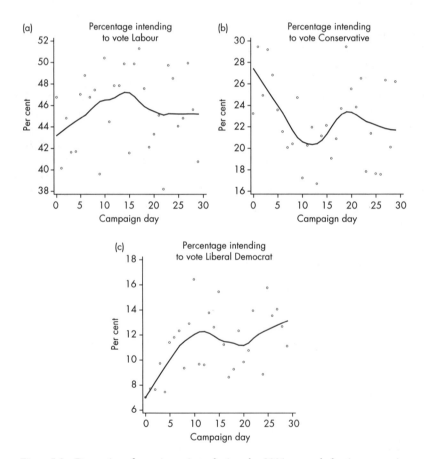

Figure 5.3 Dynamics of vote intentions during the 2001 general election campaign

Source: 2001 BES campaign survey.

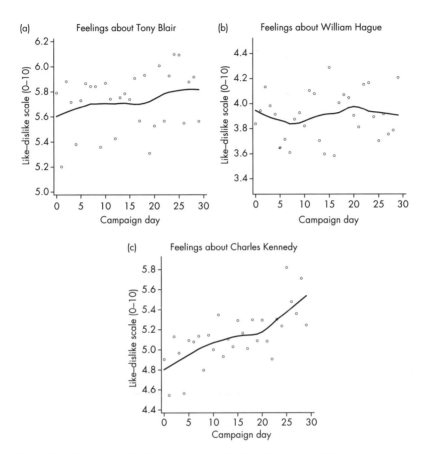

Figure 5.4 Dynamics of feelings about party leaders during the 2001 general election
campaign

Source: 2001 BES campaign survey.

leaders' average 'like–dislike' scores (measured on 0–10 scales) for every day of the
campaign.[10] Again, nearest neighbour regression lines are used to depict underlying
trends. The story of public feelings about the leaders is very simple. Both Tony
Blair and Charles Kennedy received lukewarm receptions at the beginning of the
campaign, but their likeability ratings increased as polling day approached. Blair's
gains were quite modest, but Kennedy's were more substantial. Thus, campaign
exposure enhanced the popularity of both the Labour and Liberal Democrat leaders. In contrast, public feelings about William Hague started at a much lower level,
and remained firmly rooted in the negative zone. As media commentator Jeremy
Paxman put it during a campaign interview with Mr. Hague, many voters simply
did not like the Conservative leader.

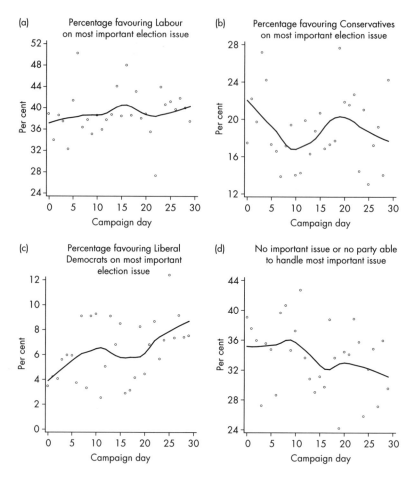

Figure 5.5 Dynamics of party best able to handle most important issue, 2001 general election campaign

Source: 2001 BES campaign survey.

Figure 5.5 shows the dynamics of links between issues and parties during the campaign. Respondents in the rolling cross-section survey were asked which election issue they thought was most important, and which party was best able to handle that issue.[11] Paralleling findings reported in Chapter Four, a large percentage of people stated either that no party was able to handle the most important issue or that there were no important issues. Although such 'no issue/no party' answers declined slightly over time, on the eve of the election the trend line indicates that nearly a third of the electorate had either not selected an important issue or failed to connect an issue with a party. Regarding connections that were made, Figure 5.5 shows that Labour had a large lead on the issues throughout the campaign, and that the dynamics of this lead were modest. The party gained in the early part of the campaign, lost a little ground, but then recovered by polling day. The pattern for the Conservatives is the reverse; the party initially lost ground, rallied slightly, and then fell back again. Overall, the Conservatives finished in an even weaker position on the issues than when the election was called. In contrast, Liberal Democrats gained on the issues both at the beginning and towards the end of the campaign.

Figure 5.6 shows the dynamics of the direction of party identification.[12] As demonstrated in Chapter Four, party identification was a strong predictor of electoral choice in 2001, and it is not surprising that movements in partisanship are basically similar to the dynamics of vote choice. The pattern of Labour gaining during the first third of the campaign only to lose ground subsequently is repeated. Nevertheless, the party finished with slightly more identifiers than it had at the start. Similarly, the trend in Conservative support is repeated; the Conservative share of identifiers trended downwards during the first third of the campaign, recovered somewhat in late May, but ended lower than where it began. The Liberal Democrats had far fewer partisans than Labour or the Conservatives. However, they made some small gains during the first half of the campaign, before finishing about where they began. Finally, contrary to what is often argued about the mobilization of partisanship during elections, Panel D of Figure 5.6 shows that there was virtually no downward trend in the proportion of nonidentifers. This failure of the 2001 campaign to energize partisan attachments is also evident in Figure 5.7, which depicts movements in the strength of party identification. The visual evidence suggests there was very little upward movement in the percentage of 'very strong' party identifiers as the campaign progressed.

Data showing that the 2001 campaign did little to mobilize partisan attachments foreshadow what is perhaps the most striking finding to emerge from the cross-section campaign survey. Figure 5.8 displays levels of interest in the election. Contrary to what might be expected, Panel A reveals that, for much of the campaign, there was a downward trend in the percentage of people who were 'very interested' in the election.[13] And, as Panel B shows, there was a parallel upward trend in the percentage who said that they were 'not very' or 'not at all' interested. These patterns reversed only in the week before polling day. Analyses presented in Chapter Eight indicate that interest in the election strongly influences the likelihood of voting. If interest had not rallied in the campaign's final stage, then it is safe to say that turnout would have been even lower than the 59 per cent figure that actually obtained.

Up to this point, we have examined data on the timing of voting decisions, changes in patterns of party support, and trends in key variables in models of

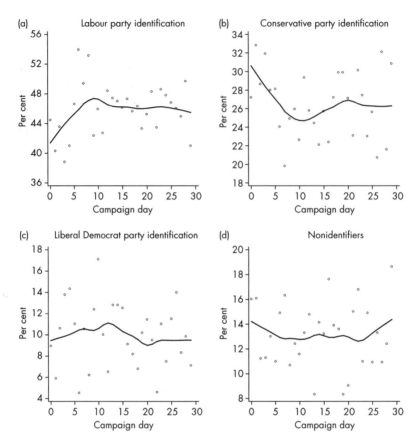

Figure 5.6 Dynamics of party identification during the 2001 general election campaign
Source: 2001 BES campaign survey.

turnout and electoral choice during the short (official) 2001 election campaign. Taken together, these data suggest that the campaign may have had significant effects on political attitudes and voting behaviour. The next steps are to analyze data on how the parties allocated their campaign spending in 2001, and to test dynamic models of the influence of campaigns on party choice.

MULTIVARIATE MODELS OF CAMPAIGN EFFECTS

This section investigates various types of campaign effects on party choice in 2001. One type of effect involves whether the campaign activated or converted

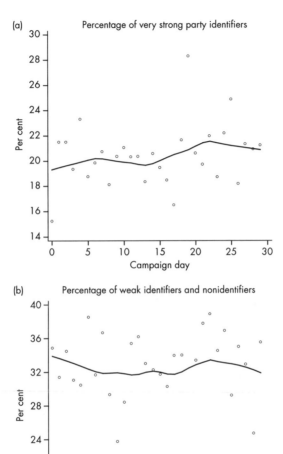

Figure 5.7 Dynamics of strength of party identification during the 2001 general election campaign

Source: 2001 BES campaign survey.

voters—reinforcing decisions already made or encouraging voters to switch to another party. Another is whether the campaign influenced voters directly or indirectly. Direct campaign influences refer to parties' mobilizing activities, as well as constituency-level campaign spending. Indirect influences refer to changes in

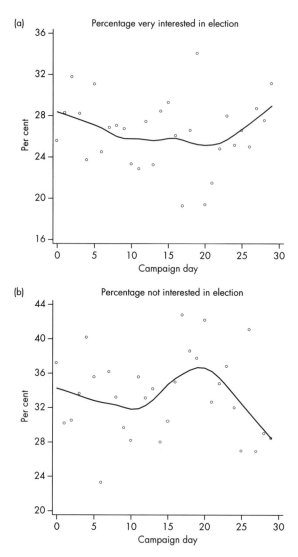

Figure 5.8 Dynamics of interest in the election during the 2001 general election campaign

Source: 2001 BES campaign survey.

attitudes towards parties, issues, and leaders. As shown in Chapter Four, these variables significantly affect electoral choice, and changes in them may occur as a result of information that voters receive during the campaign. Before estimating the campaign effects models, we first consider patterns of campaign spending in 2001.

Campaign Spending in 2001

Constituency-level campaign spending can be thought of as an indicator of capital investment in the various local campaigns and, as discussed earlier, as a proxy measure of party activity at the local level. It typically is measured in terms of the percentage of the legal maximum spent by each party in each constituency. Table 5.7 displays information on campaign expenditures in 2001 in seats won and lost by Labour, the Conservatives, and the Liberal Democrats in 1997. On average, Labour and Conservative spending exceeded that for the Liberal Democrats by considerable margins. This is true both in an absolute sense (Panel A) and relative to the legal maximum that could be spent in various constituencies (Panel B). All three parties concentrated their efforts in seats they had won in 1997. In keeping with the defensive tone of its campaign, on average, Labour spent 77 per cent of the legal maximum in seats it had won in 1997, and only 41 per cent in seats it had lost. The Liberal Democrats concentrated their resources even more heavily, spending an average of 91 per cent of the legal maximum in seats they had captured in 1997, and only 28 per cent in seats they had lost. The Conservatives were less discriminating, allocating, on average, 88 per cent of the legal maximum to constituencies where they were incumbent, and 63 per cent to ones where they were a challenger.

The data in Table 5.7 suggest considerable variation in spending by all three parties. The fact that the parties concentrated their resources in constituencies that they held reflects an element of rationality—these were places where the parties knew they could win. In 1997, investments in these constituencies had yielded demonstrable returns. In some cases, these seats were held by the parties' parliamentary leaders, and protecting their seats made good political sense. More generally, incumbent MPs appear to be motivated by varying combinations of pride and paranoia that lead them to demand resources to fight for their re-election, regardless of the competitive status of their seats. However, it may be hypothesized that party strategists behave rationally. They do not simply distinguish between seats where they are incumbents or challengers when making decisions about how to spend scarce funds. Rather, they optimize their political fortunes by taking into account their party's competitive position in various constituencies. Investment is concentrated in seats where a close contest in the last general election provides tangible evidence of a realistic possibility of winning this time around (e.g. Denver and Hands 1997; Johnston and Pattie 1997, 2002).

The conjecture that marginality attracts money can be investigated by analyzing candidate expenditures in 2001 in terms of the margins by which parties won or lost various constituencies in 1997. To control for constituency differences in legal limits on candidate spending, these expenditures are measured as percentages of legal maximums. Consonant with the observation of large differences in the amount of money spent in seats won and lost in 1997, separate analyses are performed for the two types of seats. Regression analyses show that marginality of a seat in 1997 had a significant impact on candidate expenditures years later—the

Table 5.7   Candidate expenditures in 2001

	Labour	Conservatives	Liberal Democrats
A. Candidate expenditure in £ sterling			
Overall			
Mean	5860	6486	3062
Standard deviation	2356	2866	2809
(N)	(640)	(638)	(632)
By 1997 election outcome			
Mean: Won seat	6897	8575	8547
Lost seat	3921	5758	2632
η	0.61	0.43	0.55
p	0.00	0.00	0.00
B. Candidate expenditure as per cent of legal maximum			
Overall			
Mean	64	70	33
Standard deviation	26.1	29.0	29.5
(N)	(640)	(638)	(632)
By 1997 election outcome:			
Mean: Won seat	77	88	91
Lost seat	41	63	28
η	0.66	0.37	0.56
p	0.00	0.00	0.00

Source: Electoral Commission (2002), Election 2001—Campaign Spending.

closer the contest in 1997, the more money spent in 2001 (see Table 5.8). Although this pattern obtains for all three parties, it is stronger for the Conservatives and the Liberal Democrats than for Labour. The sharply varying steepness of the regression lines displayed in Figure 5.9 illustrates that the impact of marginality on spending is quite different in seats that the parties lost in the previous election than ones that they won. Indeed, in the Conservative case, the influence of marginality on spending is statistically significant only in seats the party lost in 1997 (see Table 5.8). This reinforces the finding that parties tend to spend heavily in constituencies where they have incumbent MPs, regardless of their margin of victory in the previous election. In seats parties lost, the margin of defeat does much to dictate how much they spend this time around.

Thus, constituency-level spending in 2001 reflected an interaction between the closeness of the contest in the previous election and a party's incumbent/challenger status. Where they were incumbents, Labour and, especially, the Conservatives and Liberal Democrats, spent heavily. Where they were challengers, all three parties paid close attention to how well they had done four years earlier. In this regard, the regression coefficients in Table 5.8 indicate that Labour and the Liberal Democrats

Table 5.8 Effects of constituency marginality on candidate expenditures

	1997 Outcome					
	Overall		Seat won		Seat lost	
Predictor variables	β	SE	β	SE	β	SE
A. Labour candidate expenditures						
Marginality	−0.24***	0.06	−0.54***	0.04	−1.07***	0.12
Constant	70.39***	1.98	93.46***	1.53	61.46***	2.64
R^2	0.02		0.27		0.27	
(N)	(638)		(417)		(221)	
B. Conservative candidate expenditures						
Marginality	−1.34***	0.04	−0.09	0.11	−1.40***	0.04
Constant	103.90***	1.15	89.01***	1.60	105.43***	1.55
R^2	0.67		0.004		0.68	
(N)	(636)		(165)		(471)	
C. Liberal Democrat candidate expenditures						
Marginality	−1.28***	0.05	−0.34*	0.15	−1.06***	0.05
Constant	79.40***	1.94	94.98***	2.07	69.21***	2.11
R^2	0.53		0.10		0.43	
(N)	(630)		(46)		(584)	

*** $p \leq 0.001$; ** $p \leq 0.01$; * $p \leq 0.05$; one-tailed test.

Source: Electoral Commission (2002). Election 2001—Campaign Spending.

responded to constituency-level competition by increasing their spending by slightly over 1 per cent for every 1 per cent decrease in the margin between themselves and the party that won the seat in 1997. Conservative spending was more responsive, increasing by nearly one-and-a-half per cent for every 1 per cent decrease in the margin by which they lost a seat four years earlier. By investing their money to boost vote shares where it mattered most, the parties clearly demonstrated that *they* thought local campaigning could make a difference.

Modelling Direct Effects

This section investigates if exposure to direct campaign activities influenced party choice in the 2001 election. These are activities like canvassing, exposing people to party political broadcasts, and reminding them to get out to the polls. In each case the party appeals directly to the electorate. In what is referred to as the *minimal effects model* of campaigning, the emphasis is on calibrating conversion and reinforcement effects. Conversion refers to convincing supporters of other parties to switch their votes, and reinforcement refers to mobilizing existing supporters to turn out (Alsop and Weisberg 1988; Farah and Klein 1989; Finkel 1993). An obvious methodological problem with estimating either type of effect is to identify the influence of campaigning separately from the many longer-term factors that can influence voting behaviour. Finkel (1993; see also Johnston and Brady 2002) suggests that one way to deal with this problem is to use panel data. With panel data one can specify a model of party choice that contains a lagged endogenous (dependent) variable to control for forces on the vote operating before the official campaign begins. Accordingly, we test a direct effects model of electoral choice in 2001 using data from the BES pre-post panel, the first wave of which was conducted before the start of the official campaign, and the second, after polling day. Measuring vote intention in the first wave controls for factors influencing party choice before the official campaign started, thereby making it possible to estimate campaign effects accurately.[14] The variables that measure direct campaign effects are the party mobilization indices discussed above (see Figure 5.2), and the campaign-spending measures (see Table 5.7).

We estimate separate models for Labour, Conservative, and Liberal Democrat voting. Since the dependent variable in each model is a dichotomy, binomial logit (Long 1997: ch. 3) is used for estimation purposes. As an example, the specification of the model of Labour voting is as follows:

$$\text{VOTELAB}_t = f(\beta_0 + \beta_1 \text{VINTLAB}_{t-1} + \Sigma\beta_{2\text{-}3}\text{MLAB}_t + \Sigma\beta_{4\text{-}5}\text{MCON}_t + \Sigma\beta_{6\text{-}7}\text{MLDEM}_t)$$

where

VOTELAB_t = vote, scored 1 if individual voted Labour and 0 otherwise,

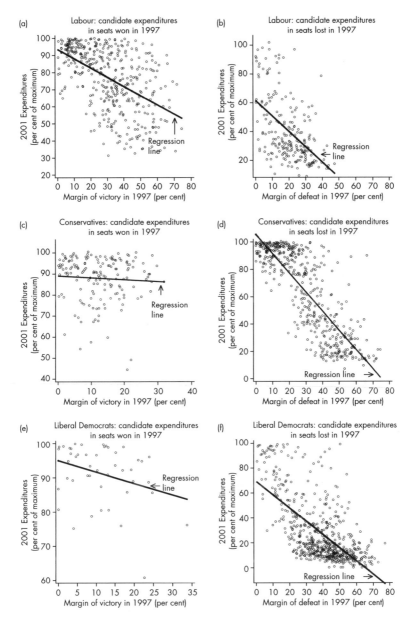

Figure 5.9 Candidate expenditures in 2001 by margin of victory in 1997 general election, controlling for seats won and lost in 1997

Source: Electoral commission (2002), *Election 2001—campaign spending*.

VINTLAB_{t-1} = vote intention before official campaign began, scored 1 if individual intended to vote Labour and 0 otherwise;

MLAB_t = exposure to mobilizing activities and constituency spending by Labour;

MCON_t = exposure to mobilizing activities and constituency spending by the Conservatives;

MLDEM_t = exposure to mobilizing activities and constituency spending by Liberal Democrats;

β_0 = a constant;

$\beta_{1\text{-}7}$ = coefficients to be estimated.

In this specification, VINTLAB_{t-1} (the lagged endogenous variable) summarizes pre-campaign forces predisposing an individual to vote for the Labour Party. Coefficients associated with the other predictor variables measure effects that result from parties' efforts during the campaign. Depending upon whether a voter was already inclined to support a particular party, these coefficients capture either reinforcement or conversion effects. If these coefficients are not significant, this means that party activities aimed directly at influencing vote choice did not affect voters' decisions.

Tables 5.9–5.11 contain logistic regression estimates of the direct effects of the mobilization and constituency-level spending measures on voting in 2001, controlling for pre-campaign vote intentions. The first column in Table 5.9 shows that, apart from the Conservative mobilization scale, all of the campaign measures significantly affected the Labour vote. As expected, Labour mobilization and spending increased the likelihood that a voter would cast a Labour ballot; and Conservative spending and Liberal Democrat mobilization and spending decreased that likelihood. The third column in Table 5.9 illustrates how each predictor variable affects the *probability* of voting Labour.[15] Not surprisingly, the variable that has the strongest influence is pre-campaign intention to support Labour. However, both the mobilization and spending variables have highly significant impacts on the likelihood of actually voting Labour. For people in the pre-campaign survey who did not intend to vote Labour but were exposed to all four mobilizing activities, the probability that they would end up choosing Labour increases by 50 points. This probability increases by 25 points if they lived in a constituency where Labour spent the legal maximum, as opposed to a constituency where it spent only the minimum amount.

Column 3 of Table 5.10 indicates that the variable with the biggest impact on the probability of casting a Conservative ballot is vote intention prior to the campaign. Indeed, the probability (0.73) associated with this variable is exactly the same as the equivalent figure in the Labour voting model. For the Conservatives, the difference between no exposure and maximum exposure to their campaign activities increased the probability of voting for them by 35 points. Similarly, the

Table 5.9 Logit model of constituency-level campaign effects on Labour vote

Predictor variables	β	SE	Probabilities
Prior intention to vote for party	3.67★★★	0.16	0.73
Labour mobilization index	0.56★★★	0.15	0.50
Conservative mobilization index	−0.06	0.15	0.01
Liberal Democrat mobilization index	−0.40★★	0.17	−0.29
Labour campaign spending	0.01★★★	0.00	0.25
Conservative campaign spending	−0.01★★★	0.00	−0.19
Liberal Democrat campaign spending	−0.01★★★	0.00	−0.29
McFadden R^2	0.46		
Per cent correctly classified	87		

★★★ $p \leq 0.001$; ★★ $p \leq 0.01$; ★ $p \leq 0.05$; one-tailed test.

Source: 2001 BES pre–post election panel survey.

Table 5.10 Logit model of constituency-level campaign effects on Conservative vote

Predictor variables	β	SE	Probabilities
Prior intention to vote for party	4.03★★★	0.18	0.73
Labour mobilization index	−0.72★★★	0.18	−0.25
Conservative mobilization index	0.57★★★	0.17	0.35
Liberal Democrat mobilization index	−0.10	0.19	−0.02
Labour campaign spending	−0.00	0.00	0.00
Conservative campaign spending	0.02★★★	0.00	0.17
Liberal Democrat campaign spending	−0.01★★	0.00	−0.04
McFadden R^2	0.49		
Per cent correctly classified	90		

★★★ $p \leq 0.001$; ★★ $p \leq 0.01$; ★ $p \leq 0.05$; one-tailed test.

Source: 2001 BES pre–post election panel survey.

maximum difference in Conservative campaign spending raised this probability by 17 points. Exposure to Labour mobilizing activities reduced the probability of voting Conservative by 25 points. Although the results for the Conservative analysis are generally similar to those for Labour, there are some noteworthy differences. First, Liberal Democrat mobilization efforts had little impact on Conservative voting, whereas Conservative and Labour mobilization efforts were influential. Second, as measured by the change in probabilities, the mobilization and spending variables have weaker impacts on the probability of voting Conservative than the comparable Labour measures have on the probability of casting a Labour ballot. This is consistent with the earlier evidence that the

Table 5.11 Logit model of constituency-level campaign effects on Liberal Democrat vote

Predictor variables	β	SE	Probabilities
Prior intention to vote for party	3.45★★★	0.22	0.66
Labour mobilization index	−0.19	0.16	−0.09
Conservative mobilization index	−0.62★★★	0.16	−0.21
Liberal Democrat mobilization index	0.59★★★	0.17	0.49
Labour campaign spending	−0.01★★★	0.00	−0.13
Conservative campaign spending	0.00	0.00	0.03
Liberal Democrat campaign spending	0.01★★★	0.00	0.16
McFadden R^2	0.29		
Per cent correctly classified	87		

★★★ $p \leq 0.001$; ★★ $p \leq 0.01$; ★ $p \leq 0.05$; one-tailed test.

Source: 2001 BES pre–post election panel survey.

Conservatives did not target their canvassing efforts very effectively. Finally, Liberal Democrat, but not Labour, spending is a significant predictor in the Conservative model.

Table 5.11 presents the results of the Liberal Democrat analysis. Liberal Democrat voting was boosted by their own campaigning and inhibited by Conservative campaigning. Labour spending also had a negative influence, and Liberal Democrat spending had a positive one. Column 3 of the table indicates that prior voting intention had a slightly weaker impact on the probability of voting Liberal Democrat than is true for other parties. This is consistent with the fact that the Liberal Democrats have significantly fewer committed partisans than do Labour or the Conservatives and, hence, Liberal Democrat vote intentions are less strongly tethered by long-term forces. As a result, campaigning is very important for the Liberal Democrats, and exposure to all four campaign activities raises the probability that an individual will opt for the party by 49 points. The estimates also show that the Liberal Democrats were more strongly affected by Conservative campaigning than by Labour campaigning. In contrast, Labour spending had a larger influence than did Conservative spending.

Overall, these analyses demonstrate that all parties benefited from their own mobilizing and spending efforts and, thus, direct campaigning was consequential. As measured by changes in the probability of voting for a party, it appears that mobilization efforts had larger effects than spending, although both types of activity were significant. Rival parties' efforts were also influential, although the effects were not as consistent as those of a party's own campaign. These results suggest that parties neglect local campaigns at their peril. In the next section, we provide a more comprehensive picture of the influence of campaigns by considering both direct and indirect effects.

Electoral Choice and the 2001 Campaign

Modelling Direct and Indirect Effects

We now consider the hypothesis that voting behaviour is influenced by variables that measure direct appeals from the parties during mostly local campaigns, as well as by variables, such as party identification, party leader images, issue priorities, and economic evaluations, that proxy what goes on during the national campaign. Accordingly, we respecify the model of party choice presented above to include both direct and indirect campaign effects. For example, the extended model of Labour voting is written as follows:

$$\text{VOTELAB}_t = f(\beta_0 + \beta_1 \text{VINTLAB}_{t-1} + \Sigma\beta_{2\text{-}3}\text{MLAB}_t + \Sigma\beta_{4\text{-}5}\text{MCON}_t + \Sigma\beta_{6\text{-}7}\text{MLDEM}_t + \Sigma\beta_{8\text{-}k}\text{ICAMP}_t)$$

where

$\quad$ VOTELAB_t = vote in 2001 general election, scored 1 if individual voted Labour and 0 otherwise;

$\quad$ VINTLAB_{t-1} = vote intention before official campaign began, scored 1 if individual intended to vote Labour and 0 otherwise;

$\quad$ MLAB_t = exposure to mobilizing activities and constituency spending by Labour;

$\quad$ MCON_t = exposure to mobilizing activities and constituency spending by the Conservatives;

$\quad$ MLDEM_t = exposure to mobilizing activities and constituency spending by Liberal Democrats;

$\quad$ ICAMP_t = variables such as party identification, party leader images, party-issue linkages, and reactions to economic conditions. Controlling for prior vote intention, these variables proxy the impact of exposure to the national-level activities of the parties during the official campaign.

Again, the vote intention variable in the pre-campaign survey (VOTEINT_{t-1} in this example) controls for the effects of various predictor variables before the campaign begins. The effects of the constituency-level activities of the parties are measured using the summary indices in Figure 5.2 and the constituency-level spending variables. Effects of national-level activities are proxied by the variables that appear in the composite vote model in Chapter Four (see Table 4.10). Here, all of these variables are measured using data gathered in the post-election survey. This makes it possible to estimate the impact of the determinants of party choice at the end of the campaign, while controlling for their influences at the start. With this specification, if a predictor variable is statistically significant, then it means that changes in that variable during the campaign have influenced the voters. For this reason, the findings differ from those of Chapter Four, which focussed on explaining the *overall* effects of various determinants of party choice, not just those associated with the official

161

campaign. As in the analyses above, the dependent variables are dichotomies (e.g. vote Labour, vote for other party), so binomial logit is used to estimate model parameters.

Tables 5.12–5.14 display the effects of the campaign variables on the probability of voting for the three parties. There are three models in each table. The first (Model A) contains all the statistically significant predictor variables from the analyses in Table 4.10, together with the direct campaign measures. The second (Model B) contains only the statistically significant variables from Model A. The third (Model C) provides multi-level estimates of the effects of variables in Model B, with the spending measures defined as second-level variables.[16] The multi-level models are used as a check on the robustness of the effects estimated in Models A and B. It bears emphasis that the coefficients reported in Tables 5.12–5.14 do not measure the overall or total effect of each independent variable on the likelihood of voting for a given party. Rather, they estimate the portion of the effect of the predictor variables produced by the short (official) campaign, controlling for pre-campaign vote intentions. For example, the last column of Table 5.12 shows that if an individual was persuaded to become a Labour party identifier during the short campaign, *ceteris paribus*, this would increase the probability that he or she would vote Labour by 39 points.

As reported in Chapter Four, two components of the valence model—party identification and party leader images—are the most powerful predictors of Labour voting in 2001. Model A in Table 5.12 shows that the campaign influenced both partisanship and party leader evaluations, but not issue perceptions, in ways that affected Labour support. If this model is compared with the one in Table 5.9, then it can be seen that prior vote intention is a much weaker predictor of voting behaviour than was true in the earlier model. This indicates, not surprisingly, that some indirect campaign factors had important influences on Labour support.

All of the predictor variables in Table 5.12 have the correct signs. Activation of Labour partisanship increases the probability of voting Labour, and activation of Conservative or Liberal Democrat partisanship reduces it. Labour party identification has approximately the same impact on the likelihood of voting Labour as does prior intention to vote Labour—and both effects are large. Table 5.12 also indicates that feelings about Tony Blair have a larger impact on the likelihood of voting Labour than do any other variable. If a hypothetical voter moved from giving the Labour leader a score of zero to a score of ten on the Blair 'like–dislike' scale during the campaign, then this increased the probability of voting Labour by a massive 70 points. This is further evidence to support the conclusions of Chapter Four that party leader images have strong effects on party choice. In this regard, trends during the campaign in feelings about the party leaders (see Figure 5.4) may have helped Labour; Blair made modest gains in popularity while feelings about Conservative leader William Hague remained stalled in the negative zone. Feelings about Liberal Democrat leader Charles Kennedy became increasingly positive throughout much of the campaign, but feelings about him are not a significant predictor of Labour voting.

Table 5.12 Logit models of constituency-level and other campaign effects on Labour vote

Predictor variables	Model A		Model B		Model C		
	β	SE	β	SE	β	SE	Probabilities
Prior intention to vote for the party	1.71***	0.21	1.73***	0.21	1.89***	0.27	0.39
Labour party identification	1.75***	0.26	1.73***	0.26	2.41***	0.31	0.39
Conservative party identification	−1.28***	0.34	−1.32***	0.33	−0.97**	0.40	−0.27
Liberal Democrat party identification	−1.23***	0.36	−1.26***	0.36	−1.07**	0.45	−0.24
Affect scale for Tony Blair	0.39***	0.05	0.40***	0.05	0.45***	0.06	0.70
Tactical voting	−0.78***	0.26	−0.80***	0.26	−0.46	0.41	−0.17
Labour mobilization index	0.11	0.19	x	x	0.15	0.22	x
Conservative mobilization index	−0.13	0.36	x	x	−0.02	0.23	x
Liberal Democrat mobilization index	0.15	0.25	x	x	−0.24	0.25	x

Table 5.12 Continued

Predictor variables	Model A		Model B		Model C		
	β	SE	β	SE	β	SE	Probabilities
Labour campaign spending	0.01★★★	0.00	0.01★★★	0.00	0.02★★★	0.01	0.24
Conservative campaign spending	−0.01★	0.00	−0.01★★	0.01	−0.02★★★	0.01	−0.16
Liberal Democrat campaign spending	−0.02★★★	0.01	−0.02★★★	0.00	−0.02★★★	0.01	−0.36
McFadden R^2	0.64		0.64				
Per cent correctly classified	92		90				

Note: Parameters in Model C are estimated using multilevel analysis, with spending indicators as second-level variables.

x—variable not included in model.

★★★ $p \leq 0.001$; ★★ $p \leq 0.01$; ★ $p \leq 0.05$; one-tailed test.

Source: 2001 BES pre–post election panel survey.

Table 5.13 Logit models of constituency-level and other campaign effects on Conservative vote

Predictor variables	Model A		Model B		Model C		
	β	SE	β	SE	β	SE	Probabilities
Prior intention to vote for the Party	1.94***	0.33	1.95***	0.27	0.23***	0.04	0.20
Labour party identification	-2.76***	0.52	-2.56***	0.41	-0.08**	0.04	-0.18
Conservative Party identification	1.15***	0.38	1.35***	0.31	0.40***	0.05	0.12
Liberal Democrat Party identification	-2.41***	0.63	-2.09***	0.54	-0.11**	0.05	-0.08
Affect scale for William Hague	0.30***	0.07	0.33***	0.06	0.01**	0.01	0.33
Affect scale for Charles Kennedy	-0.24***	0.09	-0.18***	0.07	-0.01**	0.01	-0.15
Conservatives best at most important issue	-0.68*	0.38	x	x	0.03	0.04	x
Liberal Democrats best on most important issue	-1.79***	0.65	-1.71***	0.57	-0.07	0.05	-0.06
Party issue proximity–Labour	-0.09	0.06	x	x	-0.01	0.01	x
Party issue proximity–Conservatives	0.15**	0.06	x	x	0.00	0.00	x
Labour best on economy	-1.14***	0.32	-1.08***	0.27	-0.09***	0.03	-0.08
Tactical voting	-1.13***	0.35	-0.95***	0.32	-0.05	0.04	-0.05
Labour mobilization index	-0.58**	0.29	x	x	-0.01	0.02	x

Table 5.13 Continued

Predictor variables	Model A		Model B		Model C		
	β	SE	β	SE	β	SE	Probabilities
Conservative mobilization index	0.20	0.29	x	x	0.01	0.02	x
Liberal Democrat mobilization index	0.52*	0.30	x	x	0.00	0.02	x
Labour campaign spending	−0.01	0.01	x	x	−0.001*	0.00	x
Conservative campaign spending	0.02***	0.01	0.03***	0.01	0.003***	0.00	0.12
Liberal Democrat campaign spending	−0.02***	0.01	−0.01***	0.01	−0.00	0.00	−0.06
McFadden R^2	0.75		0.72				
Per cent correctly classified	94		92				

Note: Parameters in Model C are estimated using multilevel analysis, with the spending indicators as second-level variables.

x—variable not included in model.

*** $p \leq 0.001$; ** $p \leq 0.01$; * $p \leq 0.05$; one-tailed test.

Source: 2001 BES pre–post election panel survey.

Table 5.14 Logit models of constituency-level and other campaign effects on Liberal Democrat vote

Predictor variables	Model A		Model B		Model C		
	β	SE	β	SE	β	SE	Probabilities
Prior intention to vote for the party	2.11***	0.30	2.10***	0.30	1.01***	0.16	0.39
Ethnicity	−0.67*	0.38	x	x	0.87	0.16	x
Liberal Democrat party identification	3.13***	0.32	3.18***	0.32	2.39***	0.17	0.62
Affect scale for William Hague	−0.06	0.04	x	x	−0.04***	0.01	x
Affect scale for Charles Kennedy	0.24***	0.07	0.26***	0.06	0.06***	0.02	0.27
Liberal democrats best on most important issue	1.68***	0.36	1.62***	0.35	1.00***	0.20	0.30
Party issue proximity– Liberal Democrats	0.11**	0.05	0.12**	0.05	0.02*	0.01	0.17
Tactical voting	1.25***	0.25	1.34***	0.25	0.67***	0.15	0.22
Labour mobilization index	−0.40*	0.23	−0.42**	0.18	−0.13**	0.06	−0.14
Conservative mobilization index	−0.24	0.22	x	x	−0.06	0.05	x
Liberal Democrat mobilization index	0.21	0.23	x	x	−0.07	0.08	x

Table 5.14 Continued

Predictor variables	Model A		Model B		Model C		
	β	SE	β	SE	β	SE	Probabilities
Labour campaign spending	−0.01	0.01	x	x	−0.01	0.00	x
Conservative campaign spending	−0.00	0.01	x	x	0.00	0.00	x
Liberal Democrat campaign spending	0.02★★★	0.00	0.02★★★	0.00	0.01★★★	0.00	0.24
Mcfadden R^2	0.52		0.54				
Per cent correctly classified	90		91				

Note: Parameters in Model C are estimated using multilevel analysis, with spending indicators as second-level variables.

x—variable not included in model.

★★★ $p \leq 0.001$; ★★ $p \leq 0.01$; ★ $p \leq 0.05$; one-tailed test.

Source: 2001 BES pre–post election panel survey.

There is also evidence in Table 5.12 of local campaign effects on Labour voting, even when the influence of the national campaigns is taken into account. The local campaign effects work exclusively through the campaign spending measures, and the coefficients are similar to those in the model reported in Table 5.9. The multi-level model estimates assess the robustness of these effects. As noted in the earlier table, the Labour and Liberal Democrat mobilization indices significantly influenced Labour voting, but these effects disappear when national-level effects are taken into account. Similarly, tactical voting appeared to reduce the probability of voting Labour in the initial estimates, but this is not confirmed by the multi-level model.

Table 5.13 contains estimates of local and national campaign effects on Conservative voting. Once again, Model A contains the statistically significant variables from Table 4.10, together with the several local campaign measures.[17] Model B includes only the significant predictors from the analysis of Model A. These models are more elaborate than their Labour equivalents in Table 5.12, with more campaign effects in evidence. In addition to partisanship and leadership effects, the campaign affected Conservative support via economic competence judgments. These results, which are confirmed by the multi-level model (Model C), involve perceptions of Labour's managerial competence. The negative sign on the coefficient for this variable is as anticipated, with Conservative support being reduced by the judgement that Labour was the best party on the economy. Conservative support was also significantly influenced by feelings about Hague and Kennedy, but not by feelings about Blair. It is important to note that this does not mean that public reactions to Blair failed to influence the probability of casting a Conservative ballot. What it means is that feelings about him had no influence *during the official campaign*—Blair's impact on Conservative voting occurred before the campaign started.

Prior voting intention has a weaker impact on the probability of voting Conservative than does its counterpart in the Labour model. This can be seen from the column showing how the predictor variables affected the probability of voting Conservative. It is also the case that Conservative partisanship has a weaker effect than Labour identification has in the Labour model. These findings suggest that the Conservative campaign was less effective in activating existing predispositions than was the Labour campaign. This interpretation is consistent with the issue effects in these models. The Conservatives essentially fought a campaign in which they needed to convert people who were not predisposed to support them. As the election outcome and the earlier evidence indicates, they failed to achieve this objective.

Direct local campaign effects are significant in the Conservative models, and again they operate via the spending variables. However, their influence is weaker than in the Labour models. For example, Conservative constituency-level spending increased the probability of voting Conservative by 12 points compared with an equivalent effect of 24 points in the Labour model. In Models A and B, it appears that tactical voting was influential, but this is not confirmed by the multi-level analysis (Model C). However, the multi-level model results are generally very similar to those for the individual-level ones (Models A and B). One noteworthy difference is that the multi-level model suggests that Labour constituency-level campaign spending influenced Conservative voting and Liberal Democrat spending did not—the reverse of the findings in the individual-level models. This means that the Conservative campaign spending estimates are robust, but that the estimates for the other two parties are less so.

Table 5.14 reports the analyses of Liberal Democrat voting. Consistent with the increasingly positive feelings voters expressed about Kennedy as the campaign progressed (see Figure 5.4), feelings about him are significant in all three models in Table 5.14. This finding indicates that his performance during the campaign had a positive impact on Liberal Democrat support. Prior vote intention has a similar effect as it does in the Labour and Conservative models, thereby indicating that activating predispositions significantly affected Liberal Democrat voting. This point is reinforced by the very large influence of partisanship. The Liberal Democrats have substantially fewer party identifiers than their rivals, but activating a Liberal Democrat identification does much to prompt a vote for the party. Perceptions that the Liberal Democrats are best able to handle the most important issue and the Liberal Democrat issue–proximity variable are also significant predictors. These findings indicate that reactions to issues during the campaign affected the likelihood of choosing the Liberal Democrats. Liberal Democrat campaign spending also has a highly significant effect, a finding confirmed by the multi-level analysis (Model C).

Finally, there is evidence that the Liberal Democrats benefited from tactical voting. Although the tactical voting variable does not have robust effects in the Labour and Conservative models, in the Liberal Democrat analysis its effect is both statistically and substantively significant. Net of other considerations, being a tactical voter increased the likelihood of supporting the Liberal Democrats by 22 points. An interesting question concerns the extent to which tactical voting is the product of campaign appeals or, alternatively, something that voters do without being prompted by the parties.[18] This question may be addressed by analysing how the campaign variables affect tactical voting.

Table 5.15 shows the relationship between the campaign variables and tactical voting, controlling for predispositions to vote for the various political parties. The results reveal that a prior commitment to support either of the major parties significantly lessened the likelihood of a tactical vote.[19] Controlling for these effects, Liberal Democrat local campaigning is a strong predictor of tactical voting—exposure to all four direct Liberal Democrat mobilization activities increased the probability that a voter behaved tactically by 32 points. Liberal Democrat constituency-level campaign spending also has a significant, but smaller, influence, increasing the probability of a Liberal Democrat vote by 9 points. These results suggest that a good deal of the tactical voting that took

Table 5.15   Logit model of constituency-level campaign effects on tactical voting

Predictor variables	β	SE	Probabilities
Prior intention to vote for Labour	−0.60★★★	0.22	—
Prior intention to vote for Conservatives	−0.71★★★	0.24	—
Prior intention to vote for Liberal Democrats	−0.12	0.26	—
Prior intention to vote for other party	−0.12	0.54	—
Labour mobilization index	−0.13	0.16	—
Conservative mobilization index	−0.19	0.15	—
Liberal Democrat mobilization index	0.43★★★	0.16	0.32
Labour campaign spending	−0.00★	0.00	−0.08
Conservative campaign spending	0.00	0.00	—
Liberal Democrat campaign spending	0.01★★★	0.00	0.09
Marginality of seat	−0.02	0.20	—
McFadden R^2	0.04		
Per cent correctly classified	87		

★★★ $p \leq 0.001$; ★★ $p \leq 0.01$; ★ $p \leq 0.05$; one-tailed test.

Source: 2001 BES pre–post election panel survey.

place in 2001 was the product of direct campaigning by the Liberal Democrats. The estimates also show that the marginality of the seat did not have a direct impact on tactical voting once the other variables are taken into account.[20] This latter finding reinforces the conclusion that direct campaigning is largely responsible for tactical voting. As discussed above, marginality strongly affects how the Liberal Democrats and other parties allocate resources for constituency campaigning. Voters respond to these campaigns, but they do not spontaneously cast their ballots tactically. People need to be prompted by the parties that tactical voting is likely to pay off in their constituency.

CONCLUSION: CAMPAIGNS MATTER

The parties' campaigns significantly influenced electoral choice in 2001. A substantial amount of the impact of campaigning operated by activating predispositions. This was particularly true for Labour, which was able to target its local campaigns on sympathizers and the uncommitted more effectively than did the Conservatives. The Liberal Democrat campaign was also effective in this regard. In contrast, the Conservatives found themselves trying—with little success—to convert people who favoured other parties. An indication of the failure of their direct campaigning is the fact that they ended up reminding many of their rivals' supporters to go to the polls instead of concentrating on their own supporters. Their canvassing did not accurately identify their electoral base.

Campaign effects were associated with other major variables in the valence model of electoral choice. Party leader images were influential. However, the campaign component of the impact of the leaders differed for Labour and the opposition parties. In Labour's case, there was a large campaign-related effect of feelings about Blair, but the campaign-related effects of feelings about Hague or Kennedy were not significant. In contrast, the Liberal Democrat and Conservative leaders were clearly rivals in winning the support of their respective voters. It bears emphasis that this does not mean that feelings about Blair failed to affect Conservative and Liberal Democrat voting. In both cases, Blair's impact was substantial, but it occurred before the official campaign started. There also were campaign components in issue effects on Conservative and Liberal Democrat voting. Again, this does not mean that issue perceptions were unimportant for Labour support. As discussed in Chapter Four, Labour had a large lead as the party best able to handle the issues voters judged to be important in the election, and those competence judgements significantly influenced the likelihood of casting a Labour ballot. However, Labour had established its advantage on the issues before the official campaign began and, as shown in Figure 5.5, that lead was never threatened as the campaign progressed.

Finally, there is consistent evidence that local campaigns matter. With statistical controls for prior vote intentions and the impact of variables that proxy national campaign effects, the constituency spending indicators show predictable effects in all of the voting models. These effects are confirmed by multi-level analyses, which take into account the fact that candidate spending occurs at the level of the constituency rather than that of the individual voter. Additionally, it is clear that tactical voting is influenced by constituency campaigning, particularly by the Liberal Democrats. Thus, contrary to the suggestions of some observers, British parties are not wasting their time when they engage in vigorous local campaigning. Indeed, when a general election is closely contested, local campaigns can make the difference between winning and losing.

NOTES

1. The party contact questions are: (a) 'Did a canvasser from a party call at your home to talk with you during the election campaign?' [IF 'YES'] 'Which party or parties did they represent?' (b) 'Did anyone from a political party telephone you during the election campaign to ask you how you might vote?' [IF 'YES'] 'Which party or parties did they represent?' (c) Did any political party contact you on election day itself to see whether you had voted or intended to vote?' [IF 'YES'] 'Which party or parties did they represent?' (d) 'Did you see any of Party Election Broadcasts that were shown on television during the election campaign?' [IF 'YES'] Which parties' Election Broadcasts did you see?'

2. When working with the 2001 survey data, sample size limitations prompt us to define marginal seats as constituencies in which the winning party's majority in 1997 was less than 10 per cent of the votes cast.

3. There are too few cases to permit reliable analyses of SNP and Plaid Cymru efforts at telephone canvassing or their attempts to get their supporters to the polls on election day.

4. We use the party supporter measure (see Chapter Six) rather than the traditional party identification measure, since when the parties canvass voters they typically ask: 'Can we count on your support?' (Labour Party 1997).

5. The summary party mobilization indices are constructed by adding the number of contacts (via canvassing, telephoning, election day knocking up, watching party political broadcasts) a respondent had from each of the parties. The resulting indices range from 0 to 4, and reflect the extent of campaign contact with Labour, the Conservatives, and the Liberal Democrats.

6. The questions are: (a) 'If you do vote in the general election, have you decided which party you will vote for, or haven't you decided yet?' [IF 'DECIDED'] 'Which party is that?'

7. The question is asked of voters only: 'How long ago did you decide that you would definitely vote the way you did? Was it: (i) a long time ago, (ii) some time last year, (iii) some time this year, (iv) during the election campaign. Options (i)–(iv) were presented to the respondent on a show card.

8. The rolling cross-section vote intention question sequence is identical to that used in the pre-campaign survey (see note 6 above).

9. For details concerning nearest-neighbour (LOESS) regression, see Fox (2000). Here, the nearest neighbour regressions are computed using a polynomial of degree 1 and a bandwidth of 0.5. The regressions are computed using EVIEWS 4.1 (Lilien et al. 2003).

10. The question is: 'Using the 0–10 scale, where 10 means *strongly like* and 0 means *strongly dislike*, how do you feel about: (i) Tony Blair, (ii) William Hague, (iii) Charles Kennedy, (iv) John Swinney [asked in Scotland only], (v) Wyn Jones [asked in Wales only]'. The order in which the leader names were mentioned was randomized.

11. The questions are: 'In your opinion, what is the *single most important issue* in this election?' [IF AN ISSUE IS MENTIONED] 'Which party is best able to handle this issue?'

12. The question sequence is: (a) '*Generally speaking*, do you think of yourself as Conservative, Labour, Liberal Democrat, Scottish Nationalist [in Scotland only], Plaid Cymru [in Wales only] or what?' (b) [IF NO PARTY MENTIONED in (a)] 'Do you generally think of yourself as a little closer to one of the parties than the others? If yes, please tell me which party?' (c) [IF PARTY MENTIONED IN (a) OR (b)] 'Would you call yourself very strongly, fairly strongly, or not very strongly [PARTY MENTIONED]'?

13. The question is: 'How interested are you in the general election that is to be held on 7th June this year'?

14. Using the vote intention variable from the pre-election survey as the control for prior party choice can cause simultaneity bias problems (e.g. Greene 2003: 307–14). The nature of this bias is to underestimate campaign effects and to overestimate effects that occur before the (official) campaign begins (the latter effects being proxied by the lagged endogenous variable). Given this, an analysis that includes a lagged endogenous variable provides a conservative estimate of campaign effects.

15. As discussed in Chapter Four, these probabilities are calculated by setting all predictor variables in the model to their mean values. Then, the variable of interest is varied from its minimum to maximum value and the change in the vote probability is computed. The analyses are performed using the CLARIFY programme (Tomz, Wittenberg, and King 1999).

16. Multi-level modelling permits estimates of the slopes and intercepts of the individual level variables to vary across constituencies, and provides correct standard errors for variables measured at the second (constituency) level. See, for example, Kreft and de Leeuw (1998), Raudenbush and Bryk (2001). The multi-level models are analyzed using HLM 5 (see Raudenbush et al. 2001).

17. Note that regional dummy variables are not examined in this model. Their presence makes maximum likelihood estimation of the multi-level models impossible, since they are collinear with constituency-level variables. This omission has little effect on the estimates.

18. There is no doubt that the Liberal Democrats believe that tactical voting works to their advantage. The point was made in an interview conducted by one of the authors (Whiteley), with Lord Chris Rennard, Liberal Democrat Director of Campaigns and Elections. Rennard noted that, in 1997 and 2001, Liberal Democrat strategists sought to encourage tactical voting in seats where they were the main challenger to the Conservatives by distributing leaflets to Labour sympathizers warning them that a Labour vote would be wasted.

19. Since the dependent variable in the tactical voting model is highly skewed (14 per cent of the pre-post election panel respondents who voted were classified as tactical voters), the goodness of fit of the model as measured by an estimated R^2 statistic or improvement in percentage correctly classified is necessarily poor.

20. Additional analyses demonstrate that there are no significant *interaction* effects between marginality and Liberal Democrat campaigning, on the one hand, and probability of being a tactical voter, on the other.

SIX

The Dynamics of Party Identification

For nearly half a century, party identification has been a central concept in the study of electoral choice. As discussed in Chapter Two, the concept was originally developed by Angus Campbell and his colleagues at the University of Michigan in their research on American voting behaviour in the 1950s (Campbell, Gurin, and Miller 1954; Campbell et al. 1960, 1966). Imported to Britain by Butler and Stokes (1969), party identification was designated as a key element in public political psychology. According to Butler and Stokes, the process by which the political effects of a deeply divided class society were transmitted to the electoral arena was rooted in class self-identifications that were powerful, pervasive, and primordial. The vast majority of people recognized themselves as members of either the middle or the working class. These class identifications prompted the development of durable identifications with political parties that were thought to represent the economic interests of those classes. Working class people tended to be Labour identifiers who regularly voted Labour, and middle class people tended to be Conservative identifiers who regularly voted Conservative. When voters cast their ballots, they expressed their 'tribal loyalties'. These loyalties were stable products of deeply ingrained, class-based partisan allegiances.

This conception of party identification has prompted protracted debates among students of voting and elections in Britain. A fundamental issue in these controversies is the *stability* of partisan attachments. If party identification lacks stability at the aggregate and individual levels, then theories of voting behaviour and election outcomes premised on the durability of partisan attachments are problematic. Hence, we begin our analysis by investigating long-run aggregate trends in party identification using data from several British Election Study (BES) surveys. Then, these data are employed to address longstanding debates about partisan dealignment. We map trends in the strength of the relationship between social class and party identification, and in the intensity of party identification in the electorate as a whole as well as within various age groups from the time at which they first reached the age of majority.

175

Next, we use data from several BES and British Election Panel Study (BEPS) panel surveys to gauge the extent to which individual voters change their party identifications over time. Recently developed statistical techniques enable us to determine whether observed levels of instability persist once random measurement error in survey responses is taken into account. We also consider the possibility that much of the apparent individual-level instability in partisanship reflects difficulties with the traditional BES party identification question. For this purpose, we examine data gathered in the 2001 BES, the British Household Panel Surveys (BHPS), the British Social Attitudes Surveys (BSA), and other sources. The BES and BEPS panel data then are used to investigate factors affecting the individual-level dynamics of party identification. A final set of analyses returns to the aggregate level. Using data gathered in monthly Gallup surveys, we model the aggregate dynamics of party identification between January 1992 and December 2002. The chapter concludes by arguing that partisanship in Britain may be usefully conceptualized as a storehouse of party and party leader performance evaluations.

AGGREGATE TRENDS

When the first BES post-election survey was conducted in 1964, slightly over 40 per cent said that they generally thought of themselves as Labour identifiers and an equal number said they were Conservative identifiers[1] (see Figure 6.1). About one in ten was a Liberal identifier and about one in twenty did not identify with a party. Four decades later, the picture was somewhat different. An overwhelming majority of those interviewed in the 2001 BES post-election survey stated that they identified with a party. Although the combined percentage of Conservative and Labour partisans had fallen from 87 per cent to 68 per cent, virtually all of the decrease is attributable to a rapid post-1992 decline in the number of Conservatives. The percentage of Liberal Democrats in 2001 was almost exactly the same as the percentage of Liberals in 1964. Although the size of the group not professing a partisan attachment had doubled, it was only 11 per cent. In sum, as in 1964, most of those interviewed in 2001 claimed to be party identifiers, and most said that they were either Conservatives or Labour.

One might be tempted to argue that these data are compatible with the traditional Michigan theoretical perspective that says that partisan change typically is evolutionary, not revolutionary. According to Campbell et al. (1966), partisan realignments are rare, but when they occur, they involve rapid, substantial, and enduring changes in levels of identification with various parties. Realignments are driven by voters' reactions to big events, such as depressions or world wars, or the greatly enhanced salience of an issue that divides the supporters of one or more of the parties.

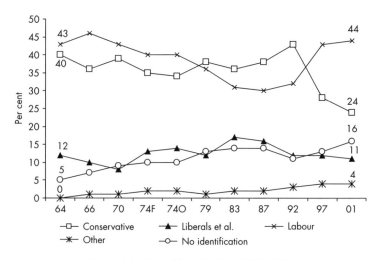

Figure 6.1   Party identification, 1964–2001

Source: 1964–2001 BES post-election surveys.

However, in Britain, there is a possible anomaly. As just observed, the number of Conservative identifiers fell precipitously after the 1992 election, and there was an accompanying large increase in Labour identifiers. To reconcile these rapid, sizeable movements in Conservative and Labour partisan shares with the Michigan perspective, one must argue that a realignment of partisan forces occurred after 1992. The Conservatives' bitter internecine conflicts in the 1990s about the Euro and other aspects of Britain's relationship with the European Union suggest that the realignment hypothesis is plausible if one accepts the Michigan model's proposition that individual-level partisan attachments are generally very stable. As observed in Chapter Two, the premise of individual-level stability in party identifications, except in the face of realigning forces, implies that swift, sizeable shifts in the aggregate balance of such identifications *must* be a product of such forces. However, as demonstrated below, partisan attachments in Britain exhibit much more individual-level movement than the Michigan account allows. This ongoing individual-level instability means that the observation of a change in the aggregate balance of party identifiers by itself is not an indicator of realignment. Thus, the concept of realignment is primarily a tool for *post-hoc* description.

Dealignment

Another aspect of the debate about the aggregate-level stability of party identification concerns dealignment. In the British context, this refers to changes in the intensity of partisan attachments and in the strength of the relationship between these attachments and social class. Soon after *Political Change in Britain* appeared, Crewe, Sarlvik, and Alt (1977) announced that BES surveys conducted in the 1970s revealed a weakening of party identification, and an erosion of the correlation between party identification and social class. As noted in Chapter Two, these findings fueled a long-lived controversy. Here, we assess changes in the strength of the relationship between party identification and social class[2] since 1964 by computing the consistency index (CI).[3] The results echo those for the correlation between social class and voting behaviour discussed in Chapter Three. As Figure 6.2 illustrates, the CI declines almost continuously across the entire 1964–2001 period. The magnitude of this long-term trend may be calibrated by regressing the CI on time while controlling for a step-shift downward in the social class × party identification relationship between 1966 and 1970. Using a 0–1 dummy variable[4] to capture this step-shift, we specify the following model:

$$CI_t = f(\beta_0 + \beta_1 Time + \beta_2 SHIFT6670)$$

where CI_t, consistency index score at time t; Time, time in years; SHIFT6670, permanent step shift in the CI beginning in 1970. The estimated coefficients, with standard errors in parentheses, are:

$$CI_t = 72.32 - 0.79\ Time - 11.84 SHIFT6670$$
$$(1.27)(0.06) \qquad (1.78)$$
Adjusted $R^2 = 0.98$, D.W. $= 2.06$

With an adjusted R^2 of 0.98, the model's explanatory power is very impressive. The linear trend and the 1966–70 step-shift coefficients have the expected negative signs and are statistically significant ($p < 0.001$). The coefficient (-0.79) for the trend term indicates that over the nearly four decades separating the 1964 and 2001 BES, the CI lost about three-quarters of a point per year in its value (on a 200-point scale). Thus, there is strong evidence of a gradual, but ultimately sizeable, erosion of the correlation between social class and party identification. This process has been going on since at least the 1960s and it has continued into the twenty-first century.

This long-term downward trend does not mean that the relationship between social class and party identification was originally strong. It bears emphasis that class defection in party identification has been widespread since at least the 1960s. Over two-fifths of middle class respondents in the 1964 BES did not identify with the Conservatives, and an equal proportion of working class respondents did not identify with Labour. Similar patterns are found in every subsequent BES survey. For example, at the high tide of Conservative electoral success in 1987, over half of the middle class respondents did not identify with that party, and nearly three-fifths of those in the working class did not identify with Labour. In 2001, nearly

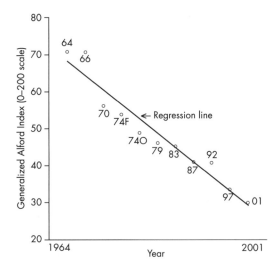

Figure 6.2 Trend in strength of relationship between social class and party identification
Source: 1964–2001 BES post-election surveys.

seven of ten middle class respondents did not identify with the Conservatives, and nearly five in ten of those in the working class did not identify with Labour.[5] The prolonged downward trend has loosened a relationship between class and party identification that already had considerable 'play' forty years ago.

A second aspect of the dealignment debate concerns the strength of party identification. In Chapter Three, we present data showing that the percentage of very strong party identifiers has decreased in every successive BES post-election survey. This pattern might be a product of a general weakening of attachments with all parties or, alternatively, a gradual weakening of attachments with some parties. Regarding the latter, one might imagine a scenario in which groups of older identifiers with a given party are not replaced by younger ones with equally strong attachments to it. Although plausible, this scenario is not what has occurred in Britain. To map the dynamics of the strength of party identification, we score 'very strong' identifiers +3, 'fairly strong' identifiers +2, 'not very strong' identifiers +1, and nonidentifiers 0. We then compute the average strength of party identification on this scale by party for each BES survey. Figure 6.3(a) shows that the erosion in the intensity of partisan attachments is generalized—identifications with the Conservatives, Labour, and the Liberals and their predecessors all decreased in strength between 1964 and 2001. And, with the exception of a relatively sharp drop in the intensity of Conservative and Liberal identifications between 1970 and 1974,[6] these long-term decreases are approximately linear.

179

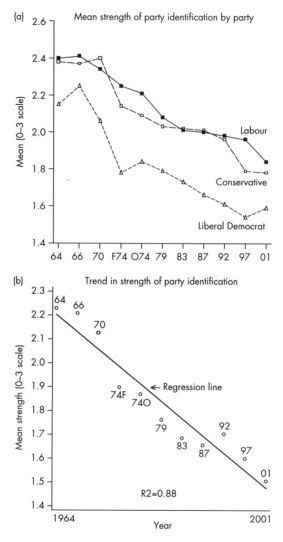

Figure 6.3 Trends in strength of party identification, 1964–2001
Source: BES 1964–2001 post-election surveys.

The overall decrease in the average strength of party identification since 1964 is depicted in Figure 6.3(b). Using a 0–1 dummy variable to allow for a possible downward shift between 1970 and 1974,[7] we specify the following model:

$$\text{SPID}_t = f(\beta_0 + \beta_1 \star \text{Time} + \beta_2 \star \text{SHIFT7074})$$

where, SPID$_t$ is the average strength of party identification at time t; Time is time in years; SHIFT7074, permanent step-shift in SPID beginning in 1974.

Estimating coefficients with OLS regression (standard errors in parentheses) yields:

$$\text{SPID}_t = 3.02 - 0.01 * \text{Time} - 0.24\text{SHIFT7074}$$
$$\text{(s.e.)} \ (0.11)(0.002) \qquad (0.04)$$
$$\text{Adjusted } R^2 = 0.97, \text{D.W.} = 1.65$$

The linear trend and the 1970–4 step-shift collectively explain virtually all of the variance in the strength of party identification over time. The trend term's coefficient (-0.01) indicates that the average intensity of party identification, as measured on the 0–3 point scale, decreased by about a tenth of a point per year. The magnitude (0.24 points) of the downward step-shift between 1970 and 1974 suggests that its effects were relatively small.

These estimates may be placed in perspective by comparing the strength of partisanship in 1964 and in 2001. In 1964, the average intensity of party identification was 2.2 points, just slightly above the score assigned to people who labelled themselves fairly strong identifiers. In 2001, the average intensity was 1.5 points, midway between fairly strong and not very strong identification. Thus, the protracted decline in the strength of partisan attachments has moved the electorate somewhat less than one-fifth of the way across the entire four-point (0–3) scale. Rather than documenting a wholesale abandonment of party identifications, the 1964–2001 BES data show that the erosion of partisan attachments has been ongoing, but incomplete—a dealignment of degree.

Of Age and Partisan Intensity

Dealignment of degree does not speak strongly against a Michigan-style conceptualization of party identification. However, the several BES surveys do provide evidence that the strength of party identification has not behaved in accordance with what the Michigan theorists would predict. Particularly important in this regard is an assessment of Converse's argument (1969, 1976) that, at the individual level, party identifications normally strengthen the longer they are held. Two processes are said to explain this. First, behavioural reinforcement of a psychological orientation occurs as party identifiers repeatedly vote for 'their' party, and subsequently justify their behaviour to themselves. Second, party identification performs a 'perceptual screening' function (Campbell et al. 1960; see also Bartels 2002). Incoming information about parties' issue positions, performance in office, leaders, and the political world more generally is neither accurate nor unbiased; rather it is selected on the basis of, and filtered through, a 'lens of partisanship'. The result is that voters possess information favourable to their parties and unfavourable to other parties. This combination of positively biased information about the party voters identify with, and negatively biased information about other parties, feeds back to strengthen existing party identifications. These reinforcement processes are repeated throughout a voter's political life cycle. The result is a positive correlation between the strength of party identification and age.

Positive relationships between party identification and age are present in the several BES surveys. However, cross-sectional correlations between party identification and age are not conclusive evidence of life-cycle effects such as those proposed by Converse. It is possible that these correlations reflect generational differences, that is, for whatever reasons, voters in different age cohorts vary in the strength of their partisan attachments. Age cohorts may undergo distinctive socialization experiences that affect the strength of their party identifications in the long-run. The picture is further complicated by the possibility of 'period' effects, whereby at a particular point in time the strength of party identification in several age groups is affected either positively or negatively by events. Although life-cycle, generational, and period effects are conceptually distinct, they cannot be separated empirically in a single cross-section; this requires very long-term panel surveys (Glenn 1977). Unfortunately, such long-term panels are unavailable.[8] There are several multi-wave BES panel surveys, but they cover only four to seven years—a modest fraction of the political life cycle.

An alternative way of obtaining a long-term perspective on partisan change in various age groups is to construct 'pseudo-panels' (e.g. see Abramson 1976, 1979). This involves dividing respondents in successive cross-sectional surveys into several age groups. The strength of party identification in each of these groups can be tracked in subsequent surveys. For example, if one wished to monitor the strength of party identification for a group aged 18–21 in the 1992 BES, then one would examine a group aged 23–26 in the 1997 survey. These groups comprised different individuals, but they are samples of the larger population of people who, by ageing, have moved from the first of these groups to the second. If the number of cases available for analysis is reasonably large, then this approach provides useful estimates of changes in the strength of party identification in various age cohorts.

We compute the percentages of very strong party identifiers in groups first eligible to vote in successive general elections held between 1970 and 2001.[9] We also do this for three older groups who arguably constitute distinct political generations. These are the Atlee generation (who entered the electorate between 1945 and 1950), the Churchill–Macmillan generation (1951, 1955, or 1959), and the Wilson generation (between 1964 and 1966). These analyses are presented in Table 6.1. Overall, there is little evidence of a tendency for the proportion of very strong party identifiers to grow within age cohorts over time. Over the entire 1970–2001 period, only two cohorts have more very strong party identifiers, and seven have fewer very strong identifiers. This result is not an artefact of choosing 2001 as the end-point for the analysis. Using 1997 as the end-point, two cohorts have at least 1 per cent more

Table 6.1 Percentages of 'very strong' party identifiers among groups of voters first entering the electorate between 1945 and 2001

	Election at which 18–21 year-old age groups entered electorate							
	1970	*Feb 1974*	*1979*	*1983*	*1987*	*1992*	*1997*	*2001*

A. Percentages of 'very strong' party identifiers among successive 18–21 year-old age groups entering the electorate between 1970 and 2001[a]

Years after initial entry

	1970	*Feb 1974*	*1979*	*1983*	*1987*	*1992*	*1997*	*2001*
0	18.2	18.8	12.4	8.9	6.1	8.0	9.4	8.2
4		16.9	13.6	12.4	10.7	8.6	7.2	7.5
9			16.5	15.5	14.2	13.6	9.9	7.8
13				13.7	11.2	10.2	8.8	9.0
17					16.2	15.9	14.9	10.6
22						17.5	13.5	7.0
27							16.0	10.9
31								10.4

	Election							
	1970	*Feb 1974*	*1979*	*1983*	*1987*	*1992*	*1997*	*2001*

B. Percentage of 'very strong' party identifiers among 'Post-War', 'Macmillan', and 'Wilson' era age groups[b]

Age group (dates first entering electorate)

	1970	*Feb 1974*	*1979*	*1983*	*1987*	*1992*	*1997*	*2001*
Wilson era (1964–66)	26.1	18.7	15.8	17.2	15.4	17.9	14.5	15.7
Macmillan era (1951–59)	36.2	25.7	20.4	21.7	22.5	23.6	19.8	17.8
Attlee era (1945–50)	39.8	24.1	20.7	24.0	23.8	25.6	29.3	21.7

Note:

[a] Read table *diagonally* to determine percentage of very strong party identifiers among a specific age group at time of subsequent elections. For example, the percentage of very strong party identifiers among the 18–21 year-old age group entering the electorate in 1970 was 18.2. In 1974 the percentage of very strong party identifiers among *that* group was 16.9, in 1979, it was 16.5, etc.

[b] Read table *horizontally* to determine percentage of very strong party identifiers among specific age group at time of subsequent elections. For example, the percentage of very strong party identifiers among the Wilson era group was 26.1 in 1970, 18.7 in 1974, 15.8 in 1979, etc.

Source: 1970–2001 BES post-election surveys.

very strong identifiers and five have at least 1 per cent fewer very strong identifiers. The results when 1992 and 1987 are used as end-points are identical. Also, recalling the 1970–4 downward shift in the strength of party identification documented earlier, we note that there has been no general tendency for the percentage of very strong identifiers to increase, regardless of when the analysis *begins*.

We next compute the average strength of party identification on the 0–3 scale described above for the several age groups. Again, there is little evidence to indicate that party identification strengthens over the life cycle (see Table 6.2A and B). Consider the people first eligible to vote in 1970. At that time, the average strength

Table 6.2 Mean strength of party identification among groups of voters first entering the electorate between 1945 and 2001

		Election at which 18–21 year-old age groups entered electorate							
		1970	Feb 1974	1979	1983	1987	1992	1997	2001

A. Mean strength of party identification on 0–3 scale[b] for successive 18–21 year-old age groups entering the electorate between 1970 and 2001[a]

Years after initial entry									
	0	1.62	1.54	1.39	1.31	1.20	1.38	1.45	1.30
	4		1.71	1.58	1.42	1.43	1.51	1.31	1.34
	9			1.66	1.52	1.46	1.58	1.36	1.23
	13				1.50	1.59	1.56	1.46	1.36
	17					1.57	1.58	1.63	1.37
	22						1.65	1.64	1.38
	27							1.65	1.42
	31								1.64

		Election							
		1970	Feb 1974	1979	1983	1987	1992	1997	2001

B. Mean strength of party identification on 0–3 scale[b] for Wilson, Macmillan, and Post-War era age groups entering the electorate between 1945 and 1966[c]

Age group (dates first entering electorate)	1970	Feb 1974	1979	1983	1987	1992	1997	2001
Wilson era (1964–66)	1.80	1.65	1.60	1.64	1.61	1.76	1.60	1.60
Macmillan era (1951–59)	2.00	1.84	1.78	1.74	1.74	1.77	1.69	1.73
Attlee era (1945–50)	2.14	1.89	1.79	1.85	1.84	1.86	1.90	1.78

Note:

[a] Read table *diagonally* to determine mean strength of party identification for a specific age group at time of subsequent elections. For example, the mean strength of party identification for the 18–21 year-old age group entering the electorate in 1970 was 1.62. That group's mean strength of party identification was 1.71 in 1974, 1.66 in 1979, etc.

[b] Strength of party identification measured as: non-identification = 0, weak = 1, fairly strong = 2, very strong = 3.

[c] Read table *horizontally* to determine mean strength of party identification for a specific age group at time of subsequent elections. For example, the mean strength of party identification for the Wilson era group was 1.80 in 1970, 1.65 in 1974, 1.60 in 1979, etc.

Source: 1970–2001 BES post-election surveys.

of party identification for this group was 1.62. Thirty years later, it was essentially unchanged at 1.64. More generally, using 2001 as the end-point for the analysis, there was only one group whose average strength of party identification increased by at least one-tenth of a point, and six groups for which it decreased by at least that much. Using other years as end-points also indicates that there has not been a generalized tendency for party identification within particular age cohorts to strengthen over time. Over the three decades encompassed by the 1970–2001 BES surveys, the intensity of partisanship within age cohorts has varied—sometimes increasing, but more often decreasing. The partisanship-reinforcement mechanisms hypothesized by Converse are not apparent in these data. If they exist, their effects have been overwhelmed by other forces that have decreased the overall intensity of partisanship.

The pseudo panel data suggest what these other forces might be. First, it is evident that there are generational differences—successive cohorts of young people entering the electorate have not been as strongly partisan as once was the case. For example, Table 6.1 shows that 18 per cent of first-time voters in 1970 were very strong identifiers. In 2001, this figure had fallen to 8 per cent. The pattern is the same when one considers the average strength of party identification for first-time voters (Table 6.2). Even if, *ceteris paribus*, there are tendencies for party identification to strengthen over the political life cycle, the fact that successive groups of newly eligible voters have been less partisan than once was the case helps to explain the overall decline in the intensity of party identification. Second, period effects are also evident. For example, Table 6.2 shows that partisanship diminished by at least a tenth of a point in eight of ten age groups between 1997 and 2001. In contrast, between 1987 and 1992, there was an equally clear tendency for partisanship to increase. Data on the percentage of very strong identifiers show the same patterns for these 1997–2001 and 1987–92 comparisons (see Table 6.1). These results indicate that events and conditions associated with particular elections affect the strength of partisanship across multiple age groups.

INDIVIDUAL-LEVEL INSTABILITY

Aggregate-level data presented above do not make a conclusive case for or against the Michigan model of party identification. Data on *individual-level dynamics* constitute the 'acid test' for understanding the nature of party identification. As noted above, it would be ideal to have very long-term panels that track individual-level partisanship over a span of several decades. Although such data do not exist, several multi-wave panel surveys have been conducted since the 1960s. These panels are particularly useful for statistical analyses when they span four or more points in time. Figure 6.4 summarizes the individual-level dynamics of party identification in six four-wave panels. Contradicting what the Michigan model predicts, there is abundant evidence of substantial individual-level instability in party identification. In the most recent (1998–2001) panel, less than two-thirds of the respondents consistently identified with the same party. An additional, but very small, group (2 per cent) consistently denied that they were party identifiers. The remaining respondents—over one-third of all those interviewed—exhibit partisan instability of various kinds. Twenty per cent switched from one party to another, and an additional 14 per cent moved between being an identifier and being a non-identifier. These numbers are typical of those for other four-wave panel surveys conducted in the 1990s (see Figure 6.4).

Although the 1990s panel data reveal impressive dynamics in individual-level party identification, it might be conjectured that they reflect the dealigning trend discussed above. The proposed story is one in which substantial instability in party identification is a recent phenomenon and, if one examines panel data gathered in earlier decades, then the incidence of partisan instability is much smaller. However, this story is not true. Over one-third of the respondents in the 1974–9 BES panel reported changing their party identifications one or more times. Moreover, although British voters may once have lived in a 'golden age' of Michigan-style party identification, the 1964–70 BES panel data strongly contradict this idea. Figure 6.4 shows that the percentage of unstable identifiers in the 1964–70 panel approaches two-fifths of all those interviewed, with 28 per cent switching identifications one or more times and an additional 10 per cent moving between

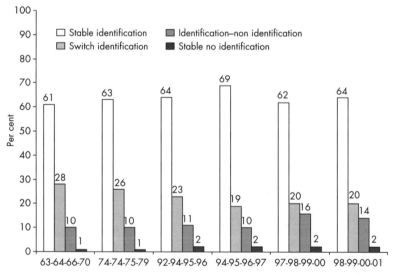

Figure 6.4 Dynamics of party identification in four-wave panels, 1963–2001
Source: 1963–2001 BES and BEPS panel surveys.

identification and nonidentification. Indeed, by a small margin, the percentage of unstable partisans in this panel exceeds that for any of the subsequent four-wave panels. Thus, partisan attachments in Britain have demonstrated considerable individual-level dynamism since at least the time that Butler and Stokes imported the concept of party identification from Ann Arbor to Nuffield.

Some analysts have expressed the idea that being a supporter of the Liberals or one of the minor parties is the British equivalent of American voters saying that they are 'independents' (e.g. Clarke and Zuk 1989). If so, then one might conjecture that partisan instability is largely confined to identifiers with the smaller parties who shift their declared partisan attachments in response to a changing mixture of short-term forces operating in the electoral arena at particular points in time. In contrast, those reporting that they are Conservatives or Labour are 'true identifiers' whose partisan attachments manifest impressive durability. Figure 6.5 shows that, in fact, identifiers with the Liberals or other smaller parties consistently report higher levels of instability than Conservative or Labour identifiers. However, rates of instability among the latter two groups are substantial. Across the 1963–70, four-wave panel, about three Conservative identifiers in ten abandoned their party, almost exactly the same proportion as in more recent panels. In the 1992–7 panel, instability in Conservative identification reached fully 44 per cent. Rates of instability in Labour identification are also substantial, ranging from 27 per cent to 31 per cent across various panels. Thus, instability has long been characteristic of major, as well as minor, party identifiers.

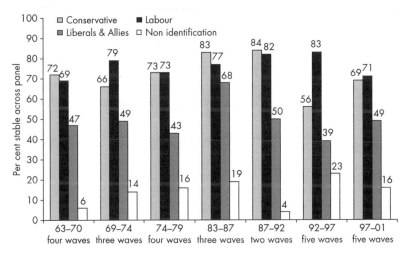

Figure 6.5 Stability of party identification across panel by initial party identification
Note: Switching patterns involving other parties included in calculations, but not shown in figure.
Source: 1963–2001 BES and BEPS panel surveys.

Dynamics of Party Identification

Latent Dynamics

The data in Figures 6.4 and 6.5 testify that party identification in Britain is much more mutable than many analysts have assumed. But, can we believe what these panel data are saying? As noted in Chapter Two, Green and his colleagues have argued that the *observed* instability in panel surveys is misleading because researchers fail to consider the effects of random measurement error (e.g. Green, Palmquist, and Schickler 2002). When random measurement error is taken into account, the dynamics of party identification in panel surveys are reduced to the low levels hypothesized by the Michigan model. Although most of the analyses by Green et al. have used American data, they report the same results using data from other countries including Britain (see Schickler and Green 1997).

Green et al. are not the first to advocate models of survey responses that incorporate random measurement error (Zaller 1992; Alvarez and Brehm 2002). Perhaps best known is Converse's (1964) famous 'black–white' model. Converse's core conjecture is that some people ('blacks') have real and stable orientations towards particular political objects, whereas others ('whites') do not have any real orientations. When asked about these orientations, people in the first group report them accurately, whereas members of the second group answer randomly. Applied to party identification, the 'black–white' model implies that some respondents do not have partisan attachments but, when queried, they invent one. These 'door-step' or 'top-of-the-head' party identifications are chosen at random from the options provided by the interviewer. When interviewed in the subsequent wave of a panel survey, people without real party identifications again answer randomly. Assuming several response categories (e.g. 'Conservative, Labour, Liberal Democrat, or what' in the traditional BES party identification question) are available, there is only a small probability that a respondent without a real party identification will select the same party on multiple occasions.[10] Assuming also that there is a sizeable number of random choosers in the surveys, one will observe considerable instability in party identification across several waves of interviewing. But, most of this observed instability is artefactual. This hypothesis deserves careful scrutiny. If party identification really is stable net of random measurement error, then the panel data reviewed above are misleading, and partisan attachments in Britain resemble what the Michigan model predicts.

We begin our assessment of the random measurement error hypothesis with a simple construct-validation analysis of observed individual-level dynamics of party identification in conjunction with the dynamics of other measures of partisan orientations. If movements in party identification are mostly random, then we would not expect them to correlate consistently and strongly with movements in these other measures. But, consistently strong correlations are exactly what we find. In BES and BEPS panels conducted over the past four decades, individual-level, over-time variations in party identification have strong and predictable relationships with over-time variations in the affective and evaluative components of party images.[11] For example, between 1997 and 2000, the mean change in feelings about the Conservative Party on a 1–5 point scale among people adopting a Conservative identification is positive (0.57) (see Table 6.3). Among those abandoning a Conservative identification, the mean change in such feelings is negative (−0.41). The correlation is strong and highly significant (eta = 0.46, p < 0.001). The pattern for comparable groups of Labour identifiers

Table 6.3 Patterns of changing party identification and changing party images in panel surveys

Panel	
A. 1966–70	Mean change in number of likes and dislikes about party
Party identification	
To Conservative	1.16
From Conservative	0.09
$\eta = 0.30, p = 0.000$	
To Labour	−0.08
From Labour	−1.31
$\eta = 0.29, p = 0.000$	
B. 1992–94	Mean change in feelings about party
Party identification	
To Conservative	−0.01
From Conservative	−1.64
$\eta = 0.46, p = 0.000$	
To Labour	1.14
From Labour	−0.64
$\eta = 0.62, p = 0.000$	
C. 1997–98	Mean change in feelings about party
Party identification	
To Conservative	0.57
From Conservative	−0.41
$\eta = 0.46, p = 0.000$	
To Labour	0.32
From Labour	−0.94
$\eta = 0.52, p = 0.000$	
D. 1997–98	Mean change in overall party image score
Party identification	
To Conservative	0.90
From Conservative	−0.39
$\eta = 0.39, p = 0.000$	
To Labour	0.19
From Labour	−0.89
$\eta = 0.34, p = 0.000$	

Source: 1966–70 BES panel survey; 1992–94 and 1997–2001 BEPS panel surveys.

is similar. Once more, the correlation is strong and significant (eta $= 0.52, p < 0.001$). Similar relationships also obtain in other panels, including the early 1966–70 one. The patterns are inconsistent with the hypothesis that partisan change is wholly random.

Although these analyses are suggestive, mixed Markov latent class models (MMLC) enable us to control for random measurement error and to analyze directly the stability of party identification at the latent variable level (see van der Pol, Langeheine, and Jong 1999; Hagenaars and McCutcheon 2002). Unlike the structural equation models used by Green, Palmquist, and Schickler,[12] MMLC does not require that the analyst impose an ordering on the categories of party identification. Thus, MMLC is useful in polities such as Britain where there are multiple parties, and ordering parties on a single underlying continuum may require problematic assumptions.[13] MMLC is also attractive because it is explicitly designed for estimating the parameters of 'mover-stayer' models in which some, but not all, of the participants in a panel survey change their responses one or more times. Converse's black–white model is a special case of such mover-stayer models where the movers shift randomly across the choice set provided by the interviewer. Here, we employ MMLC to investigate the latent-level dynamics of party identification in Britain using data for the six four-wave panels displayed in Figure 6.4.

We begin by specifying a general mover–stayer model for party identification in the 1997–2000 BEPS panel. Unlike Converse's black–white model, the general mover–stayer model does not assume that movers (unstable partisans) have an equal probability of shifting across various party identification categories. To ensure sufficient cases for analysis, we consider three party identification categories, Conservative, Labour, and others (Liberals/Liberal Democrats, Nationalists, minor party identifiers, and nonidentifiers). Controlling for random measurement error, this general mover–stayer MMLC model estimates that the proportions of unstable and stable party identifiers (called the 'mixture proportion' in Table 6.4) are 0.34 and 0.66, respectively, in the 1997–2000 panel. Stated otherwise, these numbers indicate that 34 per cent of the panel respondents had a non-zero probability of changing their party identifications, and 66 per cent had a zero probability of doing so, at some time between 1997 and 2000. The analysis shows that no type of party identifier is immune from change. Specifically, 43 per cent of those in the mover chain (group) were initially other party identifiers, 37 per cent were Conservatives, and 20 per cent were Labour.[14]

Although the mover chain in the 1997–2000 panel is sizeable, the transition probabilities for the movers indicate that identifiers with a given party were more likely to stay where they were than to go elsewhere. For example, Conservative identifiers in wave one of the panel had a 0.78 probability of being Conservative but a 0.14 probability of moving to Labour in wave two. Wave-one Labour identifiers had a 0.79 probability of remaining Labour and a 0.21 probability of shifting to the Liberal Democrats or another smaller party. For respondents in the 'other' category, the wave one/wave two probability of staying in that category was slightly less, 0.69. Thus, the MMLC analysis of the 1997–2000 panel data clearly

Table 6.4 Mixed Markov latent class model of the dynamics of party identification, 1997–2000 four-wave panel

	Movers	Stayers	
Mixture proportion (π)	0.34	0.66	
Initial state (δ)			
Conservative	0.37	0.28	
Labour	0.20	0.52	
Other	0.43	0.20	
Response probability (ρ)	True	True	
Conservative	0.78	0.99	
Labour	0.88	0.96	
Other	0.84	0.97	

Transition probabilities (τ) *for movers*

		Conservative	Labour	Other
Conservative:	1997–98	0.78	0.14	0.08
	1998–99	0.92	0.04	0.04
	1999–2000	1.00	0.00	0.00
Labour:	1997–98	0.00	0.79	0.21
	1998–99	0.08	0.92	0.00
	1999–2000	0.08	0.88	0.04
Other:	1997–98	0.10	0.21	0.69
	1998–99	0.00	0.02	0.98
	1999–2000	0.00	0.00	1.00

Latent turnover table—1997–2000 (row percentages)

		2000		
		Conservative	Labour	Other
1997	Conservative	73.9	14.6	11.5
	Labour	11.9	63.9	24.2
	Other	12.1	18.2	69.6

Model fit: $\chi^2 = 92.448$, $df = 55$, $p = 0.001$, AIC $= 10886.919$.

Source: 1997–98–99–2000 BEPS panel survey.

indicates that, although the dynamics of party identification in the mover group were substantial, they do not resemble the pattern that would be expected if movements between categories were random, as in Converse's black–white model. For Converse's model with three partisan categories, the transition probability for each would be 0.33. The latent-level turnover table tells the same story.[15] Across wave one to wave four of the panel, 74 per cent of the Conservative identifiers remained Conservative, 64 per cent of Labour identifiers remained Labour, and 70 per cent of those in the 'other' category stayed there.

MMLC analyses of other four-wave panels yield similar results. For example, the estimated proportion of respondents in the mover chain in the 1992–96 panel is quite sizeable, 0.37 (see Table 6.5). However, the transition probabilities are again far from equal levels (0.33) that would obtain if Converse's black–white model held. Also, in keeping with the fact that this panel spans the period when the aggregate share of Conservative identifiers fell sharply (see Figure 6.1), the initial state estimates indicate that a majority of those in the mover chain are Conservatives.[16] And the transition probabilities for the Conservatives across the first two waves of the panel (1992–4) suggest that a Conservative identifier *in the mover group* in 1992 had only a slightly better than 50–50 probability of being Conservative in 1994. Similarly, the latent turnover table across panel waves one to four indicates that only slightly over one-half of Conservative identifiers in the mover group in 1992 were Conservatives

Table 6.5   Mixed Markov latent class model of the dynamics of party identification, 1992–96 four-wave panel

		Movers	Stayers	
Mixture proportion (π)		0.37	0.63	
Initial state (δ)				
Conservative		0.55	0.38	
Labour		0.25	0.37	
Other		0.20	0.25	
Response probability (ρ)		*True*	*True*	
Conservative		0.98	0.97	
Labour		0.84	0.99	
Other		0.94	0.94	
Transition probabilities (τ) *for movers*				
		Conservative	Labour	Other
Conservative:	1992–94	0.56	0.15	0.29
	1994–95	0.74	0.05	0.21
	1995–96	0.95	0.04	0.01
Labour:	1992–94	0.00	1.00	0.00
	1994–95	0.00	0.99	0.01
	1995–96	0.02	0.98	0.00
Other:	1992–94	0.00	0.67	0.33
	1994–95	0.19	0.22	0.59
	1995–96	0.25	0.00	0.75
Latent turnover table—1992–96 (row percentages)				
			1996	
		Conservative	Labour	Other
1992	Conservative	52.2	25.5	22.3
	Labour	1.7	97.8	0.5
	Other	11.9	73.3	14.8

Model fit: $\chi^2 = 68.015$, $df = 55$, $p = 0.128$, AIC $= 5547.173$.

Source: 1992–94–95–96 BEPS panel survey.

four years later. Even greater change is evident for the 'other' category. Among those in this category who were in the mover chain in 1992, only slightly over one in ten was in the 'other' category in 1996. In sharp contrast, and consonant with the surge in Labour partisanship in the mid-1990s, virtually all (98 per cent) of the 1992 Labour identifiers in the mover chain were Labour identifiers in 1996.

The MMLC analyses show substantial latent-level dynamics in party identification in recent years. This is inconsistent with the high levels of partisan stability as argued by Green et al. and other proponents of Michigan-style partisanship. But, what about earlier time periods? Particularly interesting in this regard are the results of a MMLC analysis of the 1963–70 panel data. This analysis decisively rejects the conjecture that the 1960s were an era of Michigan-style partisan stability in Britain. As Table 6.6 shows, the proportion of panelists with a non-zero probability of changing party identification (the mover chain) was 0.31. There are substantial numbers of Conservative, Labour, and other types of partisans in the mover group. Once more, the transition probabilities for this 1963–70 panel are inconsistent with the idea that 'black–white' dynamics describe movements across adjacent panel waves. Between 1963 and 1964, the probabilities that Conservatives and Labour identifiers would abandon their party were nontrivial. Perhaps even more impressive are the latent level wave one to wave four mobility figures. These show that slightly over half of the Conservatives in the mover group changed their party identification between 1963 and 1970. Similarly, almost two-thirds of the Labour identifiers in the mover group changed their identification over the seven years of the panel.

MMLC analyses of other BES and BEPS four-wave panels tell similar stories. Figure 6.6 summarizes data on the estimated sizes of the mover and stayer chains in

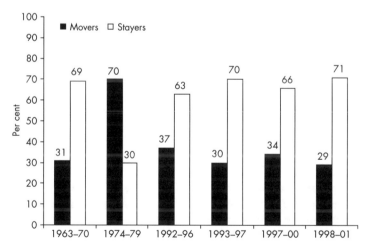

Figure 6.6 Sizes of mover and stayer groups estimated by mixed Markov latent class models
Source: 1963–2001 BES and BEPS panel surveys.

Table 6.6   Mixed Markov latent class model of the dynamics of party
identification, 1963–70 four–wave panel

		Movers	Stayers	
Mixture proportion (π)		0.31	0.69	
Initial state (δ)				
Conservative		0.22	0.45	
Labour		0.36	0.38	
Other		0.43	0.17	
Response probability (ρ)		*True*	*True*	
Conservative		0.97	0.94	
Labour		0.94	0.99	
Other		0.88	0.25	

Transition probabilities (τ) *for movers*

		Conservative	Labour	Other
Conservative:	1963–64	0.55	0.23	0.23
	1964–66	0.55	0.41	0.05
	1966–70	0.72	0.17	0.10
Labour:	1963–64	0.29	0.63	0.08
	1964–66	0.11	0.72	0.16
	1966–70	0.47	0.53	0.00
Other:	1963–64	0.00	0.00	1.00
	1964–66	0.03	0.02	0.96
	1966–70	0.22	0.07	0.71

Latent turnover table—1963–70 (horizontal percentages)

			1970	
		Conservative	Labour	Other
1963	Conservative	48.4	28.3	23.3
	Labour	48.2	35.7	16.1
	Other	23.4	08.4	68.2

Model fit: $\chi^2 = 82.618$, $df = 52$, $p = 0.004$, AIC $= 4725.681$.

Source: 1963–64–66–70 BES panel survey.

all of the four-wave panels. As the figure shows, with one exception, the mover group
varies between about three in ten (1998–2001 panel) to about four in ten (1992–6
panel). The exception is the 1974–79 panel where the size of the mover group reaches
fully seven in ten. This is the era of dealignment as studied by Crewe, Sarlvik, and Alt
(1977) (see also Sarlvik and Crewe 1983). Thus, the general conclusion of the several
MMLC analyses is straightforward. Controlling for random measurement error, party
identification in Britain has always exhibited impressive individual-level dynamics.

There have been more stayers than movers, but the latter has consistently exceeded what would be expected if partisan attachments were stable.

There is more. The general mover–stayer models can be compared with rival models of the (non)dynamics of partisanship. One rival is Converse's black–white model which, as noted, imposes equal probabilities on the transition matrices for the mover group. Another rival is a core version of the Michigan model, which does away altogether with the mover chain and specifies that everyone is a stayer. Table 6.7

Table 6.7 Rival mixed Markov latent class models of the dynamics of party identification

A. Goodness of fit

		χ^2	df	p
1963–70:	Mover–stayer: general	82.62	52	0.004
	Mover–stayer: black–white	223.02	66	0.000
	All stayer	158.79	55	0.000
1974–79:	Mover–stayer: general	48.56	52	0.610
	Mover–stayer: black–white	100.16	66	0.004
	All stayer	89.37	55	0.002
1992–96:	Mover–stayer: general	67.02	55	0.128
	Mover–stayer: black–white	295.97	66	0.000
	All stayer	190.48	55	0.000
1994–97:	Mover–stayer: general	36.15	55	0.977
	Mover–stayer: black–white	137.76	66	0.000
	All stayer	124.08	54	0.000
1997–2000	Mover–stayer: general	92.45	55	0.001
	Mover–stayer: black–white	306.67	66	0.000
	All stayer	205.75	54	0.000
1998–2001:	Mover–stayer: general	68.75	54	0.085
	Mover–stayer: black–White	256.21	67	0.000
	All stayer	234.50	54	0.000

B. Akaike information criterion (smaller is better)

		Mover–stayer Models	
Panel	General	Black–white	All stayer
1963–70	4725.68★	4824.08	4783.86
1974–79	3367.23★	3376.83	3390.04
1992–96	5547.17★	5734.12	5652.64
1994–97	4935.62★	4995.23	5005.54
1997–2000	10886.92★	11059.14	10982.22
1998–2001	8274.93★	8420.39	8422.68

★ Smallest value.

Source: 1963–2001 BES and BEPS four-wave panel surveys.

summarizes the results of estimating the alternative models for the six four-wave panels. As indicated by its smaller chi-square values, the general mover–stayer model consistently has a better fit with the data than its rivals. The Akaike Information Criterion (AIC), which discounts model fit in terms of the number of parameters estimated (Burnham and Anderson 1998; see also ch. 4), also suggests the superiority of the general mover–stayer model. In all cases, the AIC for the general mover–stayer model is smaller than those for its rivals. In sum, analyses of the several BES and BEPS panel surveys strongly indicate that party identification in Britain has dynamic properties. These dynamics are not novel—they have existed since at least the first BES panels were conducted in the 1960s.

ASKING THE WRONG QUESTION?

The evidence presented above testifies that party identification in Britain is not the unmoved mover of Michigan lore. Impressive individual-level instability in responses to the standard BES party identification questions is apparent both in simple turnover tables, as well as in more sophisticated analyses that take into account random measurement error in survey responses. However, before accepting the conclusion that there are substantial individual-level dynamics in party identification, a critic might protest that the problem with the preceding analyses is that they are based on responses to the wrong question (e.g. see Bartle 2001; Blais et al. 2002). The critique is similar to the argument motivating Converse's black–white model. The hypothesis is that the standard BES question—'Generally speaking, do you think of yourself as Conservative, Labour, Liberal Democrat, or what?'—cues respondents to accept a party label and, thus, it inflates estimates of the proportion of party identifiers in the electorate and the proportion who switch their identifications over time. More specifically, some respondents are not true identifiers, but when prompted to select a party, they oblige the interviewer and do so. When asked in a subsequent interview about their party identification, these people again provide one, but because they are not true identifiers, there is a substantial probability that they choose a different party than the first time. Wording a party identification question in a way that does not cue respondents to choose a party would reduce the number of identifiers *and* reveal that partisan stability is much more prevalent than responses to the traditional question lead one to believe.

Data gathered in successive waves of the British Household Panel Survey (BHPS) enable us to test the wrong-question hypothesis. In the BHPS, respondents are asked if they think of themselves as 'party supporters'.[17] Answers to this question sequence show that the proportion of self-acknowledged party supporters at any point in time is much lower than the proportion of party identifiers as measured by the BES question. However, analyses of responses to the BHPS question do not suggest an absence of dynamics. Although the proportion of stable non-supporters (approximately one-third of those participating in three-year rolling BHPS panels conducted between 1991 and 1997) is much larger than the proportion of nonidentifiers in the BES and BEPS panels (see Figure 6.4), overall levels of insta-bility are very substantial among BHPS panelists. The percentages changing their answers to the party supporter question range from 46 per cent in the 1995–7 panel to 52 per cent in the 1991–3 panel (Sanders, Burton, and Kneeshaw 2002).

The British Social Attitudes (BSA) surveys provide another opportunity to study the impact of using alternative question wording to measure partisan attachments.[18] The BSA surveys consistently reveal that large numbers of people do not think of themselves as party supporters. In 15 such surveys conducted between 1983 and 1999, the percentage stating that they are not party supporters ranges from a low of 49 per cent (1989, 1990) to a high of 61 per cent (1999), and it averages 54 per cent. Also similar to the BHPS, there is considerable individual-level instability in answers to the party supporter question, with slightly over 40 per cent of those in a 1983–6 BSA panel changing their responses one or more times. Rather than shifting directly between parties, nearly nine in ten of these people moved from being a party supporter to being a nonsupporter or vice versa.

To provide a direct comparison of alternative measures of partisan attachments, we asked the BSA party supporter question in the 2001 BES. To prevent mutual contamination of the two question sequences, they were widely separated in the survey instrument and their ordering was randomized. Since both sequences were asked in the pre- and the post-election surveys, it is possible to investigate differ-ences in the dynamics of responses to them.

Answers to the 2001 BES party supporter questions are similar to those in the BHPS and BSA surveys. Table 6.8 shows that, in both the pre- and post-election 2001 BES surveys, the percentage that stated that they were party supporters is much lower than the percentage selecting a party in response to the traditional party identification question. In the pre-election survey, approximately 50 per cent said they were not party supporters, but only 21 per cent did not accept a party when answering the traditional question. In the post-election survey, the compa-rable figures are 41 per cent and 16 per cent. However, as in the BHPS and BSA studies, there is considerable over-time instability in answers to the party supporter questions in the 2001 BES. Over the brief period between the pre- and post-election waves of interviewing, slightly over 26 per cent of the panelists changed their answers to the party supporter question, with an overwhelming majority of these people moving between being a supporter and being a nonsupporter. The total instability in responses to the traditional question is almost identical and, again, a large majority of switchers indicated that they had moved between identification and nonidentification.

Thus, alternative question wordings do not produce levels of partisan stability commensurate with those predicted by the Michigan model. Data gathered in a

Dynamics of Party Identification

Table 6.8 Responses to traditional party identification question and alternative party supporter question

	Pre-election survey		Post-election survey	
	Party identification	Party supporter	Party identification	Party supporter
A. Responses in pre- and post-election cross-sectional surveys				
Labour	41.6%	28.4%	44.4%	33.3%
Conservative	24.9	16.9	24.4	18.8
Liberal Democrat	8.9	3.1	11.0	5.3
Scottish Nationalist	1.6	1.0	1.6	1.2
Plaid Cymru	0.3	0.2	0.4	0.2
Greens	0.6	0.2	0.8	0.3
Other Party	1.1	0.4	1.4	0.2
None, D.K./not supporter	21.0	49.8	16.0	40.7
(N)	(3,163)	(3,191)	(2,989)	(2,994)

	Party identification	Party supporter		
B. Patterns of partisanship in pre–post-election panel survey				
Stable partisans				
Labour	37.1%	24.7%		
Conservative	20.1	13.8		
Liberal Democrat	6.4	2.3		
Scottish Nationalist	1.2	0.6		
Plaid Cymru	0.2	0.1		
Greens	0.4	0.2		
Other Party	0.1	0.1		
Total stable partisans	65.5	41.8		
Stable non-identifier/ non-supporter	8.9	32.0		
Total stable	74.4	73.8		
To<−>From identification/supporter	16.7	24.0		
Switch party identification/supported	9.9	2.2		
(N)	(2,266)	(2,282)		

Source: 2001 BES pre- and post-election cross-sectional and panel surveys.

variety of panel studies conducted over the past two decades indicate that substantial minorities switch back and forth between claiming to be a party supporter and claiming not to be one. As predicted by critics of the traditional party identification question, the BHPS, BSA, and BES surveys do reveal that levels of partisanship in Britain are lower than responses to the traditional question indicate. This finding also characterizes data gathered in several surveys conducted in 1998 and 1999 (Sanders, Burton, and Kneeshaw 2002). But, given that responses to the party supporter question also indicate that partisan attachments have considerable mutability, the lower incidence of party supporters is hardly good news for the Michigan model. One cannot use data generated by party supporter-type questions to portray partisan attachments as wide-spread, stable elements in the psychology of the British electorate. Rather, the overall impression conveyed by answers to party supporter questions is one of stable parti-sans, being the exception, not the rule. In the next section, we develop models of the forces that affect the dynamics of partisanship over time.

MODELLING DYNAMICS

The Individual Level

It is not novel to argue that party identification has dynamic properties. As discussed in Chapter Two, over the past two decades a number of analysts have rejected the idea that party identification does not change and they have devel-oped models of its individual-level dynamics. Although differing in detail, these models propose that voters are at least rough-and-ready utility maximizers who update their existing party identifications using information about the actual or anticipated performance of political parties. *Pace* Bartels (2002), these models do not require that the information used to update party identification be unbiased in the sense that it is totally free from the influence of existing party identification. It may be sensible for voters to use their existing party identification as a heuristic device to help them simplify their search for and interpretation of new informa-tion. Deliberation costs are thereby reduced (Conlisk 1996). This new information is not wholly redundant to existing party identifications; it is used to update these identifications. Since the updating process is ongoing and may reinforce or erode an existing partisan attachment, party identification becomes, in Fiorina's (1981) widely used phrase, a 'running tally' of current and past party performance evalua-tions. The process may be represented as:

$$\text{PID}_{it} = f\beta_0 + \lambda_1 \text{PID}_{it-1} + \Sigma\beta_k X_{kt}$$

where, PID_{it} is the party identification for voter i at time t; X_{kt}, party performance evaluations weighted by parameters β_k; λ, the effect of time $t-1$ party identifica-tion on time t party identification; β_0 is a constant.

In this model, a voter i begins with an initial party identification at time $t = 0$. Some analysts (e.g. Achen 2002) have interpreted this PID_{i0} as reflecting the effects of parental and other early-life socialization experiences. The λ parameter measures the rate at which voters discount information encapsulated in their existing party identi-fications. If λ equals 1.0, then existing information is never discounted, and all current and past party performance evaluations, as well as various random shocks, simply accu-mulate at their full values through time. If one hypothesizes that voters rely less on older information, then it follows that the λ parameter is less than 1.0. The β_k's capture the effects of current party performance evaluations. β_0 may be interpreted as a baseline indicator of partisanship in the electorate at time t. This would occur if voters had perfectly balanced evaluations of current and prior party performance.[19]

The BES and BEPS panels contain the data needed to estimate the parameters in this model. Here, we focus on the recent 1997–98 and 1992–94 panels and the early 1966–70 panel. We measure party identification in two ways. In one set of analyses, we construct seven-point measures of the direction and strength of Labour, Conservative, and Liberal Democrat party identification. For example, the Conservative measure ranges from very strong Conservative identifier (scored $+3$) to nonidentifier (scored 0) to very strong other party identifier (scored -3). In a second set of analyses, we focus strictly on the direction of identification with these parties. In this set, we use three-point measures, ranging, for example, from Conservative (scored $+1$), to nonidentifier (scored 0), to other party identifier (scored -1). Measures of party performance evaluations vary depending on the set of questions asked in particular surveys. These questions concern evaluations of national and/or personal economic conditions, evaluations of government performance in various policy areas, and judgements of which party leader would make the best prime minister.[20] Variables measuring social class and age cohort are also included in the model to control for the possibility that any observed effects of time $t-1$ party identification and time t party performance evaluations are, in fact, spurious—that is, products of voters' class locations or cohort-specific socialization experiences. Model parameters are estimated using an instrumental variables regression procedure.[21]

The results are presented in Table 6.9. Parameter estimates accord well with expectations. In every analysis, time $t-1$ (prior) party identification has significant, positive effects on time t (current) party identification and all coefficients are less than 1.0 in magnitude. This indicates that previous information stored in an existing party identification is progressively discounted as new information becomes available. Variables measuring the effects of new information also operate as anticipated. For example, in the 1997–98 panel, voters who judged economic conditions favourably, and evaluated government performance positively, were more likely to identify with the governing Labour Party than voters who judged economic conditions unfavourably and evaluated government performance negatively. Net of these effects, voters who thought that Tony Blair would make the best prime minister were more likely to identify with Labour, and those who favoured William Hague were less likely to do so. The results for the 1997–98 analyses of Conservative identification also make sense. As expected with a Labour government in power, favourable economic and government performance evaluations lowered the likelihood of being a Conservative identifier. Similarly, voters who thought Blair would make the best prime minister were less likely to be Conservative identifiers, and those who judged that Hague would make the best prime minister were more likely to be Conservatives.

Table 6.9 Models of the individual-level dynamics of party identification

Predictor variables	Conservative		Labour		Liberal Democrat	
	7pt	3pt	7pt	3pt	7pt	3pt
A. 1997–98 BEPS panel						
			1998 Party identification			
Party identification (t−1)	0.77***	0.81***	0.75***	0.81***	0.44*	0.42*
Government performance(t)	−0.02***	−0.01**	0.03***	0.02***	−0.02*	−0.01*
Economic evaluations(t)	−0.02*	−0.01	0.03***	0.01*	−0.01	−0.00
Best prime minister:						
Blair(t)	−0.12***	−0.06***	0.17***	0.08***	−0.10***	−0.05***
Hague(t)	0.10***	0.06***	−0.04*	−0.02*	−0.04*	−0.03**
Ashdown(t)	−0.05***	−0.03***	−0.02	−0.02*	0.16**	0.11***
Social class	0.05***	0.03***	−0.04**	−0.02*	0.01	0.01
Age cohort:						
Blair	−0.16*	−0.09	0.22*	0.15*	0.32*	0.09
Thatcher/Major	−0.05	−0.02	0.16*	0.09*	0.14	0.01
Wilson/Callaghan	−0.00	0.02	0.13*	0.07*	0.13	0.03
Macmillan et al.	0.05	0.03	−0.07	−0.00	0.11	0.01
Constant	0.58***	0.14	−1.33***	−0.55***	−0.46	−0.37*
Adjusted R^2 = (N = 2677)	0.67	0.62	0.63	0.56	0.44	0.39
B. 1992–94 BEPS panel						
			1994 Party identification			
Predictor variables						
Party identification (t−1)	0.63***	0.64***	0.76***	0.83***	0.52***	0.50***
Government performance(t)	0.03***	0.02***	−0.02**	−0.01***	0.02**	0.01
Economic evaluations(t)	0.05***	0.02***	−0.04***	−0.01**	−0.00	−0.00
Best prime minister:						
Smith/Blair(t)	−0.12***	−0.07***	0.12***	0.06***	−0.14***	−0.05***
Major(t)	0.13***	0.09***	−0.02	−0.02	−0.13***	−0.07***
Ashdown(t)	−0.10***	−0.07***	−0.04*	−0.02*	0.18***	0.12***
Social class	0.04**	0.03**	−0.05*	−0.02*	0.06***	0.02*
Age cohort:						
Thatcher/Major	−0.06	−0.05	0.16*	0.10*	0.10	−0.03
Wilson/Callaghan	0.00	−0.02	0.03	0.00	0.05	−0.05
Macmillan et al.	0.13*	0.04	−0.06	0.01	−0.00	−0.04
Constant	−1.36***	−0.67	0.93***	0.50***	−0.83***	−0.42***
Adjusted R^2 (N = 2159)	0.66	0.60	0.59	0.54	0.39	0.33

Dynamics of Party Identification

Table 6.9 Continued

Predictor variables	Conservative		Labour		Liberal Democrat	
	7pt	3pt	7pt	3pt	7pt	3pt
A. 1966–70 BES Panel						
			1970 Party identification			
Party identification($t-1$)	0.48★★★	0.47★★★	0.43★★★	0.37★★★	0.54★★★	0.49★★★
Party closest on issues(t)	0.42★★★	0.16★★★	−0.42★★★	−0.18★★★	0.01	0.01
Gov. ec. performance(t)	−0.23★★★	−0.10★★★	0.24★★★	0.09★★★	0.04	0.02
Best prime minister						
Wilson(t)	−0.15★★★	−0.05★★★	0.16★★★	0.05★★★	−0.03	−0.01
Heath(t)	0.13★★★	0.04★★	−0.14★★★	−0.05★★★	0.00	−0.00
Social class	0.09★★	0.03★	−0.13★★★	−0.06★★★	−0.00	0.01
Age cohort						
Wilson	0.07	−0.04	−0.07	0.03	0.38★★	0.07
Macmillan et al.	0.09	0.04	−0.00	0.01	0.29★★	0.06
Post-war	−0.03	−0.02	−0.07	−0.01	0.27★★	0.04
Constant	0.41	0.16	−0.48	−0.16	−1.05★★★	−0.46★★★
Adjusted R^2	0.70	0.61	0.71	0.65	0.33	0.26
($N = 1066$)						

Note: All models estimated with instrumental variables for party identification at $t-1$, except for Liberal party identification 1966–70 which is estimated using OLS.
★★★ $p \le 0.001$; ★★ $p \le 0.01$; ★ $p \le 0.05$, one-tailed test.

Source: 1966–70 BES two-wave panel survey, and 1992–94, 1997–98 BEPS two-wave panel surveys.

Similar results obtain for the 1966–70 panel. In this case, current party identification again reflects evaluations of the performance of parties and their leaders net of prior party identification and the effects of social class and age cohort. Nor is it the case that the models using the 1966–70 panel data are pale reflections of those for the 1990s. The 1966–70 models explain large percentages of the variance in 1970 Conservative and Labour party identifications, and all of the evaluation variables are correctly signed and statistically significant. The 1966–70 models do less well in accounting for the dynamics of Liberal identification, but this is also true for the 1990s panels. In this regard, the percentage of variance explained for the Liberal Democrat model is largest for the 1997–98 panel, which is the only case when a Liberal Democrat party leader evaluation variable is available.

These analyses of the individual-level dynamics of party identification contradict the spirit of the original Michigan model. Rare party realignments aside, the canonical *American Voter* version of the model says that party identification at time $t-1$ should drive party identification at time t. Current (time t) evaluations of parties and their leaders are strongly influenced by $t-1$ party identifications and, when the latter is controlled, party and leader evaluations have little, if any, effect on time *t* party identification. The results also contradict the spirit of the Butler–Stokes version of the Michigan model. In the core Butler and Stokes model, all variables, except social class, should fail to affect current (time *t*) party identification. Even prior (time *t* − 1) party identification should fail. The statistical relationship between party identification at times *t* and *t* − 1 derives from the fact that partisan attachments are stable products of enduring class identities. Hence, if class is controlled, then the statistical relationship between party identification at different points in time should disappear. But, analyses of panel data gathered since the 1960s strongly gainsay these predictions. Neither version of the Michigan model can account for the individual-level dynamics of party identification in Britain.

The Aggregate Level

Although individual-level analyses are highly informative, aggregate-level data are especially useful to assess the dynamics of party identification. To generate the time series data required for such analyses, we have included the standard BES party identification question sequence in monthly Gallup surveys conducted since January 1992. By using the BES question battery, we are able to avoid the question-wording controversy that has bedevilled research on the aggregate dynamics of party identification in the United States (see, e.g. Abramson and Ostrom 1992, 1994; MacKuen, Erikson, and Stimson 1992a). The resulting time series enables us to track short-term movements in party identification over an 11-year interval, and to investigate factors that influence those movements.

The Gallup time series data on identification with the Conservative, Labour, and Liberal Democrat parties for the January 1992–December 2002 period are displayed in Figure 6.7. As the figure shows, the percentage of Conservative identifiers fell below the Labour percentage shortly before the September 1992 ERM crisis. Subsequently, the Conservatives always had fewer identifiers than Labour. Over the entire 11-year period, the Conservative share averaged 27 per cent, as compared to 41 per cent for Labour, and 12 per cent for the Liberal Democrats. It is also noteworthy that identification with all three parties varied substantially over time. The Conservative percentage moved by 16 points, ranging from a high of 37 per cent in February 1992 to a low of 21 per cent in May 1996. As for Labour, its share varied by fully 24 points, with the cohort of Labour identifiers ranging from slightly below 30 per cent in February 1992 to nearly 54 per cent in October 1997. After that high point, Labour partisanship receded, albeit irregularly, to 36 per cent in December 2002. Liberal Democrat identification also varied considerably—climbing from a low of 7 per cent in January 1997 to a high of 19 per cent in September 1993. In December 2002, the percentage of Liberal Democrats (12 per cent) was exactly what it had been 11 years earlier.

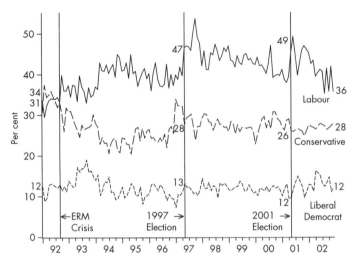

Figure 6.7 Dynamics of party identification, January 1992–December 2002
Source: 1992–2002 PSCB and P&D surveys.

To see trends in the Gallup data more clearly, we employ the nearest neighbour regression technique,[22] regressing Labour, Conservative, and Liberal Democrat party identification on time. The results show that Labour enjoyed a prolonged surge in party identification from 1992 onward, peaking shortly after its resounding general election victory in 1997 (see Figure 6.8). Afterward, although there was substantial variation in the monthly percentage of Labour identifiers, the overall pattern shows a slow downward trend. Conservative identification followed a very different course—falling sharply between 1992 and 1995, then partially recovering in the run-up to the 1997 election. Since shortly after that election, the underlying pattern has been quite stable, with the Conservative percentage of party identifiers varying between 25 and 30 per cent. The Liberal Democrat pattern was different again; although there were modest upward and downward swings, the overall trend line has been quite flat.

Can these aggregate-level movements in party identification be explained by changes in evaluations of the performance of political parties and their leaders? The Gallup surveys are useful for answering this question because they inquire about voters' national and personal economic evaluations, as well as their opinions about which party leader would make the best prime minister. These data enable us to specify models of the aggregate dynamics of party identification. However, before doing so, it is necessary to consider whether the data are characterized by trends in the technical sense of that term. In the language of time series analysis, trending variables are said to be *nonstationary*; that is, they lack constant means and/or variances.

Dynamics of Party Identification

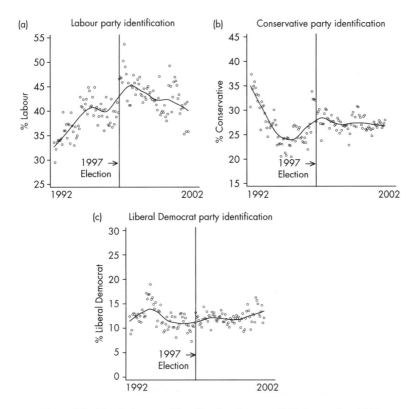

Figure 6.8　Trends in party identification, January 1992–December 2002

Note: Trend lines are generated using nearest neighbour regression, with polynomial degree 1 and bandwidth 0.3

Source: January 1992–December 2002 PSCB and P&D surveys.

As Granger and Newbold (1974) demonstrated, analyzing nonstationary variables[23] frequently produces 'spurious regressions' that pose serious threats to inference.

Some analysts (e.g. Box-Steffensmeier and Smith 1996) contend that nonstationary processes are unlikely to characterize time series data for variables such as party identification because they imply that support for particular parties could increase or decrease without limit. In substantive terms, this would mean that party systems lack mooring—no forces would be at work to restore party competition (Stokes and Iversen 1966; see also Bartolini and Mair 1990). It is more likely that the aggregate-level evolution of party support is driven by 'long memory' or 'fractionally integrated' processes (e.g. Beran 1994). If so, then levels of support for particular parties may drift upward or downward for lengthy periods of time, but will eventually move back toward a very long-run central tendency. Thus, a party's cohort of identifiers may increase for several years but not forever. Long-memory processes in time series data on party identification also are interesting because, as Granger (1980) has shown (see also Box-Steffensmeier and Smith 1997; Wlezien 2000), long-memory may result from aggregating heterogeneous individual-level data. In this regard, analyses presented above consistently indicate the presence of mover and stayer groups of party identifiers in the individual-level BES and BEPS panel data.

The simplest model for a long-memory process is: $(1-L)^d Y_t = \epsilon_t$ where ϵ_t is a random shock at time t, L is a backshift operator, and d is a fractional differencing parameter (Franses 1998). If d equals 1.0, then the process is a random walk and, hence, nonstationary.[24] If d is greater than or equal to 0.5, but less than 1.0, a long memory process is nonstationary, although it is ultimately mean reverting. As noted above, nonstationary processes invite so-called 'spurious regressions' and, hence, it is important to determine whether time series variables are nonstationary. One way of doing this is to estimate the value of their d parameters.[25] Here, we do so for the party identification series, as well as the variables measuring the monthly balance of different kinds of positive versus negative economic evaluations and monthly judgements of who would make the best prime minister.[26]

Table 6.10 shows that the d values for all of these series are greater than 0.5, thereby indicating that they are nonstationary. However, in most cases, d is significantly less than 1.0 ($p < 0.05$). As per the discussion above, such data are said to possess long memory. Substantively, the values of d for the party identification series confirm the visual impressions of trends in these series in Figure 6.8. Between 1992 and 2002, the party identification variables moved, albeit at different rates, in one direction for lengthy periods, but they did not do so indefinitely. As noted above, the presence of long memory in the party identification time series data also is consistent with the data being generated by mover–stayer processes at the individual level.

Given that the time series variables of interest have long memory and are nonstationary, we analyze the determinants of party identification by specifying fractional error correction (FEC) models (Clarke and Lebo 2003). These models enable us to study both the short- and long-term effects of various independent variables on party identification. A general FEC model for the dynamics of party identification is:

$$\Delta^d \text{PID}_t = f(\beta_0 + \beta_1 \Delta^d \text{BESTPM}_t + \beta_2 \Delta^d \text{EVAL}_t - \alpha(\text{PID}_{t-1} - \gamma_1 \text{BESTPM}_{t-1} - \gamma_2 \text{EVAL}_{t-1}) + \Sigma\beta_{3-k} \text{EVENTS}_{t-i})$$

where: PID_t = party identification t;

BESTPM_t = best prime minister at time t;

EVAL_t = economic evaluations (personal prospective, personal retrospective, national prospective, national retrospective) at time t;

EVENTS_{t-i} = various important events;

Δ^d is the fractional differencing operator;[27]

d, β, α, and γ are parameters to be estimated.

Dynamics of Party Identification

Table 6.10 Estimates of the fractional differencing parameter, d

Time series variables	d	s.e.
Party identification		
Conservative	0.63	0.07
Labour	0.54	0.07
Liberal Democrat	0.52	0.08
Best Prime Minister		
Major/Hague/Duncan-Smith	0.89[a]	0.07
Kinnock/Smith/Blair	0.85[a]	0.08
Ashdown/Kennedy	0.76	0.08
Economic evaluations		
Personal retrospective	0.74	0.07
Personal prospective	0.61	0.06
National retrospective	0.93[a]	0.08
National prospective	0.82[a]	0.09

[a] Fails to reject null hypothesis that $d = 1.0$, $p = 0.05$.

Source: January 1992–December 2002 monthly PSCB and P&D monthly surveys.

In this model, β_1 and β_2 measure the short-term effects of best prime minister judgements and economic evaluations. The term $(PID_{t-1} - \gamma_1 PM_{t-1} - \gamma_2 EVAL_{t-1})$ is an error correction mechanism (e.g. Hendry 1995) which captures the long-term effects of these variables on party identification. The α parameter measures the rate at which shocks to party identification from whatever source are eroded by the long-run relationship between party identification on the one hand, and party leader performance judgements and economic evaluations on the other.[28] If α equals 0, then this means that reactions to economic conditions and party leaders do not have long-term effects on party identification. Any effects of the former variables on the latter are short term and are captured by the β_1 and β_2 parameters.

To address controversies regarding the impact of different kinds of economic evaluations on party support (see Chapter Two), we specify four FEC models of Labour and Conservative party identification. One of the four types of economic evaluations—personal retrospections, personal prospections, national prospections, and national retrospections—appears in each model. With respect to the best prime minister judgements, the percentage selecting the Conservative leader is included in the analysis of Conservative party identification, and the percentage selecting the Labour leader is used in the analysis of Labour party identification. A parsimonious set of variables measuring the impact of important events is also included in the models. In the Labour model, these include the ERM crisis (September 1992), the change in Clause Four of Labour's constitution (April 1995), the 1997 and 2001 elections, the petrol protest (September 2000), the terrorist attack on the World Trade Center (September 2001 or 9/11), and the ensuing war in Afghanistan

(September 2001–January 2002).[29] Events in the Conservative model are the ERM crisis, Clause Four, and the 1997 election.

Table 6.11 presents parameter estimates for the Labour party identification models. The model using personal retrospective economic evaluations performs

Table 6.11   Error correction models of Labour party identification,
April 1992–December 2002

	Models			
Predictor variables	Personal retrospective β	Personal prospective β	National retrospective β	National prospective β
ΔBest prime minister (*t*)	0.25★★★	0.28★★★	0.29★★★	0.26★★★
Economic evaluations				
ΔPersonal retrospections (*t*)	0.14★★	*x*	*x*	*x*
ΔPersonal prospections (*t*)	*x*	0.04	*x*	*x*
ΔNational retrospections (*t*)	*x*	*x*	0.02	*x*
ΔNational prospections (*t*)	*x*	*x*	*x*	0.04ª
Error correction mechanism				
Party identification (*t*−1)	−0.41★★★	−0.41★★★	−0.35★★★	−0.38★★★
Best prime minister (*t*−1)	0.31★★★	0.28★★★	0.24★★★	0.15★
Personal retrospections (*t*−1)	0.17★★	*x*	*x*	*x*
Personal prospections (*t*−1)	*x*	0.12★★	*x*	*x*
National retrospections (*t*−1)	*x*	*x*	0.08★	*x*
National prospections (*t*−1)	*x*	*x*	*x*	0.04
Shocks				
ERM crisis (*t*−1)	3.28ª	3.90ª	3.42ª	3.86ª
Clause four (*t*−1)	−3.25ª	−3.39ª	−3.33ª	−3.05
1997 election (*t*)	4.25★	4.69★	4.36★	3.99ª
Petrol crisis (*t*−1)	−2.23★★★	−2.55★★★	−1.64★	−2.43★★★
2001 election (*t*)	2.29	2.60	3.57ª	3.06
9/11 and Afghan war	2.20★	3.27★★	2.96★★	3.83★★★
Constant	13.14★★★	14.49★★★	13.01★★★	15.89★★★
Adjusted R^2	0.47	0.43	0.42	0.41
AIC	−293.27	−298.12	−299.71	−300.65
DW	1.69	1.59	1.75	1.64
Serial correlation (12 lags)	17.08	21.82★	14.05	16.85
Normality	3.53	7.78★★	9.34★★	7.37★
Heteroscedasticity	0.30	0.34	1.18	1.53

x—variable not included in model.
★★★ $p \leq 0.001$; ★★ $p \leq 0.01$; ★ $p \leq 0.05$.
ª $p \leq 0.10$, one-tailed test.

Source: April 1992–December 2002 monthly PSCB and P&D surveys.

best. In addition to having the best fit as measured by the adjusted R^2 and the best AIC value (see Chapter Four), all coefficients for the long- and short-term effects of the economic and party leader evaluation variables are statistically significant and properly signed. In the other three models, either the short- or the long-term effects of economic evaluations do not achieve statistical significance ($p \le 0.10$). Party leader evaluation variables are significant in all four models. Several salient events also affected Labour partisanship. The ERM crisis, the 1997 general election, 9/11, and the subsequent war in Afghanistan had positive effects on the percentage of Labour identifiers. In contrast, the September 2000 petrol protests diminished Labour's partisan share, as did the decision to change Clause Four of the party's constitution.

As should be the case for error correction models, the α coefficients in the Labour models are statistically significant, negatively signed, and less than 1.0. The α (-0.41) for the personal retrospections model indicates that shocks to Labour party identification were eroded at the rate of 41 per cent per month by the long-term relationship between Labour identification on the one hand, and personal economic evaluations and best prime minister judgements on the other. Thus, although various events and conditions affected the size of Labour's partisan share, assessments of personal economic conditions and the performance of the Labour leader eventually offset these effects. This is what one would expect if party and party leader performance evaluations are key factors in the process that updates party identification over time.

Models of Conservative party identification are summarized in Table 6.12. Although these models are generally similar to those for Labour, there are noteworthy differences as well. First, the performance of all four models is very similar, although the adjusted R^2 and AIC values are slightly better in the case of the national prospective economic evaluation model. Second, unlike the Labour case, the short- and long-term effects of the economic and party leader evaluation variables are statistically significant and properly signed in all four models. Third, although α coefficients are significant in the four Conservative models, their values (-0.16 to -0.23) are considerably smaller than those for the Labour models. This suggests that Conservative party identification was tethered in the long run to economic evaluations and judgements of party leader performance. However, that tether was considerably looser than was the case for Labour. Net of these several effects, Conservative party identification was influenced by important events. As anticipated, the Conservative partisan share dropped in the aftermath of the ERM crisis (see Chapter Three). It also fell in the wake of the party's crushing defeat in the 1997 general election, and in response to Labour's decision to jettison Clause Four. The latter result suggests that both Labour and the Conservatives lost partisans as a result of New Labour's decision to 'modernize' the party's constitution.[30]

Diagnostics indicate that we can believe the stories that the time series models are telling us. With few minor exceptions, the models generally perform well on standard diagnostic tests for autocorrelation, heteroskedasticity, and normality (see Tables 6.11 and 6.12). Regarding which model is preferable, encompassing tests (Charemza and Deadman 1997; see also Chapter Four) confirm that the personal retrospections model provides a better account of the dynamics of Labour party identification than its rivals. The personal retrospections model encompasses all of

Table 6.12   Error correction models of Conservative party identification,
April 1992–December 2002

	Models			
	Personal retrospective	*Personal prospective*	*National retrospective*	*National prospective*
Predictor variables	*β*	*β*	*β*	*β*
ΔBest prime minister (t)	0.21★★★	0.22★★★	0.21★★★	0.22★★★
Economic evaluations:				
ΔPersonal retrospections (t)	0.07★	x	x	x
ΔPersonal prospections (t)	x	0.04★	x	x
ΔNational retrospections (t)	x	x	0.04★	x
ΔNational prospections (t)	x	x	x	0.05★★★
Error correction mechanism				
Party identification ($t-1$)	−0.21★★★	−0.23★★★	−0.16★★	−0.16★★
Best prime minister ($t-1$)	0.75★★★	0.69★★★	0.78★★★	0.87★★★
Personal retrospections ($t-1$)	0.11★	x	x	x
Personal prospections ($t-1$)	x	0.10★	x	x
National retrospections ($t-1$)	x	x	0.02	x
National prospections ($t-1$)	x	x	x	0.05
Shocks				
ERM crisis ($t-1$)	−2.85★	−2.77★	−3.64★	−3.95★★
Clause four ($t-1$)	−2.65[a]	−2.93★	−3.03★	−2.96★
1997 election (t)	−2.89★	−3.26★	−2.42[a]	−2.40[a]
Constant	3.87★	4.07★★	2.69★	2.45★
Adjusted R^2	0.30	0.30	0.30	0.33
AIC	−250.23	−250.12	−250.95	−247.89
DW	1.92	1.97	1.92	1.94
Serial correlation (12 lags)	17.85	15.00	19.44	19.46
Normality	5.42	7.67★	3.34★	0.87
Heteroskedasticity	2.84	1.75	4.05★	7.54★★★

x—variable not included in model.
★★★ $p \leq 0.001$; ★★ $p \leq 0.01$; ★ $p \leq 0.05$.
[a] $p \leq 0.10$ one-tailed test.

Source: April 1992–December 2002 monthly PSCB and P&D surveys.

the alternative models, but none of them encompass it. In contrast, encompassing tests of the rival models of Conservative party identification are inconclusive, thus providing additional testimony that the performance of the four models is very similar.

A final set of diagnostic tests investigates the exogeneity of leader effects in the party identification models. Such tests address the question of whether, at any time *t*, judgements about party leaders reflect as well as cause party identification. If so, then the party identification analyses suffer from simultaneity bias and, as a result, one cannot believe the parameter estimates (Greene 2003: 396). As in the analyses of voting behaviour in Chapter Four, exogeneity tests may be performed to determine whether simultaneity bias is, indeed, a problem. These procedures show that party leader evaluations are weakly exogenous to party identification. As required, the error correction mechanisms for the party identification models are not significant ($p > 0.05$) in the leader models. As also required, the residuals from the leader models are not significant in the party identification models. This means that the coefficients are free of simultaneity bias. A related point deserves emphasis. These results do *not* mean that party identification at time *t* never affects evaluations of party leader performance at some later time $t + i$. Indeed, it is plausible that party identification serves as a heuristic mechanism when voters seek to acquire and process information. The result is that party identification plays a kind of intertemporal 'tennis match' with party leader evaluations, with effects flowing back and forth between them over time. Sorting out that process statistically raises the question of 'strong exogeneity' (Charemza and Deadman 1997), which is not something that needs to be investigated in order to believe the testimony provided by the time series models of party identification.

CONCLUSION: VALENCED PARTISANSHIP

The analyses presented in this chapter are inconsistent with a sociological approach to party support. Rather, the evidence presented here speaks strongly on behalf of 'valenced partisanship' in the British electorate. By valenced partisanship, we mean that voters' party identifications can be thought of as a storehouse of accumulated party and party leader performance evaluations. Moreover, we show that this has been the case in Britain since at least the 1960s. To begin with, partisan attachments have considerable dynamism. Some of these dynamics involve long-term aggregate trends. Consonant with claims first advanced by Crewe et al. in the late 1970s, BES data gathered over the past four decades reveal downward trends both in the strength of party identification and in the strength of its relationship with social class. These trends are evident for the entire 1964–2001 period. However, when interpreting this finding, it would be incorrect to assume that 1960s' Britain was a nation of very strong partisans. Nor were the 1960s a time when overwhelming majorities of working class people identified with Labour, and overwhelming majorities of middle class people identified with the Conservatives. Rather, the 1960s BES data show that many voters did not claim to be intense partisans, and large minorities of working and middle class people did not identify with the 'natural' party of their class. Thus, an impressive dealignment of degree has occurred in an electorate where the intensity of partisan attachments and their linkages with social class have always been weaker than the popular image of tribal politics would suggest.

Other analyses indicate that partisan attachments do not behave in accordance with the Michigan model of party identification. Converse's (1969) conjecture concerning the strengthening of party identification across the life cycle does not fare well in Britain. BES evidence showing tendencies for party identifications to strengthen over the life cycle is very weak, and if such tendencies do exist, then it is clear that they have been overwhelmed by age-cohort and period effects. Moreover, party identifications do not manifest the individual-level stability assumed by proponents of the Michigan model. Panel data from the 1960s to the present clearly show that very sizeable minorities change their party identifications. Some move from being a party identifier to being a nonidentifier or vice versa, whereas others switch between parties. This individual-level partisan instability is not an artefact of random measurement error. Rather, mixed Markov latent class analyses show that there are large mover groups in all of the BES and BEPS panels. Nor is it the case that the apparent mutability of partisanship reflects flaws in the wording of the BES party identification question. Responses to alternative party supporter questions indicate lower levels of partisanship, but they also show considerable individual-level instability.

Evidence of large-scale, ongoing dynamics in partisan attachments accords well with the conception of valenced partisanship. This model has it origins in the updating models of party identification proposed by Fiorina (1981) and others. In these models, as voters acquire new information, they use it to reassess their existing party identifications, with previous information being progressively discounted over time. The intensity and direction of partisanship can change when new information strongly contradicts that which is stored in an existing party identification. Analyses of panel data show that such updating models of party identification perform well. Evaluations of the performance of the economy, political parties, and party leaders influence the direction and intensity of party identification in predictable ways.

Additional evidence of the nature of British voters' partisan attachments is provided by time series data gathered in monthly Gallup surveys. The long-memory dynamics of party identification in the Gallup data are consistent with the mixture of movers and stayers found in the individual-level panel data. Once more, economic evaluations and party leader performance judgements have important effects on the dynamics of party identification.

In sum, the evidence of substantial, ongoing dynamics in partisanship in Britain is strong. Party identification is not now and, at least since the 1960s, has not been an unmoved mover. Its movements are explicable in term of a simple information-updating model. This valenced partisanship model does not make strong assumptions about voter rationality but, rather, contends that voters behave sensibly. Reminiscent of the boundedly rational economic agents described by Simon (e.g. 1987) (see also Conlisk 1996), voters use current information about the performance of parties and their leaders as sensible, albeit rough and ready, guides to political action, and they reduce deliberation costs by storing that information in updated partisan attachments. This ongoing process leads some voters to stay where they are, but prompts others to move on.

NOTES

1. The 2001 BES party identification sequence is: (i) 'Generally speaking, do you think of yourself as Labour, Conservative, Liberal Democrat, Scottish Nationalist [in Scotland only], Plaid Cymru [in Wales only], or what?' (ii) [If 'None', 'Don't Know', or 'Refused'] 'Do you generally think of yourself as a little closer to one of the parties than the others?' (iii) [If 'Yes'] Which party is that?' (iv) 'Would you call yourself very strong [PARTY GIVEN in (i) or (iii)], fairly strong or not very strong?' See Appendix B for the wording of the 1964–97 BES party identification questions.

2. Social class is measured using the Market Research Society classification. People in categories A, B, and C1 are middle class, and those in categories C2, D, and E are working class.

3. The Consistency Index (CI) is a generalized version of the Alford index (see Chapter Three). The CI is computed by cross-tabulating social class (dichotomised as discussed in Note 2 above) with party identification categorized as Conservative, Labour, Liberal/Liberal Democrat, other party, none. The index is the sum of the absolute values of the differences in working and middle class respondents supporting the Labour and Conservative parties.

4. The variable is scored 0 for 1964 and 1966, and 1 for subsequent years.

5. It is not the case that simply calculating the percentages of people who fail to identify with 'their proper party' obscures strong correlations between class membership and party identification. Using the 2001 BES data, a multinomial logit analysis of party identification with social class as the predictor variable yields an estimated R^2 of only 0.02. Nor is it the case that other socio-demographic variables are powerful predictors that have been overlooked by scholars preoccupied with social class. A multinomial logit analysis of the 2001 data using age, employment sector, ethnicity, gender, home ownership, and region, as well as social class, as predictors produces an estimated R^2 of only 0.08.

6. This decrease in the strength of party identification may, in part, reflect a slight change in question wording (see Appendix B).

7. The variable is scored 0 for 1964, 1966, and 1970, and 1 for subsequent years.

8. Although the British Household Panel Surveys (BHPS) will eventually provide very long-term, individual-level data on party support, they do not ask the standard BES party identification question.

9. Since the age of majority was lowered from 21 to 18 in 1969 (Leonard and Mortimore 2001: 14), the main portion of the analysis starts with the 1970 BES data. In addition, the October 1974 data are not used since the cohort first entering the electorate at that time would be quite small, given that the preceding general election was only seven months earlier.

10. For example, if there are four equiprobable choices (Conservative, Labour, Liberal Democrat, other) and a voter chooses at random, then there is a 0.25 probability of selecting a particular party. If he or she is asked a party identification question and again chooses at random in a second survey, then probability of selecting the same party twice is $0.25 \times 0.25 = 0.063$.

11. Variables differ from one panel to the next depending on the mix of questions asked in the panel surveys. For example, for the 1997–98 panel, feelings about the Conservative and Labour parties were measured using variables ranging from 'strongly in favour' (scored +5) to 'neither/don't know' (scored +3) to 'strongly against' (scored +1). Changes in feelings about the parties were measured by subtracting a 1997 variable from its 1998 counterpart. Variables measuring party images included: (*a*) 'good for one class, good for all classes'. Responses that a party was good for all classes were scored +2, responses that a party was good for one class were scored 0, and 'don't knows'were scored 1; (*b*) 'capable of being a strong government, not capable of being a strong government'. Responses that a party was capable of strong government were scored +2, responses that a party was not capable of strong government were scored 0, and 'don't knows' were scored +1. The overall 1997 and 1998 party image variables were constructed by summing (*a*) and (*b*). Changes in party images were measured by subtracting the 1997 overall image variable from its 1998 counterpart. Details concerning construction of variables used in analyses of the 1992–94 and 1966–70 panels are available upon request.

12. The structural equation modelling procedures used by Green, Palmquist, and Schickler (e.g. 2002: ch. 3) require at least an ordinal ordering of categories. In their study of the stability of party identification in the United States, they follow a traditional practice of ordering identifiers along a seven-point scale from very strong Democrats to very strong Republicans, with independents (nonidentifiers) in the middle category. The structural equation models used by Green et al. also require multi-wave panels to have sufficient data for the purpose of identifying parameters of interest.

13. British parties might be ordered along a general 'left-right' continuum with Conservatives on the right, Liberal Democrats in the middle, and Labour on the left. However, as discussed in Chapter Four, there is evidence that the Liberal Democrats are now seen as being further to left than are Labour. The Manifestos Project data (Budge et al. 2001) echo this finding (see Chapters Three and Eight). Placement of minor parties and nonidentifiers poses additional problems.

14. Note also that all of the response probabilities are less than 1.0. This result is consistent with Green et al.'s conjecture that party identifications are measured with error.

15. A party identification 'turnover table' analysis uses panel data and cross-tabulates party identification at time *t*1 with party identification at time *t*2. All cases on the main (upper-left to lower-right) diagonal of the table are stable identifiers. Respondents in the off-diagonal cell are unstable identifiers.

16. The 'initial state' is the estimated proportions of Conservatives, Labour, and others in the mover and stayer groups in the first wave of the four-wave panel.

17. The BHPS party supporter question sequence is: (*a*) 'Generally speaking, do you think of yourself as a supporter of any particular party?' [If 'Yes', go to (c)]; (*b*) 'Do you think of yourself as a little closer to one party than to the others?' (*c*) 'Which one?' (*d*) 'Would you call yourself a very strong supporter of [PARTY], fairly strong or not very strong?'

18. The BSA party supporter question sequence is: (*a*) 'Some people think of themselves as usually being a supporter of one political party rather than another. Do you usually think of yourself as being a supporter of one particular party or not?' [If 'Yes'] 'Which party is that?'

19. Fiorina (1981) states that the constant may also be interpreted technically as a scaling device that takes into account differences in measurement of dependent and independent variables.

20. The sets of predictor variables vary from one panel to another depending upon the availability of relevant questions. For example, for the 1997–98 panel, the predictor variables are: (*a*) evaluations of how good a job the party leaders would do as prime minister, with categories ranging from 'very good' (scored $+5$) to 'don't know' (scored $+3$) to 'not at all good' (scored $+1$); (*b*) retrospective and prospective evaluations of national and personal economic conditions, with categories ranging from 'got/get a lot better' (scored $+5$) to 'stay(ed) the same/don't know' (scored $+3$) to 'got/get a lot worse' (scored $+1$). The four kinds of economic evaluation are summed to produce overall economic evaluations indices; (*c*) government performance evaluation indices based on judgements regarding how well the government has done in the areas of health, education, youth employment, taxation, spending controls, and corruption. For each area, the categories range from 'very successful' (scored $+5$) to 'don't know' (scored $+3$) to 'not at all successful' (scored $+1$). These evaluations are summed to produce the overall indices; (*d*) social class—the standard six-category measure, ranging from A (scored 6) to E (scored 1); (*e*) age: the 18–23, 24–41, 42–49, and 60–68 age-cohorts are 0–1 dummy variables with people over 69 as the reference category. The set of instruments for lagged party identification include: social class, the age cohort dummies, 1997 and 1998 economic evaluation indicies, 1997 and 1998 government performance indices, and the 1997 and 1998 party leader evaluations. Details regarding variables in the analyses of the 1992–94 and 1966–70 panels are available upon request.

21. The instrumental variables for party identification at time $t-1$ include lagged versions of the economic evaluations, party performance evaluations, and party leader evaluation variables, as well as the measures of social class and age cohort. The set of these variables varies depending upon their availability in particular panels (details available upon request). Note also that analyses that do not use instruments for lagged party identification produce substantially similar results.

22. Nearest neighbour regression of a time series variable (e.g. the percentage of Conservative party identifiers) on a time counter variable is a convenient way of mapping nonlinear trends in the data (see Fox 2000).

23. If political variables such as party identification are nonstationary, then it is likely that the data generating processes at work involve stochastic trends. The simplest stochastic trend model is the random walk, that is, $Y_t = Y_{t-1} + \epsilon_t$. In this process, the value of Y at time t is equal to its value at $t-1$ plus the value of any random shock that might occur at time t. Since the coefficient for Y_{t-1} is 1.0, the variance of the series grows without limit (Franses 1998). If the data generating process also includes a constant, that is, $Y_t = \beta_0 + Y_{t-1} + \epsilon_t$, then it is called a 'random walk with drift'. In addition to accumulating shocks, the random walk

with drift has a deterministic component such that, *ceteris paribus*, Y changes by β_0 in each successive time period.

24. To see this, note that $(1-L)^1 Y_t = \epsilon_t$ can be rewritten as $Y_t - Y_{t-1} = \epsilon_t$, which can be rewritten as $Y_t = Y_{t-1} + \epsilon_t$.

25. Unit-root tests are a popular way of testing for nonstationarity. However, these tests have been criticized for their lower power in the face of fractionally integrated and near-integrated alternatives (see, e.g. Maddala and Kim 1998).

26. The Gallup economic evaluation questions are: (*a*) personal prospections—'How do you think the financial situation of your household will change over the next 12 months?' (*b*) personal retrospections—'How does the financial situation of your household now compare with what it was 12 months ago?' (*c*) national prospections—'How do you think the general economic situation in this country will develop over the next 12 months?' (*d*) national retrospections—'How do you think the general economic situation in this country has changed over the last 12 months?' The response categories are: 'get(got) a lot better', 'get a little better', 'stay the same', 'get a little worse', 'get a lot worse'. The economic evaluation variables are constructed by subtracting the percentage offering negative responses from the percentage offering positive ones. These economic evaluation variables are multiplied by -1 starting in May 1997 to take account of the change in government from Conservative to Labour. The question measuring which party leader would make the best prime minister is: 'Who would make the best prime minister—Mr. Hague, Mr. Blair, Mr. Kennedy?' with the names of the party leaders changing as appropriate (see also Chapter Three). In the Labour analysis, the percentage selecting Smith/Blair is used; in the Conservative analysis, the percentage selecting Major/Hague is used.

27. $(1-L)^d$ can be expanded (infinitely) as $1 - dL - (1/2)d(1-d)L^2 - (1/6)d(1-d)(2-d)L^3 - \ldots - (1/j!)d(1-d)(2-d) \ldots ((j-1) - d)L^j - \ldots$ See Franses (1998: 79).

28. For example, assume a one-time shock increases Labour party identification by 10 points in month t. If $\alpha = -0.5$, this means that the effect of the shock will decrease at the rate of 50 per cent per month. Thus, the impact of the shock on party identification will be 5 points in month $t+1$, 2.5 points in month $t+2$, etc.

29. There is not a canonical list of politically important events and, ultimately, degrees of freedom will limit how many can be modelled. In the interest of parsimony, we confine attention to a small group of events that preliminary analyses suggest may have exerted significant effects on Conservative or Labour identification. With one exception, the events variables are coded 1 for the month in which they occurred, and 0 otherwise. The exception is the September 2000 petrol protest variable. Preliminary analyses suggest that this variable marked a downward 'break' in Labour partisanship. Hence, the variable is coded 1 for each month from September 2000 onwards, and 0 otherwise.

30. A plausible interpretation of the negative Clause Four parameters in the Conservative and Labour models is that its abandonment persuaded some Conservative identifiers that Tony Blair and New Labour really were different from their predecessors. Hence, they defected. But Labour paid a price as well, namely the support of some Labour's core supporters for whom Clause Four symbolized the party's historic commitment to socialism. The analyses suggest that, in net terms, Labour lost more identifiers than it gained.

SEVEN

Theories and Models of Turnout

Classic accounts of British political culture depict an active electorate. Widespread citizen participation is said to be a deeply engrained feature of political life. Thus, Almond and Verba (1963: 455) write: '[t]he political culture in Great Britain . . . approximates the civic culture. The participant role is highly developed'. Butler and Stokes (1969: 26) concur: 'Blurred ideas of popular sovereignty and universal suffrage are so interwoven in prevailing conceptions of British government that the obligation to vote becomes almost an aspect of the citizen's national identity.' The image of voters streaming to the polls could easily be accepted as a stylized fact when large majorities regularly exercised their franchise in general elections. Although turnout gradually declined after reaching a high point of 84 per cent in 1950, the downward trend was quite irregular and, as late as 1992, nearly 78 per cent cast their ballots. However, in the two most recent general elections turnout has fallen to levels not witnessed since before Second World War—to 71.5 per cent in 1997 and to 59.4 per cent in 2001. Clearly, the decision (not) to vote has become an important feature of political choice in contemporary Britain.

This chapter begins our investigation of why people in Britain do or do not vote. We are interested in voting turnout generally, but pay particular attention to the sharp decline in turnout in 2001. We first consider how two theories of democracy, the 'elite competition' and 'participatory citizenship' theories, address the importance of citizen (dis)engagement and the meaning of political participation in a democracy. This discussion is followed by an analysis of how voting fits into the broader matrix of activities that define the repertoire of political action in contemporary Britain. Then, the sociological and individual rationality frameworks presented in Chapter Two are used to organize two sets of models that have been proposed to explain the decision (not) to vote. The sociological framework includes three models—perceived equity–fairness (or relative deprivation), social capital, and civic voluntarism. The individual rationality framework also has three models— cognitive mobilization, minimal rational choice, and general incentives. Each of these six models is discussed in terms of its motivating rationale, and core concepts and 'signature variables'. The explanatory power of the models is assessed in the next chapter.

THEORIES OF POLITICAL PARTICIPATION

Interest in electoral participation and the relationship between turnout and other forms of political involvement is motivated by two variants of democratic theory. These are the theories of elite competition and participatory citizenship (for useful summaries, see Held 1996; Dalton 2002). The theory of elite competition has a lengthy pedigree and is associated with the 'responsible government' school of thought (e.g. Schumpeter 1950; Berelson, Lazarsfeld, and McPhee 1954; Almond and Verba 1963). In this theory, the key ideas are elite leadership and 'thin' democracy with limited citizen participation. More specifically, the theory recognizes 'constitutional and practical limits on the effective range of political decision', so that voting in competitive elections by a 'poorly informed and/or emotional electorate' may be seen as a *maximum* exercise of citizenship and a method that legitimizes elite decision-making (Held 1996: 197). Limited public involvement is said to help ensure effective and stable government that, in turn, bolsters public support for a democratic political order.

The theory of participatory citizenship also has many advocates. Some are liberal-democratic theorists (e.g. Mill 1859, 1861; Pateman 1970; Macpherson 1977; see also Barber 1984), whereas others may be associated with the 'reasoning public' school of thought (e.g. Neumann 1986; Lupia, McCubbins, and Popkin 2000). In this theory, the key ideas are 'untidy' governance and 'strong' democracy that requires extensive citizen involvement. A participatory society has an open institutional system with 'direct participation of citizens in the regulation of the key institutions of society, including the workplace and local community' (Held 1996: 271). In this society, voting by knowledgeable and civic-minded individuals is a *minimum* expression of citizenship. It is argued that widespread citizen involvement in political life promotes effective, open, and responsive governance, while bolstering political interest, political knowledge, and feelings of efficacy and interpersonal trust.

The two types of democratic theory thus advance sharply contrasting normative and empirical claims regarding the scope of, and possibilities for, citizen involvement in political life. These differing claims are rooted in very different philosophic anthropologies of the democratic citizen. Theories of democratic elitism are pessimistic regarding the intellectual and moral capacities of citizens, and argue that the potential for improvement is quite limited. Most people do not participate very much and, given their limited abilities, this is a 'good thing'. Theories of participatory citizenship take a much more optimistic view. Citizens can make a variety of positive contributions by engaging in various kinds of political activities. Moreover, participation creates a positive feedback loop—good citizenship begets better citizenship.

Despite these fundamental differences, there is substantial general agreement between the two theories about what political participation is. Both theories conceptualize political participation as a voluntary activity done by an individual acting alone or with others. Political participation is a means by which citizens express their political attitudes, beliefs, and opinions. It requires resources or skills, conveys information to public officials, and is purposive, that is, it attempts to achieve goals or implement policies. Political participation thus has four main elements—actions, citizens, politics, and influence—and encompasses a wide range of activities (Brady 1999: 739).

An important set of activities focus on elections. A number of analysts have argued that these electoral activities constitute a distinctive or 'unique' mode of political participation (e.g. Verba and Nie 1972: ch. 3; Verba, Schlozman, and Brady 1995: ch. 2). These activities are legally protected and socially sanctioned (Inglehart 1983; Dalton 2002: ch. 3). As such, they involve people who perform them in the political process in ways that increase their sense that the process, the decisions that it produces, and the larger institutional setting within which it is embedded are legitimate and deserving of public support. In early studies these conventional activities were often conceptualized as forming a single hierarchical dimension of political involvement (Milbrath 1965). People who do more resource-demanding activities (working for candidates or parties, attending candidate or party meetings or rallies) also do less demanding ones (voting, discussing politics with friends and family). But, those who do the latter do not necessarily perform the former.

Over the past three decades, research on political participation has expanded beyond the electoral arena to investigate a diverse range of activities. A frequent departure point for the newer generation of studies is the conceptual distinction between forms of participation that are 'conventional' and 'elite supportive' versus those that are 'unconventional' and 'elite challenging' (Barnes et al. 1979; Inglehart 1983; Dalton 2002: chs 3–4). In addition to voting and other election-centred activities, conventional forms of political participation include various kinds of community involvement, such as contacting public officials or working with friends and neighbours to try to solve a local problem (Verba and Nie 1972). Unconventional activities range from 'mild', legal forms of protest, such as signing a petition or joining a boycott of goods and services, to 'strong', possibly illegal ones, such as rallies and demonstrations where there is a risk of property damage or physical violence. Since few respondents typically engage (or are willing admit to engaging) in the stronger forms, they often are asked about protest potential, that is, how likely it is that they might perform a particular activity (Barnes et al. 1979; Jennings and Van Deth 1990; see also Dalton 2002: chs 3–4).

Theories and Models of Turnout

The idea that citizens in Britain and other contemporary democracies engage in a diverse repertoire of political activities calls into question the unidimensional conceptualization of political participation. Empirical research on the topic has delineated several dimensions or types of activity that are undertaken by different, possibly overlapping, groups. In the United States, Verba and Nie (1972) pioneered this line of inquiry when they identified four basic types of participation—voting, campaign activity, contacting, and cooperative activity. Subsequent American studies have supplemented the list (Verba, Schlozman, and Brady 1995; Brady 1999). Similar findings have been reported by researchers working in other countries. Verbal persuasion, campaign activity, nonconfrontational protest, and confrontational protest were the main types found in Canada (Kornberg and Clarke 1992: 231–41). In Britain, three dimensions—electoral-conventional, mild unconventional, and strong unconventional (Stewart 1987)—characterized participation among respondents in the Political Action Study (Marsh 1977). And, in their 1984–5 study, Parry, Moyser, and Day (1992) sorted twenty-three activities along six dimensions that included voting, party campaigning, collective action, contacting, direct action, and political violence.

To compare the frequency of voting with other ways in which British citizens may participate in politics, the 2001 British Election Study asked respondents how often they voted in general elections. As Table 7.1 shows, slightly over half (52 per cent) said that they voted in 'all' general elections, 27 per cent said 'most', 9 per cent said 'some', and 12 per cent said 'none'. Respondents also were asked to use a 0 (very unlikely) to 10 (very likely) scale to indicate how likely it was that they would engage in several other kinds of political activities.[1] Answers to this question reveal that although general election turnout was down sharply in 2001, people were still were more likely to contemplate voting than doing anything else in politics. Specifically, 80 per cent said that there was a greater than 50–50 probability that they would vote in the next local election, and 59 per cent said that there was a greater than 50–50 probability that they would vote the next election for the European Parliament (Table 7.1). Average scores on the 0–10 point scales for these items were 7.8 and 6.1, respectively. In contrast, majorities ranging from 52 to 71 per cent stated that there was *at most* a 50–50 chance that they would work with a group to solve a problem, become active in a voluntary association, discuss politics with family or friends, or boycott goods and services. Average probability scores for engaging in these activities were much lower than those for the voting items, and varied from 3.5 to 5.0. Other activities were even less popular. Large majorities indicated there that they were unlikely to take part in a rally or demonstration, give money to a political party, work for a party or candidate, or try to convince someone how to vote. Average scores for these activities on the 0–10 scale were very low, ranging from 1.2 to 2.8.

Table 7.1 Political participation in Britain

A. *Vote frequency in general elections (column percentages)*
Vote in

All elections	52
Most elections	27
Some elections	9
Never vote	12

B. *Likelihood of engaging in various political activities (horizontal percentages)*

Activity	Very unlikely 0	1–4	5	6–9	Very likely 10	Mean
Vote in the next election for the European Parliament	18	14	9	25	34	6.1
Vote in the next local election	9	6	5	26	54	7.8
Work actively with a group of people to addres a public issue/solve problem	32	29	10	22	7	3.5
Participate in a protest, like a rally or a demonstration to show concern about public issue or problem	42	28	7	18	5	2.8
Be active in a voluntary organization, like a community association, a charity group, or a sports club	22	25	10	28	15	4.6
Give money to a political party	69	19	4	5	3	1.2
Try to convince someone else how to vote	62	20	4	10	4	1.7
Work for a party or a candidate in an election campaign	66	23	3	6	2	1.2
Discuss politics with family or friends	19	23	10	33	15	5.0
Join a boycott, that is, refuse to buy a particular product or to shop at a particular store	24	23	9	29	15	4.7

Source: 2001 BES post-election survey.

The Structure of Political Participation

The 2001 BES data can be used to locate voting empirically within a broader multidimensional structure of political participation. We first note that various dimensions or 'syndromes' of activities are suggested by the correlations (r) among the several participation variables. Frequency of voting in general elections correlates strongly with voting in 2001 (0.61), and with the likelihood of voting in the next local election (0.53). And, voting in 2001 and the likelihood of voting in the next local election are also correlated quite strongly (0.49). With respect to other activities, people who say that they would work actively with a group to address a public issue or solve a problem also tend to report that they would participate in a rally or demonstration (0.49). However, there is virtually no relationship between the likelihood of protesting and voting in the 2001 general election (-0.01) or frequency of voting in general elections (0.02).

Taken together, these empirical relationships and the conceptual distinctions discussed above suggest the plausibility of a four-factor model of the structure of political participation with separate 'voting', 'party activity', 'community activity', and 'protest' dimensions. Thus, voting in the 2001 general election, reported overall rates of participation in general elections, and the probabilities of voting in the next local election and the next European parliamentary election are hypothesized to load on the voting factor. Participation variables loading on the hypothesized party activity factor include the probabilities of contributing money to a party, convincing people how to vote, and working for a political party. The likelihood of working with a group to solve a local problem and being active in a voluntary association are hypothesized to load on the community activity factor. Variables loading on the protest factor are the likelihood of joining a boycott, and the likelihood of participating in a rally or demonstration.

The adequacy of this four-factor model is assessed using confirmatory factor analysis (CFA) (see Chapter Two). For purposes of calibrating the relative goodness-of-fit of the four-factor model, we first estimate a baseline model where all eleven participation variables load on a single participation factor. As anticipated, this model has a very poor fit ($\chi^2 = 1891.71$, $df = 44$, $p = 0.000$; RMSEA $= 0.12$), thereby clearly indicating that the structure of political participation in Britain is multidimensional. We next use a random half-sample of the 2001 BES data to specify and modify aspects of the hypothesized four-factor model. With modest modifications to the error structure, the four-factor model fits the data very well. As a further test, the goodness-of-fit of the revised model is tested using the second random half-sample. The model again has a good fit, so we proceed to estimate its parameters using the entire sample. As Table 7.2 shows, the fit remains satisfactory ($\chi^2 = 119.57$, $df = 34$, $p = 0.000$; RMSEA $= 0.03$). All factor loadings are statistically significant, and the squared multiple correlations for the several variables testify that the model explains substantial amounts of item variance.

Regarding relationships among the four participation factors, all inter-factor correlations are positive but their strengths vary widely. The community activity and protest factors have a statistically significant and very strong correlation (0.85). Correlations between community activity and party activity (0.69) and between party activity and protest (0.48) are smaller, albeit substantial and statistically significant. What this means is that people who see themselves as likely community activists also are more likely than others to attend a rally or demonstration. In addition, community activists are likely to work on behalf of a party or candidate. Potential party activists are also more likely than other people to engage in various

Table 7.2   Confirmatory factor analysis of four-factor model of political participation

| | *Political participation factors* | | | |
	Voting	*Party activity*	*Communal activity*	*Protest*
Activities				
Voting in 2001 general election	0.75	0.00	0.00	0.00
Voting: all or most general elections	0.70	0.00	0.00	0.00
Vote for next European parliament election	0.66	0.00	0.00	0.00
Vote for next local election	0.88	0.00	0.00	0.00
Give money to political party	0.00	0.74	0.00	0.00
Convince someone how to vote	0.00	0.73	0.00	0.00
Work for party or candidate	0.00	0.88	0.00	0.00
Work with group to address public issue or problem	0.00	0.00	0.66	0.00
Active in voluntary organization	0.00	0.00	0.56	0.00
Join boycott	0.00	0.00	0.52	0.00
Participate in protest to show concern about issue or problem	0.00	0.00	0.00	1.00
Inter-factor correlations				
Voting	1.00			
Party activity	0.38	1.00		
Communal activity	0.36	0.69	1.00	
Protest	0.06	0.48	0.85	1.00

Note: χ^2 = 119.57, df = 34, p = 0.00; RMSEA = 0.03, p value (test of close fit) = 1.00; N = 2974.
Source: 2001 BES post-election survey.

kinds of protest activities. Although other inter-factor correlations are weaker, *pace* those who designate voting as a 'unique' activity, the voting factor has substantial, positive correlations, 0.38 and 0.36 respectively, with the party activity and communal activity factors. The voting and protest factors are essentially unrelated (0.06).

Viewed generally, the findings reinforce the results of earlier research by demonstrating that voting and other forms political participation in Britain occur along multiple, interrelated dimensions. The location of the voting dimension in this matrix of activities indicates that electoral participation is not somehow different or 'unique' in the sense of being unrelated to other forms of political action. Likely voters are more likely than nonvoters to participate in party work and various types of community action. An important implication of this finding is that theories that have been advanced to explain citizen involvement in political parties and community activities may have relevance for understanding electoral participation. The next section discusses several theoretical models that have been advanced to explain voting turnout.

EXPLAINING THE TURNOUT DECISION

The significance of voting in democratic theory, its frequency relative to other forms of participation, and the ongoing decline in turnout rates in many mature democracies have prompted interest in factors that affect the decision (not) to vote. Although some studies have focussed on basic issues having to do with how turnout rates are measured (e.g. Swaddle and Heath 1989; McDonald and Popkin 2001), others have attempted to model the individual and institutional factors that affect turnout in one or more countries at one or more time points.[2] Here, we consider these factors in terms of two overarching theoretical frameworks and two sets of competing models. As discussed in Chapter Two, the sociological and individual-rationality frameworks have shaped a great deal of the research on party choice. Although the volume of work on turnout is not as great, these frameworks also have guided a number of studies of electoral participation (e.g. Wolfinger and Rosenstone 1980; Aldrich 1993; Blais 2000). In the sociological framework, three models demand attention—perceived equity–fairness (relative deprivation), social capital, and civic voluntarism. Three significant models in the individual rationality framework are cognitive mobilization, minimal rational choice, and general incentives.

The Sociological Framework

We observed in Chapters One and Two that the sociological framework emphasizes the importance of social characteristics, social contexts, and social psychology for explaining political behaviour (Dalton and Wattenberg 1993). At one time, the prevailing approach held that social characteristics or distinctions form the basis for group awareness and experience that, in turn, shape and reinforce political preferences. Since these social factors change slowly, preferences do as well. Overlapping this approach is the social contextual approach that emphasizes processes of social identification and communication. These processes help to explain group members' use of decision-making guidelines and their mobilization to participate in politics. In contrast to these two approaches, the social–psychology model presumably is more capable of aligning people's attitudes with their perceptions and evaluations of the ongoing flow of politically relevant events and conditions (Dalton and Wattenberg 1993). As discussed in Chapter Four, according to this model group and early life socialization experiences imprint political psychological attachments, most notably party identifications. Once formed, these identifications tend to become stable elements in public political psychology that serve as 'perceptual screens' influencing other political beliefs, attitudes and behaviour. Given its nature and functions, party identification constitutes a long-term force on party choice and the likelihood of voting.

224

Theories and Models of Turnout

Here, we examine three participation models in the sociological framework. The relative deprivation or *perceived equity–fairness model* draws heavily on socio-demographic characteristics and social psychology. A number of social historians have employed this model (e.g. Hobsbawm 1962; Skocpol 1979). In social science, its several forms include the J-curve, frustration–aggression, and related hypotheses (Davies 1962; Runciman 1966; Gurr 1970; Walker and Smith 2002). The key idea is that people with particular socio-demographic characteristics compare themselves to others or to an idealized standard. If these comparisons are unfavourable, then they become frustrated, angry, and either withdraw or protest (Walker, Wong, and Kretzschmar 2002). The basic story is that members of various social groups develop expectations about how economic, political, and social systems should operate in terms of equity–fairness. They also evaluate how equitably and fairly they are treated by these systems. The greater the gap between expectations and evaluations, or the more unfavourable the comparison, the more likely they are to experience frustra-tion and anger. These emotional responses are a 'potent, volatile, instigator of action' (Marcus, Neumann, and MacKuen 2000: 26) and a stimulus to obtaining and processing information (Conover and Feldman 1986; Marcus 1988). However, whether people do act may depend on their attributions of responsibility. Self-attribution leads to withdrawal whereas system attribution erodes political support and motivates participation in social movements and, possibly, the electoral arena as well (Walker, Wong, and Kretzschmar 2002; see also Sniderman and Brody 1977). As a result, relative deprivation is a potential source of nonvoting.

The core concepts in the relative deprivation or perceived equity–fairness model are a sense of general deprivation, a sense of economic deprivation and an emotional reaction to this, a sense of policy dissatisfaction, and membership in a deprived group. General deprivation involves an individual's sense that she or he has not received a fair share in life or that political or social arrangements are inequitable and unjust. Economic deprivation is a person's judgement that her or his house-hold financial condition has deteriorated (retrospective) or is unlikely to improve (prospective), and his or her attribution of government responsibility for this condition. Emotional responses are 'negative' reactions to personal economic con-ditions. Policy dissatisfaction involves negative evaluations of government perfor-mance in various policy domains. Membership in a deprived group may be operationalized in terms of several social and economic characteristics, including ethnic minority membership, gender (female), and employment status (i.e. retired or unemployed). These characteristics index the extent to which individuals are vulnerable to economic hardship, diminished life chances, and social status losses.

The *social capital model* hinges on social trust in both its earlier, rational cost–benefit and later, socio-cultural versions (Jackman and Miller 1998). In the rational version, the key idea is that social trust is the basis of individual action. An important consideration here is the ability of groups and institutions to produce desired outputs and, by so doing, generate trust (Becker 1975, 2001; Coleman 1988).

If an institution repeatedly provides benefits, then it builds a reputation and a record for being trustworthy (Jackman and Miller 1998). Trust itself is a person's expectation of receiving a needed (individualized) benefit from a group or an institution. This expectation provides the motivation that spurs participation in a group or institution that is capable of providing the benefit.

In the socio-cultural version, social capital 'refers to connections among individuals—social networks and the norms of reciprocity and trustworthiness that arise from them' (Putnam 2000: 19). The key hypothesis is that 'honesty, civic engagement, and social trust' form a 'mutually reinforcing' syndrome (Putnam 2000: 137). Social capital is important because trusting people focus their attention less on themselves and close groups and more on society at large. Moreover, trusting people are willing to risk cooperation with others who are not well known to them, and to participate with them in community activities (Granovetter 1973; Uslaner 1999). This trust–participation relationship has many benefits—'[o]ther things being equal, people who trust their fellow citizens volunteer more often, contribute more to charity, participate more often in politics and community organizations, serve more readily on juries, give blood more frequently, comply more fully with their tax obligations, are more tolerant of minority views, and display many other forms of civic virtue' (Putnam 2000: 137). In the aggregate, many social, economic and political benefits are said to flow from high levels of social capital. It is claimed that countries with high levels of social capital will enjoy, *inter alia*, lower crime rates, lower transaction costs, higher rates of compliance with government laws and regulations, and higher rates of economic growth (Putnam 1993, 2000; Fukuyama 1995; Inglehart 1997; see also Brehm and Rahn 1997; Sullivan and Transue 1999).

Core concepts in the social capital model(s) are social trust and voluntary participation. We define social trust as a person's sense that other people are trustworthy and fair (for a discussion, see Levi and Stoker 2000). Voluntary participation refers to whether an individual offered to become active in community or public matters or was asked to do so.

In the *civic voluntarism model*, social characteristics, contexts, and psychology come into play. In both the older and newer versions of this model, the key idea is that social contexts help individuals to acquire politically relevant resources and skills. In turn, these resources and skills encourage people to have a sense of 'attitudinal engagement' and to participate in various political activities (Verba, Schlozman, and Brady 1995: 269 and ch. 9). An important aspect of the story of the civic voluntarism model is that people with the requisite educational, income, and temporal resources, and/or those located in voluntary associations, workplaces, churches, or other social settings, are likely to volunteer or to be recruited as political participants. By participating in voluntary associations, people acquire information, civic skills and other resources that predispose them to engage in politics. Harkening back to an earlier generation of studies (e.g. Milbrath 1965), the civic voluntarism model also advances several other hypotheses about factors prompting political participation. In particular, people who are more politically interested and efficacious, and those with strong ideological or partisan motivations are more likely to be active. Viewing the several explanatory factors that it incorporates negatively, the civic voluntarism model provides a three-fold account of why people do not vote: 'because they can't; because they don't want to; or because nobody asked' (Verba, Schlozman, and Brady 1995: 15).

The core concepts in the civic voluntarism model are resources, recruitment, voluntary activity, and psychological engagement. We view educational attainment, social class, and time as vote-relevant resources in Britain. Education increases people's access to information and enhances their ability to think about information in a way that is useful for making a political choice. Social class proxies skills which are useful political resources. Recruitment refers to whether people were mobilized by political parties or were asked by others to vote a particular way or to participate otherwise. Voluntary activity refers to the extent to which an individual has been involved in various kinds of community or public organizations. Psychological engagement in the political process is defined in terms of political efficacy, political interest, and strength of partisanship. Political efficacy is defined here as a person's sense that she or he has the skills and resources that are necessary to influence the political process (for a review, see Acock, Clarke, and Stewart 1985). Political interest is a curiosity that a person has about the political world, that is, the motivation to learn about government and politics and about what is going on during an election. Strength of partisanship is the intensity of an individual's identification with a political party (see Chapter Six).

Each of the three sociological models presented above offers an account of voting turnout. The perceived equity–fairness model draws on social characteristics and psychology to explain why feelings of deprivation may lead a person to protest or to withdraw and not vote. The social capital model uses social context and psychology to extend the trust–participation relationship to voting behaviour. The civic voluntarism model employs social characteristics, contexts, and psychology to develop a tri-fold explanation of (not) voting. In this account, resources, social interaction, and psychological engagement are what matter.

The Individual Rationality Framework

As discussed in Chapters One and Two, the individual rationality framework is a set of decision-making models motivated by a core or standard, expected utility model. Here, we discuss three specific individual rationality models of voting turnout. In comparison with the standard model, these cognitive mobilization, minimal rational choice, and general incentives models make less stringent demands on human decision making. The standard model explains decision making in terms of an expected utility-maximizing strategy. Since preference plays a key role in this strategy, many experimental, formal, and other types of studies have attempted to explain preference formation, ordering, and change, and to assess the power of the standard model to account for decisional problems. As is well known, these decisional problems arise in bargaining situations, committee and jury deliberations, foreign policy making, and electoral settings. These problems have important implications for collective action, (non)cooperative behaviour, goal seeking, institutional design, and rule making (for reviews, see Thaler 1993, 1994; Laver 1997; Shepsle and Bonchek 1997).

Although the standard model has received a great deal of attention in political science, one of its best-known applications involves electoral turnout and, in particular, the calculus of voting. This calculus has three aspects (Downs 1957: 271–2; Riker and Ordeshook 1968, 1973: 62–5; Grofman 1993). *Pivotality* is the calculated probability of casting a deciding vote that enables a most preferred (utility-providing) party to win and prevents less preferred (less utility-providing) parties from doing so. To make the calculation, the voter must be informed about the size of the electorate, the degree of party competition, and the system by which individual votes are translated into collective decisions (Blais 2000: ch. 3). Regarding *benefits*, the voter is interested in 'utility income' and seeks to determine which of the competing parties has implemented policies that have increased this income the most, or proposes policies that will do so. When making this determination, the voter is not adverse to consulting parties' past records, but does so only as a guide to what the future might bring should one party rather than another hold the reins of power. In assessing benefits, the voter must calculate party differentials and estimate the expected benefits of voting; that is, the difference that it makes to him or her whether one candidate or party is elected as opposed to another—the bigger the difference, the bigger the expected benefit. Pivotality *interacts* with benefits; that is, benefits are discounted by the probability that an individual can exert a crucial, that is, pivotal, effect on the outcome. The voter must also calculate the *costs* of voting, particularly the time that is needed to acquire information and to act, that is, 'to discover what parties are running, to deliberate, to go to the polls, and to mark the ballot. Since time is a scarce resource, voting is inherently costly' (Downs 1957: 265).

In the calculus of voting, the voter may decide that parties differ in the policy benefits being offered, that is, she or he will receive different amounts of utility income from them. If so, the individual prefers the party that can provide the greatest amount of utility. But, the individual will not necessarily vote. Pivotality and costs are taken into account. If the result of an individual's pivotality calculation times expected benefits exceeds anticipated costs, then the individual votes. However, there are other possibilities. The voter may think that all parties are equal in the policy improvements that they will provide. Since she or he will receive the same amount of utility income from them, the individual does not vote. Also, if the individual thinks that the probability of casting a pivotal ballot is small, even if expected benefits are large, then anticipated costs may prompt nonvoting. In this case, the product of pivotality × expected benefits is less than costs. Given the enormous size of electorates in modern democracies, the pivotality probability for any general election will (almost certainly) be very small (e.g. Gelman, King, and Boscardin 1998; Gelman and Katz 2001). This is very important for individual rationality models of turnout. As Riker and Ordeshook (1973: 63) observe, '[s]ince P is assumed to equal one divided by the number of voters, it is asserted that PB must be a very small number, so that C outweighs PB, leaving R [voting] negative. Thus the expected utility of abstaining is greater than the expected utility of voting, in which case it is irrational to vote.' Of course, if everyone thought this way, then no one would vote.

But, many people *do* vote. Why they do, when they have little chance of influencing the outcome, is a paradox of participation that has long challenged rational choice theory (Riker and Ordeshook 1973; Green and Shapiro 1994; Laver 1997). This and other 'paradoxes in rationality' have attracted considerable interest among behavioural decision theorists, cognitive psychologists, and experimental economists (e.g. see Simon, 1987; Kahneman and Tversky 1979, 2000; Plous 1993). Critics have argued that individual rationality explanations provide inaccurate representations of how decision-making environments work, how people make decisions, and how decisions affect outcomes. With respect to how people make decisions, two points are relevant. First, the use of heuristics, that is, 'general rules of thumb' applied when making a complicated decision, can reduce effort and time costs while producing 'fairly good estimates' (Plous 1993: 109). However, heuristics can also lead to biases and inconsistencies, particularly when they are employed unknowingly and without the knowledge and information needed to use them well (Kuklinski and Quirk 2000: 156–7, 167). Second, in politics, 'various and sometimes severe distortions can occur . . . . [People] hold inaccurate and stereotyped factual beliefs, hold their beliefs overconfidently, resist correct information, prefer easy arguments, interpret elite statements according to racial or other biases, and rely heavily on scanty information about a candidate's policy positions' (Kuklinski and Quirk 2000: 179).

In sum, critics of the individual rationality approach, as operationalized by the standard model, argue that the typical individual is not a 'supercitizen' (Dalton 2002: 13–14). That is, many people are not attentive to, interested in, and knowledgeable about politics and public affairs. They also are not capable of processing copious amounts of information, developing coldly calculated preferences, and making unbiased decisions. However, citizens are not afflicted by low emotional intelligence and poor memory function that impair decision making in everyday life (Tetlock 2000: 240–1; see also Kuklinski and Quirk 2000). Rather, the average citizen is a decision-maker who uses a hybrid 'psychological' rational or a 'rational' psychological model (e.g. Quattrone and Tversky 1984; Lupia, McCubbins, and Popkin 2000; Ghirardato and Katz 2002). This decision-maker 'deploy(s) mental resources strategically as a function of the perceived importance and tractability of the problem' (Tetlock 2000: 240). According to these accounts, the voter judiciously uses information from a running, affect-laden tally of events and conditions (for a review, see Druckman and Lupia 2000: 8–12) that becomes part of a large mix of emotions and evaluations that guides electoral choices (Tetlock 2000; see also Kuklinski and Quirk 2000).

Three models motivated by the individual rationality approach are particularly useful for understanding the voting decision. The *cognitive mobilization model* does not require a utility-maximizing assumption (Dalton 2002). In this model, the key idea is that more educated, media reliant, and politically interested and knowledgeable people tend to be more dissatisfied with policy outcomes. Hence, they are more inclined to protest. The story told by this model begins with two cognitive-mobilizing developments (Dalton 2002: 19–24; see also Skocpol 1979: ch. 2; Nie, Junn, and Stehlik-Barry 1996). One is that people now have enhanced access to higher education and to sophisticated communications and computer technology. This improves their ability to process large amounts of politically relevant information. A second and related development is that the cost of acquiring this information has declined with its increasing availability in electronic, print, and web-based forms. Taken together, these developments mean that more well-educated media users have become more interested in and knowledgeable about prevailing social and economic conditions, and more aware of how norms, principles, and rules of the game actually work in a democracy. The result is enhanced dissatisfaction with government performance in important policy areas. This dissatisfaction triggers protest, but its implications for voting are less straightforward. One possibility is that policy dissatisfaction prompts voting for opposition parties. However, another possibility is that dissatisfaction generalizes beyond the performance of the incumbent government to all political parties, and perhaps to the larger political system. The result is abstention from the electoral arena.

In the cognitive mobilization model, the core concepts are education, media use, political interest, political knowledge, and policy (dis)satisfaction. Education is conceptualized in terms of educational achievement, such as whether individuals have attended university or have other advanced qualifications. Media use is the frequency with which people use various mass media, notably newspapers in the United Kingdom, to get information about election campaigns, politics, and public affairs. Political interest, as defined in the civic voluntarism model, is curiosity about the political world, notably about elections, politics, and government. Political knowledge refers to vote-relevant information, such as basic facts about who is eligible to cast a ballot, when the polls are open, and which party policies are useful to making a decision (for a discussion, see Lupia and McCubbins 1998). Policy dissatisfaction is the sense that the governing party has done a bad job of addressing particular issues and providing important goods and services.

The next model considered is the *minimal rational choice model*. This model modifies the standard rational choice model discussed above by substituting political efficacy for the pivotality calculation (Riker and Ordeshook 1973: 53–7).[3] Thus, the minimal rational choice model allows for the possibility that exerting influence on an election outcome is determined not by a purely egocentric, computationally accurate, probability calculation, but rather by a person's more general sense that she or he, perhaps acting together with others, can affect politics and public affairs in meaningful ways. If someone thinks that she or he can be influential, this enhances the size of the efficacy × benefits term in the calculus of turnout. If this term is greater than the estimated cost of going to the polls, the individual votes. However, as in the standard rational choice model, an individual does not vote if she or he thinks that there is no chance of being influential, even if expected benefits are extremely large. In this case, costs, however small, dominate.

As the above discussion suggests, the core concepts in the minimal rational choice model are political efficacy, collective benefits, and the perceived costs of voting. As in the civic voluntarism model, political efficacy is a person's sense of being able to exert political influence. Feelings of political efficacy are grounded in estimations of resources and perceptions of the responsiveness of the political system. Although it might be argued that, given their limited resources, the vast majority of people should not feel politically efficacious, it is possible that such feelings are heightened by being 'collectivized'. That is, people think about the potential influence of themselves and others who they view as being 'like themselves'. Regarding other explanatory variables in the minimal rational choice model, (collective) benefits pertain to expectations regarding differences in public policy goods that would be provided by various political parties, should they win the election. Costs refer to estimates of the amount of time and effort required to go to the polls and cast a ballot.

The *general incentives model* (Whiteley et al. 1994; Whiteley and Seyd 2002) addresses the paradox of participation for rational choice theory by incorporating ideas about why rational individuals might engage in collective action. These ideas recognize that people may join several types of groups, including large, 'latent' ones. Given the size of the latter groups, a person 'cannot make a noticeable contribution to any group effort, and since no one in the group will react if he makes no contribution, he has no incentive to contribute' (Olson 1965: 50). Accordingly, the group must try to change a rational individual's preferences so that she or he will participate in a 'group-oriented way'. These efforts involve mobilizing the 'capacity for action . . . with the aid of "selective incentives"' (Olson 1965: 51). These incentives increase the sense of benefit or utility received over the perception of cost incurred. To receive the utility unrelated to the collective goods being produced by the group, the individual must participate.

As in well known, many different kinds of incentives for voting have been suggested, including those that are material, social, and moral (e.g. Olson 1965) or instrumental, expressive, and normative (Butler and Stokes 1969: 24–5). However, in the general incentives model, the key idea is that calculation and psychology combine in human decision making to motivate people to participate. Construction of the general incentives model begins by incorporating the three explanatory variables used in the minimal rational choice model. These variables are political efficacy, collective benefits, and costs. The general incentives model then adds four incentive variables that constitute alternative benefits as well as specific norms. These benefits and norms reflect the idea that an individual's sense of 'being implicated' in the political system is fundamental to the determination of the costs and benefits of participation.

The incentives consist of individual, group, system, and expressive benefits. Individual benefits refer to one's sense of personal or private reward that comes from voting. In contrast, group benefits go neither to only members of one's family and other primary groups nor to everyone in the electorate. Rather, they flow to people who are seen as similar to oneself or in need of a 'helping hand'. System benefits are benefits that accrue to a democratic political order when citizens vote. Recognition that a healthy democracy requires citizen involvement prompts people to vote. Expressive benefits are also relevant. These benefits are the sense of satisfaction that people receive when they demonstrate their support for political actors, institutions, or processes. Social norms are yet another component of the model. The argument is that social norms are important parts of the socio-political context in which people make choices about whether to vote, to participate in other ways, or to do nothing. Norms may be internalized or externalized by the individual and they must be credible to have an effect. This effect results from communication of which behaviours are appropriate, expected, and rewarded by others, and which behaviours are not. What matters is that significant others in one's environment think that voting is—or is not—an important activity.

In sum, the core concepts in the general incentives model include three elements of the minimal rational choice model, a set of incentives or benefits, and the expression of social norms. The three elements of the minimal rational choice model are political efficacy, collective benefits, and the perceived costs of voting. Individual benefits are the personal satisfaction that comes from voting and the anticipated guilt that results from not voting. Group incentives involve wanting to get benefits for people who resemble oneself or are perceived as needing help. System benefits are defined as the sense that voting is necessary to the proper functioning of democracy. An expressive benefit is the sense of satisfaction experienced by supporting a favoured candidate or party or some political institution or process. Social norms refer to people's views of what others think about voting and whether others around them vote.

Overall, each of the three individual rationality models tells an interesting story about voting turnout. In the cognitive mobilization model, cognitive skills and policy dissatisfaction may encourage people to stay home or, alternatively, prompt them to go to the polls to support an opposition party. In the minimal rational choice model, the difference between benefits discounted by efficacy and costs determines whether people will go to the polls. These calculations, together with an expanded, multi-level set of incentives or benefits, comprise the general incentives model.

SOCIOLOGY, RATIONALITY, AND TURNOUT

Sociological models have important implications for scholarly thinking about why attitudinal and behavioural change occurs, and how organizations inform voters and mobilize their participation during elections. Such models typically use social group membership and identity to explain attitudinal reinforcement in decision making and party strength in the electorate. These models also use social psychology to explain political choice. In the British case, proponents of class-based models generally have had little to say about the decision (not) to vote.[4] However, some analysts have concluded that sociology, in general, and social psychology, in particular, has a useful role to play in explanations of turnout. For example, Pattie and Johnston (1998: 266) offer the following summary: '(f)rom past research, the archetypal abstainer is a socially isolated, working class, private tenant who lives in a safe seat, is not a member of local or national organizations, and who has few distinctive political views beyond doubt over their own (and the system's) political efficacy'. Clearly, several of the explanatory variables in this account of nonvoting are located in the sociological framework.

But, there are good reasons to suspect that sociological models can tell only part of the story of why people choose to vote as they do or, indeed, why they choose to vote at all. One reason has to do with the general character of these models. They are ill equipped to deal with information that does not have a (social) group referent or with short-term contextual and political change (Dalton and Wattenberg 1993). Accordingly, they cannot accommodate short- and medium-term movements in their own explanatory variables or in the outcome variables that they purport to explain. Indeed, social characteristics and expectations, social relationships, social trust, and social resources and networks are assumed to change slowly and, in some cases, not at all. Sociological models could not possibly explain an abrupt, large-scale, change in turnout such as that which occurred between the 1997 and 2001 general elections.

A second reason involves reliance on social characteristics, contexts, and psychology. There are several points here. If social characteristics and contexts drive participation, puzzling anomalies arise. For example, as levels of education and economic resources have increased throughout the populations of mature democracies, turnout also should have increased. In fact, however, it has declined (Nie, Junn, and Stehlik-Barry 1996; Maloney, Smith, and Stoker 2000; Dalton 2002).

Similarly, if Hall (1999) is correct to claim that social capital has increased in Britain, one would expect that turnout would be trending upward. But, the long-term trend has been just the opposite. A further point is that society does not always determine the psychology of choice. In this regard, various constituency- and individual-level factors have been used to analyze voting decisions in British general elections since the 1960s (Denver and Hands 1974, 1985, 1997; Crewe, Sarlvik, and Alt 1977; Swaddle and Heath 1989; Pattie and Johnston 1998). Constituency differences in turnout rates and political choice can be explained by spatial variations in perceived economic performance and political efficacy, or by the presence of competitive parties and high-interest campaigns. Social psychology alone cannot provide unique insights into why (strong) party identifiers or politically interested people are more likely to turnout than those who are not (Pattie and Johnston 1998).

The third reason for suspicion is that sociological models are noteworthy for what they exclude as well as what they include. It has been argued that '[t]he SES model is weak in its theoretical underpinnings . . . there is no clearly specified mechanism linking social statuses to activity' (Verba, Schlozman, and Brady 1995: 281). The social capital model is also sparse: social interactions presumably ensure compliance with norms that motivate social behaviour (Putnam 2000: 336–44). In a democracy, one of these norms is civic duty, but the social capital model rarely addresses it whereas, paradoxically, some individual rationality models do. Given their difficulty in accommodating short- and medium-term change, it is not surprising that sociological models have various kinds of causal specification problems. Again, the social capital model is illustrative. Levels of trust help to diffuse information, resources, and norms necessary for participation, but social interaction and participation can also affect social trust (Rahn, Brehm, and Carlson 1999). Which way does the causal arrow flow? More basically, all three models—perceived equity–fairness, social capital, civic voluntarism—do not provide educated, resourced, efficacious, socially interconnected individuals with incentives to participate or benefits from doing so. This is not the case with the individual rationality models of cognitive mobilization, minimal rational choice, and general incentives.

In the last four decades, the erosion of traditional social anchors, such as the class-party nexus, ongoing changes in the composition of the electorate, and the changing mix of salient forces operating in the public arena at various points in time have led students of voting behaviour in Britain and elsewhere to question whether sociological models can explain electoral choice and political change. This questioning has been accompanied by a growing interest in the explanatory power of models located in the individual rationality framework. In this chapter, we have presented six models of voting turnout. Three of the models are located in the sociological framework and three are located in the individual rationality framework. In the next chapter, we will conduct a tournament to see which model tells the most convincing story of voting turnout in Britain.

NOTES

1. The question was: '[N]ow, a few questions about how active you are in politics and community affairs. Let's think about the next few years. Using a scale from 0–10, where 0 means very unlikely and 10 means very likely, how likely is it that you will [engage in each one of ten activities].'

2. In the research literature, some of the basic institutions that affect turnout levels are ballot forms (simple versus complex), voting procedures, and election systems (e.g. Jackman 1987; Blais and Carty 1990; Jackman and Miller 1995; Shepsle and Boncheck 1997; Blais and Dobrzynska 1998; Franklin 1999, 2002; Bowler, Brockington, and Donovan 2001). Voter-friendly procedures include the construction and frequent updating of permanent lists of the eligible electorate, 'motor-voter' and other go-to-the-voter registration and enumeration techniques, longer polling hours, weekend or holiday voting, and internet, wireless telephone, and kiosk voting technology. It is also argued that electoral systems affect turnout rates. Plurality systems presumably produce mismatches between seats and votes that, in turn, discourage people, particularly those who support small or minor parties, from feeling efficacious and voting (Duverger 1954; see also Powell 2000). In contrast, turnout levels arguably are higher in systems that have more numerous, ideologically identifiable, and competitive parties that offer more real choices. In sum, '[t]urnout is likely to be highest in a small, industrialized, densely populated country, where the national lower house election is decisive, voting is compulsory and the voting age is 21, having a PR system with relatively few parties and a close electoral outcome' (Blais and Dobrzynska 1998: 251).

3. Other modifications to the basic rational voter model include the specification of complex relationships among explanatory variables, the introduction of the minimax regret criterion, and considerations of the quality of information available to the voter. For example, Eubank (1986) specifies a turnout model in which the voter's sense of civic duty affects the calculation of the probability of influencing the outcome and, in turn, this calculation affects civic duty. Minimax regret requires the voter to calculate how much regret would be experienced if she or he did not vote and the preferred candidate or party lost what turned out to be an extremely close contest where their vote could have proved decisive (e.g. Aldrich 1993). Ghirardato and Katz (2002: 3) recently have argued that the quality of information matters as well: '[V]oters consider abstention strictly optimal when the candidates' policy positions are both ambiguous and they are "ambiguity complements", that is, one looks better in one scenario but the other does in another . . . the voter becomes afraid that voting for one is a mistake and for voting for the other would have been the right thing to do.'

4. For example, although Butler and Stokes (1969: 278) argued that differential abstention rates across classes could affect election outcomes, their attention to factors affecting turnout is confined to a brief bivariate analysis of the relationship between union membership and turnout (1969: 164–5).

E I G H T

The Decision (Not) to Vote

In Chapter Seven, we presented six alternative models that have been proposed to explain voting turnout. This chapter employs these models to analyze turnout in the 2001 general election. We first specify the six models and discuss their explanatory variables. The models' parameters are estimated, and their explanatory power is compared using encompassing tests of the type introduced in Chapter Four. These tests show that two models dominate their rivals, although they do not formally encompass them. We then estimate a composite or 'best' model that includes the most powerful predictor variables from specific models. The results of these analyses are used to inform an investigation of sources of change in voting rates over time. We test two variants of a hypothesis advanced to account for the sharp decline in turnout between 1997 and 2001, and then conduct a more general analysis of factors relevant for understanding the short- and long-term dynamics of electoral participation. The conclusion considers what the findings tell us about possible future trends in turnout in British general elections.

SPECIFYING RIVAL MODELS OF TURNOUT

The first model presented in Chapter Seven is the *perceived equity–fairness* or relative deprivation model. As the discussion in that chapter indicated, the key idea motivating this model is that individuals who perceive that a gap exists between what they expect and what they get out of life suffer a sense of deprivation. In turn, this stimulates them to protest. We also expect an impact on electoral participation that very likely takes the form of voting against the incumbent government if it is seen as the source of the deprivation.

The perceived equity–fairness model is specified as follows:

$$V = f(\beta_0 + \beta_1 \text{SENDEP} + \beta_2 \text{ECDEPR} + \beta_3 \text{ECDEPP} + \beta_4 \text{ECMOT} + \beta_5 \text{GOVDIS} + \Sigma\beta_{6-9}\text{MEMDEP})$$

where

$V =$ voting turnout (scored 1 if voted, and 0 otherwise);

SENDEP = generalized sense of relative deprivation;

ECDEPR = retrospective economic deprivation attributed to government;

ECDEPP = prospective economic deprivation attributed to government;

ECMOT = negative emotional reactions to personal economic circumstances;

GOVDIS = extent of dissatisfaction with the government's policy performance;

MEMDEP = member of a deprived group.

β_0 is a constant and β_{1-k} are coefficients for the effects of independent variables $1-k$.

The measure of a generalized sense of relative deprivation in the perceived equity–fairness model is constructed from two Likert-scale statements designed to capture the perception that people's expectations and their life experiences do not match, and that government does not treat them fairly. Thus, one measure links deprivation to government action, whereas the other is more general. Responses to these statements by people interviewed in the 2001 British Election Study (BES) pre- and post-election panel appear in Table 8.1. The table shows that nearly one-quarter of respondents disagreed with the statement that 'the government treats people like me fairly', and slightly over half felt that there was a big gap between their expectations of life and their actual experiences. Responses to the two statements are aggregated, with a high score denoting high levels of perceived deprivation and a low score, the opposite.[1]

Table 8.1 also contains the indicators of perceived economic deprivation. The first measures an individual's perception of the trend in his or her personal financial situation over the past year, that is, a retrospective egocentric evaluation. The second measures expectations of personal economic circumstances over the year ahead, that is, a prospective egocentric evaluation. Slightly over one-fifth of the 2001 BES panelists reported that their personal financial situation had deteriorated during the past year, and slightly fewer thought that they would experience harder times in the year ahead. When building the economic deprivation variable, responses to the two statements are weighted by respondents' assessments of government responsibility for the financial situation of their households. Thus, a high score on the economic deprivation index means that the respondent is pessimistic about their past and future economic prospects, and blames the government.[2] The expectation is that this combination of negative economic evaluations and government responsibility attributions mobilizes people to turn out, very likely to vote for an opposition party.

An additional economic indicator in the equity–fairness model is based on responses to questions in the 2001 BES that tap positive and negative emotional

Table 8.1   Indicators in the equity–fairness model (Horizontal percentages)

	Strongly agree	Agree	Neither	Disagree	Strongly disagree
Perceptions of relative deprivation					
The government generally treats people like me fairly.	4	45	26	20	4
There is often a big gap between what people like me expect out of life and what we actually get.	11	41	23	21	2
	Lot worse	*Little worse*	*Same*	*Little better*	*Lot better*
Perceptions of economic deprivation					
How does the financial situation of your household now compare with what it was 12 months ago?	5	17	46	27	6
How do you think the financial situation of your household will change over the next 12 months?	2	16	48	26	4
	Word applies				
Emotional reactions to personal economic conditions					
Which, if any, of the following words describe your feelings about the financial condition of your household?					
Angry	15				
Disgusted	11				
Uneasy	30				
Afraid	15				
	Very well	*Fairly well*	*Neither*	*Fairly badly*	*Very badly*
Policy satisfaction					
How well do you think the present government has handled each of the following issues?					
Crime	2	24	33	27	12
Education	4	39	28	19	6
The national health service	3	23	26	31	15
Transport	1	16	25	35	18

Source: 2001 BES pre–post election panel survey.

reactions to personal economic circumstances. Here, we are interested in the latter. As Table 8.1 shows, about 30 per cent of the panelists said that they felt uneasy about their economic circumstances, 15 per cent felt angry, 15 per cent were afraid, and 11 per cent were disgusted. To summarize negative emotional reactions to personal economic conditions, we construct an additive index, with high scores (4) accorded to individuals who expressed all four of the negative emotions, and low scores (0) to those who expressed none of them. The expectation is that these negative emotions prompt people to go to the polls independently of their cognitive assessments of their financial situations.

Another indicator is satisfaction or dissatisfaction with government performance in selected policy areas. The policy areas chosen were the most salient ones in the election campaign, that is, health, education, crime, and transport. As discussed in Chapter Four, there was substantial dissatisfaction with the government's performance in these (and other) policy areas. Specifically, 53 per cent said that the government had performed 'fairly' or 'very' badly on transport, and 46 per cent and 39 per cent, respectively, were dissatisfied with how the government had handled the National Health Service (NHS) and crime. Although less dissatisfaction was expressed regarding education, 25 per cent gave the government low marks in this policy area. An overall index is constructed by combining evaluations of government performance in the four policy areas.[3]

The final component of the equity–fairness model is membership in a deprived group. Although a number of such groups can be identified, they are operationalized here as ethnic minorities, women, retired persons, and the unemployed.[4] It can be hypothesized that members of these groups have experienced economic or social discrimination because of the characteristics they share. Thus, membership in these groups should prompt feelings of deprivation that encourages either abstention or 'protest voting'.

The second, *social capital* model emphasizes the role of interpersonal trust in cooperation among individuals trying to solve collective action problems. As discussed in Chapter Seven, the most influential contemporary analysis of the origins and significance of social trust is that by Robert Putnam (1993, 2000). Putnam's argument, which recalls de Tocqueville's thesis in *Democracy in America*, is that trust derives from face-to-face interactions among individuals participating in voluntary activities. Participation engenders trust and a willingness to cooperate with others. Social engagement in the social capital model is operationalized here as volunteering or being asked to participate. The model is specified as follows:

$$V = f(\beta_0 + \beta_1 \text{TRUST} + \beta_2 \text{FAIR} + \beta_3 \text{VOLUN} + \beta_4 \text{ASKED})$$

where

$V =$ voting turnout;

TRUST $=$ the extent to which individuals think that other people are trustworthy;

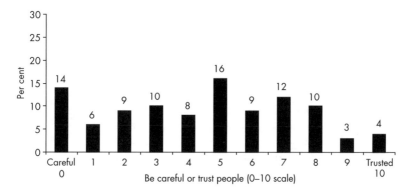

Figure 8.1 Social trust: people can be trusted or cannot be too careful
Note: Mean = 4.5, standard deviation = 2.9.
Source: 2001 BES pre–post election panel survey.

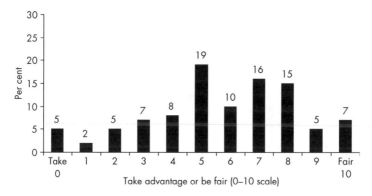

Figure 8.2 Social trust: people are fair or take advantage
Note: Mean = 5.7; standard deviation = 2.6.
Source: 2001 BES pre–post election panel survey.

FAIR = the extent to which individuals think that other people will treat them fairly;
VOLUN = volunteered to participate in politics or community affairs;
ASKED = asked to become active in a voluntary organization.

The indicators of trust and fairness appear in Figures 8.1 and 8.2. Both indicators are 11-point scales, varying from zero to ten. The trust variable is based on a BES item that asked respondents to rate their levels of trust in other people, and the fairness variable is based on an item which asked if they perceive other people to be fair or likely to take advantage of them.[5] The average trust score (4.5) is lower than the average fairness score (5.7), but both averages are close to the mid-points of the respective scales. Additionally, as Figures 8.1 and 8.2 illustrate, perceptions of trust and fairness are widely dispersed. There are minorities who strongly believe that people are trustworthy and fair, but others express considerable caution about what can be expected when dealing with others.

There are also two indicators of engagement in networks of voluntary activity in the social capital model. One is whether individuals volunteered to participate in politics or community affairs, and another is whether they have been asked to participate in such activities.[6] In this regard, 13 per cent of the respondents in the 2001 BES panel said that they had volunteered to become involved in politics or community affairs, and 20 per cent said that they had been asked to become active (see Table 8.2). Much of this activity does not take place in parties or other political organizations but, rather, occurs in sports clubs, charities, and various other groups.

The third model presented in Chapter Seven is *civic voluntarism*. It is specified as:

$$V = f(\beta_0 + \Sigma\beta_{1-4}\text{RESOURCES} + \beta_5\text{RECRUIT} + \beta_6\text{VACT} + \beta_7\text{EFFIC} + \beta_8\text{INTER} + \beta_9\text{SPID})$$

where

$$V = \text{voting turnout;}$$
$$\text{RESOURCES} = \text{educational attainment, social class, and amount of available time;}$$
$$\text{RECRUIT} = \text{an index of recruitment by others and mobilization by parties;}$$
$$\text{VACT} = \text{extent of voluntary activity;}$$
$$\text{EFFIC} = \text{political efficacy, that is, a sense of being able to influence politics;}$$
$$\text{INTER} = \text{interest in the election;}$$
$$\text{SPID} = \text{strength of partisanship.}$$

The core idea of the civic voluntarism model is that resources facilitate participation. Resources do so directly but also indirectly via their effects on a person's sense of political efficacy and his or her interest in politics. Efficacy and interest have direct effects on participation. In addition, participation is encouraged by strength of party identification, and by the activities of political parties, other groups, and individuals. Resources are measured by three variables, educational attainment, social class, and available time. Educational attainment has three categories, and social class is the standard Market Research Society scale used in earlier chapters (see Table 8.2). Available time is measured by asking people how much time they have available after they have met their work and family responsibilities.[7]

The recruitment indicators measure two types of effects. One is the influence of general face-to-face interaction, and the second is the influence of the political parties. With respect to the former, the first two variables in Table 8.2 are based on questions that explore whether someone had tried to persuade the respondent to get involved in politics or community affairs, or to vote for a particular party.

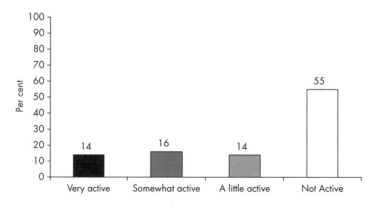

Figure 8.3   Extent of voluntary activity past few years

Source: 2001 BES pre–post election panel survey.

As discussed in Chapter Five, the party mobilization items measure whether a respondent was canvassed in person by one or more the parties, canvassed by telephone, or reminded to go to the polls.[8] As noted above, 20 per cent of the respondents said they had been asked to become involved in politics or community affairs. About one in ten said that someone they knew had tried to convince them how to vote, and slightly fewer had received a telephone call from one or more of the parties. Doorstep canvassing was the most common form of party mobilization, with nearly a quarter of the BES panelists reporting that they had been canvassed during the 2001 election campaign. And, one person in twenty reported being contacted by one or more parties on election day. The variables were factor analyzed to determine whether there are distinct social recruitment and party mobilization factors. The analysis delineated two such factors, one associated with discussions with other people and another with contacts by the parties.[9]

Another indicator in the civic voluntarism model is the extent of voluntary activity. Verba, Schlozman, and Brady (1995) and other proponents of this model argue that voluntary activity helps people to acquire skills that are useful for political participation. For example, individuals who participate in voluntary activities may develop or enhance their ability to speak in public, to negotiate with others, and to reach compromises when disagreements arise. Nearly half of the BES panelists reported that they had been at least minimally involved in voluntary activity in recent years (see Figure 8.3).[10] However, only 14 per cent described themselves as 'very active'.

Three variables in the civic voluntarism model tap psychological engagement in politics. The first variable is political efficacy which is measured by asking BES respondents to use an 11-point (0–10) scale to indicate how much influence they think they have on politics and public affairs.[11] As Figure 8.4 shows, nearly half perceived that they had no political influence at all, and most of the rest thought that

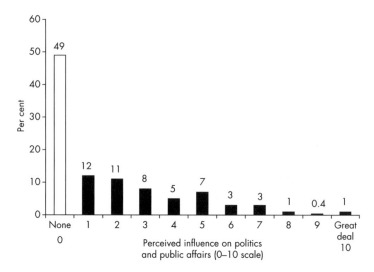

Figure 8.4   Perceived political influence scale

Note: Mean = 1.7; standard deviation = 2.2.

Source: 2001 BES pre–post election panel survey.

they had limited influence. Less than 10 per cent gave themselves scores greater than the mid-point (5) on the scale, and the average score is only 1.7 out of a possible 10. Another variable is interest in the 2001 general election. Just under one-quarter said they were 'very interested', and slightly over two-fifths were 'somewhat interested' (see Table 8.2). A third variable is strength of partisanship. This variable is measured using the traditional BES question asking about the strength of party identification. In the pre-election interview, only 9 per cent said they were 'very strong' party identifiers, and 28 per cent indicated they were 'fairly strong' identifiers.[12]

The fourth model is *cognitive mobilization*. It is specified as follows:

$$V = f(\beta_0 + \beta_1 \text{EDUC} + \beta_2 \text{MEDIA} + \beta_3 \text{INTER} + \beta_4 \text{PKNOW} + \beta_5 \text{GOVDIS})$$

where

V = voting turnout;

EDUC = educational attainment;

MEDIA = exposure to media coverage of the election;

INTER = interest in the election;

PKNOW = information relevant to voting;

GOVDIS = extent of dissatisfaction with the government's policy performance.

As discussed in Chapter Seven, the cognitive mobilization model focusses on exposure to political information, the ability and willingness to respond to that information, and reactions to its content. Media exposure captures the first of these

Table 8.2 Indicators in the civic voluntarism model (Column percentages)

Educational Qualifications		
No qualifications		48
Less than University		34
University		18
Social Class		
Middle and Upper:	A	3
	B	20
	C1	33
Working:	C2	20
	D	13
	E	11

Available Time
(Question: How much time do you have left over each week
   after you have carried out your work and family responsibilities?)

A great deal	17
A fair amount	24
Some	47
None	13

Political Mobilization	*Percentage Yes*
Over the past few years, has anyone asked you to get involved in politics or community affairs?	20
Did anyone, for example, a friend, a member of your family, or someone at work, try to convince you how to vote in the recent general election?	11
Did a canvasser from any party call at your home to talk with you during the election campaign?	23
Did anyone from a political party telephone you during the election campaign to ask you how you might vote?	8
Did any political party contact you on election day itself to see whether you had voted/intended to vote?	5

Interest in Election
(Question: How interested are you in the general election that is likely to be held soon?)

Very interested	23
Somewhat interested	41
Not very interested	24
Not at all interested	12

Strength of Party Identification
(Question: Would you call yourself very strong [PARTY], fairly strong or not very strong?)
(Pre-Election Survey)

Very strong	9
Fairly strong	28
Not very strong	48
None	14

Source: 2001 BES pre–post election panel survey.

ideas, education and political knowledge measure the ability of the individual to respond to information, and interest in the campaign and policy dissatisfaction proxy reactions to the content of information. The claims advanced by advocates of the cognitive mobilization model are straightforward—educated, interested, and knowledgeable citizens are more likely to participate than uneducated, uninterested, and uninformed ones. Additionally, dissatisfaction with government performance should affect participation. However, such dissatisfaction could 'cut either way'—increasing or decreasing the likelihood that people will go to the polls.

Regarding variables in the cognitive mobilization model, approximately one in five of the BES panelists had university qualifications, and an additional one-third had various non-university qualifications (see Table 8.2). Other variables in the cognitive mobilization model appear in Table 8.3. Political knowledge is measured using a quiz that contains three false statements and three true ones.[13] Correct

Table 8.3   Indicators in the cognitive mobilization model

	True	False	Do not know
Political Knowledge Quiz (Horizontal Percentages)			
Polling stations close at 10 PM on election day	<u>82</u>	7	10
If is official Conservative party policy that Britain should never join the single European Currency	32	<u>46</u>	22
The Liberal Democrats favour a system of proportional representation for Westminster elections.	<u>60</u>	5	35
The minimum voting age is 16.	10	<u>85</u>	5
Unemployment has fallen since Labour was elected in 1997.	<u>77</u>	13	10
Only taxpayers are allowed to vote in a general election.	3	<u>94</u>	3
Does the respondent regularly read a daily morning newspaper? (Column Percentages)			
Yes	60		
No	40		
Amount of attention respondent paid to television coverage of the 2001 general election (Column Percentages)			
A great deal of attention	9		
A fair amount of attention	23		
Some attention	42		
No attention	27		

Note: Underscored figures are correct answers.

Source: 2001 BES pre–post election panel survey.

answers to the political knowledge questions are underscored in Table 8.3. An overwhelming majority were aware of the regulations governing elections—they knew when polling stations close, that taxpayers are not the only people allowed to vote, and that the minimum age for voting is not 16. They were less knowledgeable about party policies—only 46 per cent were aware of official Conservative party policy on British membership in the European Monetary Union, and only 61 per cent knew that the Liberal Democrats favour a system of proportional representation for Westminster elections. However, a large majority had correct information about the performance of the economy—nearly four-fifths knew that unemployment had fallen since the Labour government was elected in 1997. The average number of correct answers is 4.5, suggesting that levels of relevant knowledge are reasonably high, even if some people do not know the precise content of party programmes.

Additional variables in the cognitive mobilization model concern exposure to information about politics and the election. Newspaper readership is used to measure general exposure to political information, and watching programmes about the campaign on television is used to measure information about the election.[14] Media consumption patterns suggest that attention to the 2001 campaign was quite limited. Although six of ten respondents were regular readers of a daily newspaper, less than one in ten said that they paid a 'great deal' of attention to television coverage of the election, and less than one in four said they paid a 'fair amount' of attention (see Table 8.3). The final two variables in the cognitive mobilization model involve reactions to the content of information. One measure of this is interest in the election campaign, and a second is dissatisfaction with the performance of the government.

The fifth model is the *minimal rational choice* model. The central idea of rational choice is that individuals undertake actions only if the expected benefits of doing so outweigh the costs. The model investigated here is specified as follows:

$$V = f(\beta_0 + \beta_1 \text{EFFIC} \times \text{BENEFITS} - \beta_2 \text{COSTS})$$

where

V = voting turnout;
EFFIC = political efficacy, that is, a sense of being able to influence politics;
BENEFITS = perceived collective benefits of voting;
COSTS = perceived costs of voting.

In models of this type, people's perceptions of their personal contribution to the provision of collective benefits play a key role in determining whether they participate. In the classic studies, this personal contribution is conceptualized in terms of 'pivotality', that is, the likelihood that one's contribution (vote) will decide the election outcome. Pivotality discounts the benefits (utility) expected to accrue by casting a ballot for a particular party. Thus, even if individuals perceive that enormous net benefits will result from the election of one party rather than its competitors, but they also think that their own contribution to providing these benefits is trivial (the probability that their vote will prove decisive is negligible), then it is not rational for them to vote. Since the objective probability than any single vote will, in fact, prove pivotal is exceedingly small, but millions of people do vote, this gives rise to the well-known paradox of participation that bedevils strict rational choice accounts of turnout (Green and Shapiro 1994).

In the minimal rational choice model tested here, we circumvent this problem by replacing pivotality with efficacy, that is, an individual's sense of the extent to which she or he is politically influential. Sense of personal efficacy is used to weight the collective benefits term in the model. The collective benefits variable is based on ideas in the spatial voting literature (Downs 1957; Merrill and Grofman 1999). In this literature, electors support the party that is closest to them in a policy space, which is often operationalized as a unidimensional left–right ideological continuum. By making their electoral choices in this way, voters maximize their expected utility. Applying this idea to the task of explaining turnout, if an individual assigns the same score to each party in the space, then she or he must either vote for all of the parties (which is impossible) or vote for none of them. Consequently, if an elector derives equal utility from several parties, then she or he will not vote because there is no difference in the payoff from supporting one party rather than another. In contrast, if one party is seen to provide more utility than the others, then, *ceteris paribus*, there is an incentive to go to the polls.

The efficacy variable in this model is the 11-point scale displayed in Figure 8.4. As observed above, if individuals took an objective view of their own influence on the outcome of an election, then they would give themselves a score *very* close to zero on this scale. However, as discussed in the context of the civic voluntarism model, a (small) majority of the BES respondents did not give themselves a zero score, thereby indicating that they thought they had at least some political influence. This finding can be accounted for in one of two ways. The first explanation is that voters are simply wrong about their objective level of political influence. They are 'bad statisticians' (Green and Shapiro 1994) whose calculation of the probability of casting a vote that would have a nontrivial impact on the election outcome is greatly at odds with reality. The weakness of this interpretation is that it does not accord well with a rational choice theory which is based on the assumption that people can rationally calculate the costs and benefits of different courses of action. If individuals are seriously wrong about their own influence on the outcome of an election, then they are quite likely to be wrong about the costs and benefits of voting, and the whole theory breaks down. A second explanation of perceptions of influence is more congenial with the spirit of rational choice theory, broadly defined. It suggests that when people respond to survey questions about their political efficacy, they are thinking *collectively*, that is, in terms of the influence of *groups* of people like themselves. If respondents interpret efficacy questions in these terms, then it is sensible, for example, for blue-collar factory workers to believe that they are part of a group that can influence the outcome of an election. Consequently, they are motivated to take action because they feel that they can collectively make a difference.

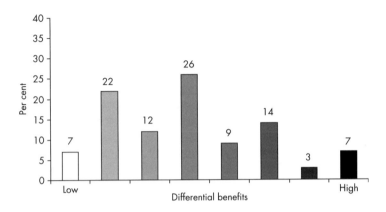

Figure 8.5 Differential party benefits index

Note: Mean squared differential benefits from various parties (pairwise comparisons between Conservatives, Labour, Liberal Democrats, and Nationalists) = 15.2, standard deviation = 15.3.

Source: 2001 BES pre–post election panel survey.

Eleven-point (0–10) party 'like–dislike' scales are used to proxy the utility that voters expect to receive from various parties (see also Chapter Four). The square of the absolute difference in these scores for each pair of parties is computed, and these quantities are averaged.[15] Scores on the resulting 'differential party benefits index' are displayed in Figure 8.5. The figure reveals that only a small minority (7 per cent) of the respondents saw little or no difference in the benefits provided by the parties. A very large majority thus had at least some minimal incentive to vote. But most people did not perceive enormous differences between the parties—only slightly over one in three had differential benefits scores that exceeded the mean value of 15.2 points, and only one in ten had scores that placed them in top two categories of the figure.

Turning next to costs, these are measured by two Likert-scale items that asked respondents about their perceptions of the amount of time that it takes to participate in politics, and whether they think people are too busy to vote.[16] Table 8.4 shows that a majority (55 per cent) of the BES panelists thought that it takes too much time and effort to get involved in politics, and only 20 per cent disagreed. Calculations about the costs of voting are quite different. A substantial majority indicated that they believe the time it takes people to vote is acceptable—nearly three-fifths disagreed with the proposition that people are too busy to vote, and only 29 per cent agreed. If time considerations were the only factor governing turnout, then the expectation would be that substantial majorities would go to the polls.

The Decision (Not) to Vote

Table 8.4   Costs of political participation (Horizontal percentages)

Statement	Strongly agree	Agree	Neither	Disagree	Strongly disagree
It takes too much time and effort to be active in politics and public affairs.	10	45	24	18	2
People are so busy that they do not have time to vote.	3	26	12	43	16

Source: 2001 BES pre–post election panel survey.

The sixth, *general incentives* model 'nests' the minimal rational choice model. That is, the general incentives model includes all of the predictor variables—efficacy × differential party benefits (EFFIC × BENEFITS) and perceived costs of voting (COSTS)—used in the minimal rational choice model. However, the general incentives model also employs predictor variables derived from social–psychological accounts of political participation. As discussed in Chapter Seven, this model was first devised to explain the 'high intensity' participation undertaken by party activists (Seyd and Whiteley 1992; Whiteley, Seyd, and Richardson 1994; Whiteley and Seyd 2002). Here, it is applied to explaining turnout, and is specified as follows:

$$V = f(\beta_0 + \beta_1 EFFIC \times BENEFITS - \beta_2 COSTS + \beta_3 INDIVB + \beta_4 GROUPB + \beta_5 SYSB + \beta_6 NORMS + \beta_7 EXPRESS)$$

where

V = voting turnout;
EFFIC = sense of being able to influence politics;
BENEFITS = perceived collective benefits of voting;
COSTS = perceived costs of voting;
INDIVB = perceived benefits or private returns provided by participation itself;
GROUPB = perceived benefits obtained by groups which the individual supports and which occur when the individual participates;
SYSB = beliefs that citizens have a duty to support the political system by voting;
NORMS = perceptions that other people expect one to vote;
EXPRESS = sense of satisfaction received by voting for a party that one supports.

Table 8.5 contains data on variables in the general incentives model that have not been discussed already. It can be seen that most people said that they feel a sense of satisfaction when they vote, which is a classic individual incentive for

Table 8.5 Additional indicators in the general incentives model (Horizontal percentages)

Statements	Strongly agree	Agree	Neither	Disagree	Strongly disagree
Individual benefits					
I feel a sense of satisfaction when I vote.	17	45	19	16	4
I would feel very guilty if I did not vote in a general election.	23	37	10	20	9
Group benefits					
Being active in politics is a good way to get benefits for groups that people care about like pensioners or the disabled.	11	58	18	12	1
When people like me vote, they can really change the way that Britain is governed.	4	36	22	29	7
System benefits					
It is every citizen's duty to vote in an election.	47	33	8	9	3
Democracy only works properly if most people vote.	25	60	8	6	1
Social norms					
Most of my family and friends think that voting is a waste of time.	4	16	12	43	25
Most people around here voted in the general election.	4	44	21	26	5

Source: 2001 BES pre–post election panel survey.

participation. The second indicator of individual benefits puts the idea the other way around and shows that many feel guilty if they do not vote.[17] Similarly, a large majority thought that voting can bring benefits to groups that they care about, and a sizeable plurality believed that if people like them vote they can really change Britain.[18] These are the measures of group benefits in the model, and they are designed to capture beliefs that such benefits can result from participating with others in an election. There also is very broad agreement with the ideas that voting is an obligation of citizenship, and that doing so has important system-level consequences. Thus, 80 per cent endorsed the proposition that it is every citizen's duty to vote, and fully 85 per cent agreed that democracy only works properly if most people vote.[19] Including these variables in the general incentives model enables us to test the hypothesis that people show up at the polls because they believe it is in the interests of the political community as a whole that citizens participate.

The survey data also suggest that social norms may play a role in motivating people to go to the polls. As Table 8.5 shows, two-thirds of the respondents disagreed with the statement that most of their family and friends think that voting is a waste of time, and less than one-third perceived that most of their neighbours did not bother to vote.[20] Both statements are designed to test the hypothesis that people act in response to perceptions of the beliefs of others they care about. The several Likert-scale statements in Table 8.5 are coded such that a high score denotes a strong sense of selective, group, and system benefits and social norms supportive of voting. The expectation is that people with high scores on these variables will be more likely to turnout than people with low scores.

Finally, the general incentives model contains the strength of partisanship variable that appears in Table 8.2. In terms of the logic of the model, this variable is conceptualized as an indicator of expressive benefits. The idea is that a psychological attachment to a political party motivates people to vote for reasons not directly linked to the calculations of the differential benefits currently being provided by various political parties. The realization of such an expressive benefit by voting is compatible with a social–psychological conception of party identification, as well as an individual rationality account of partisanship that views its strength as reflecting a tally of present and past party and party leader performance evaluations. If the latter conception of partisanship is adopted, then the inclusion of strength of party identification in the general incentives model may be justified in terms of its proxying a person's desire to express approval of the overall performance of a particular party and its leaders.

In the next section, we test the six turnout models using methods similar to those employed in Chapter Four. The rival models of turnout are tested against each other to determine which ones, if any, encompass the others. It is possible that some of the models may encompass at least some of the others, or that none of them encompasses any other. There is also the possibility that, even if a model does not formally encompass its rivals, it may nonetheless dominate in the sense of providing a statistically more powerful explanation of turnout. The analyses enable us to consider these alternative possibilities.

ANALYZING RIVAL MODELS OF TURNOUT

Binomial logit analyses (Long 1997) are used to estimate the parameters in the six turnout models. The dependent variable in these analyses is the measure of *verified turnout* in the 2001 BES, which is the most accurate indicator of individual electoral participation available.[21] Each model contains controls for age, gender, and ethnicity, all of which could influence the relationships between the predictor variables and turnout.[22] In the case of the equity–fairness model, ethnicity and gender are also part of the specification. We consider this model first.

Table 8.6 shows that several variables in the equity–fairness model affect turnout. Individuals who believed that there is a large gap between what they

Table 8.6 Rival models of turnout in the 2001 general election

Predictor variables	Civic voluntarism β	SE	Social capital β	SE	Rational choice β	SE
Education	0.03	0.09				
Social class	0.15★★★	0.04				
Leisure time	0.01	0.06				
Political efficacy	0.04★	0.03				
Party mobilization	0.15★★★	0.05				
Interest in the campaign	0.61★★★	0.06				
Voluntary activity	0.11★★	0.05				
Strength of partisanship	0.27★★★	0.06				
Asked to participate	0.08	0.05	0.46★★★	0.15		
Volunteering			0.09	0.18		
Trust in others			0.08★★★	0.02		
Perceived fairness			0.05★★	0.02		
Efficacy × benefits					0.01★★★	0.00
Perceived costs					−0.25★★★	0.03
Age	0.03★★★	0.06	0.03★★★	0.00	0.03★★★	0.00
Gender	−0.26★★	0.10	−0.12	0.10	−0.06	0.10
Ethnicity	0.42★★	0.17	0.20	0.16	0.18	0.16
Percentage correctly classified	75		71		72	
McFadden R^2	0.15		0.07		0.10	

Predictor variables	General incentives β	SE	Cognitive mobilization β	SE	Equity–fairness β	SE
Efficacy × benefits scale	0.01★★★	0.00				
Perceived costs	−0.20★★★	0.04				
Individual benefits	0.11★★★	0.04				
Group benefits	0.06	0.04				
System benefits	0.29★★★	0.04				
Social norms	0.16★★★	0.03				
Expressive benefits	0.13★★	0.06				
Education			0.10	0.08		
Election interest			0.56★★★	0.07		
Political knowledge			0.30★★★	0.05		
Attention to campaign on TV			0.19★★★	0.07		

Table 8.6 Continued

Predictor variables	General incentives		Cognitive mobilization		Equity–fairness	
	β	SE	β	SE	β	SE
Newspaper readership			−0.03	0.11		
Policy dissatisfaction			−0.03**	0.01	−0.07***	0.01
Perceived relative deprivation					−0.08***	0.03
Economic evaluations						
Prospective					0.05***	0.02
Retrospective					0.01	0.01
Emotional economic reactions					−0.07*	0.01
Age	0.02***	0.00	0.03***	0.00	0.03***	0.00
Gender	−0.08***	0.10	−0.39***	0.11	−0.14	0.10
Ethnicity	0.50***	0.17	0.28	0.18	−0.16	0.16
Retired					−0.19	0.19
Unemployed					−0.71***	0.22
Percentage correctly classified	76		75		71	
McFadden R^2	0.16		0.15		0.08	

Note: *** $p \leq 0.001$; ** $p \leq 0.01$; * $p \leq 0.05$; one–tailed test.

Source: 2001 BES pre–post election panel survey.

expect out of life and what they receive were less likely to vote. Dissatisfaction with government policy performance also inhibited electoral participation. The effects of reactions to economic conditions are mixed. On the one hand, people who were afraid, angry, uneasy, or disgusted about their personal economic circumstances were less likely to go to the polls. On the other hand, individuals who were pessimistic about their future economic prospects and blamed the government for this unhappy state of affairs were more likely to vote. A combination of negative personal economic expectations and government responsibility attributions helps to trigger participation.

Regarding the effects of socio-demographic characteristics, unemployed persons were less likely to vote, and gender and ethnicity are not statistically significant. Similarly, controlling for the general effect of age, retirement status is not significant. Age has a positive impact on the likelihood of voting, net of the effects of all other variables. But, this effect is not consistent with the perceived equity–fairness model since older voters in general, unlike the retired, are not particularly deprived in terms of income or social status. In sum, although the model does not have a very good fit with the data, some of its predictions are supported by the evidence.

The social capital model has a marginally poorer fit than its equity–fairness rival. However, three variables in the social capital model have statistically significant effects. They are trust in others, perceptions that others are fair, and being asked to participate (see Table 8.6). These findings indicate that interpersonal trust and the mobilizing activities of social networks have positive effects on the likelihood of voting. Age is also significant, but gender and ethnicity are not influential. Additionally, volunteering to become active is not a significant predictor when the other variables are included.

With respect to the civic voluntarism model, Table 8.6 shows that six of its variables—social class, party mobilization, voluntary activity, political efficacy, interest in the campaign, and strength of partisanship—are statistically significant. All of the effects are positive. People who are in higher social grades, have been contacted by political parties, are active in voluntary organizations, and are politically efficacious, interested, and strong party identifiers are more likely to go to the polls. These results suggest that people's resources, the extent to which they are mobilized by face-to-face contacts, and their psychological engagement with the political process help to explain the propensity to vote. In addition, the three control variables—age, gender, and ethnicity—have significant effects. *Ceteris paribus*, older persons, women, and members of the ethnic majority are more likely to participate. Controlling for other factors, educational level, leisure time, and being asked to participate are not influential. Overall, with an estimated R^2 of 0.15 and 75 per cent of the cases correctly classified, the civic voluntarism model fits the data better than do the equity–fairness and social capital models.

Parameter estimates for the cognitive mobilization model indicate that attention to the campaign on television, interest in the campaign, and political knowledge all promote turnout (see Table 8.6). Dissatisfaction with government performance is another significant predictor, and the negative sign on its coefficient indicates that it discourages people from voting. This result is consistent with the idea discussed above that dissatisfaction may promote withdrawal from the electoral arena and other conventional forms of political action. Regarding other predictors, newspaper readership and education are not influential. Of the socio-demographic variables, age and gender are significant—older people and women were more likely to go to the polls. Ethnicity is insignificant. As measured by the estimated R^2 and percentage of cases correctly classified, the goodness of fit of the cognitive mobilization model is identical to that of the civic voluntarism model.

The other two models displayed in Table 8.6 are minimal rational choice and general incentives. In the former, the interaction of political efficacy (perceived political influence) and collective benefits has the expected positive impact on turnout, and costs have the expected negative effect. As noted earlier, the minimal rational choice model is nested within the general incentives model. Parameter estimates for the latter model reveal that the efficacy × benefits interaction variable as well as costs continue to have a highly significant impact on turnout even when a variety of other factors are taken into account. All of the other predictors in the general incentives model, apart from perceptions of group benefits, also have significant effects. In 2001, individuals were motivated to go to the polls if they experienced a sense of personal satisfaction from voting, and if they believed that voting is a civic duty and important for the proper functioning of a democratic polity. They were also motivated by social norms, by perceptions that other people take voting seriously, and by expressive benefits, as measured by strength of partisan attachments. With one exception, the coefficients for all of the significant predictors are positive. The exception is perceived costs, which has a negative coefficient. As anticipated, people who thought that voting is costly were less likely to go to the polls. Of the control variables, only age is significant—older people were more likely than younger ones to vote.

The results in Table 8.6 are interesting, but they do not provide definitive guidance regarding which model gives the best account of turnout. Some of the models have a better fit than their rivals, but this alone cannot determine which is best. Apart from anything else, these models have very different underlying theoretical explanations of citizen participation. For example, the cognitive mobilization model predicts that voters are likely to be relatively well-educated people who are interested in and knowledgeable about government and politics. But, it has nothing to say about incentives for participation. In contrast, the general incentives model sees citizen participation arising from a wide-ranging cost-benefit calculation, but it neglects political interest and political knowledge. More generally, it is possible that each model might make a unique contribution to explaining why some people, but not others, go to the polls. Simply choosing the model with the best fit runs the risk of discarding important insights provided by the alternatives.

To shed additional light on the contributions of the alternative models, we conduct a series of encompassing tests to see if one or more of the models is superior to its rivals. We also calculate additional model selection criteria, namely the Akaike Information Criterion (AIC) and the Bayesian Information Criterion (BIC). These latter statistics, which discount a model's nominal explanatory power by the number of parameters it contains, are presented in Table 8.7. The table shows that the general incentives model has the best fit statistics of all six models, with smaller information statistics (AIC and BIC) and a larger estimated R^2 than any of the other models. By a slim margin, the general incentives model also does best in terms of correctly classifying voters and non-voters. It is closely followed by the cognitive mobilization and civic voluntarism models. By all of the criteria presented in the table, the social capital and equity–fairness models are inferior to their rivals.

A 'tournament of models' similar to that conducted in Chapter Four reveals that no one model encompasses its rivals, and all of the models have something to contribute. However, it is also clear that the pattern displayed in Table 8.7 is confirmed

Table 8.7   Comparison of the performance of rival models of turnout

Models	AIC	BIC	McFadden R²	Percentage correctly classified
Civic voluntarism	2335.74	2403.72	0.15	75
Social capital	2523.24	2562.89	0.07	71
Rational choice	2446.36	2474.68	0.10	72
General incentives	2276.30	2332.92	0.16	76
Cognitive mobilization	2318.08	2369.04	0.15	75
Equity–fairness	2511.38	2568.02	0.08	71

Source: 2001 BES pre–post election panel survey.

by the results of the tournament. Table 8.8 presents encompassing tests that compare the general incentives, cognitive mobilization, and civic voluntarism models with each other and with their weaker rivals. The table displays the reduction in the deviance statistics arising when one model is incorporated into its rivals[23]—the larger the reduction, the more powerful the model. Panel A shows that when the general incentives model is incorporated into its rivals, the improvement in fit is always *very much* larger than when the rival is added to the general incentives model. The one exception is the cognitive mobilization model. When the cognitive mobilization model is added to the general incentives model, the deviance is reduced by 100 points. When the general incentives model is added to the cognitive mobilization model, the result is quite similar, with the deviance falling by 144 points. Panel B in Table 8.8 shows that the cognitive mobilization model always enhances the fit more when it is added to a rival than is true in reverse, with the sole exception of the general incentives model. Finally, Panel C indicates that the civic voluntarism model improves the fit of the social capital and equity–fairness models more than is true in reverse, but this is not true in the case of the general incentives and cognitive mobilization models. More generally, it is evident that, although no one model formally encompasses the others, some models dominate the tournament. It is possible to rank order the models in terms of their ability to account for turnout and to add to the explanatory power of their rivals. The general incentives model is the most powerful, followed by cognitive mobilization and civic voluntarism. Minimal rational choice, equity–fairness, and social capital are weaker, with the latter being the weakest of all.

These results suggest that our ability to explain voting turnout can be enhanced by specifying a general model that includes elements of the six specific ones. To this end, we first construct a global model that includes all of the variables in the six models. Then, we reduce it to a more parsimonious composite specification by means of a general-to-specific modelling methodology similar to that advocated by

Table 8.8   Encompassing tests of rival models of turnout

Given Models	When the general incentives model is added to the given model	When the given model is added to the general incentives model
Panel A		
Civic voluntarism	129.8	74.4
Social capital	275.2	22.2
Rational choice	180.1	n.a.[a]
Cognitive mobilization	144.0	100.2
Equity–fairness	273.8	38.7
	When the cognitive mobilization model is added to the given model	When the given model is added to the cognitive mobilization model
Panel B		
Civic voluntarism	53.0	41.4
Social capital	222.0	12.9
Rational choice	193.7	57.4
General incentives	100.2	144.0
Equity–fairness	209.9	18.6
	When the civic voluntarism model is added to the given model	When the given model is added to the civic voluntarism model
Panel C		
Social capital	209.4	13.1
Rational choice	168.1	43.5
General incentives	74.4	129.8
Cognitive mobilization	41.4	53.0
Equity–Fairness	203.2	23.6

Note: [a] Not applicable since the rational choice model is nested within the general incentives model.
Source: 2001 BES pre–post election panel survey.

Hendry (1995).[24] This involves eliminating all variables which are not statistically significant at the 0.05 level or less. Parameter estimates for the resulting composite model are displayed in Table 8.9. These statistics confirm that the general incentives and cognitive mobilization models dominate. Altogether, five of the variables in the composite model—efficacy × benefits, costs, individual benefits, system benefits, and social norms—come from general incentives or minimal rational choice models. Four variables come from cognitive mobilization, that is, attention to the campaign on television, election interest, political knowledge, and dissatisfaction with the

Table 8.9   Composite model of turnout in the 2001 general election

Predictor variables	β		SE
Election interest	0.30***		0.07
Trust in others	0.05**		0.02
Efficacy × benefits scale	0.004***		0.001
Perceived costs	−0.15***		0.04
Individual benefits	0.10***		0.04
System benefits	0.23***		0.04
Social norms	0.13***		0.03
Policy dissatisfaction	−0.03**		0.01
Political knowledge	0.21***		0.05
Personal economic expectations	0.04***		0.01
Social class	0.08*		0.04
Party mobilization	0.11*		0.06
Attention to campaign on TV	0.14*		0.07
Perceived relative deprivation	0.07*		0.04
Age	0.02***		0.003
Gender	−0.37***		0.11
Ethnicity	0.43**		0.19
Percentage correctly classified		75	
McFadden R^2		0.21	
AIC		2174.88	
BIC		2271.11	

Note: *** $p \leq 0.001$; ** $p \leq 0.01$; * $p \leq 0.05$; one-tailed test.

Source: 2001 BES pre-post election panel survey.

government's performance. Civic voluntarism contributes social class, party mobilization, and interest in the campaign which it shares with cognitive mobilization. Social capital supplies interpersonal trust, and equity–fairness adds feelings of relative deprivation and prospective economic evaluations. The three control variables—age, ethnicity, gender—also are statistically significant in the composite model.

Figure 8.6 illustrates the change in the probability of voting associated with each of the variables in the composite model.[25] The largest effect is associated with the system benefits index. This effect (41 points) is more than twice as large as the individual benefits measure (17 points). These figures indicate that system benefits are substantially more important than private returns from voting, even though the latter are also significant. The strength of system benefits provides an explanation for why the paradox of participation does not prevent people from voting; namely, that they perceive voting is an obligation of citizenship that helps to make democracy work. However, it is also apparent that efficacy-discounted benefits and perceived costs have sizeable effects on the likelihood of casting a ballot. The former can increase the probability of voting by 30 points, and the latter can reduce

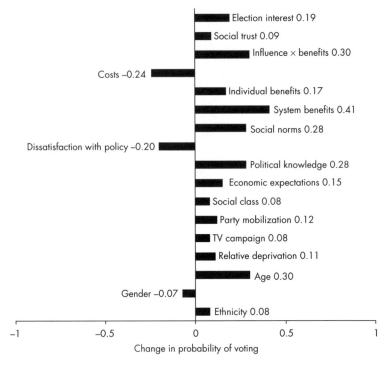

Figure 8.6 Effects of significant predictors on probability of voting, composite turnout model

it by 24 points. These results indicate that the cost–benefit calculations in the minimal rational choice and general incentives models are important components of the explanation of turnout provided by the composite model. More generally, the strong contribution of the general incentives model is apparent. On average, its variables can alter (increase or decrease) the probability of casting a ballot by 28 points.

Figure 8.6 also shows that variables associated with the cognitive mobilization model have an important story to tell. Changes in the probability of voting vary from 28 points in the case of political knowledge to 20 points in the case of dissatisfaction with the government's policy performance, to eight points in the case of attention to television coverage of the campaign. The average effect for variables in the cognitive mobilization model is 19 points. Other models speak less forcefully. On average, variables associated with the civic voluntarism model can change the probability of voting by 13 points, and variables associated with the social capital and equity–fairness models can do so by 9 and 13 points, respectively.

The control variables are also influential, with the impact of age being especially powerful. With other variables set at their means, the oldest voters have a 30-point greater probability of casting a ballot than the youngest ones.

Taken together, analyses of the composite model suggest that turnout can be explained by three classes of factors. First, there are *demographic characteristics.* As just noted, the age effect is sizeable, with younger people being much less likely to vote than their older counterparts, even with all other factors controlled. Gender and ethnicity are less important; however, women were more likely to vote than men, as were those in the ethnic majority. The second set of variables involves *incentives* that are contributed by the minimal rational choice and general incentives models. Some of these variables pertain to calculations of private costs and benefits, but the most important is a sense of obligation to the political community at large. The third class of variables refers to *mobilization* which is linked to the traditional notion of the 'good citizen' who pays attention to the political campaign, is informed about politics, and evaluates the performance of the government. Taking into account the explanatory power of various predictors, the overall message is clear. Turnout is basically about incentives and mobilization, with demographics—apart from age—playing only modest roles. In the next section, we consider how these findings help us to understand the dramatic change in turnout between 1997 and 2001 as well as more general variations in turnout over time.

CHANGING TURNOUT OVER TIME

Any attempt to investigate factors affecting participation in British general elections before 2001 encounters a problem. Until quite recently, turnout was not an important concern and, accordingly, most of the explanatory variables analyzed above were not included in the 1997 or earlier BES surveys. Hence, data from these surveys cannot be used in conjunction with those gathered in 2001 to measure over-time changes in the values of most of the significant predictor variables. However, it is possible to study some of the factors that influence the long-term dynamics of turnout, as well as two variants of a hypothesis that has been proposed to explain the especially large decline that occurred in 2001. We consider the latter topic first.

Turnout in 2001: Losing the Heartlands?

Several commentators argue that the dramatic fall in turnout in 2001 reflects the fact that Labour 'lost its heartlands'. There are two versions of this argument. One is rooted in spatial Downsian-style theories of party competition (Downs 1957). Variations in turnout are explained using the concept of differential party benefits

261

that motivates the specification of the minimal rational choice and general incentives models. Reminiscent of a conjecture advanced by Butler and Stokes (1969: 121) over three decades ago, the Downsian heartlands hypothesis claims that New Labour's policy positions alienated the party's traditional working class base. By moving his party to the right (e.g., see Figure 8.7), Tony Blair substantially narrowed the ideological distance between Labour and its principal competitor, the Conservatives. This may have made New Labour more attractive to the middle class, but it made it less attractive to the party's heartlands. In this account, turnout plummeted in 2001 because many working class Labour supporters saw no reason to vote when their party offered 'a Tory echo' rather than 'a socialist choice'.

A puzzle associated with this Downsian heartlands hypothesis is why the effect operated weakly, if at all, in the preceding 1997 general election. By the time that people prepared to go to the polls in that election, the New Labour project should have been readily apparent. Blair was clearly and correctly labelled a modernizer when he ran for the party leadership in 1994. After becoming leader, he repeatedly emphasized that he and his party would campaign and govern as New Labour (Bara and Budge 2001). Just in case anyone had doubts, Blair's determination to break with Labour's past was underscored when he routed the left opposition and removed 'Clause IV' (committing Labour to the 'common ownership of the means of production, distribution, and exchange') from the party's constitution. Given the wide publicity generated by New Labour's efforts to separate itself from Old Labour, a pronounced Downsian-style heartlands effect might have been expected in 1997. In the event, turnout *was* down. But, the drop was not huge by historical standards, with the percentage going to the polls being only slightly less than a number of other post–Second World War elections.

A second version of the heartlands hypothesis emphasizes performance in office, not commitments made in advance. Implicitly rehearsing Stokes (1963, 1992) critique of spatial models and his emphasis on valence rather than positional issues (see Chapter 2), this hypothesis focusses on New Labour's failure to 'deliver the goods'. Blair and Chancellor of the Exchequer, Gordon Brown, had adhered to a programme of tightly controlled public spending, and thereby had frustrated many in Labour's heartlands who had high hopes that 'their' government would revitalize the national health service, education, transport, and other cherished public services. The desireability of generous funding for these services had long been an article of faith among Labour partisans, and their disappointment with New Labour was especially bitter because the requisite funds were available. Unlike the Wilson and Callaghan governments whose policy ambitions had been thwarted by stagflation and associated economic ills, Blair and his colleagues enjoyed the luxury of governing with a vibrant economy.

New Labour's failure to deliver left their party's supporters with nowhere to go. Expanding public services was hardly a credible priority for a Conservative party that was promising large tax cuts and was widely seen to have run down the public sector during nearly two decades in office. The Liberal Democrats' credibility problem was not their policy positions. Indeed, as discussed in Chapter Four, respondents in the 2001 BES were slightly closer on average on the general 'left–right' and 'more services–less taxation' scales to the Liberal Democrats than to Labour. But, the Liberal Democrats had a political problem—they had no chance to win, and voters knew it. When asked about who would win in their local constituency, only 6 per cent of those interviewed in the 2001 BES pre-election survey chose the Liberal Democrats. Faced with the unpalatable alternatives of one party that was an ideological anathema, and a second that was a sure loser, a sizeable number of Labour's erstwhile supporters decided to stay at home in 2001.

The Downsian version of the heartlands hypothesis requires that the difference in perceived benefits provided by Labour as compared to other parties decrease among heartlands people (working class Labour partisans) *relative* to other voters between 1997 and 2001. Data from the 1997 BES show that the average differences for heartlands and other respondents were 4.3 and 3.3 points, respectively ($\eta = 0.22$, $F = 126.66$, $p = 0.000$). In 2001, the comparable figures were 3.5 and 2.7 points ($\eta = 0.17$, $F = 90.53$, $p = 0.000$). In both years, heartlands people saw a bigger benefits gap between Labour and other parties than did other voters, but the *size of the gap* between the two groups decreased by only one-fifth of a point between 1997 and 2001. More generally, perceived differential party benefits were smaller among both groups in 2001 than they had been four years earlier, but decreases were not sufficient to have a major effect on turnout. Across all voters, the party differential averaged 3.5 points in 1997 and 3.0 points in 2001. Assuming other predictors in the composite model are set at their means, such a small decrease in the party differential would be sufficient to lower the probability of voting by only a miniscule amount—one-fifth of a point.

The Stokesian version of the heartlands hypothesis also fails, at least if the effect at issue is restricted to working class Labour partisans. To test the hypothesis, we construct an interaction variable that measures the extent of performance dissatisfaction among working class Labour identifiers.[26] Adding this variable to the composite model of turnout shows that its effect (-0.03) is correctly signed but statistically insignificant ($p > 0.05$). However, it may be that a Stokesian-type effect works for Labour supporters generally, not just those in the working class. To investigate this possibility, we construct an interaction variable that measures performance dissatisfaction among all Labour identifiers. When added to the composite model, this more general interaction variable is negatively signed and statistically significant ($p < 0.05$). Thus, the influence of dissatisfaction with New Labour's performance in office on suppressing turnout was discernibly stronger among Labour partisans than in the rest of the electorate. With other predictor variables set at their means, changing the value of the interaction variable from its minimum to its maximum decreases the likelihood of casting a ballot by 13 points. Labour supporters did not need to be part of the party's traditional working class base to have disappointment with their party's performance dampen their enthusiasm for voting in 2001. However, this generalized Stokesian heartlands effect cannot account for a large proportion of the overall decline in turnout between 1997 and 2001. The 13-point decline in the probability of voting applies only to Labour identifiers who expressed the maximum level of government performance dissatisfaction. Only a minority of people were Labour partisans, and their levels of dissatisfaction with government performance varied widely.

Turnout over Time: Inter-Party Competition and Age

Using a logic similar to that motivating the inclusion of the political efficacy ✕ expected benefits term in the minimal rational choice and general incentives models, observers frequently argue that a competitive election among parties with distinctive policies is more likely to motivate participation than an uncompetitive one among parties with similar policies. As Anthony King (2001) commented after the 2001 election: 'Just provide the voters with a closely fought election at which a great deal is at stake and, make no mistake, they will again turn out in their droves.' King's reference to 'a great deal is at stake' clearly maps into the notion of differential expected benefits, and the extent of inter-party competition ('a closely fought election') is related to levels of political efficacy. Consider a situation when an election is a foregone conclusion, with one party expected to win easily. This will discourage participation, since people will be more inclined to believe that they are not influential—the election is a 'done deal', and their votes will not affect its outcome. In contrast, if the contest is likely to be close, then this will mobilize people to turn out. They feel a heightened sense of efficacy because they perceive that their votes and those of people like them can make a difference. The hypothesized relationship is the same as that between party competition and turnout at the constituency level (see Chapter Five), except it is applied to the anticipated result across the country as a whole.

To test the hypothesis, we employ aggregate data on general elections between 1945 and 2001. We measure inter-party competition using opinion polls available to the public in the period immediately preceding an election. If one party is well ahead of its rivals, then this implies that the contest will be seen as uncompetitive and, accordingly, the incentive to participate is reduced. In contrast, if the rival parties are running 'neck and neck', then this implies a very competitive situation, and the incentive to participate increases. We operationalize inter-party competition in the run-up to an election by computing the natural logarithm of the absolute distance in the polls between the leading party and its closest rival for the three months before election day.[27] Taking the natural logarithm reflects the assumption that an increase in party competition has a greater effect on turnout when the difference between parties is small than when it is large. As the gap between a leading party and its closest competitor narrows, the incentive to participate grows, and it does so at an increasing rate.

Inter-party competition provides a useful proxy for political efficacy, which is the *P* variable in the $P \times B - C$ expression in the minimal rational choice and general incentives models analyzed above. But, what about the *B* (benefits) and *C* (costs) terms? Although the survey data needed to measure these variables directly are unavailable, without being unduly heroic one may assume that the aggregate costs of voting are roughly constant over time. This leaves the *B* term, which is proxied using data on parties' left–right ideological positions gathered in the Party Manifestos Project (Budge et al. 2001). Recalling our earlier discussion of the minimal rational choice model, the idea is that larger policy differences among the parties should enhance the incentive to vote. Thus, in any given election, aggregate turnout should be positively related to the magnitude of the difference in the parties' policy positions as revealed by their manifesto commitments. The evolution of these positions over the 1945–2001 period is displayed in Figure 8.7. As shown, New Labour's sharp shift in 1997 put Labour to the right of centre, substantially narrowing the distance separating it from the Conservatives. The gap narrowed again four years later. In 2001, Labour hardly changed its position, but the Conservatives became somewhat more moderate. For their part, the Liberal Democrats drifted slightly to the right and were almost at dead centre. The overall result was that the average ideological distance among the three parties (9.8 points) was smaller in 2001 than at any time since 1945.

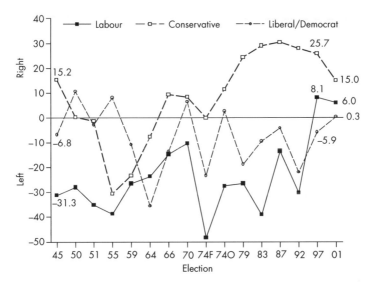

Figure 8.7 Party positions on left–right ideological scale, 1945–2001
Source: Bara and Budge (2001); Budge et al. (2001).

Similar to the benefits term for the individual-level analyses reported earlier, we measure B (for each election) by computing the average value of the absolute squared distances between pairs of parties. To reflect the likelihood that the effects of a unit difference in ideological distance diminishes when the distance is very large, we take the natural logarithm of this average. Finally, we multiply the resulting ideological proximity variable by the inter-party competition variable to yield a proxy for $P \times B$ (efficacy $\times$ differential benefits) interaction term. For this purpose, we reflex the scores on the party competition variable to capture properly its joint effects with ideological proximity.

To gauge the effects of inter-party competition and ideological proximity accurately, we need to control for other factors that might contribute to over-time variations in turnout. Since the survey data needed to create time series variables for these factors are unavailable, we mimic their collective effects by specifying models with simple deterministic trends. As observed above, turnout in post-Second World War general elections reached a high point in 1950, and then declined slowly, albeit irregularly, from 1950 to 1997, before falling sharply in 2001. Since the precise nature of the long-term trend is not known and our aim is to have as effective a control as possible, we employ two alternative specifications: a linear trend and a quadratic trend. The models have the following form:

Linear Trend: $TURN_t = f(\beta_0 + \beta_1 PBI_t + \beta_2 TREND)$
Quadratic Trend: $TURN_t = f(\beta_0 + \beta_1 PBI_t + \beta_2 TREND + \beta_3 TREND^2)$

where

$TURN_t$ = turnout in election at time t;
PBI_t = inter-party competition $\times$ ideological–proximity interaction at time t;
$TREND$ = time counter, running from 1 to 16.

In addition to testing the interaction effect, we also examine the impact of inter-party competition and ideological proximity separately.

Table 8.10 presents parameter estimates for these models. Regardless of whether the trend is specified as linear or quadratic,[28] the party competition variable is statistically significant, with its negative sign indicating that increased competition (as reflected in a smaller distance in the polls between the two leading parties) is associated with higher turnout (Models A and D). The coefficients are very similar (-0.74 and -0.76) and indicate that the estimated effect of competition is quite robust to changes in specification of the trend. Models B and E tell similar stories for ideological proximity. Its coefficients (2.41 and 2.34) are statistically significant and, as expected, positive. As ideological distance—the proxy for perceived differential benefits—among the parties increases, the likelihood of voting rises. Finally, and consistent with the significance of the $P \times B$ interaction term in the individual-level turnout models, Models C and F show that the inter-party competition $\times$ ideological proximity variable is statistically significant and correctly

Table 8.10   Effects of inter-party competition and ideological proximity on turnout in 1945–2001 general elections

Predictor variables	Model A		Model B		Model C	
	β	SE	β	SE	β	SE
A. Linear trend models						
Constant	81.19***	2.08	65.65***	7.61	64.76***	6.68
Party competition	−0.74*	0.34	x	x	x	x
Ideological proximity	x	x	2.41*	1.12	x	x
Competition × proximity interaction	x	x	x	x	0.028**	0.01
Time (linear trend)	−0.64***	0.22	−0.72***	0.22	−0.70***	0.20
Adjusted R^2	0.48		0.48		0.53	
D.W.	1.63		1.93		1.94	

Predictor variables	Model D		Model E		Model F	
	β	SE	β	SE	β	SE
B. Quadratic trend models						
Constant	79.59***	1.38	64.10***	7.08	62.95***	6.07
Party competition	−0.78**	0.31	x	x	x	x
Ideological proximity	x	x	2.34*	1.06	x	x
Competition × proximity interaction	x	x	x	x	0.027**	0.01
Time (quadratic trend)	−0.04***	0.01	−0.04***	0.01	−0.04***	0.01
Adjusted R^2	0.57		0.53		0.60	
D.W.	1.89		2.06		2.15	

Note: *** $p \leq 0.001$; ** $p \leq 0.01$; * $p \leq 0.05$; one-tailed test. x—variable not included in model.

Source: Budge et al. (2001); Butler and Kavanagh (2002: appendix 1); King and Wybrow (2001).

(positively) signed. Viewed more generally, it is evident that these models can explain a sizeable proportion of the variance in turnout rates over time. The adjusted R^2's vary from 0.48 to 0.60, being greatest for Models C and F which include the interaction effect variable. Moreover, not all of the action is in the trends. For the linear model, the R^2 increases from 0.38 to 0.48 when the interaction term is added, and for the quadratic model, it increases from 0.44 to 0.60.

To hear more clearly what these models are saying about the influence of inter-party competition and ideological proximity, we consider a counterfactual scenario where the 2001 election was basically a replay of 1992. In this scenario, the Conservatives and Labour run neck-and-neck (on average) in the polls over the three months leading up to the election, and the party manifestos indicate substantial ideological distance separates the Tories, Labour, and the Liberal Democrats (see Figure 8.7). Using the coefficient estimates from the quadratic trend model (Model F) in Table 8.10, we calculate the impact of this combination of a close contest and considerable ideological divergence. Doing so indicates that the voting rate would have been 72.5 per cent. This figure was up 1 per cent on 1997, and a very different result from the massive 11.8 per cent drop that actually occurred in 2001. The linear trend model (Model D) produces almost exactly the same result—the predicted turnout rate for 2001 is 72.4 per cent. Given that the actual voting rate in 1992 was 77.7 per cent, it is clear that the models do not tell the whole story of the recent decline in turnout. However, it is equally clear that choice-based models, such as those investigated here, can help to explain aggregate-level variations in participation across successive elections.

Another topic that can be explored with simplified models is the nature of the age effect. Age is statistically significant in all of the analyses of turnout in 2001 presented above. A key issue is whether this is a *life-cycle* or a *generational* effect. If the former, then the long-term implications of age differences in turnout are not serious, since the younger groups will eventually vote at the same rate as older fellow citizens. If, on the other hand, there are generational differences, then turnout is likely to continue to decline in the years ahead as older high-participant individuals die and younger low-participant ones take their place. A strong test of the life-cycle and generational hypotheses requires panel data gathered over many years. Such data would enable one to detect if specific individuals participate at higher rates as they grow older. However, we can gain insight into the life-cycle and generational alternatives by constructing pseudo panels (see Chapter Six) for tracking turnout rates among groups first entering the electorate in successive general elections held between 1970 and 2001.

The data in Table 8.11 reveal that turnout in the 18 to 21 year-old group which first entered the electorate in 1970 was 67.9 per cent, and this increased to 78.8 per cent four years later in February 1974. Apart from this initial jump, reading along the diagonal of the table indicates that the group continued to participate at about the same rate in subsequent elections. For example, in 2001, some thirty-one years after they had reached the age of majority, slightly over 79 per cent of them reported voting. Moving on four years from 1970 we can see that 79.7 per cent of the group who entered the electorate for the first time in 1974 reported going to the polls that year. In 2001, some twenty-seven years later, 75.8 per cent did so. A similar picture emerges for other age cohorts. Although some fluctuations occur, various groups continue to vote at roughly the same rate as they did when they first reached the age of majority. The picture is very different if we read the first row of Table 8.11. This provides information on turnout among successive 18 to 21 year-old groups as they first entered the electorate. It is apparent that, during the 1990s, the electoral participation of young people started to decline. As noted above, nearly 80 per cent of the group that became eligible for the first time in 1974 claimed to have voted. This contrasts sharply with participation rates of 60.5 per cent and 55.7 per cent for groups first eligible in 1997 and 2001, respectively.

Table 8.11   Percentages of people first entering the electorate between
1970 and 2001 voting in successive general elections

Year after initial entry	*Election at which 18–21-year-old age group entered electorate*							
	1970	Feb 1974	1979	1983	1987	1992	1997	2001
0	67.9	79.7	72.1	74.1	72.8	75.2	60.5	55.7
4		78.8	78.2	72.9	80.7	79.6	67.6	46.5
9			76.5	77.7	83.4	87.9	66.8	55.2
13				79.0	87.5	87.5	71.3	62.1
17					86.9	91.1	74.5	59.5
22						88.0	82.2	75.8
27							87.3	75.8
31								79.4

Note: Read table *diagonally* to determine the percentage of a specific group reporting that they voted in subsequent elections. For example, the percentage of 18–21-year-old age group entering electorate between 1970 and 2001, reporting that they voted in 1970 was 67.9. In 1974 the percentage of that group reporting that they voted was 78.8, in 1979 it was 76.5, etc.

Source: 1970–2001 BES post-election surveys.

Comparing initial participation rates with participation rates in 2001 shows that turnout fell among virtually all of the groups entering the electorate in successive elections since 1970. This is indicative of a more general *period* effect that was working to suppress turnout in 2001. However, the extent of the change between rate at first entry and rate in 2001 varies substantially. Among those entering the electorate in 1970, turnout in 2001 was actually 11.5 per cent greater in 2001 than it had been thirty-one years earlier. For those entering in 1974 and 1979, there were modest decreases, less than 4 per cent in both cases. However, for those entering in 1983, 1987, 1992, or 1997, the decreases are much larger. For these groups, the decrease ranges from 10.7 per cent to 20 per cent, and it averages fully 14.8 percent. Taken together, these numbers indicate that younger age groups were considerably more susceptible to forces working to suppress turnout in 2001. This, in turn, suggests the possibility of generational differences.

We can develop this analysis further. The life-cycle hypothesis states that individuals, regardless of generation, are more likely to vote as they age. We can approximate this effect by specifying three alternative models based on different hypotheses about how it might work (Johnston 1992; Blais 2003). The first hypothesis is that the life-cycle effect is linear, that is, the probability that individuals will vote V_i increases by β_1 each year as they grow older:

$$V_i = f(\beta_0 + \beta_1 \text{AGE})$$

The second model assumes that the life-cycle effect, or the relationship between age and turnout, is non-linear. Turnout increases initially, reaches a maximum value, and then begins to decline, as captured by a quadratic function of the following type:

$$V_i = f(\beta_0 + \beta_1 \text{AGE} + \beta_2 \text{AGE}^2)$$

The third model also assumes that the relationship is non-linear. In this case, the expectation is that turnout increases with age, but at a declining rate which is captured by the logarithm of age:

$$V_i = f(\beta_0 + \beta_1 \ln(\text{AGE}))$$

We also estimate possible generational effects by first defining a series of 'political generations'. The first group is the post-Second World War generation—people who reached the age of 18 or adulthood before 1950. Prior to 1969, the minimum voting age was 21 (Leonard and Mortimore 2001: 14), but it is plausible that the age of 18 is the point at which individuals begin to be aware of politics and to take an interest in elections. The second is the 'Macmillan' generation—people who reached the age of majority between 1951 and 1964, when the Conservatives were continuously in office. The third is the 'Wilson/Callaghan' generation—those who became adults between 1964 and 1979, an era of Labour government interrupted by the 1970–4 Conservative interregnum. The fourth is the 'Thatcher' generation who entered the electorate between 1979 and 1992 during a period of Conservative hegemony. Finally, there is the Blair generation. These are people who became eligible to vote after 1992, the last year in which the Conservatives won a general election.

Dummy variables for the Macmillan, Thatcher, and Blair age groups are added to the three life-cycle models of turnout just described (the post-war generation is the reference category). Logit estimates of the coefficients (see Table 8.12) suggest two conclusions. First, there are no life-cycle effects (i.e. the 'age' variables are not statistically significant), net of controls for the possible generational effects. This is consistent with the patterns in the pseudo-panel data presented in Table 8.11. Second, there are significant generational effects, with the decline in turnout across political generations starting with people who entered the electorate during the Thatcher era. This pattern has continued during the Blair years. When considering these results, we reiterate that only multiple-wave panel data collected over decades could provide conclusive evidence that age differences in turnout largely reflect generational processes. Nevertheless, the available evidence is quite consistent with the idea that the Thatcher era—a period characterized by insistent advocacy of market rather than government solutions to societal problems, and a more general emphasis on individual rather than collective goods—had important negative effects on public attitudes towards electoral participation. It also appears that these effects have not abated since New Labour came to power in 1997.

Table 8.12   Age and turnout in 2001: logit estimates of life-cycle and generational effects

Predictor variables	Model A		Model B		Model C	
	β	SE	β	SE	β	SE
Age	−0.001	0.01	0.04	0.03	x	x
Age squared	x	x	−0.0004	0.0002	x	x
Age logged	x	x	x	x	0.05	0.42
Political generations						
Blair	−1.64***	0.44	−1.36**	0.48	−1.54***	0.46
Thatcher	−1.07**	0.32	−1.00***	0.32	−1.00***	0.29
Wilson/Callaghan	−0.24	0.20	−0.29	0.20	−0.21	0.18
Macmillan	−0.22	0.23	−0.48*	0.29	−0.19	0.19
Constant	1.53*	0.81	0.80	0.94	1.21	1.82
McFadden R^2	0.06		0.06		0.06	
Percentage correctly classified	67.5		67.5		67.5	

Note: x—variable not included in model. *** $p \leq 0.001$; ** $p \leq 0.01$; * $p \leq 0.05$; one-tailed test.
Source: 2001 BES post-election survey.

The hypothesis that the Thatcher and Blair generations were less civic minded than their predecessors can be investigated more directly by considering the relationship between age and sense of civic duty. As shown earlier, system benefits, one component of which is civic duty, have a strong impact on the probability of voting in 2001. As Figure 8.8 illustrates, sense of civic duty is positively correlated with age. The percentage of BES respondents agreeing with the statement 'It is every citizen's duty to vote in an election' rises from 63 per cent among the youngest group (the Blair group) to 93 per cent among the oldest group. Levels of agreement with another civic duty statement, 'I would be *seriously* neglecting my duty as a citizen if I didn't vote', have an even stronger age gradient. Although only a minority (41 per cent) of the youngest group (the Blair generation) believed nonvoting is a serious dereliction of duty, fully 86 per cent of the oldest group (the post-war generation) did so. Moreover, differences in percentages of respondents agreeing with both statements are consistently related to age, being largest for the youngest group (22 per cent) and smallest for the oldest one (7 per cent). Younger groups were not only less likely to believe that voting is a duty, they also were *proportionately less likely* to take that duty seriously.

Analyses similar to those for turnout suggest that the relationship between age and civic duty reflects generational differences. Table 8.13 presents the results of regressing an overall index of civic duty on the set of generation dummy variables, plus age in years.[29] Regardless of how the impact of the latter variable is specified, two of the

271

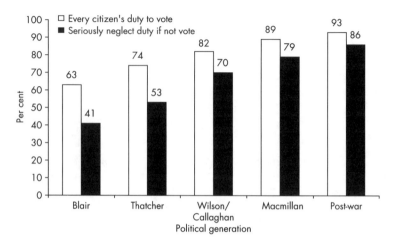

Figure 8.8 Sense of civic duty across political generations

Source: 2001 BES post-election survey.

Table 8.13 Age and civic duty in 2001: OLS estimates of life-cycle and generational effects

Predictor variables	Model A		Model B		Model C	
	β	SE	β	SE	β	SE
Age	0.008*	0.005	0.02	0.02	x	x
Age squared	x	x	−0.001	0.000	x	x
Age logged	x	x	x	x	0.35	0.21
Political generations						
Blair	−0.53**	0.21	−0.46*	0.24	−0.51*	0.23
Thatcher	−0.32*	0.15	−0.29*	0.15	−0.35**	0.14
Wilson/Callaghan	−0.12	0.09	−0.12	0.09	−0.15*	0.08
Macmillan	0.02	0.10	−0.02	0.12	−0.03	0.09
Constant	2.05***	0.38	1.86***	0.49	1.20	0.92
Adjusted R^2	0.10		0.10		0.10	

Note: x—variable not included in model. *** $p \leq 0.001$; ** $p \leq 0.01$; * $p \leq 0.05$; one-tailed test.

Source: 2001 BES pre- and post-election panel survey.

generational dummy variables—those for the Blair and Thatcher cohorts—have significant negative effects. With one marginal exception, none of the other generational variables is significant. This means that, controlling for a more general age effect, the two youngest groups have lower levels of civic duty than any of the older groups. Thus, it again appears that people who have entered the electorate during the Thatcher and Blair eras constitute distinct political generations whose relatively low levels of civic mindedness help to explain their greater reluctance to go to the polls.

The importance of individual choice for both turnout and party support is a strong theme of this book, but it carries a paradox—namely, the paradox of participation. If, in an individualistic world, people do things for private benefits and they do not worry about society, then they are not inclined to vote. As our analyses indicate, the impact of this paradox does not drive turnout rates to zero because many people are motivated by a sense of duty to the political community of which they are a part, and many evidently think collectively in terms of 'people like me' when assessing their political influence. If these attitudes weaken across the electorate, then turnout will continue to decline. As argued, one way this may occur is via generational change, with older, civic-minded groups gradually being replaced by younger, egocentric ones. However, as also demonstrated, the closeness of the contest and the ideological distance between the parties are important factors in explaining variations in turnout across elections, so an increase in participation in a closely contested future election when the parties take quite different policy positions is quite possible. The processes that drive turnout overlay one another and have different dynamics. Levels of party competition and parties' policy positions are potentially highly changeable, varying markedly from one election to the next. In contrast, generational replacement is slowly paced, inducing long-term trends that are not easily reversed. The age-cohort analyses suggest that the positive effects of close inter-party competition and enhanced policy divergence are necessary to prevent even lower levels of turnout in the future than in the recent past.

CONCLUSION: BRITAIN AT THE POLLS?

This chapter has investigated the ability of six alternative models to explain turnout in the 2001 general election. The analyses indicate that no single model formally encompasses its rivals; all of them have 'something to say'. However, two models—general incentives and cognitive mobilization—dominate the others in the sense of having superior explanatory power. The conclusion is that choice- and knowledge-based models do the best job at explaining turnout in contemporary British general elections. However, the choice to vote or abstain is not based wholly on expectations of the benefits that competing parties will provide. Evaluations of a party's performance in office also matter. Although not irrelevant, resource-based accounts of turnout exemplified by the civic voluntarism and social capital models do not fare well when compared with their choice- and knowledge-based rivals. These results suggest that resource-based models continue to be very popular in the political participation literature, at least when they are applied to the task of

273

explaining electoral turnout, because they are typically privileged by methodological strategies which ignore their rivals.

A related point is that, with the noteworthy exception of age, sociological variables such as class, ethnicity, and gender, are of marginal relevance for explaining turnout in 2001. Sociological variables also are of little value for explaining aggregate-level variations in turnout from one election to the next. In particular, such factors cannot account for major changes in turnout across successive elections, such as the massive drop that occurred between 1997 and 2001. Trends in the composition of the class structure or the size of ethnic minority populations are simply too slowly paced to account for such large-scale changes over a four-year span. Thus, an individual rationality framework that emphasizes the importance of voter choices and that delineates the factors that affect those choices must take centre stage when explaining large inter-election differences in turnout. In this regard, analyses show that the interacting effects of party competition and ideological distance are both statistically significant and substantively important. These variables are aggregate-level analogues for the political efficacy × differential party benefits term, which is a core component of the minimal rational choice and general incentives models.

An emphasis on choice should not obscure the possibility that some influential variables in the dominant models of turnout may vary slowly, if at all, at the individual level. Age-cohort analyses indicate that long-term change may be taking place in the likelihood that new generations will exercise their electoral franchise. Differences in civic duty are particularly interesting. Younger people—members of what we term the Thatcher and Blair generations—are less likely than older people to believe that voting is a civic duty. Younger people also are much less likely to think that nonvoting is a serious violation of their responsibilities as citizens. This lack of a strong sense of civic duty helps to explain why there is a strong relationship between age and turnout. Moreover, it appears that these age differences in civic mindedness are not simply life-cycle phenomena; rather, they have significant generational components. The clear implication is that, *ceteris paribus*, turnout may continue to be a problem in future elections.

The analyses in this chapter delineate the relevant variables for explaining electoral participation. What matters is partly a matter of calculations of the costs and benefits of certain courses of action, and partly a matter of characteristics which define the 'good citizen', such as attentiveness to the campaign, political knowledge, and especially, civic duty. The latter finding underscores the point that understanding the nature and consequences of electoral choice requires that attention be paid to the matrix of political beliefs, attitudes, and opinions within with voting and other forms of political action occur. Accordingly, in the next chapter, we explore the evolution of British voters' orientations towards themselves as political actors, as well as their evaluations of the performance of parties, elections, and the more general functioning of democracy in Britain.

NOTES

1. Responses to the 'government treats people like me fairly' statement are scored 'strongly agree' = 1, 'agree' = 2, 'neither' = 3, 'disagree' = 4, and 'strongly disagree' = 5. Responses to the 'there is often a big gap' statement are scored: 'strongly agree' = 5, 'agree' = 4, 'neither' = 3, 'disagree' = 2, and 'strongly disagree' = 1. The general relative deprivation index is created by summing the two recoded variables

2. Responses to the two questions regarding retrospective and prospective evaluations of one's personal economic condition are scored: 'lot worse' = 5, 'little worse' = 4, 'same' = 3, 'little better' = 2, and 'lot better' = 1. Each resulting variable is multiplied by a variable based on recoded responses to the question: 'To what extent do you think that the government's policies affect the financial situation of your household?' Responses to this question are recoded: 'great deal' = 5, 'fair amount' = 4, 'do not know' = 3, 'not very much' = 2, and 'not at all' = 1.

3. Respondents were asked: 'How well do you think the present government has handled each of the following issues?' For each issue, the response categories are scored: 'very well' = 5, 'fairly well' = 4, 'neither well nor badly' = 3, 'fairly badly' = 2, and 'very badly' = 1. The resulting variables for crime, education, the NHS, and transport are summed to create the government performance index.

4. These variables are scored—gender: men = 1, women = 0; (self-reported) ethnicity: 'white British' = 1, other ethnic groups = 0; employment status: unemployed = 1, else = 0; retirement status: retired = 1, other = 0.

5. The trust question is: 'Generally speaking, would you say that most people can be trusted, or that you can't be too careful dealing with people? Please use the 0–10 scale to indicate your view, where 0 means "can't be too careful" and 10 means "most people can be trusted." ' The fairness question is: 'Do you think that most people you come into contact with would try to take advantage of you if they got the chance or would they try to be fair? Please use the 0–10 scale again where 0 means "would try to take advantage" and 10 means "would try to be fair." '

6. The questions are: (*a*) 'Over the past few years, has anyone asked you to get involved in politics or community affairs?' (*b*) 'Over the past few years, have you volunteered to get involved in politics or community affairs?' Affirmative answers to (*a*) and (*b*) are scored 1, and other answers are scored 0.

7. Responses to the leisure time question are scored: 'great deal' = 4, 'fair amount' = 3, 'some' = 2, 'none' or 'do not know' = 1.

8. The party mobilization variables are scored: canvassed = 1, not canvassed = 0; telephoned = 1, not telephoned = 0; contacted on election day = 1, not contacted = 0. Responses to the question: people trying to convince respondent how to vote are scored: friend = 4, family = 3, co-worker = 2, other person = 1, no one = 0.

9. The analysis yields two factors with eigenvalues greater than 1.0, and which collectively explain 54% of the item variance. The 'asked to become active' and 'people tried to convince respondent how to vote' items loaded on one factor. The party mobilization variables loaded on another factor. Factor scores are used to create social recruitment and party mobilization variables.

10. The extent of voluntary activity question is: 'Over the past few years, how active have you been in a voluntary organization, like a local community association, a charity, or a sports club?' Responses are scored: 'very active' = 4, 'somewhat active' = 3, 'a little active' = 2, 'not at all active' or 'do not know' = 0.

11. The perceived political influence question is: 'On a scale from 0 to 10 where 10 means a great deal of influence and 0 means no influence, how much influence do you have on politics and public affairs?'

12. Strength of party identification is scored: 'very strong' = 3, 'fairly strong' = 2, 'not very strong' = 1, and 'no identification' = 0.

13. Each correct answer is scored 1, and incorrect and 'do not know' answers are scored 0. The six resulting 0–1 variables are summed to create the political knowledge index.

14. Print media consumption is measured by scoring respondents who regularly read a daily newspaper 1, and other respondents, 0. Attention to television coverage of the campaign is scored: 'great deal of attention' = 4, 'fair amount of attention' = 3, 'some attention' = 2, and 'no attention' = 1.

15. Squaring the absolute differences in the scores given to each pair of parties is consistent with practice in the spatial voting literature (e.g. see, Merrill and Grofman 1999).

16. The two costs variables are recoded as: 'strongly agree' = 5, 'agree' = 4, 'neither' = 3, 'disagree' = 2, and 'strongly disagree' = 1. An overall costs index is constructed by summing the two recoded variables.

17. The two individual benefit variables are recoded as: 'strongly agree' = 5, 'agree' = 4, 'neither' = 3, 'disagree' = 2, and 'strongly disagree' = 1. An overall individual benefits index is constructed by summing the two recoded variables.

18. The two group benefit variables are recoded as: 'strongly agree' = 5, 'agree' = 4, 'neither' = 3, 'disagree' = 2, and 'strongly disagree' = 1. An overall group benefits index is constructed by summing the two recoded variables.

19. The two system benefit variables are recoded as: 'strongly agree' = 5, 'agree' = 4, 'neither' = 3, 'disagree' = 2, and 'strongly disagree' = 1. An overall systems benefits index is constructed by summing the two recoded variables.

20. The 'voting is a waste of time' variable is coded: 'strongly agree' = 1, 'agree' = 2, 'neither' = 3, 'disagree' = 4, and 'strongly disagree' = 5. The 'most people voted' variable is recoded: 'strongly agree' = 5, 'agree' = 4, 'neither' = 3, 'disagree' = 2, and 'strongly disagree' = 1. The two variables are summed to create the social norms index.

21. The turnout variable is based on the validated vote variable (named VOTED in the 2001 BES data set). Respondents with the following codes are considered to have voted: 'said voted and did' = 1, 'said did not vote, yet did' = 2, 'proxy vote' = 6. These codes are recoded to 1. Respondents with the following codes are considered to have not voted: 'said voted, but found not to have done so' = 2, 'said did not vote and did not' = 3, 'said did not vote and not registered' = 9, 'said did not vote and address not found' = 10. These codes are recoded to 0. Other codes are declared to be missing data.

22. Age is recorded in years, and gender and ethnicity are described in Note 4 above.

23. As described in Chapter Four, the deviance statistic is $-2 \times$ log likelihood, that is, $-2 \times \ln(L(\theta \mid x))$.

24. This involves specifying a global model that 'jointly nests' a set of rival models, and then reducing it to include only those variables which are statistically significant.

Hendry (1995: ch. 9) argues that this procedure is superior to the conventional approach of starting with a simple model, and then respecifying it by adding variables in a stepwise fashion.

25. As done in several other chapters, the change in probabilities is calculated by allowing a variable of interest to vary from its minimum to its maximum value while other variables are held at their means. Calculations are done using the CLARIFY programme (Tomz, Wittenberg, and King 1999).

26. The interaction effect variable is computed by multiplying the government performance dissatisfaction index (see note 14) by social class (scored working class (categories C2, D, E) = 1, middle class (categories A, B, C_1) = 0) by party identification (scored Labour = 1, other identifiers and nonidentifiers = 0).

27. The poll data were gathered in Gallup surveys (see King and Wybrow 2001).

28. The first-order term in initial estimates of the quadratic trend models was insignificant (all other variables were significant) and, hence, the models were re-estimated, retaining the second-order term.

29. The civic duty index varies from 0 to 3, and is constructed by counting the number of 'strongly agree' or 'agree' responses to three statements. One of the statements, 'It is every citizen's duty to vote in an election', was asked in both the pre- and post-election surveys. The other statement, 'I would feel very guilty if I did not vote in a general election', was asked in the post-election survey only.

NINE

The 2001 Election and Democracy in Britain

In previous chapters, we sought to explain the party choices British voters make—and why some people choose not to vote at all. In this chapter, our focus widens to consider the health of British democracy more generally. In part, this broadening of focus stems from the fact that turnout fell to a post-World War II low in 1997, and then plummeted in 2001. Analyses presented in Chapter Eight reveal that a substantial portion of the declines in the two most recent elections can be explained by a combination of the one-sided nature of these contests and the relative lack of policy distance between the major parties. But equally clearly, the significance of trend terms in these analyses suggests that other factors were at work. Thus, it is important to assess the extent to which the decrease in turnout reflects more general disillusionment with the political system. The focus of this chapter also reflects the changed institutional context of British politics. The 1997 parliament witnessed the creation, following popular referendums, of the Scottish Parliament in Edinburgh and the Welsh Assembly in Cardiff. This extension of the mosaic of democratic institutions raises significant questions about the possible fragmentation or rejuvenation of the British political system.

Our departure point is recognition that healthy democracy must receive the support of its citizens. Following Easton (1965; see also Kornberg and Clarke 1992), we distinguish among support for public officials responsible for making policy decisions, including those who are part of the 'government of the day' (the political authorities); support for the rules of the political game and core institutions of the state (the regime); and support for the binding together of individuals 'by a political division of labour' into an overarching collectivity (the political community) (Easton 1965: 177). This chapter concentrates on support at the regime and community levels, bracketed together as 'system support' for presentational purposes. We argue that there are two sources of political support. One source of support is a generalized sense of political identity that develops as a result of protracted socialization processes. A second source of support derives from evaluations of the performance of the political system and its various components. If citizens identify with the political system and are satisfied with its performance, then they are likely to lend it their support.

Four organizing themes structure the analysis. The first concerns the *engagement of the individual citizen with the political system.* How interested are people in the interplay of party politics? Do they think that politicians respond to their concerns? To what extent is their engagement with politics driven by a sense of duty? And, are they prepared to engage in various different forms of political activity? The second theme concerns *evaluations of various components of the political system.* What are people's beliefs about political parties? How do they view elections? To what extent do they respect the principal political institutions of the state? What do they think democracy means? The third and fourth themes address, respectively, *forces from above* and *forces from below* the state. Forces from above include both supranational institutions such as the European Union, as well as the complex of social and economic processes commonly labelled 'globalization'. Forces from below refer primarily to growing demands for national and regional devolution that have developed over the past two decades. Analyses consider the extent to which citizens' reactions to these forces from above and below have affected both their degree of engagement with the political system and their evaluations of it.

The chapter first outlines arguments for supposing that public support for the British political system has declined significantly since the 1960s. We argue that, on the contrary, no such decline in support has occurred; that, in the minds of its citizens, British democracy is no less healthy now than it was in the past. The empirical analyses begin with an examination of data on citizens' engagement with the political process. We find that levels of engagement in the early twenty-first century differ little from those observed in the 1960s. The next section investigates evaluations of the political system. This evidence suggests that people in Britain are *more* satisfied with their political system now than they were a generation ago. The fourth and fifth sections deal with the changes in the way that people have viewed forces from above and below over the last three decades. Analyses indicate that, in general, there have been no secular trends in the way that these forces have been perceived. The sixth section examines public beliefs about parties, elections, and democracy. The final section develops and tests a model of the extent of (dis) satisfaction with the practice of democracy in Britain. Analyses indicate that assessments of British democracy are influenced more by forces from above than by forces from below, but that evaluations of institutional performance are most important. This pivotal role of performance evaluations echoes findings in earlier chapters about the importance of valenced judgements for understanding political attitudes and electoral choices.

DECLINING LEVELS OF POLITICAL SUPPORT SINCE THE 1960S?

Circa the mid-twentieth century, many observers were favourably impressed by the workings of Britain's parliamentary democracy. Universal suffrage was enshrined in a famously unwritten constitution. Civil liberties were protected by both statute and common law, and the rule of law prevailed. Governments formed and dissolved in accordance with established precedent, which required (except during wartime) the holding of a general election at least every five years. The first-past-the-post electoral system helped to ensure that the largest party in parliament could usually form a government without recourse to coalition, a condition that, in turn, helped to promote government stability. Although there was certainly intense competition over which party or parties would form the government of the day, there was also a high level of agreement about both the rules of the democratic game and the boundaries of the political system itself. And, as noted in Chapter Seven, in their pioneering study, Almond and Verba (1963) lauded Britain for having a 'participant–allegiant' political culture. Levels of turnout and other forms of conventional political participation were relatively high, and British citizens (or, to be more precise, 'subjects') exhibited high levels of allegiance to both the regime and the political community.

In the ensuing decades, new challenges have arisen—some applicable to many countries, others more specific to Britain—that have potential to reshape the syndrome of political attitudes and behaviour that collectively constitute Britain's 'civic culture'. In principle, each challenge could have weakened citizens' support for their democratic political system. The first derives from the UK's membership of the European Community (EC), latterly the European Union. Britain joined the EC in 1973 after its two previous applications failed in 1962 and 1967. The primary motive for membership was economic (Sanders 1990). Britain's growth rate had stubbornly lagged behind those of 'the Six' since the mid-1950s, and it was widely believed that access to the 'larger internal market' would provide an important boost to British productivity and growth. It had always been recognized that joining the EC would involve the ceding of some decision-making powers from the nation-state to Brussels. But this was considered to be a price worth paying for membership in what appeared to be a highly successful economic club. However, what a substantial proportion of the British electorate had not bargained for was the stipulation in the EC's founding charter, the 1957 Treaty of Rome, that the peoples of Europe would move towards 'an ever closer political and economic union'. The Single European Act of 1986 and the Maastricht Treaty of 1992 moved this process forward significantly, by extending the scope of majority decision-making in the Council of Ministers and by establishing the conditions and timetable for the move to a single European currency by January 2002. Although the British were allowed to opt out of membership of the Euro zone, this progressive strengthening of the supranational component of the European Union, combined with the voluntary relinquishing of authority in some policy areas, has inevitably reduced the decision-making autonomy of national governments. In turn, this implies that national governments now have less freedom to manoeuvre in response to the specific needs of their citizens than in earlier times.[1]

Two features of recent British political life have given focus to UK citizens' concerns about this 'loss of sovereignty'. First, for almost two decades, a significant part of Britain's national daily press has consistently delivered a strongly 'Eurosceptic' message to readers. In particular, readers of the *Sun, Express, Mail*, and *Telegraph* (papers which collectively have a 55 per cent share of the UK market) have been consistently supplied with stories about the real or imagined damage that Brussels has inflicted on the British way of life. Second, and particularly since 1997, the leadership of one of the major national parties has been strongly Eurosceptic and vigorously opposed to any further extension of supranational decision making within the European Union. These two conditions have politicized the question of national versus EU policy 'competence' to a degree not encountered in other European countries.[2] In turn, this politicization has had two potentially important implications. First, if the state can do less for citizens now, then they have less incentive than before either to engage with its institutions or, in Easton's sense, to support it. Therefore, as the policy scope of the European Union has increased, especially after the amendments to the Treaty of Rome introduced in 1986 and 1992, one might expect to find that public support for the British political system has declined over time at the aggregate level (Richardson 2001). Second, there may be differences in the responses of people who take a critical view of the EU as opposed to those who are either pro-European or broadly neutral. Eurosceptics are likely to view the diminution in national decision-making autonomy associated with Britain's continued EU membership in very negative terms. And precisely because, in their view, the British state has allowed its powers to be usurped by Brussels, Eurosceptics are less likely than their more pro-EU counterparts to have respect for UK political institutions. In turn, this implies that Eurosceptics are likely to exhibit lower levels of support for the political system than are citizens who are either sympathetic or neutral in their stance towards the European Union.

A second development with potential to affect public attitudes in a similar way is the process of globalization. Although globalization has many facets and meanings, one of its key features is the increased influence and autonomy of non-state economic actors that have derived from the deregulation of financial and capital markets that occurred during the 1980s and 1990s. The ability of multinational corporations to move capital, labour, goods, and services across national borders has increased enormously over the last two decades. This increased flexibility has made it much more difficult for national governments to monitor, let alone control, these activities. As with the extension of EU policy-making authority, the increased commercial autonomy and sheer size of the major multinationals have served to reduce the decision-making powers of the nation-state. In these circumstances, it would be unsurprising if citizens accorded less support to the political system. The reason for this is that the government's ability to improve their lives has declined in comparison with the damage inflicted by the decisions of multinational corporations. As with the European Union, this implies that, at the aggregate level, the increased globalization of recent years should be associated with decreased support for the political system. At the individual level, citizens most critical of globalization and of the state's failure to counter its impact should exhibit lower levels of support for the political system.

A third development that could have reduced support for the British political system over the last 30 years concerns the increased pressures for national/regional autonomy that have arisen in Scotland and Wales. The reasons for this upsurge in nationalist sentiment are complex but two factors are particularly noteworthy. First, the rapid and sustained economic growth enjoyed by the Irish Republic inside the European Union after 1973 provided a model of Celtic success—independent of England—that nationalists in Scotland and Wales could point to as evidence that independence was a realistic economic option. Second, between 1979 and 1997, Scotland and Wales were ruled from Westminster by a Conservative government that received a small and diminishing share of Scottish and Welsh votes.[3] For the Scots and Welsh to be ruled from Westminster by a party that they so insistently rejected raised serious questions about the accountability of general elections. A direct response to these concerns was the creation of the Scottish Parliament and the Welsh Assembly in 1999. It remains to be seen whether devolution will strengthen Scottish and Welsh commitment to the UK political community or encourage further demands for national autonomy. In either event, it is important to assess how far the centrifugal pressures that created the demand for devolution in the first place have weakened Scots and Welsh support for the UK political community and the parliamentary political regime that operates within it.

A fourth reason for supposing that regime and political community support in the United Kingdom might have declined relates to increasing ethnic diversity in Britain over the past forty years. Ethnic minorities now comprise approximately 7 per cent of the UK population and 20 per cent of the population in Greater London. This change in the composition of the population has two implications. One is that, for some members of the indigenous European population, it represents a failure of the established regime to protect the homogeneity of British society. As such, it represents a potential source of dissatisfaction with the democratic process itself. Another implication is that members of the ethnic minorities may feel that the democratic process is unresponsive to their concerns given that the top positions in British politics, justice, and administration are overwhelmingly populated by ethnic Europeans. Again, disillusionment with the democratic process may be the result.

In sum, expectations that public support for the political regime and community may have weakened since the 1960s are grounded in four considerations. Forces from above the nation-state—Britain's membership of the European Union and the increased autonomy of multinational corporations—have restricted the decision-making scope of the UK government. In principle, this has provided an incentive for all citizens to downgrade their assessments of the performance of British political institutions. Forces from below the state—the increased support for autonomy in Scotland and Wales and increasing ethnic diversity throughout the United Kingdom—have provided incentives for particular groups to downgrade such assessments as well. We next investigate whether these developments have affected how the British think about their political system.

ENGAGEMENT WITH THE POLITICAL SYSTEM

One way of assessing the extent to which citizens are engaged with the political system is to ask them if they are interested in politics, care about election outcomes, feel politically efficacious, consider voting as a civic duty, and are willing to undertake various forms of political activity.[4] In several studies, respondents in British Election Study (BES) and British Social Attitudes (BSA) surveys have been asked about their interest in politics. BES respondents also have been asked whether they care about the general election outcome.[5] The results are reported in Figure 9.1. Although the measures used in the various surveys are not identical, they still provide a useful basis for discerning a lack of systematic change in political interest between 1964 and 2001. Indeed, when the 'positive' responses to the political interest question are combined, we find that typically 60–65 per cent of the respondents over the 1974–2001 period expressed at least 'some' interest in politics. The figure was 62 per cent in February, 1974 and barely changed at 64 per cent in 2001. A similar pattern emerges when views of the election outcome are considered. Figure 9.1 reports the percentages of respondents who said that they 'cared a good deal.' Although the figure shows that the percentage who 'cared' fell by 9 points to 66 per cent in 2001, it also reveals that the 2001 figure barely differs from the level reported in the early 1970s when the figure was 68 per cent for three successive elections. The simple conclusion is that there is little, if any, systematic variation in either interest or concern with election outcomes over the 1964–2001 period. Contrary to the conjectures offered by some observers, there is no evidence to suggest that engagement with the political system has declined significantly since the early 1960s.

Another important indicator of individual engagement is political efficacy. As noted in Chapter Seven, a distinction is often made between 'internal efficacy' (people's sense that they can influence the political process) and 'external efficacy' (people's perceptions of government responsiveness to their concerns). The 2001

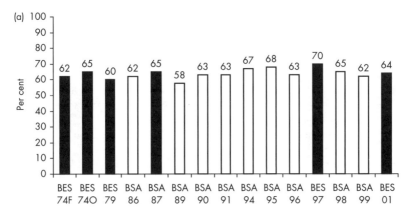

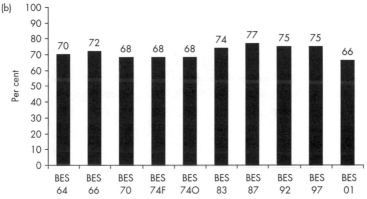

Figure 9.1 Indicators of political engagement, 1964–2001. (a) Percentages of survey respondents with at least some interest in politics, 1974–2001. (b) Percentages of survey respondents caring which party won election, 1964–2001

Note: Shaded bars indicate election year.

Source: 1964–2001 BES post-election surveys, and 1986–99 BSA surveys.

BES respondents were asked whether they agreed or disagreed with four statements, two relating to the internal and two to the external dimensions of efficacy. Table 9.1 gives the statement wordings, and its extreme right column reports the percentage in 2001 who agreed with each statement. These data indicate that approximately 55 per cent felt internally inefficacious, whereas approximately 65 per cent felt externally inefficacious. Accordingly, majorities of those interviewed in 2001 did not believe that they could affect the political system or that it responded adequately to them. However, comparing the 2001 figures with those for earlier years reveals that many British citizens have felt similarly inefficacious

285

The 2001 Election and Democracy in Britain

Table 9.1 Political efficacy, 1963–2001 (percentages agreeing with statement)

	A&V 1963	BSA 1986	BES 1987	BSA 1987	BSA 1991	BSA 1994	BSA 1996	BES 1997	BSA 1998	BES 2001
A. Internal Efficacy										
People like me have no say in what government does	59	71	49	69	60	66	62	58	60	55
Politics and government are too complicated for me to understand	59	69	57	n.a.	66	70	66	n.a.	64	54
B. External Efficacy										
MPs soon lose touch with the people who elected them	n.a.	70	n.a.	71	68	74	76	n.a.	72	65
Parties are only interested in votes, not voter's opinions	n.a.	66	55	64	66	72	75	64	69	64

Note: n.a.—data not available. There are slight differences in statement wordings in various surveys.

Source: 1987, 1997, 2001 BES surveys; 1986, 1987, 1991, 1994, 1996, 1998 BSA surveys; 1963 Civic Culture survey.

for a long time. In Almond and Verba's 1963 study, internal inefficacy levels (i.e. 59 per cent agreeing with both internal statements in Table 9.1) were somewhat higher than in 2001. A similar pattern emerges from the evidence provided by BES and BSA surveys conducted over the last two decades. In all cases, levels of internal and external inefficacy were higher than they were in 2001. There appears to have been brief periods when the average sense of inefficacy seemed to increase (e.g. the 1991–6 figures are higher that those for 1964 or 2001). However, there is no evidence of a progressive growth in disillusionment with the political system as far as the average citizen's sense of political efficacy is concerned.

A fourth indicator of engagement with the political system is the belief that voting is a civic duty. In general, in the early twenty-first century, duty is not a widely used concept in social or political discourse. It—like fortitude and shame—is often seen as an anachronistic value in times that emphasize personal fulfilment, instrumentality, rights, and market forces. But, is it the case that people felt differently at an earlier time? Some four decades ago, Almond and Verba (1963) asked their respondents about the duty to vote. However, they couched the question in a way that gave respondents the choice of saying either that they voted *only* out of a sense of duty or they voted because it gave them a feeling of satisfaction. In response, 45 per cent opted for duty, 44 per cent for satisfaction, and the rest said that they did not know. Since it is possible that performing one's duty also provides satisfaction, the responses to Almond and Verba's question may have substantially understated the actual incidence of the sense of duty to vote among British citizens. As discussed in Chapters Seven and Eight, the 2001 BES asked respondents two questions about their sense of civic duty. Comparisons are also made with a question asked in the Citizen Audit (CA) survey conducted in 2000, and questions asked in BSA surveys conducted between 1994 and 1998.[6] The results are in Figure 9.2. Regardless of how the question is worded, data for the 1994–2001 period reveal that very large majorities of British citizens believed that voting is a civic duty. Thus, at a time when the language of duty is not widely used, the fact that at least two thirds of the electorate still regard voting as a duty suggests a relatively high level of psychological engagement with the political system.

The remaining indicator of degree of political engagement is the extent to which people are prepared to participate in 'complementary' or 'substitute' political activities. This refers to behaviour that is a part of the democratic process and can, in principle, serve either to complement, or to substitute for, voting. In Chapter Seven, we discussed the frequency with which people engage in different types of political activity and the general structure of contemporary political participation in the Britain. Here, we compare evidence from the 2001 BES with that gathered in earlier surveys.[7] The probabilities that respondents in 2001 would undertake different

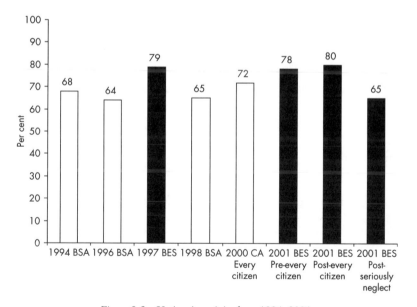

Figure 9.2   Voting is a civic duty, 1994–2001

Note: Shaded bars indicate election year.

Source: 2001 BES pre- and post-election surveys; 2000 CA survey; 1994, 1996, and 1998 BSA surveys.

types of activity are shown in the extreme right-hand column of Table 9.2. Giving money to, or working for, a political party was part of the action repertoire of only 8 per cent. However, more than 40 per cent were prepared to boycott goods and services. Surveys conducted between 1979 and 1998 show substantial members also are prepared to sign or collect petitions.

Another activity for which comparable data exist over time is willingness to participate in protests and demonstrations. In recent years, it appears that the British public has become more inclined to be politically active. In the mid-1980s, approximately 10 per cent said that they were likely to participate in a protest or demonstration. This figure climbed gradually during the 1990s so that, by 2001, nearly one in four claimed that they were likely to do so. However, data from 1977 and 1979 put this recent increase in context. In the late 1970s, the potential for protest was very similar to that recorded in 2001. This suggests that the 1980s may have been a period of unusually low protest potential and that we may have now returned to 'normal times'. In any event, it is unclear whether a relatively high level of willingness to protest connotes a high level of disillusionment with the democratic process. As discussed in Chapter Seven, people who were more likely to protest were also more likely to engage in other activities. We conclude that levels of engagement in complementary or substitute activities do not appear to have changed significantly in Britain since the 1970s.

Table 9.2   Willingness to engage in various political activities, 1973–2001
(percentages doing/willing to do various activites)

	POLACT 1973–4	BES 1979	BES 1987	PMD 1984	BSA 1984	BSA 1986	BSA 1989	BSA 1991	BSA 1994	BSA 1998	BES 2001
Sign or collect a petition	55	45	74	63	57	65	71	78	67	67	n.a.
Join a protest or a demonstration	32	21	13	15	9	11	14	14	16	21	23
Join or form a group	n.a.	n.a.	8	11	8	8	10	7	10	9	n.a.
Work with a group to solve a problem	n.a.	n.a.	n.a.	n.a.	n.a.	n.a.	n.a.	n.a.	n.a.	n.a.	29
Give money to a political party	n.a.	n.a.	n.a.	n.a.	n.a.	n.a.	n.a.	n.a.	n.a.	n.a.	8
Work for a political party	n.a.	n.a.	n.a.	n.a.	n.a.	n.a.	n.a.	n.a.	n.a.	n.a.	8
Boycott goods or services	24	n.a.	n.a.	n.a.	n.a.	n.a.	n.a.	n.a.	n.a.	n.a.	45

Note: n.a.—data not available.

Source: 1979, 1987, 2001 BES surveys; 1984, 1986, 1989, 1991, 1994, 1998 BSA surveys; Barnes, et al. (1979: 548, table TA.3); Parry, Moyser, and Day (1992: 44, table 3.1).

This analysis of political engagement yields a simple conclusion. Overall, there is little evidence to suggest that British citizens have become more disengaged from the political process over the last several decades. They vote less in elections but they are as concerned about election outcomes now as they were in the 1960s. Their levels of political efficacy have changed little over the past forty years. Their willingness to protest is higher now than in the 1980s but is no higher than it was in 1979. Finally, differences in question wording make it difficult to make precise comparisons of beliefs about voting as a civic duty over time, and analyses presented in Chapter Eight indicate that there may now be significant generational differences in such beliefs. These caveats notwithstanding, it is the case that large percentages of survey respondents have always indicated that they think voting is a duty. In short, if forces from 'above' and 'below' the nation-state have reduced support for the British political system, it has certainly not been manifested in the extent of citizen engagement.

EVALUATIONS OF THE POLITICAL SYSTEM

We observed in Chapter Seven that democratic theory attaches considerable importance to what citizens think about themselves as political actors and how they judge public officials and institutions of the political system. Above, we find that levels of citizen engagement in Britain have not changed in major ways over the past four decades. In this section, we investigate whether evaluations of the regime and its institutions have also remained relatively impervious to decline. To assist us in doing so, the 2001 BES asked a series of questions about attitudes towards political parties in general, towards elections, and towards democracy. The results are reported in Tables 9.3–9.6.

Table 9.3 Beliefs about political parties, 2001

	% Agreeing
Parties are more interested in winning elections than in governing afterwards.	60
The main political parties in Britain do not offer voters real choices in elections because their policies are pretty much all the same.	47
The main political parties do more to divide the country than unite it.	40
Political parties spend too much time bickering with each other.	83
There is often a big difference between what a party promises it will do and what it actually does when it wins an election.	80
In elections, political parties do not tell people about the really important problems facing the country.	60

Source: 2001 BES post-election survey mailback questionnaire.

Table 9.4   Feelings about political parties, 1974–2001 (mean scores on 10-point scales)

Parties	1974F	1974O	1979	2001
Conservatives	5.7	5.8	6.2	4.0
Labour	6.0	6.1	6.1	5.5
Liberals/Liberal Democrats	4.8	4.8	5.4	4.8
SNP (Scotland only)	4.6	5.2	3.6	5.0
PC (Wales only)	3.2	3.8	3.3	4.4
Average, all parties	4.8	5.1	4.9	4.7

Source: 1974, 1979, 2001 BES post-election surveys.

Table 9.5   Beliefs about elections, 2001

	% Agreeing
Elections help to keep politicans accountable for the promises they make.	69
Elections allow voters to express their opinions but do not really change anything.	59
Elections give voters an opportunity to tell politicans what they think is really important.	63
All things considered, most elections are just a big waste of time and money.	23

Source: 2001 BES post-election survey mailback questionnaire.

Democratic theory assigns a variety of important tasks to political parties. *Inter alia*, parties formulate policy proposals, mobilize political participation, recruit candidates for public office, organize elections by structuring choices among policies and candidates, form the government of the day or serve as critical but 'loyal' opposition to that government, and link citizens psychologically to the larger political order (for a discussion, see Kornberg and Clarke 1992: 62). These tasks are crucial for the successful functioning of a democratic polity and, as in other mature democracies, parties in Britain traditionally have been deeply involved in performing them. However, data gathered in the 2001 BES indicate that there appears to be a fairly high level of public cynicism as to how well the parties discharge their responsibilities. As reported in Table 9.3, many respondents thought that parties spend too much time bickering (83 per cent) and fail to deliver on their election promises (80 per cent). Many respondents also agreed that parties do not discuss the most important issues facing the country (60 per cent), and are more interested in winning elections than in governing well afterwards (60 per cent). Sizeable minorities also believed that parties fail to offer real choices because their policies are so similar (47 per cent) and that they do 'more to divide the country than unite it' (40 per cent).

The 2001 Election and Democracy in Britain

Table 9.6   Beliefs about democracy in Britain, 2001

	% Agreeing
A. Beliefs about democracy	
In a democracy, the majority has a right to pass laws to protect its own language and culture.	66
A democracy has the right to ban violent political groups, even if it means restricting some individual's rights.	64
In a true democracy, the majority has a responsibility to protect the rights of all minorities.	81
There is nothing more to democracy than giving people the right to vote in free elections.	26
In a true democracy, income and wealth are redistributed to ordinary working people.	34
B. Satisfaction with way democracy works in Britain (Column percentage)	
Very satisfied	9
Fairly satisfied	57
A little dissatisfied	26
Very dissatisfied	9

Source: Beliefs about democracy, 2001 BES post-election survey mailback questionnaire; satisfaction with democracy, 2001 BES post-election survey.

One indication that things may not have changed much in the last 30 years is provided by Table 9.4. This table uses data from BES surveys in the 1970s which asked respondents to give each party a mark out of ten, as well as data from the 2001 BES which asked respondents to indicate how they felt about each party on a 1–10 scale.[8] Two features of the data are noteworthy. First, the average ratings for Labour and especially for the Conservatives are lower in 2001 than in the 1970s, whereas the average ratings for the two nationalist parties are higher. The Liberal Democrat rating is identical in 2001 to that observed for the Liberals in the two elections of 1974. Although this pattern reflects some unhappiness with the two major parties, it also suggests the rising support for nationalist parties in Scotland and Wales since the mid-1970s. But, note the second feature of Table 9.4. The average rating of all five parties together in February 1974 was 4.8. Although this rating went up slightly in the two subsequent elections, the 2001 figure is very similar to that recorded three decades earlier. In sum, although British voters may be somewhat more dissatisfied with the Conservatives and Labour now than they were in the 1970s, there is no reason to think that they are more disaffected with parties in general. As parties' changing shares of votes in general elections and seats in the House of Commons suggest, disillusionment with the two main parties has found expression in increased support for the Liberal Democrats and for the Scottish and Welsh nationalists.

291

The 2001 Election and Democracy in Britain

Like parties, elections perform important functions in a democracy (e.g. see Kornberg and Clarke 1992). In theory, elections serve to select candidates for public office, to authorize the implementation of public policy, to produce accountability of politicians to citizens, and to build support for the larger political system. Elections also provide at least one formal means for achieving political equality, and they perform an educational function, helping people learn about political issues and competing parties' policy proposals. Indeed, it has been argued that elections are so important—particularly in terms of their accountability function—that they constitute the *sine qua non* of democratic government. Table 9.5 summarizes the findings of the 2001 BES regarding whether public beliefs about elections accord with the functions ascribed to elections by democratic theory. The pattern of responses is mixed. On the one hand, 59 per cent of the respondents thought that 'elections allow voters to express their opinions but do not really change anything'. On the other hand, only 23 per cent agreed with the statement that 'most elections are just a big waste of time and money'. And, approximately two-thirds believed that 'elections give voters an opportunity to tell politicians what they think is important', and that 'elections help to keep politicians accountable for the promises they make'.

The finding that a substantial majority of the British electorate thought that elections ensure accountability is not novel. The 1964 and 1966 BES surveys posed a similar (but not identical) question. Respondents were asked whether they agreed or disagreed with the statement that 'elections ensure that governments are responsive to what people want'. In 1964, 71 per cent agreed; in 1966, 72 per cent. Although the 1960s' question is about elections and responsiveness whereas the 2001 question is about elections and accountability, the meaning of the questions is probably quite similar for the average person. The implication is clear. Voters in 2001 were not noticeably different from their counterparts in the mid-1960s in terms of views of the accountability function of elections.

As is well known, the meaning of democracy has been the subject of longstanding and intense theoretical discussions (for a review see Held 1996). A reading of this literature indicates that conceptions of democracy are inevitably characterized by tensions over individual and community rights, freedom and equality, and government intervention in economy and society. Table 9.6 reports our findings regarding citizens' beliefs about democracy in Britain. Citizen and community rights feature prominently. Approximately two-thirds of the 2001 respondents believed that the majority has the right to protect its own language and culture, and violent groups should be banned even if it means restricting the rights of some individuals. However, only slightly over a quarter of those interviewed agreed that 'there is nothing more to democracy than giving people the right to vote in free elections'. At the same time, they did not think that democracy requires a relatively even distribution of material rewards. Only about a third concurred with the idea that 'in a true democracy, income and wealth are redistributed to ordinary working people'.

The 2001 Election and Democracy in Britain

A critical feature of Table 9.6 is the data on satisfaction with democracy. Sixty-six per cent of the 2001 BES respondents said they were 'very satisfied' or 'fairly satisfied' with 'the way that democracy works in this country'. An effective way of putting this figure in perspective is to compare it with responses recorded at earlier points in time. This can be done since the BES question is identical to that asked in successive Eurobarometer surveys since 1973. Figure 9.3 reports the average satisfaction levels recorded in these surveys and the 2001 BES. The results are striking. Although there have been fluctuations, *the average level of satisfaction with democracy in Britain has risen since the early 1970s.* This evidence clearly challenges the view that support for the political system has fallen over the last four decades as a result of forces from above or below. We investigate the sources of satisfaction with democracy later in this chapter.

Citizens' views of parties, elections, and democracy do not provide a complete picture of political support. Given that the institutions of the state continuously attempt to respond to public concerns and demands, we need to know how people evaluate various institutions. Over the years a number of attempts have been made to study these evaluations. Between 1974 and 1990, BES and BSA surveys asked respondents how 'satisfied' they were with certain state institutions. In 1991, the BSA survey asked respondents how 'confident' they were in a subset of institutions. And, from 1994 to 1998, the BSA asked respondents about the extent to which they could 'trust' different institutions to undertake particular tasks (see Table 9.7 for details).

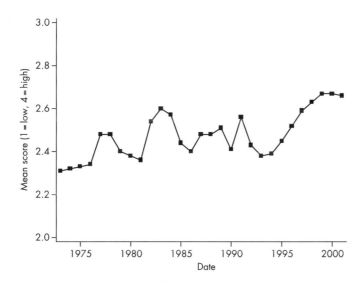

Figure 9.3   Democracy satisfaction in Britain, 1973–2001

Source: 1973–99 Eurobarometer surveys; 2000 P&D survey; 2001 BES post-election survey.

Table 9.7 Attitudes towards political institutions, 1974–2001 (percentages expressing satisfaction, confidence, trust or respect)

	Satisfaction				Confidence, BSA 1991	Trust			Respect, BES 2001
	BES 1974	BES 1983	BSA 1984	BSA 1990		BSA 1994	BSA 1996	BSA 1998	
Parliament					18				51
Civil service			53		11	27	28		55
Local government	37		49			31	29		38
Police		79	79	71		47	51		69
Courts					19				57
Politicians	18					9	8	9	24
Scotish Parliament									60
Welsh Assembly									62
European Union									26

Source: 1984, 1990, 1991, 1994, 1996, 1998 BSA surveys; 1974, 1983, 2001 BES surveys.

One problem with this latter approach was that, because the tasks cited were different, it is difficult to compare the responses across institutions. To facilitate cross-institutional comparison, the 2001 BES asked respondents how much they 'respected' several institutions on a 0–10 scale. The highest UK-wide levels of respect were accorded to institutions associated with the legal system—that is, the police and the courts. With regard to forces from below, levels of respect for the Scottish Parliament and for the Welsh Assembly were higher than that for the Westminster Parliament. In terms of forces from above, one of the lowest levels of respect was registered for the European Union. Politicians also fared badly in terms of public respect.

Table 9.7 also describes the results of earlier efforts to gauge public attitudes towards some of the more important political institutions in Britain. Several broad patterns in these attitudes are evident. Whenever the police were included in the list of institutions, they tended to receive relatively high ratings. Orientations towards the civil service and local government were substantially less favourable. Politicians were consistently accorded the lowest ratings. Viewed more generally, the important feature of these data is the absence of any discernible trend over time. Given this, it is reasonable to infer that the British are no less supportive of their major political institutions now than they were three or four decades ago.

FORCES FROM ABOVE: THE EUROPEAN UNION AND GLOBALIZATION

We noted earlier that the twin processes of increased EU policy 'competence' and globalization could have served to undercut the ability of the nation-state to respond to the specific needs of its citizens. In turn, we speculated that this 'hollowing-out' of the nation-state could have led to a decline in support for the political system. The evidence presented thus far does not bolster this conclusion. Citizens seem no less supportive of the political system now than they were a generation or more ago. Evaluations of elections, parties, and other institutions do not seem to have become more negative. And satisfaction with democracy has increased since it was first measured in the early 1970s. These political attitudes appear to have withstood strong downward pressures exerted by the forces from above in the form of Britain's membership in the European Union and the process of globalization. But, how do people themselves perceive these forces?

Data collected in several surveys help us to address this question (Table 9.8). The questions posed have changed over time because the circumstances surrounding Britain's membership themselves have changed. Backed by a cross-party consensus, support for Britain's membership in the European Union grew during the 1960s to 76 per cent in 1966. It plummeted after Britain's second application to join failed in 1967, but then rose progressively during the 1970s. After the United Kingdom had already joined, two-thirds of those participating in a retrospective referendum voted to remain inside what was then called the EC. Support for continuing membership fell in the early 1980s but thereafter rose steadily. However, in 1992, in response to a new question, a substantial proportion of people indicated a preference for a reduction in EU powers. This option became increasingly attractive during the 1990s, rising to 43 per cent in 1999. The rise in Euroscepticism was accompanied by a lack of enthusiasm for the abolition of

Table 9.8 Attitudes towards forces from above: the EC/EU and globalization, 1964–2001 (percentages agreeing)

	BES 1964	BES 1966	BES 1970	BSA 1983	BSA 1987	BSA 1990	BES 1992	BSA 1995	BES 1997	BSA 1999	BES 2001
Go into/stay in EEC/EC	51	76	25	53	63	76	72				
Stay out/leave EEC/EC	44	20	53	42	32	19	22				
Leave EC/EU							10	14	17	14	
Reduce EC/EU powers							30	23	43	43	
Keep £ rather than the €							54	62	62	58	54
Disapprove of EU											31
Approve of EU											43
Multinationals weaken democracy											33

Source: 1964, 1966, 1970, 1992, 1997, 2001 BES surveys; 1983, 1987, 1990, 1995, 1999 BSA surveys.

sterling and its replacement by the Euro. In essence, by the early 1990s, the British public had firmly accepted their membership in the European Union but a majority thought that there should be some reining back of the power that the United Kingdom had ceded to Brussels.

Similar oscillations in the pattern of British support for membership in the EC/EU are evident in Figure 9.4. The figure reports the percentages in 1973–99 Eurobarometer surveys who thought that EC/EU membership was good for Britain. After the euphoria of the referendum in 1975, the percentage taking a positive view fell progressively until 1980. From 1982, this percentage steadily increased until a second period of decline began in 1990. This continued through to the late 1990s.

There is considerable evidence to suggest that the pattern in Figure 9.4 was driven in part by the condition of the UK economy. Between 1975 and the mid-1990s, the trend in attitudes towards the European Union broadly matches the movement in inflation. For example, the simple correlation between EU support and the average annual inflation rate between 1974 and 1999 is $r = -0.52$ ($N = 26$). When the economy was going well, people tended to think that EU membership was good for Britain, and *vice versa*. However, this political economy argument fails to explain the continued Euroscepticism in the mid- and late-1990s

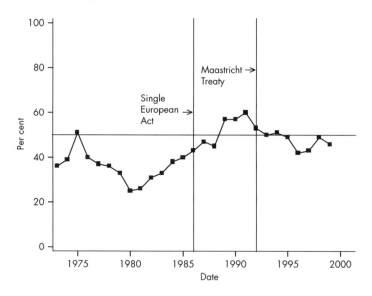

Figure 9.4 Percentage believing membership in European Union has been good for Britain, 1973–2000

Source: 1973–99 Eurobarometer surveys; 2000 P&D survey; 2001 BES post-election survey.

that occurred in the face of a sustained economic recovery (and a decline in inflation) after 1992.

One possible explanation for the post-1992 incongruence between attitudes towards the European Union and economic conditions is that, over and above any macro-economic effects, these attitudes were also conditioned by the long-term growth of EU responsibility for policy formulation and implementation. However, such an effect appears to be unrelated to the *objective* 'step' rises in such EU policy 'competence'. If objective change had mattered, then there would have been clear declines in the view that EU membership is good for Britain at precisely the points when EU policy responsibility increased—after the introduction of the Single European Act (SEA) in 1986 and in the wake of the signing of the Maastricht Treaty in 1992. However, objective changes may be less important than subjective perceptions of change. It could be the case that public awareness of increases in EU policy competence lagged behind the changes in policy reality. It may have taken the British public a few years to realize the full implications of the constitutional changes that the SEA and the Maastricht Treaty entailed. Margaret Thatcher herself claims not to have appreciated the extent to which the SEA reinvigorated the supranational momentum of the European Union until after she had retired from office in 1990 (Thatcher 1993). In these circumstances, it is perhaps unsurprising that the British public did not immediately downgrade its view of the European Union in 1986. However, the possibility that there was a time lag between the objective growth in EU policy responsibility in 1986 and the subsequent recognition of that growth, particularly after the signing of the Maastricht Treaty, has important implications. It means that the increased Euroscepticism of the 1990s observed in both Table 9.8 and Figure 9.4 could have been a delayed response to the growth of the scope of the EU's policy authority. Indeed, by the time of Labour's victory in the 1997 general election, over a third of the electorate thought that the European Union, as opposed to the British government, had primary responsibility for managing the British economy. This was nearly 10 percentage points higher than had been the case five years earlier.[9] In sum, the hollowing out of the nation-state associated with the European Union may not have affected British voters' perceptions of their own domestic political system, but it does seem to have adversely affected their attitudes towards the European Union.

Reservations about the European Union are echoed in attitudes towards an even larger force from above—globalization. We measured these attitudes indirectly in the 2001 BES by asking respondents about the extent to which they agreed with the statement that 'big international companies now have more influence on daily life in Britain than our own government does'. We assume that agreement connotes a negative view of globalization, and that disagreement implies a positive view. As the final row of Table 9.8 shows, 33 per cent of those interviewed viewed globalization in negative terms. Although no comparable questions have been asked in previous surveys, as discussed below, we can relate individual variations in perceptions of globalization to more general questions about the sources of (dis)satisfaction with democracy.

FORCES FROM BELOW: DEMANDS FOR NATIONAL AUTONOMY

As argued earlier, demands for national autonomy directly challenge both the composition of the *political community* and the character of the established *regime*. This section first considers attitudes towards the integrity of the political community. This is done by investigating the extent to which pressures for autonomy in Scotland and Wales have varied over the last two decades—the period for which reliable data are available. We then determine whether these pressures have resulted in distinctive perceptions of the regime among the English, Scots, and Welsh.

Table 9.9 reports variations in 'national' (i.e. English, Scots, or Welsh) identity versus British identity between 1979 and 2001. Panel A of the table shows the consequences of presenting respondents with a simple choice among a national identity, a British identity, some other identity, or none at all. Although a longer cross-time comparison is not possible for England, it is clear that, in 1999, the English were the most likely to consider themselves British. However, cross-time

Table 9.9   National identity versus British identity, 1979–2001

	England	Scotland		Wales	
	1999	*1979*	*1999*	*1979*	*1999*
A. Responses to Questions Posing Simple Choice between National and British Identity, 1979–99					
English/Scots/Welsh identity	44	66	78	56	55
British identity	44	31	17	32	33
Other identity/none	12	3	5	12	12

	England		Scotland			Wales	
	1997	*2001*	*1992*	*1997*	*2001*	*1997*	*2001*
B. Responses to 'Graduated' Identity Question in 1992–2001 BES							
English/Scots/Welsh not British	7	14	19	23	46	12	16
More English/Scots/Welsh than British	17	13	40	38	18	29	23
English/Scots/Welsh and British equally	45	41	33	27	18	25	31
More British than English/Scots/Welsh	14	10	3	4	5	9	9
British not English/Scots/Welsh	9	14	3	4	8	18	18
Other/none	7	7	2	4	5	7	4

Source: 1979, 1992, 1997, 2001 BES surveys; 1999 BSA survey.

comparisons can be made for both Scotland and Wales between 1979, when the first referendum on Scottish devolution was held, and 1999, the year in which the newly devolved national assemblies were created. Over this period, national identification remained virtually unchanged in Wales (at 55–56 per cent), while it rose in Scotland (from 66 to 78 per cent). This pattern of change is confirmed in panel B of Table 9.9, which reports the results of posing a more graduated question on national identity in the 1992, 1997, and 2001 BES surveys. It is clear that levels of national identity increased in all three countries between 1997 and 2001. However, the most noticeable feature of panel B is the increase in exclusively nationalist identifiers in Scotland after 1997. Those considering themselves 'Scottish not British' increased from 23 per cent in 1997 to 46 per cent in 2001. It seems likely that this result is in no small measure due to the creation of the Scottish Parliament. This institutional arena for Scottish politics has strengthened the Scots' sense of belonging to a distinctive community. The Welsh Assembly—with its more restricted powers—has yet to produce a similar mobilizing effect in Wales.

But if national identity, at least in Scotland, has developed significantly since devolution, then what effect has devolution itself had on people's demands for national autonomy? Table 9.10 reports opinions on the main constitutional options for devolving power in Scotland and Wales. Panel A distinguishes between the UK-wide view and the Scottish view of these options. It shows how support for both Scottish independence and for an elected Scottish assembly rose in Scotland *and* across the United Kingdom more generally after 1979. Support for

Table 9.10 Attitudes towards forces from below: support for devolution options, 1979–2001 (percentages in favour)

	BES 1979	BES 1992	BSA 1994	BES 1997	BSA 1999	BES 2001
A. Scotland constitutional options						
UK-wide view						
Independence for Scotland	7	14	15	16	20	17
Elected assembly	15	55	47	59	58	55
Scottish view						
Independence for Scotland	8	23	29	27	18	21
Elected assembly	22	74	45	54	65	75
B. Wales constitutional options						
Welsh view[a]						
Independence for Wales	4	13	12	10	12	6
Elected assembly	11	40	49	56	74	63

[a] UK-wide view not recorded.

Source: 1979, 1992, 1997, 2001 BES surveys; 1994, 1999 BSA surveys.

independence in Scotland peaked in 1994, when almost one-third of Scots chose the independence option. However, after the Scottish Parliament was established, support for independence fell to 18 per cent. At the same time, the number favouring the elected assembly option rose to 65 per cent. By 2001, support for independence had risen slightly to 21 per cent, but support for the assembly had reached an overwhelming 75 per cent. This suggests that devolution, at least for the time being, has renewed Scottish confidence in the desirability of maintaining the current boundaries of the political community.

Panel B of Table 9.10 reports the corresponding views of devolution options among the Welsh. The pattern over time is similar to that in Scotland. The popularity of independence, though never as great as in Scotland, more than tripled between 1979 and 1992. Similarly, the number favouring an assembly almost quadrupled in the same period. However, as in Scotland, the creation of a Welsh Assembly thus far seems to have 'bought off' support for independence. By 2001, when enthusiasm for the assembly stood at 63 per cent, support for independence had fallen to 6 per cent—only marginally higher than the 4 per cent recorded in 1979.

But, if devolution has stabilized the boundaries of the political community, have the pressures which produced demands for autonomy led the Scots and Welsh to feel more disengaged from and critical of the existing political regime? Table 9.11 reports data from the 2001 BES on the views of United Kingdom, English, Scots, and Welsh respondents on various aspects of individual engagement and the

Table 9.11 Mean scores on political orientation scales, 2001

	Among respondents living in			
	Britain	*England*	*Scotland*	*Wales*
Internal efficacy index (1–5 scale)	2.6	2.6	2.5	2.6
External efficacy index (1–5 scale)	2.4	2.4	2.3	2.4
Civic duty (1–5 scale)	3.6	3.6	3.6	3.5
Protest probability (0–10 scale)	2.7	2.6	2.7	2.8
Positive attitudes towards parties (1–5 scale)	2.5	2.5	2.5	2.5
Positive attitudes towards elections (1–5 scale)	3.3	3.3	3.2	3.3
Satisfaction with democracy (1–4 scale)	2.6	2.6	2.6	2.7
Respect for parliament at Westminster (0–10 scale)	5.5	5.5	5.0	5.6
Respect for civil service (0–10 scale)	5.3	5.3	5.1	5.4
Respect for local government (0–10 scale)	5.0	5.1	4.9	4.8
Respect for the police (0–10 scale)	6.9	7.0	6.8	6.9
Respect for the courts (0–10 scale)	5.8	5.9	5.5	5.6
Respect for politicians (0–10 scale)	4.0	4.0	4.0	4.1
Respect for Scottish/Welsh Assembly (0–10 scale)			5.4	4.3
Respect for the European Union (0–10 scale)	3.9	3.7	4.1	4.0

Source: 2001 BES survey.

political system. The numbers shown in the table are average scale scores, broken down by country.[10] The dominant pattern is immediately evident.[11] In terms of internal and external efficacy, civic duty, protest potential, attitudes towards parties, attitudes towards elections, democracy satisfaction, and respect for institutions, there are *very few differences* among English, Scots, and Welsh voters. The only cases for which there are noticeable differences concern the European Union (the Scots and Welsh tended to be more respectful than the English) and the Westminster Parliament (unsurprisingly, Scots were less respectful than the English and Welsh). These minor differences underscore how similar all the other responses are. In sum, Table 9.11 shows that the 'forces from below' have not produced a situation in which citizens in Scotland and Wales have substantially different attitudes about the individual's engagement in politics or about the UK political system. On the contrary, English, Scots, and Welsh are, on average, remarkably similar.

Evidence provided in Figure 9.5 reinforces this point. The figure shows how the summary measure of satisfaction with democracy varied by country between 1973 and 2001. The results indicate a gentle upward trend, with some oscillation along the way. Notwithstanding pressures for devolution, satisfaction levels in England, Scotland, and Wales have tended to move upwards together over time. There is no indication either of declining satisfaction in Scotland or Wales or of a divergence in average satisfaction levels. And, there is certainly no evidence of 'damage' being inflicted by the 'forces from below'.

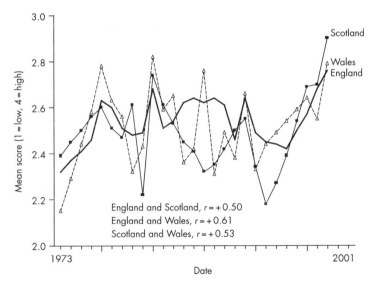

Figure 9.5 Democracy satisfaction in England, Scotland, and Wales, 1973–2001
Source: 1973–99 Eurobarometer surveys; 2000 P&D survey; 2001 BES post-election survey.

EXPLAINING SATISFACTION WITH DEMOCRACY IN BRITAIN

The foregoing discussion has assessed how far support for the British political community and regime have changed in recent decades. Our conclusion is that surprisingly little has changed at the UK level and that, in the wake of devolution, support remains quite evenly distributed across England, Scotland, and Wales. In this section, we investigate the extent to which citizens are satisfied with the practice of democracy in Britain. We focus on democracy satisfaction for two reasons. First, we argue that it is an important indicator of political support at the authority, regime, and community levels. There is some debate about whether democracy satisfaction refers to support for the government of the day or for the larger political community. However, there is evidence that the democracy satisfaction measure correlates equally well with indicators of authority, regime, and community support and, thus, it acts as a useful summary of all three (Kornberg and Clarke 1992; see also Clarke, Dutt, and Kornberg 1993). Second, there is directly comparable data over time which show that democracy satisfaction has increased across Britain in recent years. In this part of our discussion, we specify a model of democracy satisfaction, and then test it using individual-level data from the 2001 BES. Our purpose in doing so is to establish the relative importance of the explanatory factors discussed above.

Table 9.12 summarizes hypothesized influences on satisfaction with democracy.[12] In the table, the explanatory variables are grouped in terms of individual engagement, evaluations of system performance, attitudes to forces from above, and attitudes to forces from below. The *individual engagement* variables correspond closely to those discussed earlier in the chapter. Interest in politics is included because, following the logic of Norris's 'virtuous circle' (Norris 2001), we hypothesize that, *ceteris paribus*, interested individuals are more engaged with and supportive of the democratic process in general. Regarding political efficacy, individuals who feel that they can have an influence on the political system and that it is relatively responsive are more likely to register higher levels of democracy satisfaction. With respect to civic duty, it is hypothesized that people who regard voting as a civic duty are expressing a commitment to the political system and, thus, are more likely to have high levels of democracy satisfaction. Party identification is also included here; it is expected that people who identify with a political party are more likely to have a stronger commitment to the political system than those who do not.[13]

The rationale that underpins the inclusion of each of our measures of system performance evaluations assumes that citizens make judgements about the (un)successful functioning of the democratic process partly in valence or performance terms. If people think that the political system performs well, then they are more likely, other things equal, to express support for it. Accordingly, we hypothesize that

Table 9.12 Possible influences on satisfaction with democracy

	Predicted effect
Explanatory variables	
Individual's engagement with political system	
Voting is a civic duty	+
Party identifier	+
Sense of political efficacy	+
Interest in politics	+
Performance of the existing system	
Institutional satisfaction	+
Economic policy satisfaction	+
Social policy satisfaction	+
Overall party leader evaluations	+
Attitudes to forces that affect democracy 'from above'	
Support for the European Union	+
Multinational companies perceived as a threat to democracy	−
Attitudes to forces that affect democracy 'from below'	
Scottish national identifier	−
Welsh national identifier	−
Prefers single UK parliament	−
Support Scots/Welsh independence	−
Demographic characteristics that reflect 'forces from below'	
Lives in Scotland/not	0
Lives in Wales/not	0
Ethnic minority/not	−
Control variables	
View of incumbent government	
Feelings towards the Labour Party	+
General sense of economic and social satisfaction	
Relative deprivation	−
Life satisfaction	+
Demographics	
Social class (ABC1/C2DE)	+
Owner occupier/not	+
Gender (male/not)	+
Graduate qualification/not	+
Age	+

Note: A + sign indicates a predicted positive effect, a − sign indicates a predicted negative effect, and a zero (0) indicates a prediction of no effect.

satisfaction with economic and social policy, with the performance of the main political institutions, and with the overall quality of national political leadership disposes individuals to exhibit higher levels of satisfaction with democracy.

Justification of the specification of the effects of the forces from above is anticipated earlier. Those who take a negative view of the European Union are also likely to be relatively dissatisfied with democracy precisely because the established system has failed to protect the decision-making autonomy of the nation-state. Accordingly, we hypothesize that those who disapprove of the European Union are more likely to register low scores on democracy satisfaction. An analogous logic underpins the likely impact of perceptions of globalization. Those who view multinational companies in negative terms, as a threat to democracy, are also likely to be critical of the existing democratic order—on the grounds that it has failed to address the challenges that globalization has presented. Therefore, we expect that negative views of globalization are associated with low levels of democracy satisfaction.

Reasoning with regard to forces from below is based partly on national identities, partly on the positions taken on the main Scots and Welsh constitutional options, and partly on demographic characteristics. With regard to identities, we hypothesize that individuals whose primary identity is either Scottish or Welsh are less inclined to be satisfied with the operation of what they regard to be the *British* democratic system. This is because they are likely to feel dominated by the English majority. As for constitutional options, it is expected that people who favour either a single UK parliament or independence for Scotland are unhappy with the *status quo* and, therefore, exhibit lower levels of democracy satisfaction. Given our earlier finding that there are no significant regional variations in democracy satisfaction, we hypothesize that levels of democracy satisfaction among people living in Scotland and Wales will not differ from those for people living in England. In terms of other demographic characteristics, we also consider the effects of ethnic minority status. One possible implication of the relative exclusion of ethnic minorities from mainstream political activity in the United Kingdom is that members of such minorities are less satisfied with democracy.

Finally, a set of control variables is included. These variables fall into three categories: views of the incumbent government; a general sense of economic and social well-being (which is operationalized as 'relative deprivation' and 'life satisfaction'); and miscellaneous other socio-demographic characteristics. The inclusion of feelings about the Labour Party (on a 0–10 scale) is intended to capture the tendency of individuals who voted for 'winners' in an election to have higher levels of system support (Kornberg and Clarke 1992; see also Acock and Clarke 1989; Anderson and Tverdova 2001). A relative deprivation variable is specified on the grounds that people who think that they have not benefited duly from the existing political system should exhibit less support for it. The life satisfaction variable is intended to control for the possibility that people who are generally satisfied with their lives are also likely to be satisfied with the political system itself. Additional socio-demographic variables are included to capture the extent to which members of particular groups have a larger 'stake' in the existing political system. Accordingly, owner-occupiers, middle-class men, and better educated people are more likely to be satisfied with how democracy operates. We also expect that older voters are more satisfied as a result of reinforcing their attachments to the political system over a lengthy period of time.

The model of democracy satisfaction may be summarized as follows:

$$\text{DEMOSAT} = f(\beta_0 + \Sigma_{1-4} \text{ ENGAGE} + \Sigma\beta_{5-8}\text{EVAL}$$
$$+ \Sigma\beta_{9-10}\text{ABOVE} + \Sigma\beta_{11-14}\text{BELOW} + \Sigma\beta_{15-17}\text{BELDEM}$$
$$+ \Sigma\beta_{18-25} \text{ CONTROL})$$

where

DEMOSAT = level of satisfaction with democracy in Britain;
ENGAGE = variables measuring engagement with the political system;
EVAL = variables measuring evaluations of system performance;
ABOVE = attitudes towards forces from above;
BELOW = attitudes towards forces from below;
BELDEM = demographic characteristics reflecting forces from below;
CONTROL = control variables.

The β's are parameters to be estimated. Since the dependent variable, democracy satisfaction, is a four-category ordinal scale, ordered logit is used to estimate model parameters (Long 1997: ch. 5).[14]

Table 9.13 summarizes the effects of engagement, evaluations, and attitudes towards forces from above and below on satisfaction with democracy in Britain. The model is reasonably well determined, with an estimated R^2 of 0.14. The column marked ΔP represents the change in the probability that an individual will be fairly or very satisfied with democracy as the value of the independent variable changes from its minimum to its maximum value, holding all other variables constant at their respective means. For example, the change in probability of 0.38 for economic policy satisfaction means that a person who scores 10 on the 0–10 economic policy satisfaction scale is 0.38 more likely, *ceteris paribus*, to be satisfied with democracy than someone who scores 0 on it. The change in probability scores gauge the relative importance of each of the independent variables in the model.

Results of the analysis generally support the expectations outlined in Table 9.12. Measures of individual engagement all have significant or near-significant effects. As predicted, civic duty and party identification both contribute positively and significantly to democracy satisfaction. The effect of efficacy is also positive, although it is only significant at the 0.10 level in a one-tailed test. However, contrary to expectations, interest in politics exerts a significant *negative* effect. This suggests that, over and above the other effects specified in the model, increased political interest renders people more, rather than less, dissatisfied with the performance of the political system.[15] Thus, the effect of political interest (a cognitive mobilization

Table 9.13   Ordered logit model of satisfaction with democracy in Britain, 2001

	β	SE	ΔP
Explanatory variables			
Engagement with political system			
Voting is a civic duty	0.15★★★	0.05	0.14
Party identification (very/fairly strong)	0.14★★	0.07	0.09
Sense of political efficacy	0.14	0.09	0.11
Interest in politics	−0.17★★★	0.06	−0.15
Evaluations of system performance			
Institutional satisfaction	0.21★★★	0.04	0.44
Economic policy satisfaction	0.44★★★	0.10	0.38
Social policy satisfaction	0.41★★★	0.11	0.32
Party leader evaluations	0.11★★	0.05	0.25
Attitudes to forces 'from above'			
Support for the European Union	0.01	0.05	0.01
Multinational companies a threat to democracy	−0.33★★★	0.06	−0.28
Attitudes to forces 'from below'			
Scottish national identifier	0.15	0.34	0.02
Welsh national identifier	0.08	0.47	0.00
Prefers single UK parliament	−0.05	0.14	−0.01
Supports Scots/Welsh independence	−0.21	0.14	−0.05
Demographics reflecting 'forces from below'			
Resident of Scotland	−0.02	0.25	0.00
Resident of Wales	−0.00	0.30	0.00
Member of ethnic minority	−0.06	0.26	0.00
Control variables			
Attitude toward incumbent government			
Feelings about Labour Party	0.08★★	0.03	0.18
General sense of satisfaction			
Relative deprivation	−0.07	0.05	−0.02
Life satisfaction	0.35★★★	0.08	0.23
Socio-demographic controls			
Age	0.01★★	0.00	0.12
Education	−0.21	0.14	−0.04
Gender	0.02	0.10	0.00
Owner occupier	0.18	0.13	0.04
Social class	−0.13	0.12	−0.03

Notes: Estimated cut points: $1 = 2.81$ (★★★); $2 = 5.01$ (★★★); $3 = 8.55$ (★★★); likelihood ratio $\chi^2 = 500.87$; estimated $R^2 = 0.14$.

★★★ $p \leq 0.001$; ★★ $p \leq 0.01$; ★ $p \leq 0.05$; one-tailed test.

ΔP is change in probability as predictor variables change from minimum to maximum values.

Source: 2001 BES post-election survey.

variable) is decidedly a double-edged sword in British politics. As discussed in Chapter Eight, it makes individuals more likely to participate but, as just indicated, it also tends to make them less satisfied with democracy. Performance evaluations also figure prominently in the model. As anticipated, institutional satisfaction, economic policy satisfaction, social policy satisfaction, and leader evaluations all exert highly significant and positive effects on satisfaction with democracy. These effects are consistent with our general argument about the importance of valence politics in Britain, and they are discussed more fully below.

With regard to forces from above, democracy satisfaction is negatively influenced by perceptions of globalization. However, attitudes towards the European Union are not influential. Finally, none of the variables relating to the forces from below exerts a significant effect. The terms for Scots and Welsh identity are both insignificant. The same is true for those that measure respondents' preferences for a single UK parliament or for independence for Scotland or Wales. Living in Scotland or Wales or being a member of an ethnic minority has no effect on democracy satisfaction. This latter finding contradicts the prediction that ethnic minorities should be more dissatisfied. However, the more general pattern of insignificant effects for the forces from below strongly confirms the earlier observation that the pressures for national autonomy in Scotland and Wales have yet to undermine support for the UK political system. Finally, none of the socio-demographic variables included as controls exerts a statistically significant effect.

The explanatory power of variables in the model of democracy satisfaction is illustrated in Table 9.14. This table provides an example of how the independent effects identified in the model can work collectively to produce dramatic differences in levels of democracy satisfaction. The first row of the table reports the 'baseline' democracy satisfaction probabilities associated with setting each independent variable to its mean. The second row assumes that a particular individual is a 23-year-old non-graduate who feels no sense of civic duty and does not identify with a political party. It also assumes that this person is very dissatisfied with Britain's political institutions, with its policy performance, and with life in general. The model predicts that this individual has a 75 per cent chance of being very dissatisfied with democracy, a 21 per cent chance of being fairly dissatisfied, and no chance of being very satisfied. The third row of the table reports results for a very different kind of person—a 55-year-old graduate who has a strong sense of civic duty, is a strong party identifier, and is very satisfied with Britain's political institutions, with its policy performance, and with life in general. This person has a 59 per cent chance of being very satisfied with democracy in Britain, a 39 per cent chance of being fairly satisfied, and almost no chance of being dissatisfied.

The message of this analysis is consistent with that reported in other studies of support for democracy. Democracy satisfaction in the United Kingdom derives both from a sense of engagement with the political system and from evaluations of its performance. Three of the significant variables in the democracy satisfaction

Table 9.14 Democracy satisfaction scenarios: probabilities of having different levels of democracy satisfaction (based on model in Table 9.13)

| | Democracy satisfaction | | | |
| | Dissatisfied | | Satisfied | |
	Very	Fairly	Fairly	Very
Baseline assumption: all predictor variables set to mean values	0.05	0.27	0.62	0.06
Set institutional satisfaction, economic policy satisfaction, social policy satisfaction, strength of partisanship, civic duty, graduate status, life satisfaction to *minimum* values; all others to mean values	0.75	0.21	0.04	0.00
Set institutional satisfaction, economic policy satisfaction, social policy satisfaction, strength of partisanship, civic duty, graduate status, life satisfaction to *maximum* values; all else to mean values	0.00	0.02	0.04	0.59

model can be regarded as measuring various aspects of engagement. Three of them—civic duty, partisanship, and political efficacy—have significant, positive effects. Thus, the more engaged that individuals are, the more likely it is that they have a high level of satisfaction with democracy. In addition, the results indicate a significant role for age. It was included in the model as a control variable and as a surrogate indicator of prolonged experience with the political system. Net of all other considerations, older people are more likely to display high levels of democracy satisfaction than their younger counterparts.[16]

What is also clear is that strong statistical effects on democracy satisfaction derive from evaluations of performance. These evaluations are manifested in two ways. The more satisfied that citizens are with institutions, with economic and social policies, and with leaders, the more utility they derive from the existing system. And the more utility they receive, the greater their level of political support. Also, individuals who are critical of globalization presumably think that the growing power of multinational corporations has been accompanied by a diminished ability of the existing regime to protect their interests and, thus, they are less satisfied with democracy.

For policy-makers, the results reported here are a source of both comfort and potential concern. They are a source of comfort because system performance is the basis of the most consistent effects on satisfaction with democracy in Britain. Current institutional arrangements, including the devolved assemblies in Scotland and Wales, generate relatively high levels of satisfaction. As long as policy-makers continue to respond to citizens' concerns and to ensure relatively high levels of institutional, policy, and leadership performance, then people will respond by continuing to support the political system.

The source of concern involves citizens' sense of civic duty and party identification. As shown in Chapter Eight, sense of civic duty has a very strong age gradient, with older cohorts exhibiting progressively higher levels of duty.[17] It is possible that this is almost entirely a life-cycle effect—as people get older, they develop a stronger sense of civic duty. But, the analyses presented in Chapter Eight indicate there may be generational effects as well. People entering the electorate during the 1980s and 1990s—what we call the Thatcher and Blair generations—have significantly lower levels of civic duty than a life-cycle model would anticipate. If this is the case, then it would imply that as older voters die, civic duty will decline. And, as a sense of civic duty declines, we would also expect political support to decline—unless there is an offsetting increase in evaluations of system performance. With regard to partisanship, as shown in Chapters Three and Six, the incidence and strength of party identification have fallen over the past four decades. If this gradual decline continues, then it follows that there will be even fewer partisans in the electorate to lend their support to the existing regime. Again, *ceteris paribus*, satisfaction with democracy may be set to decline—unless there are compensating increases in system performance or new forms of commitment to the political regime and community emerge.

CONCLUSIONS: DISAFFECTION WITH BRITISH DEMOCRACY?

The marked decline in turnout in the 2001 general election inevitably raises questions about the health of the contemporary British political system. In this chapter, we have explored the extent to which the fall in turnout can be regarded as an indication of a wider malaise in British democracy. There are certainly good *a priori* reasons for supposing that support for the UK political community and regime might have declined in recent decades. EU membership and the process of globalization have restricted the decision-making autonomy of the nation-state, thereby reducing the incentives for citizens to support either the political community or the regime. At the same time, new sources of nationalist and ethnic identity have arisen that could have reduced levels of attachment to the political system.

In fact, levels of political support appear not to have changed substantially since the 1960s. If we look beyond the act of voting, survey data indicate that the British electorate is just as engaged with the political system now as it was forty years ago. The extent to which British citizens are satisfied with democracy has risen across the United Kingdom. And, since the creation of the devolved assemblies in Scotland and Wales, demands for Scottish and Welsh independence appear to have abated.

But, if there is little evidence to suggest that levels of political support have changed much over the past four decades, then what do we know about the sources of support? And, what sort of prognosis does an analysis of these sources offer for the future? Analyses show that satisfaction with democracy in Britain is influenced by evaluations of institutional, policy, and leadership performance and, to a lesser degree, by the extent to which citizens are engaged in the political system itself. To the extent that policy-makers are seen to be responsive and to perform well, support is likely to be relatively high. With regard to the political community, it is particularly noteworthy that Scots, Welsh, and members of Britain's ethnic minorities do not exhibit lower levels of democracy satisfaction than their English and ethnic majority counterparts. These groups are statistically indistinguishable from one another. However, the prognosis looks less optimistic when civic duty and party identification are considered. The latter is in long-term decline and both vary significantly across age groups—with the possible implication that turnover in the electorate over time will result in lower overall levels of civic duty and partisanship. Such secular declines, should they occur, will work to reduce support for the political system.

In sum, the government's ability to 'deliver the goods' and citizens' willingness to grant it support constitute fundamental features of political life in contemporary Britain. Notwithstanding the decline in turnout between 1997 and 2001, by recent historical standards, public support for British democracy is relatively high. The political system has proved that it can respond to public demands. Voters are not especially interested in politics, but they can recognize genuine efforts by policy-makers to respond to their concerns. If future policy-makers can continue to deliver the responsiveness and performance that is required, then future voters who subscribe to a valence view of politics may, in due course, acquire a deeper sense of involvement in, and commitment to, the political life of British democracy.

NOTES

1. There are a number of policy areas where national government's freedom to make policy has been curtailed and where the rules operated by national government's own state agencies are often subject to control by EU directives. These include the forms and levels of indirect taxation that governments may levy on both firms and individuals. Value added tax (VAT) is the universal form of indirect taxation within the EU. Once VAT has been applied to a particular category of items, it is not within the purview of a national government either to remove it or reduce the percentage rate at which VAT is applied. Another possible, and related, source of citizen dissatisfaction with government is the tendency of the modern state to depoliticize certain policy areas by abdicating responsibility (often with good reason) in favour of other agencies, such as quangos or local government. A recent example of such an abdication in the United Kingdom was the decision of the Labour government in June

1997 to hand over control of interest rate policy to the Bank of England. Although the Treasury still determines the target for inflation, it is up to the Bank, and its panel of advisers, to set interest rates at a level that will achieve that target.

2. The term 'policy competence' is often used in the sense of 'policy scope'. The term refers to a particular level of government that is acknowledged as responsible for the formulation and implementation of policy in a particular sphere. The term does not necessarily refer to the quality of the government's performance in that sphere.

3. For example, in 1979, the Conservatives received 36% of the popular vote in Scotland and 20% in Wales. By 1997, these shares had fallen to 17% and 12%, respectively.

4. An additional indicator of political engagement is party identification. It is investigated in detail in Chapter Six and its impact on democracy satisfaction is analyzed further in this chapter.

5. The response options to the political interest question reported in Figure 9.1 have varied over time. For the 1974–9 BES, 'interested' responses combine 'a great deal' and 'some', and the 'uninterested' responses combine 'not much' and 'none at all'. For the 1997–2001 BES, 'interested' responses combine 'a great deal', 'quite a lot', and 'some'; 'uninterested' responses combine 'not very much' and 'not at all'. For the 1986–97 BSA, 'interested' responses combine 'very', 'fairly', and 'somewhat' interested', and 'uninterested' responses combine 'not very' and 'not at all' interested. 'Cared about the outcome' entries represent the percentage of BES respondents who 'cared a lot' about the election outcome.

6. The 2001 BES entries are the percentages of respondents who 'strongly agree' or 'agree' that: (*a*) 'It is every citizen's duty to vote in an election', and (*b*) 'I would be *seriously* neglecting my duty as a citizen if I did not vote.' The entry for the 2000 CA survey is the percentage from the first wave of the CA national panel who 'strongly agree' or 'agree' that: 'It is every citizen's duty to vote in elections' (Pattie, Seyd, and Whiteley 2004, forthcoming). The 1997 BES question is: 'Thinking now about voting in general elections, generally speaking, do you think: people need not vote unless they really care who wins, or, is it everyone's duty to vote.' The BSA civic duty data are from the following question: 'Which of the following statements comes closest to your view about general elections? In a general election: (*a*) 'It's not really worth voting', (*b*) 'People should vote only if they care who wins', (*c*) It is everyone's duty to vote.'

7. The 2001 BES data are the percentages of respondents who scored 6 or more on the 0–10 likelihood-of-participation scale. The 1979 BES data are the percentages of respondents who said that it was either 'very' or 'quite' likely that they would do various activities. The 1987 BES data are the percentages of respondents who said that they 'have done' various activities. The 1984, 1989, 1991, and 1992 BSA data are percentages of respondents who said they 'would do' various activities. The 1984 PMD data are percentages who 'have done' various activities (Parry, Moyser, and Day 1992: 44, Table 3.1). The 1973–4 data are percentages of respondents in the British Political Action survey who said that they 'have done' or 'would do' various activities (Barnes, Kaase et al. 1979: 548, Table TA.3).

8. Respondents in the 1974 and 1979 BES were asked to give each party a mark out of ten. In 2001, respondents were asked: 'On a scale that runs from 0 to 10, where 0 means *strongly dislike* and 10 means *strongly like*, how do you feel about the [. . .] party?'

9. The question is: 'Which one of the following do you think affects the general economic situation in this country most? Would you say the British Government or the European Union?'

10. The 1–5 scales shown in Table 9.11 are based on Likert-scale questions where the response options are 'strongly agree', 'agree', 'neither agree nor disagree', 'disagree', and 'strongly disagree'. Variables were recoded as necessary to ensure that, for positive statements, strong agreement was coded 5, and for negative statements, strong disagreement was coded 5. Indices were constructed by adding variables together and dividing by the number of variables. For example, the internal efficacy scale (internal and external items are shown in Table 9.1) is constructed by combining the responses to the 'no say' and 'difficult to understand' statements. The responses are first recoded so that a response that implies high inefficacy (e.g. strong agreement with the first statement) receives a score of 1, while a response that implies high efficacy (e.g. strong disagreement with the statement) is scored as 5. The internal efficacy scale is the sum of the two sets of responses divided by 2. The civic duty item is, 'It is every citizen's duty to vote in an election.' The beliefs about parties and beliefs about elections items are shown in Tables 9.3 and 9.5, respectively. The satisfaction with democracy scale is based on responses to the question 'On the whole, are you satisfied or dissatisfied with the way that democracy works in this country?' The response options are 'very satisfied' (scored 4), 'fairly satisfied' (scored 3), 'a little dissatisfied' (scored 2), and 'very dissatisfied' (scored 1).

11. Equivalent analyses of earlier BES and BSA surveys yield findings almost identical to those reported here (details available from the authors on request).

12. The independent variables in the democracy satisfaction analysis are measured as follows: (a) *civic duty*—an additive index based on responses to two measures of civic duty in the post-election survey; (b) *party identification*—respondents indicating that they identify 'fairly' or 'very' strongly with a political party are scored 1, others, 0; (c) *political efficacy*—an additive index based on 'strongly agree' to 'strongly disagree' responses to the following statements: (i) 'People like me have no say in what government does', (ii) 'It often is difficult for me to understand what is going on in government and politics', (iii) 'Those elected to Parliament soon lose touch with the people', (iv) 'Parties are only interested in people's votes, not in their opinions', (v) 'Government does not care much what people like me think'; (d) *political interest*—a 0–4 scale based on responses to the question 'Generally speaking, how interested are you in politics?'; (e) *institutional satisfaction*—an additive index that averages responses to a question about levels of respect for various institutions. The question is 'Now, thinking about institutions like Parliament, please use the 0–10 scale to indicate how much respect you have for each of the following, where 0 means no respect and 10 means a great deal of respect.' The institutions asked about were the Parliament at Westminster, the civil service, the police, local government in the respondent's area, the European Union, the courts, the Scottish Parliament, the Welsh Assembly. Respondents were also asked about their respect for 'politicians generally'; (f) *economic policy satisfaction*—an additive index based on responses to the following question: 'How well do you think the present government has handled each of the following issues . . . very well, fairly well, neither well nor badly, fairly badly, very badly.' Issues used in building the index were: 'the economy in general', 'inflation', 'taxes', and 'unemployment'. (g) *social policy satisfaction*—an additive index based on responses to the question posed in (f) above regarding the following issues: 'asylum seekers', 'crime', 'education', 'national health service', 'pensions', and 'transport'; (h) *feelings about party leaders*—an additive index that combines responses to the following question: 'Using a scale that runs from 0 to 10, where 0 means strongly dislike and 10 means strongly like, how do you feel about: Tony Blair, William Hague, Charles Kennedy,

The 2001 Election and Democracy in Britain

[in Scotland only] John Swinney, [in Wales only] Wyn Jones'; (*i*) *support for European Union*—a 5-point scale based on the following question: 'Overall, do you approve or disapprove of Britain's membership in the European Union?' Response options ranged from 'strongly approve' to 'strongly disapprove'; (*j*) *attitude towards multinational corporations*—a 5-point scale based on responses to the following statement: 'Big international companies are a threat to democratic government in Britain. Response categories range from 'strongly agree' to 'strongly disagree'; (*k*) *national identity*—a dummy variable scored 1 if respondent identifies self as exclusively Scottish/Welsh, or more Scottish/Welsh than British, and 0 otherwise; (*l*) *preference for single UK parliament*—a dummy variable based on responses to the following question: 'Which statement comes closest to your view? Scotland/Wales should: (i) become independent, separate from the United Kingdom, (ii) remain part of the United Kingdom, with its own elected parliament, (iii) be part of the United Kingdom without an elected parliament. Respondents choosing (iii) are scored 1, respondents choosing (i) or (ii) are scored 0; (*m*) *preference for Scots/Welsh independence*—respondents choosing (i) in (*l*) above are scored 1, respondents choosing (ii) or (iii) are scored 0; (*n*) *ethnic minority*—a dummy variable, with persons in the 'white British' ethnicity category scored 0, and all other respondents scored 1; (*o*) *Scotland resident*—a dummy variable, with residents of Scotland scored 1, and residents of other parts of Britain scored 0; (*p*) *Wales resident*—a dummy variable, with residents of Wales scored 1, and residents of other parts of Britain scored 0; (*q*) *attitude toward incumbent government*—rating of Labour Party on 0 ('strongly dislike') to 10 ('strongly like') scale; (*r*) relative deprivation—a 5-point scale based on responses to the statement 'There is often a big gap between what people like me expect out of life and what we actually get.' Answers are scored from 5 ('strongly agree') to 1 ('strongly disagree'); (*s*) *life satisfaction*—a four-point scale based on responses to the question: 'Thinking about your life as a whole, are you very satisfied (scored 4), fairly satisfied (3), a little dissatisfied (2), very dissatisfied(1)?'; (*t*) *socio-demographics*: (i) social class—nonmanual occupations (A, B, C1) scored 1, manual occupations (C2, D, E) scored 0; (ii) housing tenure—owner/occupiers scored 1, others, 0; (iii) gender—men scored 1, women, 0; (iv) education—respondents with graduate qualifications scored 1, others, 0; (v) age—in years.

13. Although we hypothesize that party identification is a basis for building an attachment to the larger political system, this does not imply that the sources of party identification are anything other than the Fiorina-style running tally of retrospective performance evaluations as discussed in Chapter Six.

14. Model parameters are estimated using STATA 7.1's ordered logit procedure.

15. The plausibility of this finding is reinforced by the negative, although insignificant, coefficient on the education control variable. This indicates that, other things being equal, graduates are likely to register lower levels of satisfaction with democracy than non-graduates.

16. For example, the ΔP (change in probability) figure for age in Table 9.13 indicates that, other things being equal, a 65-year-old is 12% more likely to be satisfied with democracy than an 18-year-old.

17. This strong relationship persists when controls are applied for a range of other variables.

TEN

Valence Politics

The core claim of this book is that, although the economic and social context of electoral choice in Britain has changed considerably since the 1960s, the basic calculus of voters' decisions has not. We argue that voters have been concerned consistently and primarily with valence—the ability of governments to perform in those policy areas that people care about most. Central to this argument is the idea that perceptions of party leaders crystallize people's thoughts about the likely performance of political parties in office. Leadership is obviously not the only thing that matters but, in our view, it has always mattered much more than previous studies of British voting behaviour have allowed.

In this concluding chapter, we summarize the main substantive findings that emerge from the empirical analyses. This involves examining party choice, turnout, and the public's views of the democratic process. We next present a set of simulations designed to illuminate how patterns of party support might change over different circumstances. These simulations are based on the models of party choice developed in Chapter Four. The simulations illustrate how changes in economic evaluations, leader images, and perceptions of issue competence—particularly when they occur in combination—can have substantial effects on voters' electoral decisions. We conclude with a discussion of our view of the nature of political choice in contemporary Britain.

PARTY CHOICE, TURNOUT, AND ATTITUDES TOWARDS DEMOCRACY

Our analyses compare models of electoral choice located in two overarching theoretical approaches or frameworks—the sociological and the individual rationality frameworks. Although models from both frameworks feature in our statistical estimations, the most powerful effects are associated with individual rationality models and, in particular, with a set of variables that collectively comprise what we call the valence model. When we examine the effects of a range of 'signature variables' associated with various models subsumed by the two frameworks, the strongest predictors of party choice are partisanship and images of leaders. This finding is not confined to voting behaviour in 2001; rather it has been the case since at least the 1960s. Perceptions of parties' issue competence and relative closeness to the main parties on a left–right ideological continuum are also significant, although less important. The most marked change has been the erosion of the impact of social class. Although our analysis of British Election Study (BES) data indicates that class effects were not as strong in the 1960s as many observers believed, the relationship between class and vote clearly has weakened since that time. Although the decline was especially evident in the 1970s, it continued thereafter, particularly after Tony Blair's election as leader of the Labour Party in 1994. In the past decade, the major change in the class–vote nexus has been the decrease in support for the Conservatives among the middle class. By 2001, class effects on voting were negligible.

The implications of these findings for the two approaches to electoral choice are not straightforward. The sociological approach has always claimed party identification, together with social class, as key signature variables. Notwithstanding the diminished effect of class, it could be argued that the more general explanatory power of the sociological approach has remained strong over time because of the continuing importance of party identification. However, we show that partisan attachments in Britain are characterized by significant individual- and aggregate-level dynamics. Analyses demonstrate that partisanship conforms more closely to Fiorina's idea of an accumulation of party performance assessments than it does to the social–psychological concept of an enduring affective attachment. Party identifications are potentially mutable, being influenced by assessments of economic conditions and by perceptions of the competence of rival parties and their leaders. This leads us to conclude that partisanship in Britain is fundamentally connected to notions of performance. It is a continuously updated storehouse of judgements about the ability of parties and their leaders to deliver sound economic and political management.

The finding that party identification reflects party and leader performance evaluations has important implications for the competing theoretical perspectives under consideration. The sociological account was founded on the twin notions of stable long-term class-linked partisan identities and class-based voting. Voters were said to acquire class and partisan identities early in life. Once formed, these identities were stable and they exerted powerful effects on voting behaviour in successive elections. Our analyses dispute these claims. Perhaps most simply, BES data gathered since the 1960s consistently reveal that approximately one-half of the electorate do not think of themselves in class terms. Moreover, multi-wave BES and British Election Panel Study (BEPS) panel data demonstrate that partisanship is not as deeply embedded and highly stable as the sociological approach claims. In all of the multi-wave panels conducted over the past four decades sizeable minorities exhibit flexible partisan attachments—changing their party identifications one or more times across successive waves of interviewing. Analyses also reveal that another main pillar of the sociological account—the relationship between class and partisanship—has weakened significantly since the 1960s. Similar to the class × vote relationship, BES data indicate that the linkage between class and partisanship was never as strong as many have surmised. Although several other socio-demographic characteristics—notably homeownership and region—correlate with party choice, their combined influence has not increased sufficiently to compensate for the declining power of class. In sum, the sociological approach can no longer claim to play a major role in explaining electoral choice in Britain.

In contrast, a Downsian spatial or issue–position/proximity model fares better. Analyses using issue–position and left–right measures in the 2001 BES reveal that the distances between voters and parties influence electoral choice. However, these effects are not as strong as those associated with the valence model. The outcomes of the last four general elections are consistent with the statistical evidence. Since 1987, the average voter has consistently placed her or himself closer to the Labour and Liberal Democrat (Alliance) parties than to the Conservatives—yet the Conservatives won in both 1987 and 1992. The key to these two Conservative successes, and to Labour's subsequent victories in 1997 and 2001, was that, on each occasion, the loser was tainted with an image of managerial incompetence, while the winner was viewed as capable of delivering sound management in the policy areas that voters cared about.

The analyses of electoral choice strongly indicate the importance of variables that collectively comprise what we call a valence voting model. Voters use partisanship and leader images as cognitive short cuts to make judgements about which party is most competent to govern and which party, in turn, they should support. Leader images are especially important. Not only do perceptions of leaders exert powerful direct effects, they also shape electoral choice indirectly by influencing partisanship. Economic evaluations also have indirect effects on voting as they, too, affect partisanship. Consonant with a core proposition in the economic voting literature, people who have positive assessments of the economy are more likely to support the incumbent party and its leader, whereas those with negative assessments are more likely to support the opposition.

Campaigns also matter. Their potential to influence both individual voting behaviour and the overall election result is considerable because a substantial minority of voters report that they do not make up their minds until an election is in the offing. Some campaign effects are the result of local party organizations' constituency-level mobilization efforts, whereas others are products of what is happening nationally. In this regard, analyses reveal that part of the impact of important variables such as party leader images, economic evaluations, and perceptions of party competence on important issues occurs before the official campaign begins, and part takes place during the campaign. Finally, there is evidence that some voters are influenced by tactical considerations; they support a less-preferred party to reduce the chances that a party they least prefer will be elected. Approximately 14 per cent of those voting in 2001 behaved tactically—and generally to the benefit of the Liberal Democrats.

Although the main focus of our analyses of party choice is support for the two major parties, it is not silent about increasingly important minor parties. Models of support for the Liberal Democrats and various other parties tell very similar stories to those for Labour and Conservative support. Socio-demographic factors always have been relatively unimportant for Liberal (Democrat) voting, so the decline in class-based voting has left the calculus that prompts voters to choose the party largely undisturbed. Support for the Liberal Democrats and other parties is influenced by partisanship, assessments of party leaders, perceptions of competence to handle important issues, tactical voting considerations, and, in the Liberal Democrats' case, assessments of the government's economic performance. In short, support for these parties is driven by many of the same factors that determine voting for Labour and the Conservatives—valence matters most.

A second major component of our analyses involves the determinants of turnout in the context of widespread concern that electoral participation in Britain, as in other advanced democracies, is undergoing an accelerating, long-term decline. In the British case, turnout trended gently, if irregularly, downwards between 1945 and 1992, before falling significantly in 1997 and then dramatically in 2001. The post-1992 decline in turnout appears to be very broadly based, affecting virtually all socio-demographic and political groups. This suggests that there may have been something distinctive about the two most recent general elections that produced a significant change in people's willingness to go to the polls. Aggregate analysis shows that a key factor was the lack of inter-party competition, acting in combination with a pronounced policy convergence between the Conservatives and Labour. A substantial part of the fall in turnout was caused by the fact that Labour held a large lead in public opinion polls in the runups to these two elections. It was also important that, under Tony Blair's leadership, Labour dramatically reduced the policy distance between itself and the Conservatives, hence reducing differences in the perceived benefits that could be expected should one or the other of these parties form a government. In circumstances when the outcomes appeared to be foregone conclusions, and the leading contenders were offering 'echos' rather than 'choices', why bother to vote at all?

The idea of voting as a broadly rational response to a set of perceived circumstances underpins the individual-level analyses of the decision to participate in the 2001 election. Chapter Eight identifies five important variables in what we call the general incentives model that are critical determinants of the decision to vote. First, people who think that the political authorities respond to their needs *and* that there are important differences between the political parties, are more likely to go to the polls. Second, the perception that there are direct personal costs associated with the act of voting deters turnout. A third, and particularly important, influence is a sense of civic duty; that is, the belief that participation confers benefits on the political system as a whole. A fourth influence is a set of norms that are prevalent in the individual's immediate social environment. People are more likely to cast a ballot when they believe that their families and friends value voting, and when they think that voting is what most people do in the area in which they live. Expressive benefits also matter.

Older people are much more likely than younger ones to vote, and the former are much more likely to believe that voting is a civic duty that should be taken seriously. Although the absence of very long-term panel surveys means that conclusive evidence is unavailable, analyses suggest that there are significant generational components to these relationships. 'Thatcher's children'—the cohort of people who entered the electorate during the Thatcher and Major years—are less likely to vote than older generations, and less likely to believe that not voting is a serious neglect of their civic duty. The comparatively low levels of turnout and civic mindedness in the Thatcher generation is consistent with the fact that this group came of political age during an era that gave full expression to the principles of individualism and marketization. People who joined the electorate more recently—the Blair generation—exhibit similar tendencies. 'Blair's children' have a relatively weak sense of civic duty, and their turnout rate is lower than would be expected if the relationship between age and electoral participation were purely a life-cycle phenomenon.

A third main area of inquiry explores public attitudes towards elections and the democratic process more generally. This analysis is motivated in part by the low turnout levels in local, European, and by-elections throughout the 1990s and, more particularly, by the falloff in turnout in the 1997 and 2001 general elections. Reacting to these trends, media commentators and politicians have become concerned that falling turnout might indicate growing disillusionment with the electoral process and the political system more generally. In fact, available evidence reveals that public attitudes towards politics have changed very little over the last four decades. Levels of interest in politics and concern with the outcomes of general elections have barely changed. And, levels of political efficacy are virtually indistinguishable from those recorded by Almond and Verba in the late 1950s. To be sure, Britain is not now, nor was it then, a nation of keenly interested, highly efficacious citizens. It remains a place where many people have at most 'some' but not a 'great deal' of interest in government and politics, and many feel powerless to influence what goes on in the political arena. At the same time—and despite the weakening of a sense of civic duty among younger voters discussed above—a large majority continues to believe that they have a responsibility to participate in general elections, and a smaller, but still sizeable, majority cares about the results of those contests. However, the latter findings are not cause for complacency. If relationships such as those between age and civic duty do signify significant

319

generational differences, then there is clearly potential for levels of political engagement and civic mindedness to decline in the years ahead. Whether that potential will be realized remains to be seen.

Although people's orientations toward themselves as political actors are presently much the same as when Britain's 'civic culture' was first mapped several decades ago, their orientations towards the political system actually have become more positive. Satisfaction with democracy, which has been measured regularly since 1973, has gradually *increased*. The positive trend has occurred in a context where substantial majorities typically state that they are 'very' or, at least, 'fairly' satisfied with the way democracy works in Britain. This suggests that British citizens are less disapproving of their political system than is sometimes supposed. Levels of satisfaction with democracy are distributed more or less evenly across all socio-demographic groups. For example, ethnic minorities are not more likely to be dissatisfied than members of the ethnic majority; the Scots and Welsh are no more likely to be dissatisfied than the English. Significantly, the main sources of satisfaction are related to evaluations of various aspects of institutional and policy *performance*. People are satisfied because they believe that state institutions deserve respect, and because they think that government generally delivers the right sorts of economic and social policy outcomes. Satisfaction with the way democracy works, like party support, is contingent on performance.

POTENTIAL CHANGES IN THE BRITISH ELECTORAL LANDSCAPE

Despite evidence that many people are favourably disposed to the way democracy is practiced in Britain, there is still potential for political change. Likely changes take two forms: those relating to political institutions and to the party system, and those relating to patterns of party support. New Labour initiated major institutional changes shortly after it took office in 1997. The creation of assemblies in Scotland and Wales, to be elected on the basis of proportional representation (PR), produced more than just a new, devolved layer of government. The new institutions simultaneously created new party systems in Scotland and Wales, in which the nationalist parties found a much stronger voice. Indeed, in Scotland, the party fragmentation invoked by PR led directly, in 1999, to the formation of an Executive in which Labour and the Liberal Democrats were in formal coalition—at a time when Labour enjoyed an overwhelming majority at Westminster.

There is clearly considerable potential for devolved coalition government to be held up as a model of 'how things could be at Westminster'. It seems likely that parties that are able to perform well under PR in Scotland and Wales will continue to press for the introduction of PR for the Westminster parliament. And it is entirely possible that their arguments will receive a more sympathetic hearing across the United Kingdom if the experience of devolved coalition government is demonstrably positive. A possible complication stems from any future reform of the House of Lords. New Labour reduced the number of hereditary peers to ninety-nine in its first efforts at reform. At the time of writing, the reform process has stalled. However, there is still a chance that a fully elected second chamber, perhaps elected on the basis of PR, could result from the current round of deliberation. All of this suggests that the pressures to introduce PR in Westminster elections have not been entirely dispelled. And, if PR was introduced at Westminster, then the potential for a transformation of voting patterns and the party system would be considerable.

However, for the foreseeable future, elections to the Westminster parliament will continue to be based on the first-past-the-post principle. Accordingly, we can use evidence from our analyses of electoral choice to investigate what would produce significant changes in the fortunes of the main parties. We consider three scenarios. The first explores what Labour would have to do 'wrong' to lose the commanding popular vote lead that it established over its opponents in 1997 and 2001. The second considers what would have to happen for the Conservatives to return to within striking distance of Labour. The third reviews the Liberal Democrats' chances of overtaking the Conservatives and becoming the second largest party in terms of vote share. We offer these simulations *not as forecasts of future election outcomes* but as illustrations of the way in which we think that voters make decisions about party choice. The simple message that emerges from the simulations is that the parties' 2001 vote shares are 'soft'. It does not take much change in the key explanatory variables in our models to produce significant changes in party choice. In this sense, British electoral politics, notwithstanding Labour's current dominance in the House of Commons, remains potentially volatile.

The simulations are based on the models presented in Chapter Four. Those models sought to identify the key long- and short-term influences on voters' decisions to support one party rather than another. In the scenarios developed here, we manipulate the values of the three main short-term determinants of party choice.[1] These variables are all strongly linked to valence—to the idea that voters tend to choose the party that they think is likely to outperform its rivals in managing the complex political and economic issues facing the country.

First, we consider reactions to economic conditions. The analyses in Chapter Four demonstrate that several of these variables significantly influence party support: *emotional responses to the economy*; prospective and retrospective *evaluations of the national economy*; and assessments of the *party best able to manage the economy*. The underlying reason for examining these variables is to assess the general proposition that the incumbent party tends to benefit electorally when the economy is going well, and *vice versa*. To gauge the likely impact of an economic downturn on party fortunes, we assume that there are decreases in the proportions of voters who register positive economic emotions and positive economic evaluations. We also assume that there is a reduction in the proportion of people who regard Labour as the party best able to deal with the economy. Although different assumptions could be made about the extent of these declines, for ease of presentation, we make a *single* set of assumptions about economic change. We assume that the overall condition of the economy worsens sufficiently for average economic emotion scores and average economic evaluation scores to fall below 2001 levels by half of one standard deviation.[2] It is further assumed that the percentage regarding Labour as best able to handle economic difficulties falls to 39.7 per cent. This figure represents the mid-point between Labour's average monthly score on this variable before the September, 1992 Exchange Rate Mechanism (ERM) crisis and its monthly average score thereafter.[3] Taken together, these assumptions about public reactions to the economy do not imply the occurrence of an economic catastrophe under Labour. Rather, they involve modest but significant negative shifts in assessments of the condition of the economy and Labour's ability to handle it. This shift is roughly half the size of what occurred when the Conservatives were in power between 1992 and 1997.

The second short-term influence on party support examined in the simulations is leader images. As discussed in earlier chapters, party leader images provide voters with useful cognitive shortcuts for making judgements about the likely performance of parties in office. The more positive is a leader's image, the more likely it is that voters will regard that leader's party as capable of performing well in government. Our simulations make fairly modest assumptions about changes in leader evaluations. Given that Charles Kennedy had a reasonably positive leader-image rating in 2001 (his average score on our 0–10 scale was 5.9), we assume that his (or his successor's) ratings remain unchanged. Tony Blair achieved an average image rating in 2001 of 5.7. We assume that the 'cost of ruling' (Nannestad and Paldam 2002) gradually erodes Blair's image, and that his ratings fall moderately to the 'neutral' position of 5.0. William Hague's average rating in 2001 was 4.2. Although polls indicate that his successor, Ian Duncan-Smith, was not warmly received, we assume that the average rating of the Conservative leader rises to the neutral point of 5.0.

The third short-term factor considered is the perceived competence of competing parties to handle important issues facing the country. This again involves judgements that are quintessentially concerned with valence. In the post-election wave of the 2001 BES, 39 per cent of the respondents thought that Labour was best able to handle the issue they believed was most important, 14 per cent favoured the Conservatives, and 7 per cent, the Liberal Democrats. The rest thought either that there were no important issues or that no party was competent. Two scenarios are considered. In the first scenario, we assume that the Conservatives moderate their policy stances and campaign sufficiently convincingly that they are able to persuade the public that they are at least as competent as Labour to perform satisfactorily in those policy areas that most people prioritize. We also assume that the Liberal Democrats, because of their greater representation in the 2001 Parliament, are able to raise their policy profile modestly. As a result, the pattern of party competence evaluations shifts to 25 per cent for Labour, 25 per cent for the Conservatives, and 10 per cent for the Liberal Democrats. The remaining 40 per cent continue to think either that no party is competent or that there are no important issues. In the second scenario, we assume that the Conservatives make inroads regarding the party competence lead that Labour held in 2001, and that the Liberal Democrats do the same. Accordingly, the three parties enter the election with equal status in voters' eyes with regard to their respective abilities to handle the most important issues. This implies a 20/20/20 split on party competence, with the remaining 40 per cent again taking no view.

The results of the simulations are displayed in Tables 10.1 and 10.2.[4] Table 10.1 reports changes in the probability that the average voter would support each party that are implied by making a *single* assumption about changes in the values of the independent variables. Table 10.2 makes different *combinations* of assumptions that correspond to the three scenarios described above.

The single-change effects in Table 10.1 reveal the extent of Labour's reliance on Tony Blair for its electoral success. A relatively modest decline in Blair's leadership rating implies a significant decrease (10 points) in the probability that the average voter will support Labour. However, note that the Liberal Democrats and various smaller parties benefit more than the Conservatives as a result of such a change. Unfortunately for the Conservatives, an *increase* of a similar magnitude in the Conservative leader's ratings does not produce a symmetric increase in the Con-servatives' fortunes. A modest improvement in the Tory leader's image would increase the chances of the average voter supporting the Conservatives by only three points. Moreover, this is primarily at the expense of the Liberal Democrats rather than Labour. The other single effects shown in Table 10.1 produce broadly similar changes in voting probabilities. A modest economic downturn reduces the probability of supporting Labour by 4 points, with the Conservatives as the main

Table 10.1 The dynamics of electoral choice: single-factor scenarios

| Scenario | Change in the probability that the average voter will support | | | |
	Labour	Conservatives	Liberal Democrats	Other parties
Economic downturn	−0.04	+0.03	0.00	0.00
Blair's leader image 'neutral'	−0.10	+0.02	+0.04	+0.03
Conservative leader's image 'neutral'	−0.01	+0.03	−0.03	0.00
Issue–competence split 20/20/20	−0.05	0.00	+0.04	0.00
Issue–competence split 25/25/10	−0.03	+0.01	+0.01	+0.01

Table 10.2 The dynamics of electoral choice: multiple-factor scenarios

| Scenarios | Change in the probability that the average voter will support | | | |
	Labour	Conservatives	Liberal Democrats	Other parties
Labour in trouble				
Economic downturn				
+ Blair's image neutral	−0.13	+0.06	+0.03	+0.03
Replay of late 1970s				
Economic downturn				
+ Blair's image neutral +				
issue–competence split 20/20/20	−0.15	+0.07	+0.05	+0.03
Confidence restored				
Economic downturn				
+ Blair's image neutral				
+ Conservative leader's image				
neutral + issue–competence				
split 20/20/20	−0.21	+0.16	−0.02	+0.06
Equal credibility				
Issue–competence split 20/20/20				
+ Blair's image neutral	−0.14	+0.02	+0.08	+0.03

beneficiaries. A shift in the distribution of general issue–competence perceptions in the Conservatives' favour (to 25/25/10) damages Labour, although the Conservatives benefit no more than either the Liberal Democrats or other parties as a result. Finally, a shift in issue–competence perceptions towards both the Conservatives and the Liberal Democrats (to 20/20/20) helps only the Liberal Democrats. In these circumstances, the Conservatives derive no gain at all, whereas the Liberal Democrats increase their chances of attracting the average voter's support by 4 points.

All of these single-change effects appear to be quite small in absolute terms. However, it should be noted that they derive from very modest changes in the explanatory variables being manipulated. Overall, these effects suggest three conclusions. First, the economy remains a battleground primarily between Labour and the Conservatives: if Labour's economic management fails, then the Conservatives are most likely to benefit; the Liberal Democrats have yet to establish themselves as serious contenders to run the economy. Second, Labour is vulnerable to a decline in the popularity of its leader but, in these circumstances, the Liberal Democrats are most likely to reap the benefit. Third, reductions in Labour's perceived ability to deal with important issues also disproportionately benefit the Liberal Democrats. It is the latter party that has the most to gain by convincing people that it is capable of dealing effectively with their concerns.

Table 10.2 sketches three different scenarios of possible changes in party support. The 'Labour in Trouble' scenario assumes that there is an economic downturn, with people becoming more negative in their economic judgements and views of Blair's competence. In these circumstances, the average voter would be 13 points less likely to support Labour, with the Conservatives being the biggest beneficiary. The next simulation, 'Labour's Not Working' is a replay of the late 1970s. Here, Labour is assumed to oversee an economic decline, experience a modest fall in its leader's image ratings, and find itself neck-and-neck with the Conservatives in terms of issue competence. According to this scenario, the probability that the average voter will support Labour falls by 15 points.

The 'Confidence Restored' scenario involves the combination of an economic downturn, a decline in Blair's leader ratings, a recovery in the Conservative leader's image scores, and a strong shift in issue–competence perceptions towards the Conservatives. This scenario produces no less than a 16-point increase in the probability that the average voter will support the Conservatives, with Labour's chances down by 21 points and the Liberal Democrats only marginally affected. Given the bias of the electoral system against them (e.g. Curtice 2001), even probability changes of this magnitude might not be sufficient to propel the Tories back into office with a solid majority government. However, they would certainly be sufficient to ensure that the party was the largest in the House of Commons.

In the 'Equal Credibility' scenario, it is simply assumed that Blair's leader ratings decline and that voters perceive the three main parties to be more or less equal in terms of issue competence. There is no assumption about economic decline because, as shown in Table 10.1, the Liberal Democrats do not gain from Labour's failing in this regard. These assumptions produce a serious (14-point) decline in the chances of the average voter supporting Labour, and an 8-point increase for the Liberal Democrats. These findings suggest that, by improving their credibility on the salient valence issues, the Liberal Democrats are capable of inflicting serious damage on Labour in future elections, although the party may not be able to garner commensurate support for itself as a result.

What do these several simulations say about electoral choice in Britain? Above all, they indicate the considerable volatility of contemporary patterns of party support. Changes in valence calculations on the part of voters—whether they involve judgements about the economy, images of leaders, or perceptions of issue competence—are all capable of producing significant changes in the probability that an otherwise average voter will support each of the rival parties. In combination, the effects are more pronounced. Relatively modest changes in the explanatory variables, when they occur together, can produce quite dramatic changes in the propensities of people to support different parties. The simulations suggest that the Conservatives, apart from hoping that Tony Blair's halo will slip of its own volition, can benefit most from an economic downturn and by going into an election with a leader whose image is either neutral or, better still, positive. For the Conservatives, William Hague's negative image in 2001 constituted a serious impediment to their putative electoral recovery. For their part, the Liberal Democrats need to establish that they can perform well in office. The party's experience in coalition in the Scottish Executive, combined with its increasing presence in local government across the United Kingdom, could provide a useful focus for the development of this image of managerial competence. In any event, the simulations show very clearly that the Liberal Democrats, in particular, cannot rely on Labour mismanaging the economy if they are to make substantial electoral progress. They need actively to demonstrate their own competence to perform adequately in relation to the issues that matter to voters.

POLITICAL CHOICE IN BRITAIN

Political choice in Britain is exactly that. Key (1968) was very much on target when he concluded that voters 'are not fools'. Rather than being life-long political captives of their class locations or other ponderous social forces, British voters are capable of making effective, if 'rough and ready', judgements regarding which party is best suited for government. In doing so, they rely heavily on evaluations of the demonstrated and anticipated performance of parties and their leaders in economic and other important policy areas. As Stokes (1963, 1992) argued, electorally consequential political debate typically is not about what are the ends, but rather who has the means. In Britain, as in other mature democracies, a strong economy characterized by vigorous growth coupled with low rates of inflation and unemployment, universal access to high quality, affordable health-care and education, safe and efficient transport, a sound national defence, and low crime rates are prominent examples of things that virtually everyone values. Thus, public opinion is heavily skewed or valenced about what the ends of government action should be. Electoral politics is largely valence politics, and public debate and inter-party competition focus on which party and which leader are best able to deliver.

When making political choices in a world of valence politics, most voters lack detailed information about parties' policy proposals and *a fortiori*, the efficacy of such proposals for achieving consensually agreed upon goals. Rather than bearing the heavy deliberation costs of acquiring and processing such information, voters rely on heuristic devices for cues about what to do. Party leader images are among the most important of these devices. Perceptions of leader competence enable voters to choose who is likely to do a good job in circumstances that are difficult, or impossible, to foresee. By emphasizing leader competence when making their electoral choices, voters wisely seek to entrust the future to 'a safe pair of hands'. Voters' competence judgements involve a variety of policy areas. However, cognitive and emotional reactions to national and personal economic conditions are fundamental. An emphasis on economic competence is eminently sensible. A healthy economy is the engine of valence politics, making the provision of cherished public services possible.

A related and important guide for political choice is party identification. As Fiorina (1981) and others have argued, voters do not throw away their evaluations about how parties and leaders have handled the economy and other important matters in the past. Rather, these evaluations are stored as a sense of party identification. As voters acquire new information about party and leader performance, they discount existing evaluations and they revise their party identifications accordingly. Depending upon the content of incoming information, party identifications can change in both intensity and direction. BES evidence gathered over the past four decades clearly shows that British voters are willing to change their partisan attachments in light of updated performance evaluations. Doing so is sensible. By incorporating fresh information, voters ensure that their partisan attachments do not 'go stale' but, rather, remain useful summary guides for the political choices they are repeatedly required to make.

An important aspect of political choice is the decision whether to go to the polls. When making this choice, contemporary British voters, like their predecessors, respond to a variety of incentives. Individual- and aggregate-level evidence combine to suggest that the turnout decision is driven, in part, by cost–benefit calculations. Eschewing a narrow, exclusively self-centred view of their potential political influence helps voters to escape the 'paradox of voting', while making turnout decisions that take into account the likelihood that the election will be a close contest between parties offering varying combinations of meaningful policy and performance choices. However, turnout is about more than cost–benefit calculations; voters also respond to broader system incentives, especially those encapsulated in a sense of civic duty. Traditionally, levels of civic duty have been high, enabling Britain to avoid being a nation of 'rational fools' (Sen 1977)— people whose self-centred instrumentalism leads them to undermine their democratic system of government by failing to participate.

Nevertheless, it should not be assumed that contemporary Britain is a place where high levels of public support for the existing political institutions and processes will necessarily prevail. It is not just that the sense of civic mindedness may erode as younger, more egocentric generations become a larger component of the electorate, although that is a troubling possibility. As discussed above, opportunities for making system support choices have expanded in recent years, as referendums have been held on proposals for major constitutional change. At the same time, continuing controversy over Britain's role in Europe clearly signals that the definition and boundaries of the political system are legitimate subjects for

327

public debate and, possibly, redesign. The scope of political choice has widened, and our analyses indicate that system support, like party support, has significant instrumental components. In particular, voters judge the performance of Britain's democratic political system much the same way as they evaluate the parties and politicians that animate it. Support at all levels of the political system is a renewable resource—but support must be renewed. Compared to earlier generations, people like Jim Hill's granddaughter, Melanie, are encountering a wider variety of consequential political choices. But, like Jim, Melanie defines what politics is about largely in valence terms. Performance is key to the political choices that she makes.

NOTES

1. These are factors that produce important short- to medium-term shifts in party support. As shown in Chapter Four, other factors, such as party identification, also exert powerful effects on the vote. However, as a cumulative reservoir of dispositions, partisanship generally changes less readily than economic perceptions, leader images, and perceptions of issue competence.

2. Specifically, these assumptions involve the following decreases in average economic perception scores: emotions towards the national economy -0.13; emotions towards the personal economy -0.56; retrospective national evaluations -0.39; retrospective personal evaluations -0.50; prospective national evaluations -0.38; prospective personal evaluations -0.52.

3. As discussed in Chapter Three, the ERM crisis was highly significant because it destroyed the Conservatives' reputation as competent managers of the economy. Thereafter, monthly Gallup opinion poll data reveal that Labour has been almost invariably regarded as the party best able to handle the situation if Britain were in economic difficulties. The difference between Labour's average economic management score before and after the ERM crisis was $(48.1 - 31.3 = 16.8)$. Half of this is 8.4. The difference between 48.1 and 8.4 is 39.7, the figure used in our simulations. We regard this as being the nearest equivalent to the half a standard deviation decreases used for the economic emotions and economic evaluations variables.

4. The simulations were performed using the multinomial logit model reported in Table 4.10. The simulations involve setting all explanatory variables in the model at their respective means and then manipulating the economic perceptions, leader image, and policy competence variables in the ways described above. These simulations are then compared with a 'core model', in which all explanatory variables are set to their respective means. The comparisons enable us, given the particular simulation assumption(s), to estimate the change in the probability, between 2001 and a future election, that the average voter would support each of the major parties or a minor party. STATA 7.1 and CLARIFY (Tomz, Wittenberg, and King 1999) were used to do the simulations.

Appendix A.
2001 BES Data Used in this Book

Several major data collections were conducted in the 2001 British Election Study (BES). Data used for the analyses in this book are as follows:

I. MAIN SURVEYS

Pre-election (Wave 1)	Post-election (Wave 2)	Self-completion (Wave 2)
Fieldwork: NOP Method: In-person CAPI Response rate: 52.8% N: 3220 Questionnaire: noppre.doc Data: prepost.sav Codebook/tables: noppre.lst	Fieldwork: NOP Method: In-person CAPI Response rate (of W1): 74.1% N: 2359 Questionnaire: noppost.doc Data: prepost.sav Codebook/tables: noppost.lst	Response rate: 69.2% N: 1628 Questionnaire: nopmailback.doc Data: prepost.sav Codebook/tables: nopmailback.lst
	Post-election (Top-up)	**Self-completion (Top-up)**
	Fieldwork: NOP Method: In-person CAPI Response rate: 46.5% N: 681 Questionnaire: noppost.doc Data: prepost.sav Codebook/tables: noppost.lst	Response rate: 55.7% N: 379 Questionnaire: Data: prepost.sav nopmailback.doc Codebook/tables: nopmailback.lst

II. ROLLING CROSS-SECTION CAMPAIGN SURVEY AND POST-ELECTION PANEL SURVEY

Campaign Rolling Cross-Section (Wave 1)	**Post-election Campaign Panel (Wave 2)**
Fieldwork: Gallup	Fieldwork: Gallup
Method: Telephone	Method: Telephone
Response rate: 28.9%	Response rate: 78.0%
N: 4810 (average = 160 per day)	*N*: 3751
Questionnaire: galluppre.doc	Questionnaire: galluppost.doc
Data: gallup.sav	Data: gallup.sav
Codebook/tables: galluppre.lst	Codebook/tables: galluppost.lst

GUIDE TO THE DATA

The file names listed above match the names of the files submitted to the University of Essex Data Archive. All of these files can also be accessed via the BES website (www.essex.ac.uk/bes). Note that data sets submitted to the UK Data Archive at the University of Essex are SPSS system files (with a .SAV suffix). Data files on the BES website are in SPSS portable (.POR) format. An Excel file (ROSETTASTONE.XLS) cross-references survey questions and variables. Anyone with questions about the data should contact Harold Clarke (email address: hclarke@utdallas.edu) or David Sanders (email address: sanders@essex.ac.uk) for additional information.

I. MAIN SURVEYS

Wave 1

Wave 1 was a pre-election benchmark survey. The fieldwork was conducted by NOP, during the period 3 March–14 May 2001 (95.7 per cent of the interviews were completed in March and April). Face-to-face interviews were conducted in the respondents' homes, via CAPI (computer-assisted personal interviews). The average length of an interview was 29.8 minutes. The following table summarizes

Appendix

the response rate to Wave 1:

	N	% issued	% in-scope
Number of addresses issued	6460	100.0	
Vacant/non-residential	366	5.7	
Number of addresses in-scope	6094	94.3	100.0
Interview obtained	3219	49.8	52.8
Interview not obtained	2875	44.5	47.2
Refusal	1408	21.8	23.1
Non-contact	910	14.1	14.9
Other	557	8.6	9.1

Wave 2

Wave 2 was a face-to-face (CAPI) interview conducted with as many respondents as possible to the pre-election benchmark survey. Fieldwork was conducted by NOP, during the period 8 June–30 July 2001. The average length of an interview was 42.4 minutes, and a self-completion questionnaire was left with respondents. The response rate is summarized in the following table:

	N	% issued	% in-scope
Number of addresses issued	3223	100.0	
Moved away [a]	40	1.2	
Number of addresses in-scope	3183	98.8	100.0
Interview obtained [b]	2354	73.0	74.0
With self-completion	1628		69.2
Without self-completion	726		30.8
Interview not obtained	829	25.7	26.0
Refusal	409	12.7	12.8
Non-contact	213	6.6	6.7
Other	168	5.2	5.3
Moved	39	1.2	1.2

Notes: [a] Of the seventy-nine respondents who moved between Waves 1 and 2, forty were designated ineligible by the fieldwork agency.
[b] During the construction of the panel, 2315 definite panel matches were identified. The N of 2354 reported in the table therefore includes thirty-nine respondents designated as 'unlikely panel matches'. These respondents are assigned a value of '3' on the pre–post panel filter variable, and so users can decide whether or not to include them in analyses. If these thirty-nine are assumed not to be part of the panel, then the response rate falls to 72.7%.

Appendix

In order to adjust for the impact of panel attrition, and to ensure that the post-election survey yielded a representative sample of the electorate comparable with previous BES post-election cross-sections, the post-election survey included an additional 'top-up' sample of respondents, to constituencies that were under-represented in the panel component of Wave 2. NOP conducted the top-up field-work over the period 23 July–30 September 2001. The response rate for the top-up sample is summarized below:

	N	% issued	% in-scope
Number of addresses issued	1548	100.0	
Vacant/non-residential	72	4.7	
Number of addresses in-scope	1476	95.3	100.0
Interview obtained	681	44.0	46.1
With self-completion	379		55.7
Without self-completion	302		44.3
Interview not obtained	795	51.4	53.9
Refusal	407	26.3	27.6
Non-contact	229	14.8	15.5
Other	154	9.9	10.4

With its panel and top-up components, the post-election survey was designed to yield a representative sample of the British electorate. Initially, a random sample of 128 constituencies was drawn, stratified by standard region. (Constituencies north of the Caledonian Canal were excluded.) Then, from within each of these con-stituencies, two wards were randomly selected. This provided the 256 clusters for sampling. Respondents within these wards were sampled from the Postcode Address File. The survey incorporates booster samples for both Scotland and Wales. Users wishing to analyze just the Scottish or the Welsh samples should select from the data set cases on which REGNALL = 9 (Scotland) or REGNALL = 4 (Wales). (Alternatively, separate data sets containing these Celtic sub-samples are available via the BES website at www.essex.ac.uk/bes/data.html.)

Weighting

There is a variety of weighting variables included in the main BES data sets. These variables offer the possibilities of weighting by region, by gender, or by age within gender. The recommended option is to use the overall weighting variables, thereby weighting by region, gender, and age within gender simultaneously. The names of the various weighting variables are listed below.

Appendix

Data Files

PREPOST.SAV—an SPSS data file containing data from the first two waves of the main British Election Study survey. Variables from the pre-election survey begin with the letter 'a'; those to the post-election survey begin with 'b', while those from the self-completion mail questionnaire begin with 'c'. Note that the structure of the BES is such that several sub-data sets are nested within this overall file. The filter variables to select these subsets, and the weight variables that they require, are set out in the following table:

	To use sub-data sets			
	Pre-election	Pre1Post panel	Post-election cross-section	Mailback
Filter variable	TOPUP = 0	PREPOST = 1	POSTRESP = 1	MAILFILT = 1
Unique respondent ID label[a]	BUNIQIDR	BUNIQIDR	BUNIQIDR	BUNIQIDR
Weight variables				
Region	REGWGTHC	BREGNWGT	REGOCTWT	MREGNWGT
Gender	GENWGTHC	BGENWGT	GENOCTWT	MGENWGT
Age/w/gender	AGEWGTHC	BAGEWGT	AGEOCTWT	MAGEWGT
Region × gender × age/w/gender	AWGTGB	BPANWGT	POSTOCTW	MAILWGT
Unweighted N	3219	2315	3035	2191[b]
Weighted N	3223	2303	3025	2195

Notes: [a] The variable 'buniqidr' links respondents through each stage of data collection: it matches the 'arespid' to the pre-survey, it is the principal ID for the post-survey (including the top-up), and it matches the 'crespid' to the mailback survey. (The variable 'brespid' does not uniquely identify respondents.)

[b] These overall Ns include mailbacks to the 'unlikely panel match' respondents. They also include 184 mailbacks to respondents involved in the pre- but not the post-interview. (These are respondents who were unwilling to be re-interviewed, but were persuaded by the interviewer to fill out the self-completion supplement in order to avoid a complete refusal and loss of information.)

PREPOSTAGG.SAV—an SPSS data file, identical to PREPOST.SAV, but also containing constituency-level information for aggregate analysis. The first 157 variables in the data set are taken from the British Parliamentary Constituency database, 1992–2001 (may be obtained via http://ksghome.harvard.edu/~pnorris.shorenstein.ksg/data.htm).

NOPPRE.DOC and NOPPRE.PDF—WORD and ADOBE versions of the questionnaire used for Wave 1 of the main BES.

Appendix

NOPPRECARDS.DOC and NOPPRECARDS.PDF—WORD and ADOBE versions of the show-cards used in conjunction with the pre-election survey.

NOPPRE.LST—an ASCII file containing summary tables of frequencies for variables generated by the pre-election wave (Wave 1) of the 2001 BES main survey.

NOPPOST.DOC and NOPPOST.PDF—WORD and ADOBE versions of the questionnaire used for the face-to-face interview in the post-election wave (Wave 2) of the 2001 BES main survey administered to panel and top-up respondents.

NOPPOSTCARDS.DOC and NOPPOSTCARDS.PDF—WORD and ADOBE versions of the show-cards used in conjunction with the post-election survey.

NOPPOST.LST—an ASCII file containing summary tables of frequencies for variables generated by the post-election wave (Wave 2) of the 2001 BES main survey (contains data for both panel and top-up respondents).

NOPMAILBACK.DOC and NOPMAILBACK.PDF—WORD and ADOBE versions of the self-completion mailback questionnaire left with panel and top-up respondents in the post-election survey.

NOPMAILBACK.LST—an ASCII file containing summary tables of frequencies for variables generated by the self-completion questionnaire left with panel and top-up respondents in the post-election survey.

ROLLING CROSS-SECTION CAMPAIGN SURVEY

Wave 1

Freestanding from the main BES surveys described above, the rolling cross-section campaign survey was conducted by the British Gallup organization during the election campaign. Fieldwork took place between 8 May and 6 June, with 4810 telephone interviews being completed during the campaign. Approximately 160 interviews were conducted each day. The average interview time was approximately 10.5 minutes. Information on response rates is summarized below:

	N	%
Numbers called	16620	100.0
Successful	4810	28.9
Unsuccessful	11810	71.1
Screened	1874	11.3
No reply/engaged/answerphone	6744	40.6
Refused	2789	16.8
Other	403	2.4

Appendix

Wave 2

Respondents interviewed in the rolling cross-section campaign survey were re-interviewed by telephone immediately after the election (8–18 June 2001). The average interview time was just over 3 min. Seventy-eight per cent ($N = 3751$) of those interviewed prior to the election were re-interviewed.

Sampling

Interviewing was conducted by random digit dialling to ensure that ex-directory households were included. Interviewers then asked to speak to the person aged 18 or over in the house who had had the most recent birthday to ensure that the sample was random within households.

Weighting

The variable WEIGHT is included in the data sets. It is calculated on the basis of five factors: gender by social class, gender by age, household car ownership, housing tenure, and population by region.

Files

GALLUP.SAV—an SPSS system file containing data to the election campaign rolling cross-sectional survey (unweighted $N = 4810$). The weight variable is WEIGHT (weighted $N = 4810$). The file also contains data gathered from post-election interviews with a panel of the pre-election respondents (unweighted $N = 3751$). To select only panel respondents for analysis, select those cases on which the filter variable PANELIST $= 1$. All post-election variables start with the letter 'Z'. Note that filters and weights are included so that analysts may construct each of the 7-day rolling cross-sectional campaign surveys. The rolling cross-sectional filters are FILT0514–FILT0606 and the respective weights are WGT0514–WGT0606.

GALLUPAGG.SAV—an SPSS data file, identical to GALLUP.SAV, but also containing constituency-level information. The first 157 variables in the data set are taken to the British Parliamentary Constituency database, 1992–2001. These aggregate data were obtained to Professor Pippa Norris' website (http://ksghome. harvard.edu/~pnorris.shorenstein.ksg/data.htm). An additional constituency-level population density variable (to Butler and Kavanagh 1997: Appendix 1, Table A1.3) also is included. Filters and weights to construct the 7-day rolling cross-sectional campaign surveys are omitted.

Appendix

GALLUPPRE. DOC and GALLUPPRE.PDF—WORD and ADOBE versions of the questionnaire used for the election campaign rolling cross-sectional survey.

GALLUPPRE.LST—an ASCII file containing summary tables of frequencies for variables generated by the campaign rolling cross-sectional survey.

GALLUPPOST.DOC and GALLUPPOST.PDF—WORD and ADOBE versions of the post-election survey questionnaire administered to respondents in the campaign rolling cross-sectional survey.

GALLUPPOST.LST—an ASCII file containing summary tables of frequencies for variables generated by the post-election survey of respondents in the campaign rolling cross-sectional survey.

Appendix B. BES Party Identification Questions, 1963–2001

1963, 1964, 1966, 1969, 1970

'Generally speaking, do you usually think of yourself as Conservative, Labour, Liberal or what?' [1963: '. . . as Conservative, Labour or Liberal?']

If respondent gives a party affiliation: 'How strongly [Conservative, Labour etc.] do you generally feel—very strongly, fairly strongly or not very strongly?'

If answers none/do not know: 'Do you generally think of yourself as [1963: 'feel'] a little closer to one of the parties than the others?' If yes: 'Which party is that?'

FEBRUARY 1974, OCTOBER 1974, 1979

'Generally speaking, do you think of yourself as Conservative, Labour, Liberal (in Scotland: Scottish Nationalist; in Wales: Plaid Cymru) or what?'

If answers conservative/labour/liberal [in 1979: If answers any party]: 'Would you call yourself (a) very strong Conservative [Labour/Liberal], fairly strong, or not very strong?

If answers none/do not know: same as 1963–70.

1983

'Generally speaking, do you think of yourself as Conservative, Labour, Liberal, Social Democrat [in Scotland: Scottish Nationalist; in Wales: Plaid Cymru] or what?'

If 'Alliance', probe: 'Liberal or Social Democrat?'

If respondent gives any party affiliation: 'Would you call yourself a very strong [name of party], fairly strong, or not very strong?'

If answers none/do not know: 'Do you generally think of yourself as a little closer to one of the parties than the others?' [If yes] 'Which party is that?' [If 'Alliance', probe] 'Liberal or Social Democrat?'

1987

The same as 1983, except that the strength of identification question is also put to respondents who, having answered 'none' or 'do not know' to the first question, say in answer to the supplementary question that they feel closer to one of the parties.

1992

'Generally speaking, do you think of yourself as Conservative, Labour, Liberal Democrat (Scotland: Nationalist; Wales: Plaid Cymru) or what?'

If answers none/do not know: 'Do you generally think of yourself as a little closer to one of the parties than the others?' [If yes] 'Which party?'

All respondents naming a party in answer to either of the above questions: 'Would you call yourself a very strong [party named], fairly strong or not very strong?'

1997

'Generally speaking, do you think of yourself as Conservative, Labour, Liberal Democrat (if Scot: SNP; if Wales: Plaid Cymru) or what?'

If answers none/do not know: 'Do you generally think of yourself as a little closer to one of the parties than the others?' [If yes] 'Which party?'

All respondents naming a party in answer to either of the above questions: 'Would you call yourself very strong [party named], fairly strong or not very strong?'[1]

2001

'Generally speaking, do you think of yourself as Labour, Conservative, Liberal Democrat, Scottish Nationalist [in Scotland only], Plaid Cymru [in Wales only], or what?'

Appendix

If answers none/do not know: 'Do you generally think of yourself as a little closer to one of the parties than the others?' [If yes] 'Which party is that?'

All respondents naming a party in answer to either of the above Questions: 'Would you call yourself very strong [party named], fairly strong or not very strong?'

NOTES

1. In the document deposited at the data archive the 'very strong' option is omitted. However, the data set indicates respondents answered 'very strong' so one can assume that the question was actually asked in full.

SOURCES

1963–92—Crewe, Fox, and Day (1996); 1997—UK Data Archive at the University of Essex: www.data-archive.ac.uk/doc/3887/mrdoc/word/besxs.doc; 2001 BES pre- and post-election study questionnaires.

Appendix C. Vote in 2001 by Socio-Demographic Characteristics (Validated Voters)

Socio-demographic characteristics	Vote (Horizontal percentages)			
	Labour	Conservative	Liberal Democrat	Other
Age				
18–25	34	17	43	6
26–35	51	25	20	5
36–45	50	23	22	6
46–55	44	26	23	7
56–65	47	35	14	3
66 and older	47	37	14	3
Cramer's $v = 0.13, p \leq .001$				
Education (age completed)				
Still in school	39	19	39	4
15 or younger	58	26	13	3
16	50	30	16	5
17	30	40	26	5
18	38	34	20	8
19 or older	37	28	29	6
Cramer's $v = 0.14, p \leq 0.001$				
Ethnicity				
White British	45	30	20	5
Other	59	16	20	5
Cramer's $v = 0.09, p \leq 0.01$				
Gender				
Men	47	29	19	6
Women	45	29	21	4
Cramer's $v = 0.04, p > 0.05$				
Home ownership				
Own outright	37	40	19	4
Mortgage	46	27	22	5
Rent	62	14	18	6
Cramer's $v = 0.23, p \leq 0.001$				

Appendix

Socio-demographic characteristics	Vote (in %)			
	Labour	Conservative	Liberal Democrat	Other
Occupational sector				
Public	48	26	22	5
Private, other	46	30	19	5
Cramer's $v = 0.05, p > 0.05$				
Social class (market research society)				
Non-manual				
A	27	46	23	4
B	33	37	24	5
C1	42	31	22	5
Manual				
C2	58	26	12	3
D	56	16	21	6
E	65	15	14	6
Cramer's $v = 0.15, p \leq 0.001$				
Social class (Heath-Goldthorpe)				
Salariat	33	39	24	4
Routine non-manual	28	44	24	4
Petty bourgeoisie	48	33	13	7
Foremen and technicians	25	49	22	5
Working class	18	63	13	6
Cramer's $v = 0.14, p \leq 0.001$				
Region				
East Midlands	45	37	15	2
Eastern	37	42	18	4
London	47	31	18	5
Northeast	59	21	17	3
Northwest	51	29	17	3
Southeast	29	43	24	4
Southwest	26	39	31	6
West Midlands	45	35	15	6
Yorkside and The Humber	49	30	17	4
Scotland	43	16	16	25
Wales	49	21	14	16
Great Britain (Total)	42	32	19	7
United Kingdom (Total)	41	32	18	9

Sources: 2001 BES post-election survey for all variables but region. Regional voting data are from *Election 2001: The Official Results,* Electoral Commission, 2001, pp. 224–7.

Appendix D. Turnout by Socio-Demographic Characteristics

	%	
	Voted 2001 general election[a]	*Votes 'all' or 'most' general elections*[b]
Age		
18–25	43	57
26–35	53	68
36–45	63	76
46–55	76	85
56–65	78	93
66 and older	82	94
Cramer's v, $p \leq$	0.28, 0.001	0.30, 0.001
Education (Age completed)		
15 or younger	72	84
16	58	73
17	58	75
18	65	78
19 or older	74	85
Still in school	50	71
Cramer's v, $p \leq$	0.16, 0.001	0.14, 0.001
Ethnicity		
White British	67	80
Other	57	71
Cramer's v, $p \leq$	0.06, 0.001	0.06, 0.001
Gender		
Men	65	80
Women	67	79
Cramer's v, $p \leq$	0.02, 0.500	0.02, 0.560

Appendix

	%	
	Voted 2001 general election[a]	Votes 'all' or 'most' general elections[b]
Housing tenure		
Own outright	79	89
Mortgage	67	82
Rent, other	51	65
Cramer's v, $p \leq$	0.23, 0.001	0.23, 0.001
Occupational sector		
Private	63	77
Public	74	85
Cramer's v, $p \leq$	0.10, 0.001	0.09, 0.001
Region		
Southeast/East Anglia	66	80
Southwest	69	82
Midlands	69	80
North	62	79
Wales	66	78
Scotland	66	79
Greater London	71	78
Cramer's v, $p \leq$	0.07, 0.060	0.03, 0.910
Social class (Market Research Society)		
Non-manual		
A	77	95
B	75	89
C1	68	79
Manual		
C2	62	75
D	63	74
E	53	70
Cramer's v, $p \leq$	0.15, 0.001	0.30, 0.001
Social class (Heath-Goldthorpe)		
Salariat	74	86
Routine non-manual	64	77
Petty bourgeoisie	63	78
Foremen and technicians	66	82
Working class	59	74
Cramer's v, $p \leq$	0.13, 0.001	0.12, 0.001

Notes: [a] 2001 BES post-election survey, validated voters, weighted $N = 2836$.
[b] BES post-election survey in 2001 weighted $N = 2981$.

References

Abramson, Paul R. (1976). 'Generational Change and the Decline of Party Identification in America: 1952–1974', *American Political Science Review*, 70:469–78.

—— (1979). 'Developing Party Identification: Further Examination of Life-Cycle, Generational, and Period Effects', *American Journal of Political Science*, 23:78–96.

Abramson, Paul R. and Ostrom, Charles W. Jr. (1991). 'Macropartisanship: An Empirical Reassessment', *American Political Science Review*, 85:181–92.

—— (1992). 'Question Wording and Macropartisanship', *American Political Science Review*, 86:475–86.

—— (1994). 'Question Form and Context Effects in the Measurement of Partisanship: Experimental Tests of the Artifact Hypothesis', *American Political Science Review*, 88:955–58.

Achen, Christopher (1992). 'Social Psychology, Demographic Variables, and Linear Regression: Breaking the Iron Triangle in Voting Research', *Political Behavior*, 14:195–211.

—— (2002). 'Parental Socialization and Rational Party Identification', *Political Behavior*, 24:151–70.

Acock, Alan and Clarke, Harold D. (1989). 'National Elections and Political Attitudes: The Case of Political Efficacy', *British Journal of Political Science*, 19:951–62.

Acock, Alan, Clarke, Harold D. and Stewart, Marianne C. (1985). 'A New Model for Old Measures: A Covariance Structure Analysis of Political Efficacy', *Journal of Politics*, 47:1062–84.

Aldrich, John H. (1993). 'Rational Choice and Turnout', *American Journal of Political Science*, 37:246–78.

Alesina, Alberto, Roubini, Nouriel and Cohen, Gerald D. (1997). *Political Cycles and the Macroeconomy*. Cambridge, MA: The MIT Press.

Alford, Robert R. (1964). *Party and Society*. Chicago, IL: Rand McNally.

Almond, Gabriel and Verba, Sidney (1963). *The Civic Culture: Political Attitudes and Democracy in Five Nations*. Princeton, NJ: Princeton University Press.

Alsop, Dee and Weisberg, Herbert F. (1988). 'Measuring Change in Party Identification in an Election Campaign', *American Journal of Political Science*, 32:996–1017.

Alvarez, R. Michael and Brehm, John (2002). *Hard Choices, Easy Answers*. Princeton, NJ: Princeton University Press.

Anderson, Christopher (1995). *Blaming the Government: Citizens and the Economy in Five European Democracies*. New York, NY: M.E. Sharpe.

Anderson, Christopher J. and Tverdova, Yuliya V. (2001). 'Winners, Losers, and Attitudes Toward Government in Contemporary Democracies', *International Political Science Review*, 22:321–38.

References

Bara, Judith and Budge, Ian (2001). 'Party Policy and Ideology: Still New Labour?' in Norris, Pippa (ed.), *Britain Votes 2001*. Oxford: Oxford University Press.

Barber, Benjamin (1984). *Strong Democracy: Participatory Politics for a New Age*. Berkeley, CA: University of California Press.

Barnes, Samuel H., Kaase, Max et al. (1979). *Political Action: Mass Participation in Five Western Democracies*. Beverly Hills, CA: Sage Publications.

Barry, Brian (1970). *Sociologists, Economists and Democracy*. London: Collier-Macmillan.

Bartels, Larry M. (2002). 'Beyond the Running Tally: Partisan Bias in Political Perceptions', *Political Behavior*, 24:117–50.

Bartle, John (2001). 'The Measurement of Party Identification in Britain: Where Do We Stand Now?' in Jon Tonge et al. (eds.), *British Elections & Parties Review*, Vol. 11. London: Frank Cass.

Bartle, John and Crewe, Ivor (2002). 'The Impact of Party Leaders in Britain: Strong Assumptions, Weak Evidence' in Anthony King (ed.), *Leaders' Personalities and the Outcomes of Democratic Elections*. Oxford: Oxford University Press.

Bartolini, Stefano and Mair, Peter (1990). *Identity, Competition and Electoral Availability 1885–1985*. Cambridge: Cambridge University Press.

Bean, Clive and Mughan, Anthony (1989). 'Leadership Effects in Parliamentary Elections in Australia and Britain', *American Political Science Review*, 83:1165–80.

Becker, Gary S. (1975). *Human Capital: A Theoretical and Empirical Analysis*. New York, NY: National Bureau of Economic Research.

—— (2001). *Social Economics*. Cambridge, MA: Harvard University Press.

Beer, Samuel (1965). *British Politics in the Collectivist Age*. New York, NY: Alfred A. Knopf.

—— (1982). *Britain Against Itself: The Political Contradictions of Collectivism*. New York, NY: W. W. Norton.

Belknap, George and Campbell, Angus (1952). 'Political Party Identification and Attitudes toward Foreign Policy', *Public Opinion Quarterly*, 15:601–23.

Beran, Jan (1994). *Statistics for Long-Memory Processes*. New York, NY: Chapman and Hall.

Berelson, Bernard, Lazarsfeld, Paul F. and McPhee, W. (1954). *Voting*. Chicago, IL: University of Chicago Press.

Black, Duncan (1958). *Theory of Committees and Elections*. Cambridge: Cambridge University Press.

Blais, André (2000). *To Vote or Not to Vote: The Merits and Limits of Rational Choice Theory*. Pittsburgh, PA: University of Pittsburgh Press.

—— (2003). 'Where Does Turnout Decline Come From?', *European Journal of Political Research*, forthcoming.

Blais, André and Carty R. K. (1990). 'Does Proportional Representation Foster Voter Turnout?', *European Journal of Political Research*, 18:167–81.

Blais, André and Dobrzynska, Agnieszka (1998). 'Turnout in Electoral Democracies', *European Journal of Political Research*, 33:239–61.

Blais, André et al. (2002). *Anatomy of a Liberal Victory: Making Sense of the Vote in the 2000 Canadian Election*. Toronto: Broadview Press.

Borre, Ole and Scarbrough, Elinor (eds.) (1995). *The Scope of Government*. Oxford: Oxford University Press.

Box-Steffensmeier, Janet M. and Smith, Renee (1996). 'The Dynamics of Aggregate Partisanship', *American Political Science Review*, 90:567–80.

References

—— (1997). 'Heterogeneity and Individual Party Identification', paper presented at the Annual Meeting of the Midwest Political Science Association, Chicago, IL, April 1997.

Bowler, Shaun and Donovan, Todd (1998). *Demanding Choices: Opinion, Voting and Direct Democracy*. Ann Arbor, MI: University of Michigan Press.

Bowler, Shaun, Brockington, David and Donovan, Todd (2001). 'Election Systems and Voter Turnout: Experiments in the United States', *Journal of Politics*, 63:902–15.

Brady, Henry E. (1999). 'Political Participation' in John P. Robinson, Phillip R. Shaver and Lawrence S. Wrightsman (eds.), *Measures of Political Attitudes*. Burlington, MA: Academic Press.

Brehm, John and Rahn, Wendy (1997). 'Individual-Level Evidence for The Causes and Consequences of Social Capital', *American Journal of Political Science*, 41:888–1023.

Breslaw, John A. (2002). 'Multinomial Probit Estimation without Nuisance Parameters', unpublished paper. Montreal: Concordia University, Department of Economics.

Brittan, Samuel (1983). *The Role and Limits of Government: Essays in Political Economy*. Minneapolis, MN: University of Minnesota Press.

Budge, Ian and Farlie, Dennis (1983). *Explaining the Predicting Elections: Issue Effects and Party Strategies in Twenty-Three Democracies*. London: Allen and Unwin.

Budge, Ian, Crewe, Ivor and Farlie, Dennis (eds.) (1976). *Party Identification and Beyond: Representations of Voting and Party Competition*. New York, NY: John Wiley & Sons.

Budge, Ian, Robertson, David, and Hearl, Derek (eds.) (1987). *Ideology, Strategy and Party Change: Spatial Analyses of Post-War Election Programmes in 19 Democracies*. Cambridge: Cambridge University Press.

Budge, Ian et al. (2001). *Mapping Policy Preferences: Estimates for Parties, Electors, and Governments, 1945–1998*. Oxford: Oxford University Press.

Burnham, Kenneth P. and Anderson, David R. (1998). *Model Selection and Inference: A Practical Information-Theoretic Approach*. New York, NY: Springer-Verlag.

Butler, David (1952). *The British General Election of 1951*. Basingstoke: Palgrave Macmillan.

—— (1998). 'Reflections on British Elections and Their Study' in Polsby, Nelson W. (ed.), *Annual Reviews of Political Science*, Vol. 1. Palo Alto, CA: Annual Reviews.

Butler, David and Kavanagh, Dennis (1992). *The British General Election of 1992*. London: Palgrave Macmillan.

—— (1997). *The British General Election of 1997*. London: Palgrave Macmillan.

—— (2002). *The British General Election of 2001*. London: Palgrave Macmillan.

Butler, David and Stokes, Donald (1969). *Political Change in Britain: Forces Shaping Electoral Choice*. New York, NY: St. Martin's Press.

—— (1971). *Political Choice In Britain*, College edn. New York, NY: St. Martin's Press.

—— (1976). *Political Choice in Britain*. 2nd College edn. New York, NY: St. Martin's Press.

Campbell, Angus, Gurin, Gerald, and Miller, Warren (1954). *The Voter Decides*. Evanston, IL: Row, Peterson.

Campbell, Angus, Converse, Philip, Miller, Warren, and Stokes, Donald (1960). *The American Voter*. New York, NY: John Wiley & Sons.

—— (1966). *Elections and the Political Order*. New York, NY: John Wiley & Sons.

Charemza, Wojciech W. and Derek F. Deadman (1997). *New Directions in Econometric Practice*. 2nd edn. Aldershot: Edward Elgar.

Clarke, Harold D, Kornberg, Allan and Wearing, Peter (2000). *A Polity on the Edge: Canada and the Politics of Fragmentation*. Toronto: Broadview Press.

References

Clarke, Harold D. and Lebo, Matthew (2003). 'Fractional (Co)Integration and Governing Party Support in Britain', *British Journal of Political Science*, 33:283–302.

Clarke, Harold D. and Stewart, Marianne C. (1984). 'Dealignment of Degree: Partisan Change in Britain 1974–83', *Journal of Politics*, 46:689–718.

—— (1992). 'The (Un)Importance of Party Leaders: Leader Images and Party Choice in the 1987 British Election', *Journal of Politics*, 54:447–70.

—— (1994). 'Prospections, Retrospections, and Rationality: The "Bankers" Model of Presidential Approval Reconsidered', *American Journal of Political Science*, 38:1104–23.

—— (1995). 'Economic Evaluations, Prime Ministerial Approval and Governing Party Support in Britain: Rival Models Reconsidered', *British Journal of Political Science*, 25:145–70.

—— (1998). 'The Decline of Parties in the Minds of Citizens' in Polsby, Nelson W. (ed.), *Annual Reviews of Political Science*. Vol. 1. Palo Alto, CA: Annual Reviews.

Clarke, Harold D. and Zuk, Gary (1989). 'The Dynamics of Third-Party Support: The British Liberals, 1951–79', *American Journal of Political Science*, 33:196–221.

Clarke, Harold D., Jenson, Jane, LeDuc, Lawrence, and Pammett, Jon H. (1979). *Political Choice in Canada*. Toronto: McGraw-Hill Ryerson.

Clarke, Harold D., Stewart, Marianne C., and Zuk, Gary (1988). 'Not For Turning?: Beliefs About the Role of Government in Contemporary Britain', *Governance*, 1:271–87.

Clarke, Harold D., Mishler, William, and Whiteley, Paul (1990). 'Recapturing the Falklands: Models of Conservative Popularity, 1979–83', *British Journal of Political Science*, 20:63–81.

Clarke, Harold D., Elliottt, Euel W., Mishler, William, Stewart, Marianne C., Whiteley, Paul F., and Zuk, Gary (1992). *Controversies in Political Economy: Canada: Great Britain, the United States*. Boulder, CO: Westview Press.

Clarke, Harold D., Dutt, Nitish, and Kornberg, Allan (1993). 'The Political Economy of Attitudes Toward Polity and Society in Western European Democracies', *Journal of Politics*, 55:998–1021.

Clarke, Harold D., Stewart, Marianne C., and Whiteley, Paul F. (1997). 'Tory Trends: Party Identification and the Dynamics of Conservative Support Since 1992', *British Journal of Political Science*, 26:299–318.

—— (1998). 'New Models for New Labour: The Political Economy of Labour Party Support, January 1992–April 1997', *American Political Science Review*, 92:559–75.

—— (1999). 'New Labour's New Partisans: The Dynamics of Party Identification in Britain Since 1992' in Justin Fisher, et al. (eds.), *British Elections & Parties Review*, Vol. 9. London: Frank Cass.

Clarke, Harold D., Ho, Karl, and Stewart Marianne C. (2000). 'Major's Lesser (Not Minor) Effects: Prime Ministerial Approval and Governing Party Support in Britain Since 1979', *Electoral Studies*, 18:255–74.

Coleman, James S. (1988). 'Social Capital in the Creation of Human Capital', *American Journal of Sociology*, 94:95–120.

Collins, Daniel and Seldon, Anthony (2001). 'Conservatives in Opposition' in Pippa Norris, (ed.), *Britain Votes 2001*. Oxford: Oxford University Press.

Conlisk, John (1996). 'Why Bounded Rationality?', *Journal of Economic Literature*, 34:669–700.

Conover, Pamela and Feldman, Stanley (1986). 'Emotional Reactions to the Economy: I'm Mad as Hell and I'm Not Going to Take It Any More', *American Journal of Political Science*, 30:50–78.

References

Converse, Philip E. (1964). 'The Nature of Belief Systems in Mass Publics' in David E. Apter (ed.), *Ideology and Discontent*. Glencoe, IL: The Free Press.

—— (1969). 'Of Time and Partisan Stability', *Comparative Political Studies*, 2:139–72.

—— (1976). *The Dynamics of Party Support: Cohort-Analyzing Party Identification*. Beverly Hills, CA: Sage Publications.

Crewe, Ivor (1974). 'Do Butler and Stokes Really Explain Political Change in Britain?', *European Journal of Political Research*, 2:47–92.

—— (1986). 'On the Death and Resurrection of Class Voting: Some Comments on How Britain Votes', *Political Studies*, 35:620–38.

—— (1992). 'Changing Votes and Unchanging Voters', *Electoral Studies*, 11:335–45.

Crewe, Ivor and King, Anthony (1994). 'Did Major Win? Did Kinnock Lose? Leadership Effects in the 1992 Election' in Anthony Heath et al. (eds.), *Labour's Last Chance? The 1992 Election and Beyond*. Aldershot: Dartmouth.

—— (1996). *SDP: The Birth, Life and Death of the Social Democratic Party*. Oxford: Oxford University Press.

Crewe, Ivor and Searing, Donald D. (1988). 'Ideological Change in the British Conservative Party', *American Political Science Review*, 82:361–84.

Crewe, Ivor, Sarlvik, Bo and Alt, James E. (1977). 'Partisan Dealignment in Britain, 1964–1974', *British Journal of Political Science*, 7:129–90.

Crewe, Ivor, Fox, Anthony, and Day, Neil (1996). *The British Electorate 1963–1992: A Compendium of Data from the British Election Studies*. Revised edn. Cambridge: Cambridge University Press.

Crewe, Ivor, Gosschalk, Brian, and Bartle, John (eds.) (1998). *Political Communications: Why Labour Won the General Election of 1997*. London: Frank Cass.

Curtice, John (2001). 'The Electoral System: Biased to Blair?' in Pippa Norris (ed.), *Britain Votes 2001*. Oxford: Oxford University Press.

—— (2002). 'The State of Election Studies: Mid-life Crisis or New Youth?' in Mark N. Franklin and Christopher Wlezien (eds.), *The Future of Election Studies*. London: Elsevier Science Ltd.

Curtice, John and Park, Allison (1999). 'Region: New Labour, New Geography' in Geoffrey Evans and Pippa Norris (eds.), *Critical Elections: Voters and Parties in Long-Term Perspective*. London: Sage Publications.

Curtice, John and Steed, Michael (1997). 'The Results Analysed' in David Butler and Dennis Kavanagh, *The British General Election of 1997*. London: Palgrave Macmillan.

—— (2002). 'The Results Analysed', in David Butler and Dennis Kavanagh, *The British General Election of 2001*. London: Palgrave Macmillan.

Dalton, Russell J. (2000). 'The Decline of Party Identification' in Russell J. Dalton and Martin P. Wattenberg (eds.), *Parties Without Partisans: Political Change in Advanced Industrial Democracies*. Oxford: Oxford University Press.

—— (2002). *Citizen Politics: Public Opinion and Political Parties in Advanced Industrial Democracies*, 3rd edn. Chatham, NJ: Chatham House Publishers.

Dalton, Russell J. and Wattenberg, Martin P. (1993). 'The Not So Simple Act of Voting' in Ada W. Finifter (ed.), *Political Science: The State of the Discipline II*. Washington, D.C.: American Political Science Association.

—— (eds.) (2000). *Parties Without Partisans: Political Change in Advanced Industrial Democracies*. Oxford: Oxford University Press.

References

Dalton, Russell J., Flanagan, Scott, and Beck, Paul (eds.) (1984). *Electoral Change in Advanced Industrial Democracies*. Princeton, NJ: Princeton University Press.

Dalton, Russell J., McAllister, Ian, and Wattenberg, Martin (2000). 'The Consequences of Partisan Dealignment' in Russell J. Dalton and Martin Wattenberg (eds.), *Parties Without Partisans: Political Change in Advanced Industrial Democracies*. Oxford: Oxford University Press.

Davies, James C. (1962). 'Toward a Theory of Revolution', *American Sociological Review*, 27:5–19.

Denver, David (1998). 'The Government That Could Do No Right' in Anthony King (ed.), *New Labour Triumphs: Britain at the Polls, 1997*. Chatham, NJ: Chatham House Publishers.

—— (2001) 'The Liberal Democrat Campaign' in Pippa Norris (ed.), *Britain Votes 2001*. Oxford: Oxford University Press.

—— (2003). *Elections and Voters in Britain*. London: Palgrave Macmillan.

Denver, David and Hands, Gordon (1974). 'Marginality and Turnout in British General Elections', *British Journal of Political Science*, 15:17–35.

—— (1985). 'Marginality and Turnout in General Elections in the 1970s', *British Journal of Political Science*, 15:381–88.

—— (1997). *Modern Constituency Electioneering*. London: Frank Cass.

Denver, David, Hands, Gordon, Fisher, Justin, and MacAllister, Iain (2002). 'The Impact of Constituency Campaigning in the 2001 General Election' in Lynn Bennie et al. (eds.), *British Elections & Parties Review*. Vol. 12. London: Frank Cass.

Downs, Anthony (1957). *An Economic Theory of Democracy*. New York, NY: Harper and Row.

Druckman, James N. and Lupia, Arthur (2000). 'Preference Formation' in Nelson W. Polsby, (ed.), *Annual Review of Political Science*, 3:1–24.

Dunleavy, Patrick and Husbands, Christopher (1985). *British Democracy at the Crossroads*. London: George Allen & Unwin.

Duverger, Maurice (1954). *Political Parties*. New York, NY: John Wiley & Sons.

Easton, David (1965). *A Systems Analysis of Political Life*. New York, NY: John Wiley & Sons.

Electoral Commission (2001). *Election 2001: The Official Results*. London: Politico's Publishing.

—— (2001). Website www.electoralcommission.org.uk.

—— (2002). *Election 2001—Campaign Spending*. www.electoralcommission.org.uk.

Erikson, Robert S., MacKuen, Michael B., and Stimson, James A. (1998). 'What Moves Macropartisanship? A Response to Green, Palmquist, and Schickler', *American Political Science Review*, 92:901–12.

—— (2000). 'Bankers or Peasants Revisited: Economic Expectations and Presidential Approval', *Electoral Studies*, 19:295–312.

—— (2002). *The Macro Polity*. New York, NY: Cambridge University Press.

Eubank, William Lee (1986). 'Voter Rationality: A Retest of the Downsian Model', *Social Science Journal*, 23:253–66.

Evans, Geoffrey (1999). 'Europe: A New Electoral Cleavage?' in Geoffrey Evans and Pippa Norris (eds.), *Critical Elections: Voters and Parties in Long-Term Perspective*. London: Sage Publications.

Evans, Geoffrey and Norris, Pippa (eds.) (1999). *Critical Elections: Voters and Parties in Long-Term Perspective*. London: Sage Publications.

Farah, Barbara and Klein, Ethel (1989). 'Public Opinion Trends' in Gerald Pomper (ed.), *The Election of 1988: Reports and Interpretations*. Chatham, NJ: Chatham House.

References

Farrell, David M. and Webb, Paul (2000). 'Political Parties as Campaign Organizations' in Russell J. Dalton and Martin P. Wattenberg (eds.), *Parties Without Partisans: Political Change in Advanced Industrial Democracies*. Oxford: Oxford University Press.

Finkel, Steven E. (1985). 'Reciprocal Effects of Participation and Political Efficacy: A Panel Analysis', *American Journal of Political Science*, 29:891–913.

—— (1987). 'The Effects of Participation on Political Efficacy and Political Support', *Journal of Politics*, 49:441–64.

—— (1993) 'Reexamining the "Minimal Effects" Model in Recent Presidential Campaigns', *Journal of Politics*, 55:1–21.

—— (1995). *Causal Analysis With Panel Data*. Thousand Oaks, CA: Sage Publications.

Fiorina, Morris P. (1981). *Retrospective Voting in American National Elections*. New Haven, CT: Yale University Press.

Foley, Michael (2000). *The British Presidency*. Manchester: Manchester University Press.

Fox, John (2000). *Nonparametric Simple Regression: Smoothing Scatterplots*. Thousand Oaks, CA: Sage Publications.

Frank, Robert H. (1988). *Passions Within Reason: The Strategic Role of the Emotions*. New York, NY: W. W. Norton.

Franklin, Charles H. (1984). 'Issue Preferences, Socialization, and the Evolution of Party Identification', *American Journal of Political Science*, 28:459–78.

—— (1992) 'Measurement and the Dynamics of Party Identification', *Political Behavior*, 14:297–309.

Franklin, Charles H. and Jackson, John E. (1983) 'The Dynamics of Party Identification', *American Political Science Review*, 77:957–73.

Franklin, Mark (1985). *The Decline of Class Voting in Britain*. Oxford: Oxford University Press.

—— (1999). 'Electoral Engineering and Cross-National Turnout Differences: What Role for Compulsory Voting?', *British Journal of Political Science*, 29:205–16.

—— (2002). 'Electoral Participation', in Lawrence LeDuc, Richard G. Niemi, and Pippa Norris (eds.), *Comparing Democracies: New Challenges in The Study of Elections and Voting*, 2nd edn. Thousand Oaks, CA: Sage Publications.

Franklin, Mark N., Mackie, Thomas T., and Valen, Henry (eds.) (1992). *Electoral Change: Responses to Evolving Social and Attitudinal Structures in Western Countries*. Cambridge: Cambridge University Press.

Franses, Philip Hans (1998). *Time Series Models for Business and Economic Forecasting*. Cambridge: Cambridge University Press.

Fukuyama, Francis (1995). *Trust: Human Nature and The Reconstitution of Social Order*. New York, NY: Touchstone Books.

Geddes, Andrew P. and Tonge, Jonathan (eds.) (2002). *Labour's Second Landslide: The British General Election 2001*. Manchester: Manchester University Press.

Gelman, Andrew and Katz, Jonathan N. (2001). 'How Much Does a Vote Count? Power, Coalitions, and the Electoral College'. California Institute of Technology: Social Science Working Paper 1121.

Gelman, Andrew, King, Gary, and Boscardin, W. J. (1998). 'Estimating the Probability of Events That Have Never Occurred: When Is Your Vote Decisive?', *Journal of the American Statistical Association*, 93:1–9.

Ghirardato, Paolo and Katz, Jonathan N. (2002). 'Indecision Theory: Quality of Information and Voting Behavior'. California Institute of Technology: Social Science Working Paper 1106R.

References

Glenn, Norvall D. (1977). *Cohort Analysis*. Beverly Hills, CA: Sage Publications.

Goodhart, Charles A. E. and Bhansali, R. J. (1970). 'Political Economy', *Political Studies* 18:43–106.

Granger, Clive W. J. (1980). 'Long Memory Relationships and the Aggregation of Dynamic Models', *Journal of Econometrics*, 14:227–38.

Granger, Clive W. J. and Newbold, Paul (1974). 'Spurious Regressions in Econometrics', *Journal of Econometrics*, 2:111–20.

Granovetter, Mark (1973). 'The Strength of Weak Ties', *American Journal of Sociology*, 78:1360–80.

Green, Donald P. and Palmquist, Bradley (1990). 'Of Artifacts and Partisan Instability', *American Journal of Political Science*, 34:872–902.

Green, Donald P. and Shachar, Rona (2000). 'Habit Formation and Political Behaviour: Evidence of Consuetude in Voter Turnout', *British Journal of Political Science*, 30:561–73.

Green, Donald P. and Shapiro, Ian (1994). *Pathologies of Rational Choice Theory*. New Haven, CT: Yale University Press.

Green, Donald P., Palmquist, Bradley, and Schickler, Eric (1998). 'Macrospartisanship: A Replication and Critique', *American Political Science Review*, 92:883–99.

—— (2002). *Partisan Hearts & Minds: Political Parties and the Social Identities of Voters*. New Haven, CT: Yale University Press.

Greene, William H. (2003). *Econometric Analysis*. 5th edn. New York, NY: Prentice-Hall.

Grofman, Bernard (ed.) (1993). *Information, Participation & Choice: An Economic Theory of Democracy in Perspective*. Ann Arbor, MI: University of Michigan Press.

Gurr, Ted Robert (1970). *Why Men Rebel*. Princeton, NJ: Princeton University Press.

Habermas, Jurgen (1975). *Legitimation Crisis*. Boston, MA: Beacon Press.

Hagenaars, Jacques and McCutcheon, Allan (eds.) (2002). *Applied Latent Class Analysis*. Cambridge: Cambridge University Press.

Hall, Peter (1999). 'Social Capital in Britain', *British Journal of Political Science*, 29:417–61.

Heath, Anthony and McDonald, Sarah K. (1988). 'The Demise of Party Identification Theory?', *Electoral Studies*, 7:95–107.

Heath, Anthony and Pierce, Roy (1992). 'It Was Party Identification All Along: Question Order Effects on Reports of Party Identification in Britain', *Electoral Studies*, 11:93–105.

Heath, Anthony and Taylor, B. (eds.) (1994). *Labour's Last Chance? The 1992 Election and Beyond*. Aldershot: Dartmouth.

Heath, Anthony F., Jowell, Roger M., and Curtice, John K. (1985). *How Britain Votes*. Oxford: Pergamon Press.

—— (1987). 'Trendless Fluctuation: A Reply to Crewe', *Political Studies*, 35:256–77.

—— (2001). *The Rise of New Labour: Party Policies and Voter Choices*. Oxford: Oxford University Press.

Heath, Anthony, Evans, Geoffrey, Field, Julia, and Witherspoon, Sharon (1991). *Understanding Political Change: The British Voter 1964–1987*. Oxford: Pergamon Press.

Held, David (1996). *Models of Democracy*, 2nd edn. Stanford, CA: Stanford University Press.

Hendry, David (1995). *Dynamics Econometrics*. Oxford: Oxford University Press.

Hibbs, Douglas A. (1977). 'Political Parties and Macroeconomic Policy', *American Political Science Review*, 71:1467–87.

—— (1987). *The American Political Economy: Macroeconomics and Electoral Politics*. Cambridge, MA: Harvard University Press.

References

Himmelweit, Hilde T., Humphreys, Patrick, Jaeger, Marianne, and Katz, Michael (1981). *How Voters Decide*. London: Academic Press.

Hobsbawm, E.J. (1962). *The Age of Revolution 1789–1848*. New York, NY: New American Library.

Hochschild, Jennifer L. (1981). *What's Fair? American Beliefs about Distributive Justice*. Cambridge, MA: Harvard University Press.

Hotelling, Harold (1929). 'Stability in Competition', *Economic Journal*, 39:41–57.

Huckfeldt, Robert, and Sprague, John (1995). *Citizens, Politics and Social Communication*. Cambridge: Cambridge University Press.

Ingelhart, Ronald (1983). 'Changing Paradigms in Comparative Political Behavior', in Ada W. Finifter (ed.), *Political Science: The State of The Discipline*. Washington, D.C: American Political Science Association, 433–37.

—— (1997). *Modernization and Post-Modernization*. Princeton, NJ: Princeton University Press.

Jackman, Robert W. (1987). 'Political Institutions and Voter Turnout in the Industrial Democracies', *Comparative Political Studies*, 27:467–92.

Jackman, Robert W. and Miller, Ross A. (1995). 'Voter Turnout in the Industrial Democracies During the 1980s', *Comparative Political Studies*, 27:467–92.

—— (1998). 'Social Capital and Politics' in Nelson W. Polsby (ed.), *Annual Review of Political Science*, Vol. 1. Palo Alto, CA: Annual Reviews.

Jennings, M. Kent and Niemi, Richard G. (1974). *The Political Character of Adolescence*. Princeton, NJ: Princeton University Press.

Jennings, M. Kent and Deth, Jan Van (1990). *Continuities in Political Action: A Longitudinal Study of Political Orientations in Three Western Democracies*. New York, NY: deGruyter.

Johnston, Richard (1992). 'Political Generations and Electoral Change in Canada', *British Journal of Political Science*, 22:93–116.

Johnston, Richard and Brady, Henry E. (2002). 'The Rolling Cross-Section Design', in Mark N. Franklin and Christopher Wlezien (eds.), *The Future of Election Studies*. Amsterdam: Pergamon Press.

Johnston, Ron and Pattie, Charles (1995). 'The Impact of Spending on Party Constituency Campaigns at Recent British General Elections', *Party Politics*, 1:261–73.

—— (1997). 'Where's the Difference? Decomposing the Impact of Local Election Campaigns in Great Britain', *Electoral Studies*, 16:165–74.

—— (2002). 'Do Canvassing and Campaigning Work? Evidence From the 2001 General Election in England', unpublished paper. University of Bristol: Department of Geography.

Johnston, Ron, Pattie, Charles, and Allsopp, J. G. (1988). *A Nation Dividing? The Electoral Map of Great Britain 1979–87*. Harlow: Longman.

Johnston, Ron, Pattie, Charles, and Johnston, L. C. (1989). 'The Impact of Constituency Spending on the Result of the 1987 British General Election', *Electoral Studies*, 8:143–55.

Johnston, Ron, Cowley, Philip, Pattie, Charles, and Stuart, Mark (2002). 'Voting in the House or Wooing the Voters at Home: Labour MPs and the 2001 General Election Campaign', *The Journal of Legislative Studies*, 28:9–22.

Jones, Nicholas (2001). *Campaign 2001*. London: Politico's Publishing.

Joreskog, Karl G. and Sorbom, Dag (1996). *LISREL 8: User's Reference Guide*. Chicago: Scientific Software.

353

References

Kaase, Max and Newton, Kenneth (eds.) (1995). *Beliefs in Government*. Oxford: Oxford University Press.

Kahneman, Daniel and Tversky, Amos (1979). 'Prospect Theory: An Analysis of Decision Under Risk', *Econometrica*, 47:313–27.

—— (eds.) (2000). *Choices, Values and Frames*. New York, NY: Cambridge University Press and Russell Sage Foundation.

Kahneman, Daniel, Slovic, Paul, and Tversky, Amos (eds.) (1982). *Judgment Under Uncertainty: Heuristics and Biases*. Cambridge: Cambridge University Press.

Key, V. O. (1961). *Public Opinion and American Democracy*. New York, NY: Alfred A. Knopf.

—— (1968). *The Responsible Electorate: Rationality in Presidential Voting, 1936–1960*. New York, NY: Vintage Books.

Kiewiet, D. Roderick (1983). *Macroeconomics & Micropolitics: The Electoral Effects of Economic Issues*. Chicago, IL: University of Chicago Press.

Kinder, Donald R. and Kiewiet, D. Roderick (1979). 'Economic Discontent and Political Behavior: The Role of Personal Grievances and Collective Economic Judgments in Congressional Voting', *American Journal of Political Science*, 23:495–527.

—— (1981). 'Sociotropic Politics: The American Case', *British Journal of Political Science*, 11:129–61.

King, Anthony (1975). 'Overload: Problems of Governing in the 1970s', *Political Studies*, 23:162–74.

—— (ed.) (1998). *New Labour Triumphs: Britain at the Polls 1997*. Chatham, NJ: Chatham House.

—— (2001). 'Why a Poor Turnout Points to a Democracy in Good Health' *The Daily Telegraph*, 17 May 2001.

—— (ed.) (2002a). *Britain at the Polls 2001*. Chatham, NJ: Chatham House.

—— (ed.) (2002b). *Leaders' Personalities and the Outcome of Democratic Elections*. Oxford: Oxford University Press.

King, Anthony and Wybrow (eds.) (2001). *British Political Opinion 1937–2000: The Gallup Polls*. London: Politico's.

Kornberg, Allan and Clarke, Harold D. (1992). *Citizens and Community: Political Support in a Democratic Society*. New York, NY: Cambridge University Press.

Kreft, Ita G. and Leeuw, Jan de (1998). *Introducing Multilevel Modeling*. Thousand Oaks, CA: Sage Publications.

Kuklinski, James H. and Quirk, Paul J. (2000). 'Reconsidering the Rational Public: Cognition, Heuristics, and Mass Opinion' in Arthur Lupia, Mathew D. McCubbins and Samuel L. Popkin (eds.), *Elements of Reason: Cognition, Choice, and the Bounds of Rationality*. New York, NY: Cambridge University Press.

Labour Party (1997). *General Election Handbook*. London: Labour Party.

—— (2000). *Operation Turnout Explained*. London: Labour Party.

Laver, Michael (1997). *Private Desires, Political Action: An Invitation to the Politics of Rational Choice*. London: Sage Publications.

Lazarsfeld, Paul F., Berelson, Bernard R., and Gaudet, Hazel (1948). *The People's Choice*. 2nd edn. New York, NY: Columbia University Press.

Leighley, Jan (1995). 'Political Participation: A Field Review Essay', *Political Research Quarterly*, 48:181–210.

References

Leonard, Dick and Mortimore, Roger (2001). *Elections in Britain: A Voter's Guide*. 4th Edn. London: Palgrave.

Levi, Margaret and Stoker, Laura (2000). 'Political Trust and Trustworthiness', *Annual Review of Political Science*, 3:475–507.

Lewis-Beck, Michael S. (1988). *Economics and Elections: The Major Western Democracies*. Ann Arbor, MI: University of Michigan Press.

Lilien, David et al. (2003). *Eviews 4.1*. Irvine, CA: Quantitative Micro Software.

Lipset, Martin, Seymour, and Rokkan, Stein (eds.) (1967). *Party Systems and Voter Alignments*. New York, NY: The Free Press.

Lodge, Milton and Hamill, H. (1986). 'A Partisan Schema for Information Processing', *American Political Science Review*, 80:505–19.

Long, J. Scott (1997). Regression Models for Categorical and Limited Dependent Variables. Thousand Oaks, CA: Sage Publications.

Ludlam, Steve and Martin J. Smith (2001). *New Labour in Government*. London: Macmillan Press Ltd.

Lupia, Arthur and McCubbins, Mathew D. (1998). *The Democratic Dilemma: Can Citizens Learn What They Really Need to Know?* Cambridge: Cambridge University Press.

Lupia, Arthur, McCubbins, Mathew D., and Popkin, Samuel L. (eds.) (2000). *Elements of Reason: Cognition, Choice, and the Bounds of Rationality*. New York, NY: Cambridge University Press.

Macdonald, Stuart Elaine and Rabinowitz, George (1998). 'Solving the Paradox of Nonconvergence: Valence, Position and Direction in Democratic Politics', *Electoral Studies*, 17:281–300.

MacKuen, Michael B., Erikson, Robert S., and Stimson, James A. (1989). 'Macropartisanship', *American Political Science Review*, 83:1125–42.

—— (1992a). 'Question Wording and Macropartisanship', *American Political Science Review*, 86:475–86.

—— (1992b). 'Peasants or Bankers?: The American Electorate and the U.S. Economy', *American Political Science Review*, 86:597–611.

—— (1996). 'Comment', *Journal of Politics*, 58:793–801.

Macpherson, C. B. (1977). *The Life and Times of Liberal Democracy*. Oxford: Oxford University Press.

Maddala, G. S. and Kim, In-Moo (1998). *Unit Roots, Cointegration, and Structural Change*. Cambridge: Cambridge University Press.

Maloney, William A., Smith, Graham, and Stoker, Gerry (2000). 'Social Capital and Associational Life', in Stephen Baron, John Field, and Tom Schuller (eds.), *Social Capital: Critical Perspectives*. Oxford: Oxford University Press.

Marcus, George E. (1988). 'The Structure of Emotional Response: 1984 Presidential Candidates', *American Political Science Review*, 83:737–62.

Marcus, George E., Neuman, W. Russell, and McKuen, Michael (2000). *Affective Intelligence and Political Judgement*. Chicago, IL: University of Chicago Press, 2000.

Marsh, Alan (1977). *Protest and Political Consciousness*. London: Sage Publications.

McDonald, Michael P. and Popkin, Samuel L. (2001). 'The Myth of the Vanishing Voter', *American Political Science Review*, 95:963–74.

McKenzie, Robert and Silver, Allan (1968). *Angels in Marble: Working Class Conservatives in Urban England*. Chicago, IL: University of Chicago Press.

References

Merrill, Samuel, III and Grofman, Bernard (1999). *A Unified Theory of Voting: Directional and Proximity Spatial Models*. Cambridge: Cambridge University Press.

Milbrath, Lester (1965). *Political Participation: How and Why Do People Get Involved in Politics?* Chicago, IL: Rand McNally.

Mill, John Stuart (1972/1859). *Considerations on Representative Government*, in H. B. Acton (ed.), *Utilitarianism, On Liberty and Considerations on Representative Government*. London: J.M. Dent & Sons.

—— (1972/1861). *On Liberty*, in H. B. Acton (ed.), *Utilitarianism, On Liberty and Considerations on Representative Government*. London: J.M. Dent & Sons.

Miller, Arthur H., Wattenberg, Martin P., and Malanchuk, Oksana (1986). 'Schematic Assessments of Presidential Candidates', *American Political Science Review*, 80:521–40.

Miller, John H., Page, Scott E., and Kollman, Kenneth (1998). 'Political Parties and Electoral Landscapes', *British Journal of Political Science*, 28:139–58.

Miller, Warren E. (1991). 'Party Identification, Realignment, and Party Voting: Back to Basics', *American Political Science Review*, 85:557–68.

Miller, Warren E. and Shanks, J. Merrill (1996). *The New American Voter*. Cambridge, MA: Harvard University Press.

Miller, William (1977). *Electoral Dynamics in Britain Since 1918*. Basingstoke: Palgrave Macmillan.

Miller, William, Clarke, Harold D., Harrop, Martin, LeDuc, Lawrence, and Whiteley, Paul (1990). *How Voters Change: The 1987 British Election Campaign in Perspective*. Oxford: Clarendon Press.

Milne, R. S. (1959/1977). 'Second Thoughts on "Straight Fight" ' in Eugene Burdick and Arthur J. Brodbeck (eds.), *American Voting Behavior*. New York, NY: The Free Press/ Greenwood Press.

Milne, R. S. and Mackenzie, H. C. (1954). *Straight Fight 1951*. London: The Hansard Society.

—— (1958). *Marginal Seat 1955*. London: The Hansard Society.

Milner, Henry (2002). *Civic Literacy: How Informed Citizens Make Democracy Work*. Hanover and London: University Press of New England.

Morton, Rebecca B. and Williams, Kenneth C. (2001). *Learning by Voting: Sequential Choices in Presidential Primaries and Other Elections*. Ann Arbor, MI: University of Michigan Press.

Mueller, Dennis C. (1989). *Public Choice II*. Cambridge: Cambridge University Press.

Mughan, Anthony (1993). 'Party Leaders and Presidentialism in the 1992 Election: A Post-War Perspective' in David Denver et al. (eds.), *British Elections and Parties Yearbook 1992*. London: Frank Cass.

Muller, Edward N. (1970). *Aggressive Political Participation*. Princeton, NJ: Princeton University Press.

Mutz, Diana (1998). *Impersonal Influence: How Perceptions of Mass Collectives Affect Political Attitudes*. Cambridge: Cambridge University Press.

Nadeau, Richard, Niemi, Richard G. and Amato, Timothy (1996). 'Prospective and Comparative or Retrospective and Individual? Party Leaders and Party Support in Great Britain', *British Journal of Political Science*, 26:245–58.

Nannestad, Peter and Paldam, Martin (1994). 'The V-P Function: A Survey of the Literature on Vote and Popularity Functions After 25 Years', *Public Choice*, 79:213–45.

—— (2002). 'The Cost of Ruling: A Foundation Stone for Two Theories' in Han Dorussen and Michaell, Taylor (eds.), *Economic Voting*. London: Routledge.

References

Neumann, Russell (1986). *The Paradox of Mass Politics: Knowledge and Opinion in The American Electorate*. Cambridge, MA: Harvard University Press.

Nicholas, H. G. (1951). *The British General Election of 1950*. Basingstoke: Palgrave Macmillan.

Nie, Norman H., Junn, Jane, and Stehlik-Barry, Kenneth (1996). *Education and Democratic Citizenship in America*. Chicago, IL: University of Chicago Press.

Nordlinger, Eric (1967). *The Working Class Tories*. London: MacGibbon and Kee.

Norpoth, Helmut (1987). 'Guns and Butter and Government Popularity in Britain', *American Political Science Review*, 81:949–59.

—— (1996a). 'Presidents and the Prospective Voter', *Journal of Politics*, 58:776–92.

—— (1996b). 'Rejoinder', *Journal of Politics*, 58:802–05.

—— (1997). *Confidence Regained: Economics, Mrs. Thatcher, and the British Voter*. Ann Arbor, MI: University of Michigan Press.

Norpoth, Helmut, Lewis-Beck, Michael S., and Lafay, Jean Dominique (eds.) (1991). *Economics and Politics: The Calculus of Support*. Ann Arbor, MI: University of Michigan Press.

Norris, Pippa (2000). *A Virtuous Circle: Political Communication in Postindustrial Societies*. Cambridge: Cambridge University Press.

Norris, Pippa (ed.) (2001). *Britain Votes 2001*. Oxford: Oxford University Press.

O'Connor, James (1973). *The Fiscal Crisis of the State*. New York, NY: St. Martin's Press.

Offe, Claus (1984). *Contradictions of the Welfare State*. London: Hutchinson.

Olson, Mancur (1965). *The Logic of Collective Action*. New York, NY: Schocken Books.

Page, Benjamin I. and Shapiro, Robert Y. (1992). *The Rational Public: Fifty Years of Trends in Americans' Policy Preferences*. Chicago, IL: University of Chicago Press.

Parkin, Frank (1968). *Middle Class Radicalism: The Social Bases of the British Campaign for Nuclear Disarmament*. Manchester: Manchester University Press.

Parry, Geraint, Moyser, George, and Day, Neil (1992). *Political Participation and Democracy in Britain*. Cambridge: Cambridge University Press.

Pateman, Carole (1970). *Participation and Democratic Theory*. Cambridge: Cambridge University Press.

Pattie, Charles and Johnston, Ron (1998). 'Voter Turnout at the British General Election of 1992: Rational Choice, Social Standing or Political Efficacy?', *European Journal of Political Research*, 33:263–83.

—— (2002). 'Local Battles in a National Landslide: Constituency Campaigning at the 2001 British General Election' unpublished paper. University of Sheffield: Department of Geography.

Pattie, Charles, Fieldhouse, E. A. and Johnston, Ron (1995). 'Winning the Local Vote: The Effectiveness of Constituency Campaign Spending in Great Britain, 1983–1992', *American Political Science Review*, 89:969–79.

Pattie, Charles, Seyd, Patrick, and Whiteley, Paul (2004). *Atomised Citizens: Democracy and Participation in Contemporary Britain*. Cambridge: Cambridge University Press.

Plous, Scott (1993). *The Psychology of Judgment and Decision Making*. New York, NY: McGraw-Hill.

Popkin, Samuel L. (1991). *The Reasoning Voter: Communication and Persuasion in Presidential Campaigns*. Chicago, IL: University of Chicago Press.

Powell, Jr., G. Bingham (2000). *Elections as Instruments of Democracy: Majoritarian and Proportional Visions*. New Haven, CT: Yale University Press.

References

Powell, Jr., Bingham, G. and Whitten, Guy (1993). 'A Cross-National Analysis of Economic Voting: Taking Account of the Political Context', *American Journal of Political Science*, 37:391–414.

Przeworski, Adam and Sprague, John 1986. *Paper Stones: A History of Electoral Socialism.* Chicago, IL: University of Chicago Press.

Putnam, Robert (1993). *Making Democracy Work: Civic Traditions in Modern Italy.* Princeton, NJ: Princeton University Press.

—— (2000). *Bowling Alone: The Collapse and Revival of American Community.* New York, NY: Simon & Schuster.

Pulzer, Peter (1968). *Political Representation and Elections in Britain.* London: Allen and Unwin.

Quattrone, G. A. and Tversky, Amos (1984). 'Causal versus Diagnostic Contingencies: On Self-Deception and on the Voter's Illusion', *Journal of Personality and Social Psychology*, 46:237–48.

Rahn, Wendy M., Brehm, John, and Carlson, Neil (1999). 'National Elections as Institutions for Generating Social Capital' in Theda Skocpol and Morris P. Fiorina (eds.), *Civic Engagement in American Democracy.* Washington and New York, NY: Brookings Institution and Russell Sage Foundation.

Raudenbush, Stephen W. and Bryk, Anthony S. (2001). *Hierarchical Linear Models: Applications and Data Analysis Methods.* 2nd edn. Thousand Oaks, CA: Sage Publications.

Raudenbush, Stephen W., Bryk, Anthony, Cheong, Uk Fai, and Congdon, Richard (2001). *HLM 5: Hierarchical Linear and Nonlinear Modeling.* Chicago, IL: Scientific Software International.

Richardson, Jeremy (ed.) (2001). *European Union: Power and Policymaking.* 2nd edn. London: Routledge.

Riker, William and Ordeshook, Peter C. (1968). 'A Theory of the Calculus of Voting', *American Political Science Review*, 62:25–42.

—— (1973). *An Introduction to Positive Political Theory.* Englewood Cliffs, NJ: Prentice-Hall.

Rose, Richard and McAllister, Ian (1986) *Voters Begin to Choose.* London: Sage Publications.

—— (1990). *The Loyalties of Voters: A Lifetime Learning Model.* London: Sage Publications.

Rosenstone, Steven J. and Hansen, J. M. (1993). *Mobilization, Participation and Democracy in America.* New York, NY: Macmillan.

Rossi, Peter (1959/1977). 'Four Landmarks in Voting Research' in Eugene Burdick and Arthur J. Brodbeck (eds.), *American Voting Behavior.* New York, NY: The Free Press/Greenwood Press.

Runciman, W. G. (1966). *Relative Deprivation and Social Justice.* Berkeley, CA: University of California Press.

Saari, Donald G. (2001). *Decisions and Elections: Explaining the Unexpected.* Cambridge: Cambridge University Press.

Saggar, Shamit (1997). 'Racial Politics', *Parliamentary Affairs*, 50:693–708.

Sanders, David (1990). *Losing an Empire: Finding a Role: British Foreign Policy Since 1945.* Basingstoke: Macmillan.

—— (1991). 'Government Popularity and the Next General Election', *Political Studies*, 62:235–61.

—— (1993). 'Why the Conservatives Won—Again' in Anthony King (ed.), *Britain at the Polls 1992.* Chatham, NJ: Chatham House Publishers.

References

—— (1995). 'It's the Economy, Stupid: The Economy and Support for the Conservative Party, 1979–1994', *Talking Politics*, 7:158–67.

—— (1998). 'The New Electoral Battleground' in Anthony King (ed.), *New Labour Triumphs: Britain at the Polls*. Chatham, NJ: Chatham House Publishers.

Sanders, David, Burton, Jonathan, and Kneeshaw, Jack (2002). 'Identifying the True Identifiers: A Question Wording Experiment', *Party Politics*, 8:193–205.

Sanders, David, Clarke, Harold, Stewart, Marianne, and Whiteley, Paul (2001). 'The Economy and Voting' in Pippa Norris (ed.), *Britain Votes 2001*. Oxford: Oxford University Press.

Sanders, David, Ward, Hugh, and Marsh, David, with Fletcher, Tony (1987). 'Governmental Popularity and the Falklands War: A Reassessment', *British Journal of Political Science*, 17:281–313.

Sarlvik, Bo and Crewe, Ivor (1983). *Decade of Dealignment: The Conservative Victory of 1970 and Electoral Trends in the 1970s*. Cambridge: Cambridge University Press.

Scarbrough, Elinor (1984). *Political Ideology and Voting: An Exploratory Study*. Oxford: Clarendon Press.

—— (2000). 'The British Election Study and Electoral Research', *Political Studies*, 48:391–414.

Schickler, Eric and Green, Donald P. (1997) 'The Stability of Party Identification in Western Democracies: Results From Eight Panel Surveys', *Comparative Political Studies*, 30:450–83.

Schofield, Norman (2003). 'Equilibrium in the Spatial Valence Model of Politics', unpublished manuscript. Washington University at St. Louis: Department of Political Science.

Schumpeter, Joseph A. (1950/1942). *Capitalism, Socialism and Democracy*. New York, NY: Harper & Row.

Sen, Amartya (1977). 'Rational Fools: A Critique of the Behavioral Foundations of Economic Theory', *Philosophy and Public Affairs*, 6:317–44.

Seyd, Patrick (2001). 'The Labour Campaign' in Pippa Norris (ed.), *Britain Votes 2001*. Oxford: Oxford University Press.

Seyd, Patrick and Whiteley, Paul (1992). *Labour's Grassroots: The Politics of Party Membership*. Oxford: Clarendon Press.

—— (2002). *New Labour's Grassroots: The Transformation of the Labour Party Membership*. London: Palgrave Macmillan.

Shepsle, Kenneth A. and Bonchek, Mark S. (1997). *Analyzing Politics: Rationality, Behavior and Institutions*. New York, NY: W. W. Norton.

Simon, Herbert A. (1987). 'Satisficing', in John Eatwell, Murray Milgate and Peter Newman (eds.), *The New Palgrave: A Dictionary of Economics*. London: Macmillan.

Skocpol, Theda (1979). *States & Social Revolutions: A Comparative Analysis of France, Russia, & China*. Cambridge: Cambridge University Press.

—— and Fiorina, Morris P. (eds.) (1999). *Civic Engagement in American Democracy*. Washington and New York: Brookings Institution and Russell Sage Foundation.

Sniderman, Paul M. and Brody, Richard A. (1977). 'Coping: The Ethic of Self-Reliance', *American Journal of Political Science*, 21:501–22.

Sniderman, Paul M., Brody, Richard A., and Tetlock, Phillip E. (eds.) (1991). *Reasoning and Choice: Explorations in Political Psychology*. Cambridge: Cambridge University Press.

Stevenson, Randy (2001). 'The Economy and Policy Preference: A Fundamental Dynamic of Democratic Politics', *American Journal of Political Science*, 45:620–33.

References

—— (2002). 'The Economy as Context: Indirect Links Between the Economy and Voters' in Han Dorussen and Michaell Taylor (eds.), *Economic Voting*. London: Routledge.

Stewart, Marianne C. (1987). 'Modes of Political Participation: A Covariance Structure Analysis', paper presented at the Annual Meeting of the Midwest Political Science Association, Chicago, IL, April 9–11.

Stewart, Marianne C. and Clarke, Harold D. (1992). 'The (Un)Importance of Party Leaders: Leader Images and Party Choice in the 1987 British Election', *Journal of Politics*, 54:447–70.

—— (1998). 'The Dynamics of Party Identification in Federal Systems: The Canadian Case', *American Journal of Political Science*, 42:97–116.

Stokes, Donald E. (1963). 'Spatial Models of Party Competition', *American Political Science Review*, 57:368–77.

—— (1992). 'Valence Politics' in Kavanagh, Dennis (ed.), *Electoral Politics*. Oxford: Clarendon Press.

Stokes, Donald E. and Iversen, Gudmund R. (1966). 'On the Existence of Forces Restoring Party Competition' in Angus Campbell et al. (eds.), *Elections and the Political Order*. New York, NY: John Wiley & Sons, Inc.

Sullivan, John and Transue, John (1999). 'The Psychological Foundations of Democracy: A Selective Review of Research on Political Tolerance, Interpersonal Trust and Social Capital', *Annual Review of Psychology*, 50:625–50.

Swaddle, K. and Heath, Anthony (1989). 'Official and Reported Turnout in the British General Election of 1987', *British Journal of Political Science*, 19:537–51.

Tetlock, Philip E. (2000). 'Coping with Trade-Offs: Psychological Constraints and Political Implications' in Arthur Lupia, Mathew D. McCubbins and Samuel L. Popkin (eds.), *Elements of Reason: Cognition, Choice, and the Bounds of Rationality*. New York, NY: Cambridge University Press.

Thaler, Richard (ed.) (1993). *Advances in Behavioral Finance*. New York, NY: Russell Sage Foundation.

—— (1994). *Quasi Rational Economics*. New York, NY: Russell Sage Foundation.

Thatcher, Margaret (1993). *The Downing Street Years*. London: Harper Collins.

Tomz, Michael, Wittenberg, Jason, and King, Gary (1999). *CLARIFY: Software for Interpreting and Presenting Statistical Results*. Cambridge, MA: Harvard University, Department of Government.

Toynbee, Polly and Walker, David (2001). *Did Things Get Better? An Audit of Labour's Successes and Failures*. London: Penguin Books.

Uslaner, Eric M. (1999). 'Democracy and Social Capital' in Mark E. Warren (ed.), *Democracy & Trust*. New York, NY: Cambridge University Press.

Van der Pol, Frank, Langeheine, Rolf, and Jong, Wil de (1999). *PANMARK 3 User's Manual*. 2nd Version. The Netherlands: Voorburg.

Verba, Sidney, and Nie, Norman H. (1972). *Participation in America*. New York, NY: Harper & Row.

Verba, Sidney, Schlozman, Kay Lehman, and Brady, Henry E. (1995). *Voice and Equality: Civic Voluntarism in American Politics*. Cambridge, MA: Harvard University Press.

Von Neumann, John and Morgenstern, Oskar (1947). *Theory of Games and Economic Behavior*. Princeton, NY: Princeton University Press.

References

Walker, Iain, and Smith, Heather J. (2002). 'Fifty Years of Relative Deprivation Research', in Iain Walker and Heather J. Smith (eds.), *Relative Deprivation: Specification, Development and Integration*. Cambridge: Cambridge University Press.

Walker, Iain, Wong, Ngai Kin, and Kretzschmar, Kerry (2002). 'Relative Deprivation and Attribution: From Grievance to Action' in Iain Walker and Heather J. Smith (eds.), *Relative Deprivation: Specification, Development and Integration*. Cambridge: Cambridge University Press.

Wattenberg, Martin J. (1991). *The Rise of Candidate Centered Politics*. Cambridge, MA: Harvard University Press.

—— (2000). 'The Decline of Party Mobilization' in Russell J. Dalton and Martin P. Wattenberg (eds.), *Parties without Partisans: Political Change in Advanced Industrial Democracies*. Oxford: Oxford University Press, pp. 64–76.

Weakliem, D. L. and Heath, Anthony F. (1994). 'Rational Choice and Class Voting', *Rationality and Society*, 6:243–70.

Whiteley, Paul and Seyd, Patrick (1994). 'Local Party Campaigning and Voting Behaviour in Britain', *Journal of Politics*, 56:242–52.

—— (2002). *High-Intensity Participation—The Dynamics of Party Activism in Britain*. Ann Arbor, MI: University of Michigan Press.

—— (2003). 'How to Win a Landslide by Really Trying: The Effects of local Campaigning on Voting in the 1997 British General Election', *Electoral Studies*, 22:301–24.

Whiteley, Paul, Seyd, Patrick, and Richardson, Jeremy (1994). *True Blues: The Politics of Conservative Party Membership*. Oxford: Clarendon Press.

Whiteley, Paul, Seyd, Patrick, Richardson, Jeremy, and Bissell, Paul (1994). 'Explaining Party Activism: The Case of the British Conservative Party', *British Journal of Political Science*, 24:79–94.

Whiteley, Paul, Clarke, Harold D., Sanders, David, and Stewart, Marianne (2001). 'Turnout', in Pippa Norris (ed.), *Britain Votes 2001*. Oxford: Oxford University Press.

Wlezien, Christopher (2000). 'An Essay on 'Combined' Time Series Processes', *Electoral Studies* 19:77–94.

Wolfinger, Raymond E., and Rosenstone, Steven J. (1980). *Who Votes?* New Haven, CT: Yale University Press.

Zaller, John (1992). *The Nature and Origins of Mass Opinion*. New York, NY: Cambridge University Press.

Name Index

363

Name Index

Name Index

Lodge, Milton 20
Long, J. Scott 68, 112, 126, 128, 156, 252, 305
Lupia, Arthur 21, 36, 218, 229, 230

MacKuen, Michael B. 26, 27, 28, 203, 225
Macpherson, C. B. 218
Macdonald, Stuart 36
Mackenzie, H. C. 18
Mackie, Thomas T. 33
Maddala, G. S. 216
Mair, Peter 205
Malanchuk, Oksana 35
Maloney, William A. 233
Marcus, George E. 27, 35, 225
Marsh, Alan 220
McAllister, Ian 6, 33, 131, 133
McCubbins, Mathew D. 218, 229, 230
McCutcheon, Allan 190
McDonald, Michael P. 224
McKenzie, Robert 33
McPhee, W. 18, 218
Merrill, Samuel III 248, 276
Milbrath, Lester 219, 226
Mill, John Stuart 218
Miller, Arthur H. 18, 19, 20, 21, 25, 35, 36, 226
Miller, John 36
Miller, Ross 225, 235
Miller, Warren 175
Miller, William 33, 134
Milne, R. S. 18
Mishler, William 24, 25, 60
Morgenstern, Oskar 21
Mortimore, Roger 214, 270
Moyser, George 220, 311
Mughan, Anthony 28, 35
Mutz, Diana 19

Nannestad, Peter 322
Neuman, Russell 27
Newbold, Paul 205
Newton, Kenneth 34
Nicholas, H. G. 132
Nie, Norman H. 219, 220, 230, 233
Niemi, Richard G. 19
Nordlinger, Eric 33
Norpoth, Helmut 25, 35, 60
Norris, Pippa 302

O'Connor, James 34
Olson, Mancur 231

Ordeshook, Peter C. 7, 228, 229, 231
Ostrom, Charles W. 203

Page, Scott 36
Paldam, Martin 322
Palmquist, Bradley 14, 20, 21, 188, 214
Park, Allison 33
Parry, Geraint 220, 311
Pateman, Carole 218
Pattie, Charles 34, 45, 47, 133, 134, 153, 233, 234, 311
Plous, Scott 36, 229
Popkin, Samuel L. 218, 224, 229
Powell, G. Bingham Jr. 23, 235
Przeworski, Adam 19
Pulzer, Peter 40
Putnam, Robert 226, 234, 240

Quattrone, G. A. 229
Quirk, Paul J. 229, 230

Rabinowitz, George 36
Rahn, Wendy M. 226, 234
Raudenbush, Stephen W. 174
Richardson, Jeremy 134, 250, 282
Riker, William 7, 228, 229, 231
Roubini, Nouriel 77
Robertson, David 51, 52
Rose, Richard 6, 33
Rosenstone, Steven 133, 224
Rossi, Peter 18, 19
Runciman, W. G. 225

Saari, Donald G. 36, 235
Saggar, Shamit 75
Sanders, David 11, 34, 35, 62, 197, 198, 281
Sarlvik, Bo 6, 33, 178, 194, 234
Scarbrough, Elinor 6, 17, 34
Schickler, Eric 14, 20, 21, 188, 214
Schofield, Norman 24
Schlozman, Kay Lehman 219, 220, 226, 227, 234, 243
Schumpeter, Joseph A. 218
Searing, Donald D. 51, 86
Seldon, Anthony 138
Sen, Amartya vii, 327
Seyd, Patrick 133, 134, 137, 139, 231, 250, 311
Shanks, J. Merrill 19, 21, 36, 276
Shapiro, Ian 7, 229, 248
Shepsle, Kenneth A. 22, 228, 235

Name Index

Subject Index

Subject Index

political parties:
  evaluations of 289–91
Poll Tax 62
proportional representation (PR) 320–1

relative deprivation model 237–9

Scottish Parliament 283, 294, 299, 300
Smith, John 53, 57, 61, 73, 201, 207, 210, 319
social capital 225–6
social class:
  identification with 40, 44, 79, 97, 175
  measurement of 39, 58
  and partisanship, see party identification
  and voting, see voting behaviour
social trust 232, 233, 241
sociological framework v, vi, 5, 12, 17, 18, 32,
    36, 39, 45, 68, 70, 74, 125, 224, 225, 233
Spatial models, see issue-proximity models
STATA 129, 313, 328
Swinney, John 126, 173, 313

tactical voting 81, 82, 112, 115, 116
  and campaign effects on 113, 138, 169
  and Liberal Democrats 112
tax-spend scale 81, 82, 125, 127
Thatcher, Margaret 7, 29–30, 47, 51, 60–2, 86,
    88, 270–4, 297, 309
trade unions 40, 51, 52, 54, 75
Trade Union Acts 54
turnout:
  and age cohorts 182, 268, 274
  benefits of 226, 228–9, 231–3, 247, 249,
    251, 252
  and canvassing 143, 160
  civic voluntarism model of 222, 245,
    255–61
  decline in 2001 v, 150, 217
  effects of civic duty on 218, 234–5
  cognitive mobilization model of 230, 246,
    247, 254, 257–61, 273
  costs of 228–33
  equity-fairness/relative deprivation model of
    254–61
  general incentives model of 231, 232, 250,
    254, 257–61, 273
  generational differences in 268, 270
  and heartlands hypotheses 261–4
  and inter-party competition 264–74
  and life-cycle effects 182, 269

minimal rational choice model of 231, 247,
    248, 257–61
minority group membership and 225
and paradox of voting 229, 273
period effects on 269
and policy dissatisfaction 225, 230, 232
and political efficacy 218, 227, 231–3
and political interest 218, 224, 227, 229, 230,
    234
and political knowledge 230, 247
rival models of 10, 237–53, 257–61
social capital model of 225, 226, 240,
    257–61
and social norms 251, 252
and strength of party identification 252
trends in 223, 234

unemployment, unemployment rate 51, 60
utility maximization 2, 21–2, 24, 26–8

valence politics model v, vii, 4, 8–11, 17, 21,
    23–4, 27, 35–6, 40, 57–74, 79, 94,
    124–5, 172, 211, 315–28
voluntary activity:
  extent of 243
  recruitment to 245
voting behaviour:
  and age vii, 109, 119
  dynamics of 3, 21
  economic evaluation model of 84, 85,
    99–103, 106, 107, 111, 113, 115, 116, 119
  and emotional reactions to economic
    conditions 86, 95, 99, 103, 111, 118–20
  and ethnicity 106–9, 112, 113, 115
  and gender 119
  and home ownership 47, 71, 109, 113, 115,
    116, 119
  and individual rationality framework 7, 315
  issue-position (proximity) model of 7, 99,
    100, 101, 103–7, 115, 118, 119, 124
  issue-priority model of 102
  Michigan model of 81, 175, 176
  party identification model 7–9, 99–103,
    105–7, 109, 112, 114, 119, 124
  party leader leaders vii, 66, 95, 99–101, 103,
    105–8, 110, 112–24
  and private/public sector 6, 94, 97, 98
  and public service delivery 52, 54, 55, 84,
    86–90, 118, 123–4
  and region 94, 95, 97, 98, 109

370